Translator - Lauren Na
English Adaptation - R.A. Jones
Copy Editors - Troy Lewter, Carol Fox
Retouch and Lettering - Tom Misuraca
Cover Layout - Patrick Hook
Graphic Designer - John Lo

Editor - Rob Tokar
Digital Imaging Manager - Chris Buford
Pre-Press Manager - Antonio DePietro
Production Managers - Jennifer Miller, Mutsumi Miyazaki
Art Director - Matt Alford
Managing Editor - Jill Freshney
VP of Production - Ron Klamert
President & C.O.O. - John Parker
Publisher & C.E.O. - Stuart Levy

E-mail: info@TOKYOPOP.com
Come visit us online at www.TOKYOPOP.com

A **TOKYOPOP** Manga

TOKYOPOP Inc.
5900 Wilshire Blvd. Suite 2000
Los Angeles, CA 90036

King of Hell Vol. 5

ISBN:1-59182-483-4

First TOKYOPOP printing: April 2004

10 9 8 7 6 5 4 3

Printed in the USA

KING OF HELL

VOLUME 5

BY
RA IN-SOO

&
KIM JAE-HWAN

TOKYOPOP®

LOS ANGELES • TOKYO • LONDON

KING OF HELL

WHO THE HELL...?

MAJEH:
A feared warrior in life, now a collector of souls for the King of Hell. Majeh has recently been returned to his human form in order to carry out the mission of destroying escaped evil spirits upon the earth. There are two catches, however:
1. Majeh's full powers are restrained by a mystical seal.
2. His physical form is that of a teenage boy.

CHUNG POONG NAMGOONG:
A coward from a once-respected family, Chung Poong left home hoping to prove himself at the Martial Arts Tournament in Nakyang. Broke and desperate, Chung Poong tried to rob Majeh. In a very rare moment of pity, Majeh allowed Chung Poong to live...and to tag along with him to the tournament. Chung Poong's older brother--Chung Hae--is also a student of the martial arts and is the "nephew" (martial arts inferior) of Poong Chun.

THE MARTIAL ARTS CHILD PRODIGIES

"BABY":
A mysterious, shy, 15-year-old from the infamous Blood Sect, his weapon is the deadly "snake hand" technique. Much to the relief of his fellow contestants, this fearsome ability hasn't yet reached full maturity...or has it? There's definitely much more to Baby than meets the eye!

CRAZY DOG:
A 6-year-old hellion who is partial to using a club, this wild child hails from a remote village...and he definitely lives up to his name.

SAMHUK:
Originally sent by the King of Hell to spy on the unpredictable Majeh, Samhuk was quickly discovered and now--much to his dismay--acts as the warrior's ghostly manservant.

DOHWA BAIK:
A vivacious vixen whose weapons of choice are poisoned needles. She joined Majeh and Chung Poong on the way to the tournament.

KING OF HELL:
You were expecting horns and a pitchfork? This benevolent, otherworldly ruler reigns over the souls of the dead like a shepherd tending his flock.

DOHAK:
A 15-year-old monk and a master at fighting with a rod, he is affiliated with the Sorim Temple in the Soong mountains.

POONG CHUN:
A 12-year-old expert with the broad-sword, he is affiliated with the Shaman Sect. Poong Chun is the "uncle" (martial arts superior) of Chun Hae--Chung Poong's older brother.

YOUNG:
A 15-year-old sword-master, possessing incredible speed, he is affiliated with Mooyoung Moon-- a clan of assassins, 500 strong.

Hell's worst inmates have escaped and fled to Earth. Seeking recently-deceased bodies to host their bitter souls, these malevolent master fighters are part of an evil scheme that could have dire consequences for both This World and the Next World. It is believed that the escaped fiends are hunting for bodies of martial arts experts, as only bodies trained in martial arts would be capable of properly employing their incredible skills.

To make matters even more difficult, the otherworldly energy emitted by the fugitives will dissipate within one month's time...after which, they will be indistinguishable from normal humans and undetectable to those from the Next World. The King of Hell has assigned Majeh to hunt down Hell's Most Wanted and return them to the Next World...but Majeh doesn't always do exactly what he's told.

Majeh was a master swordsman in life and, in death, he serves as an envoy for the King of Hell, escorting souls of the dead to the Next World. Majeh caught Samhuk--a servant for the King of Hell--spying on him and, after making the appropriate threats, now uses Samhuk as his own servant as well.

The King of Hell has reunited Majeh's spirit with his physical body, which was perfectly preserved for 300 years. Due to the influence of a Superhuman Strength Sealing Symbol (designed to keep the rebellious and powerful Majeh in check), Majeh's physical form has reverted to a teenaged state. Even with the seal in place, however, Majeh is still an extremely formidable warrior.

Along with the young, wannabe-warrior called Chung Poong Namgoong and a beautiful femme fatale named Dohwa Baik, Majeh has made his way to the heralded Martial Arts Tournament at Nakyang--the most likely place for the warrior demons to make their appearance.

Shortly after arriving in Nakyang, Majeh and company met Chun Hae--Chung Poong's older brother--though it was far from a happy reunion. Chun Hae berated his younger sibling and ordered Chung Poong to return home. To make matters worse, Poong Chun-- Chun Hae's "uncle" (his superior in martial arts)-- arrived and berated both siblings. Never one to miss an opportunity to make a new enemy, Majeh intervened and publicly shamed Poong Chun. Unsurprisingly, Poong Chun's vow to get even failed to impress Majeh in any way.

Now, at long last, the tournament is about to begin!

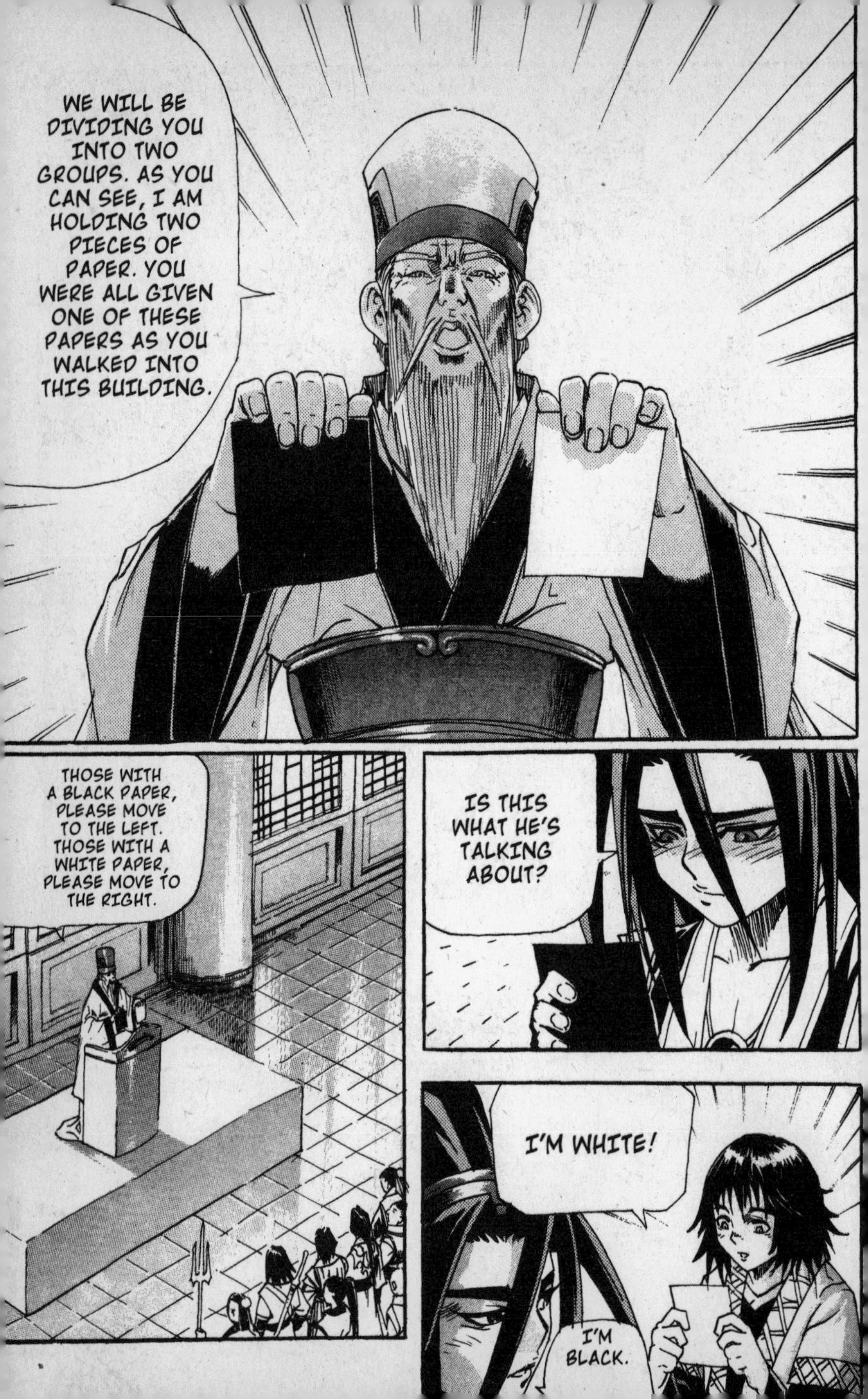
WE WILL BE DIVIDING YOU INTO TWO GROUPS. AS YOU CAN SEE, I AM HOLDING TWO PIECES OF PAPER. YOU WERE ALL GIVEN ONE OF THESE PAPERS AS YOU WALKED INTO THIS BUILDING.
THOSE WITH A BLACK PAPER, PLEASE MOVE TO THE LEFT. THOSE WITH A WHITE PAPER, PLEASE MOVE TO THE RIGHT.
IS THIS WHAT HE'S TALKING ABOUT?
I'M WHITE!
I'M BLACK.

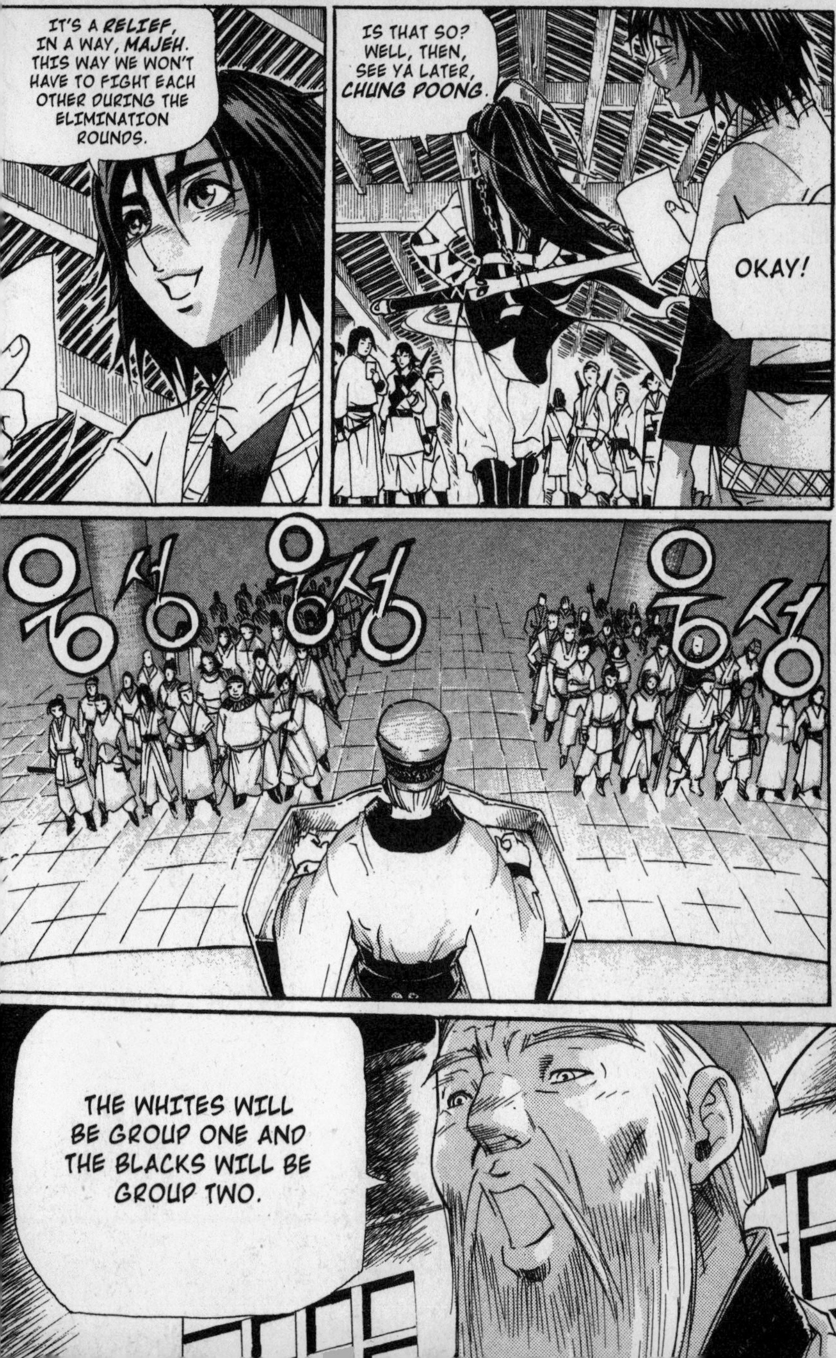

IT'S A *RELIEF*, IN A WAY, *MAJEH*. THIS WAY WE WON'T HAVE TO FIGHT EACH OTHER DURING THE ELIMINATION ROUNDS.
IS THAT SO? WELL, THEN, SEE YA LATER, *CHUNG POONG*.
OKAY!
웅성 웅성
웅성
THE WHITES WILL BE GROUP ONE AND THE BLACKS WILL BE GROUP TWO.

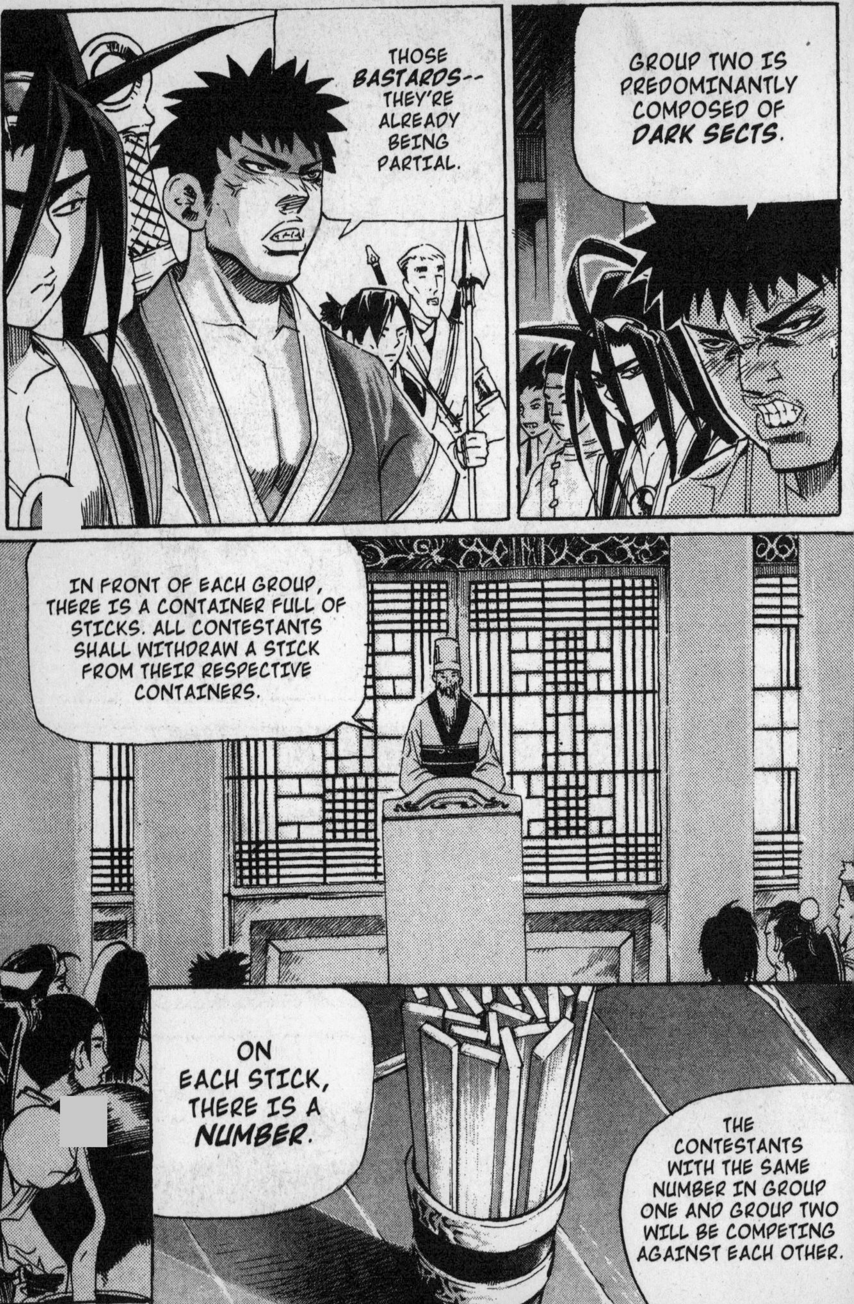
THOSE BASTARDS-- THEY'RE ALREADY BEING PARTIAL.
GROUP TWO IS PREDOMINANTLY COMPOSED OF DARK SECTS.
IN FRONT OF EACH GROUP, THERE IS A CONTAINER FULL OF STICKS. ALL CONTESTANTS SHALL WITHDRAW A STICK FROM THEIR RESPECTIVE CONTAINERS.
ON EACH STICK, THERE IS A NUMBER.
THE CONTESTANTS WITH THE SAME NUMBER IN GROUP ONE AND GROUP TWO WILL BE COMPETING AGAINST EACH OTHER.

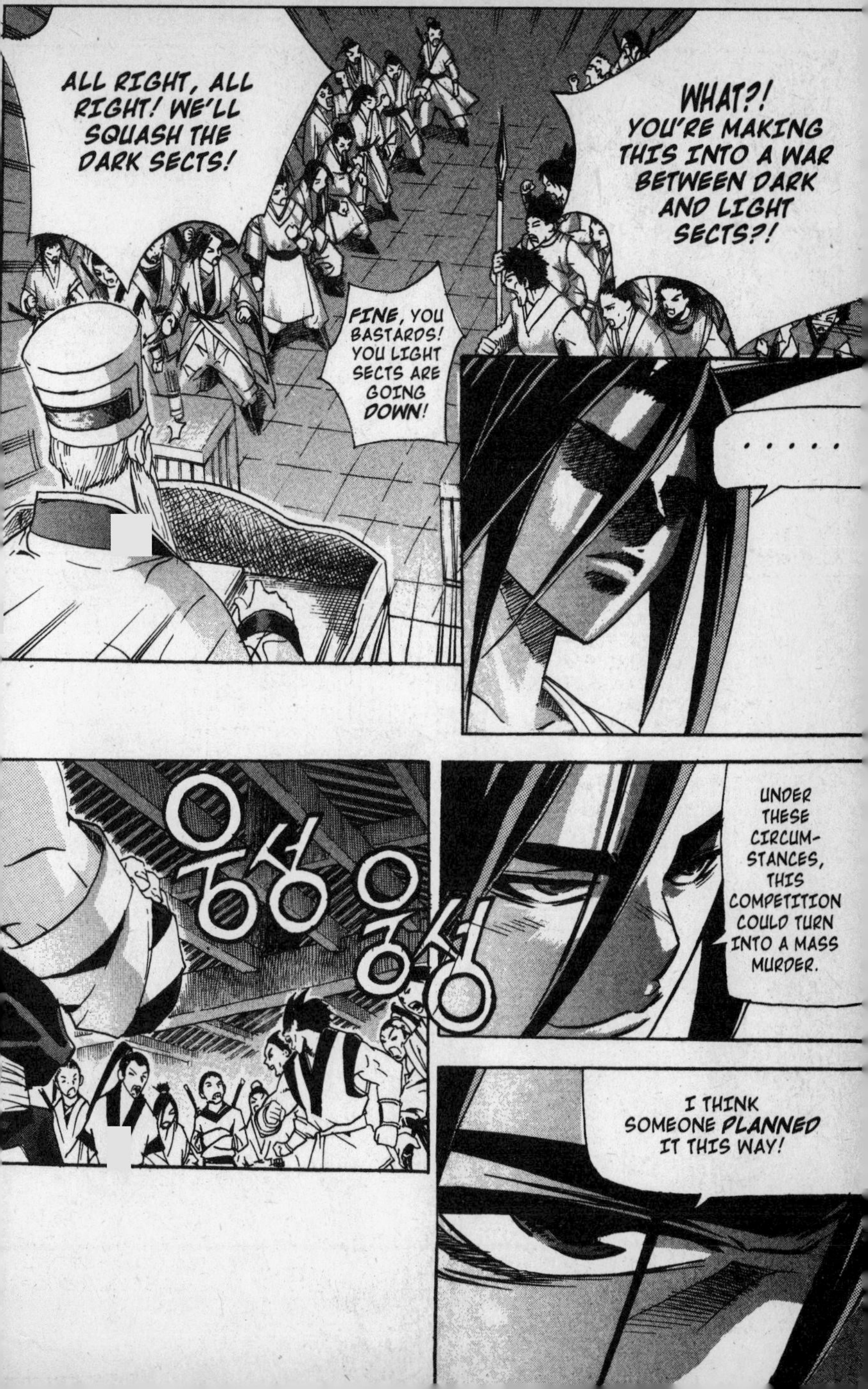
ALL RIGHT, ALL RIGHT! WE'LL SQUASH THE DARK SECTS!
WHAT?! YOU'RE MAKING THIS INTO A WAR BETWEEN DARK AND LIGHT SECTS?!
FINE, YOU BASTARDS! YOU LIGHT SECTS ARE GOING DOWN!
.....
UNDER THESE CIRCUM-STANCES, THIS COMPETITION COULD TURN INTO A MASS MURDER.
I THINK SOMEONE PLANNED IT THIS WAY!

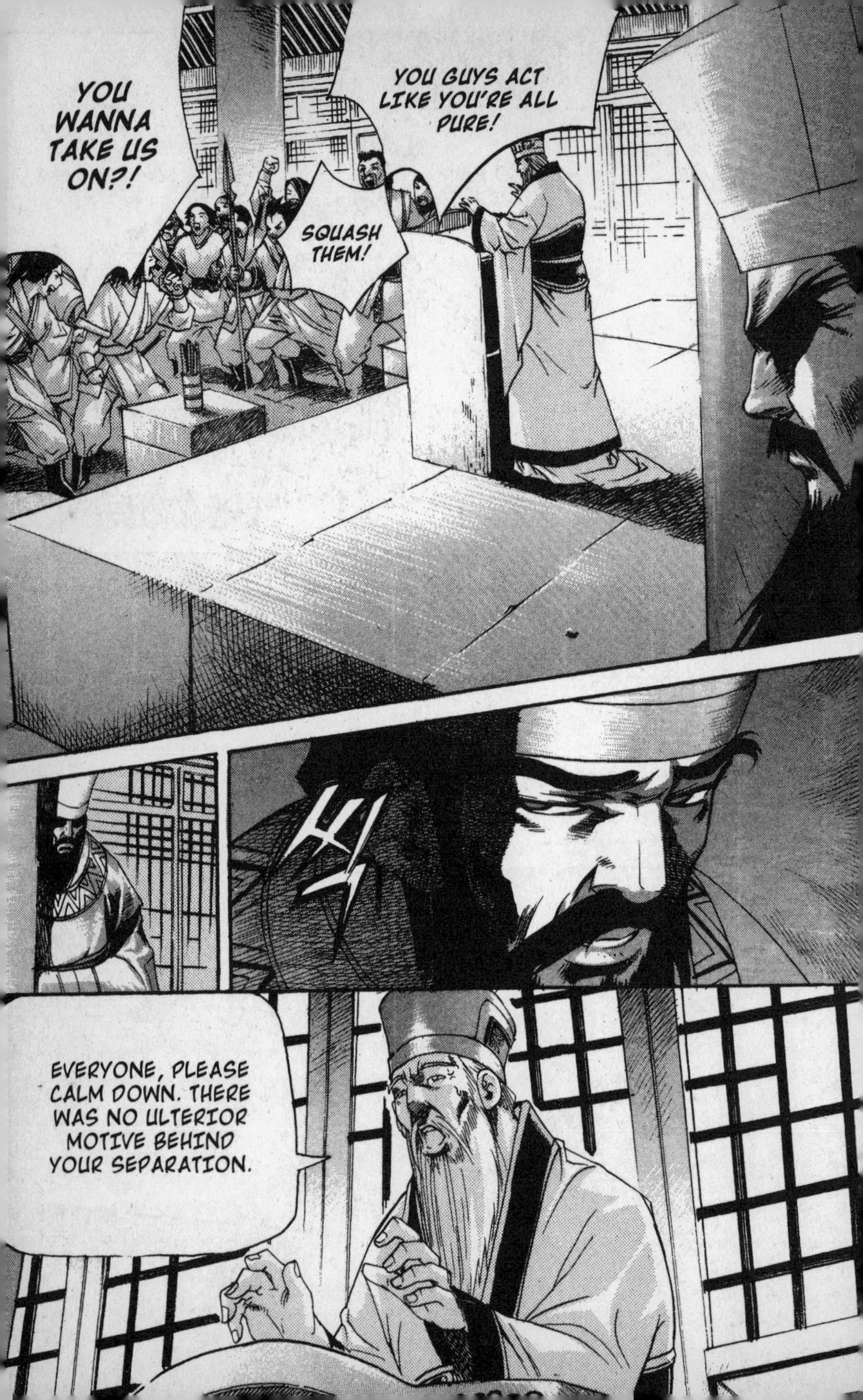
YOU GUYS ACT LIKE YOU'RE ALL PURE!
YOU WANNA TAKE US ON?!
SQUASH THEM!
EVERYONE, PLEASE CALM DOWN. THERE WAS NO ULTERIOR MOTIVE BEHIND YOUR SEPARATION.

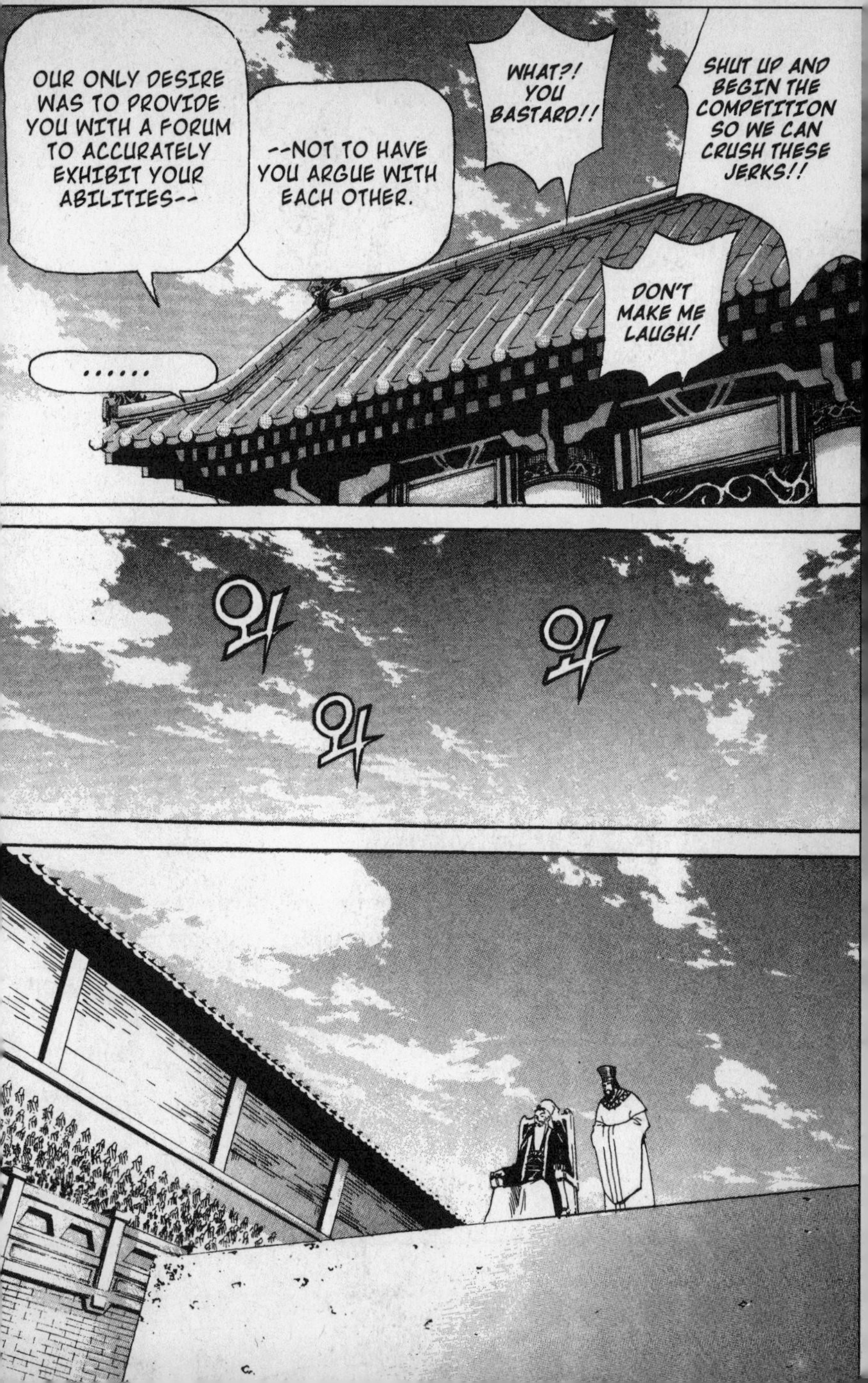
SHUT UP AND BEGIN THE COMPETITION SO WE CAN CRUSH THESE JERKS!!
WHAT?! YOU BASTARD!!
DON'T MAKE ME LAUGH!
OUR ONLY DESIRE WAS TO PROVIDE YOU WITH A FORUM TO ACCURATELY EXHIBIT YOUR ABILITIES--
--NOT TO HAVE YOU ARGUE WITH EACH OTHER.
......
와
와
와

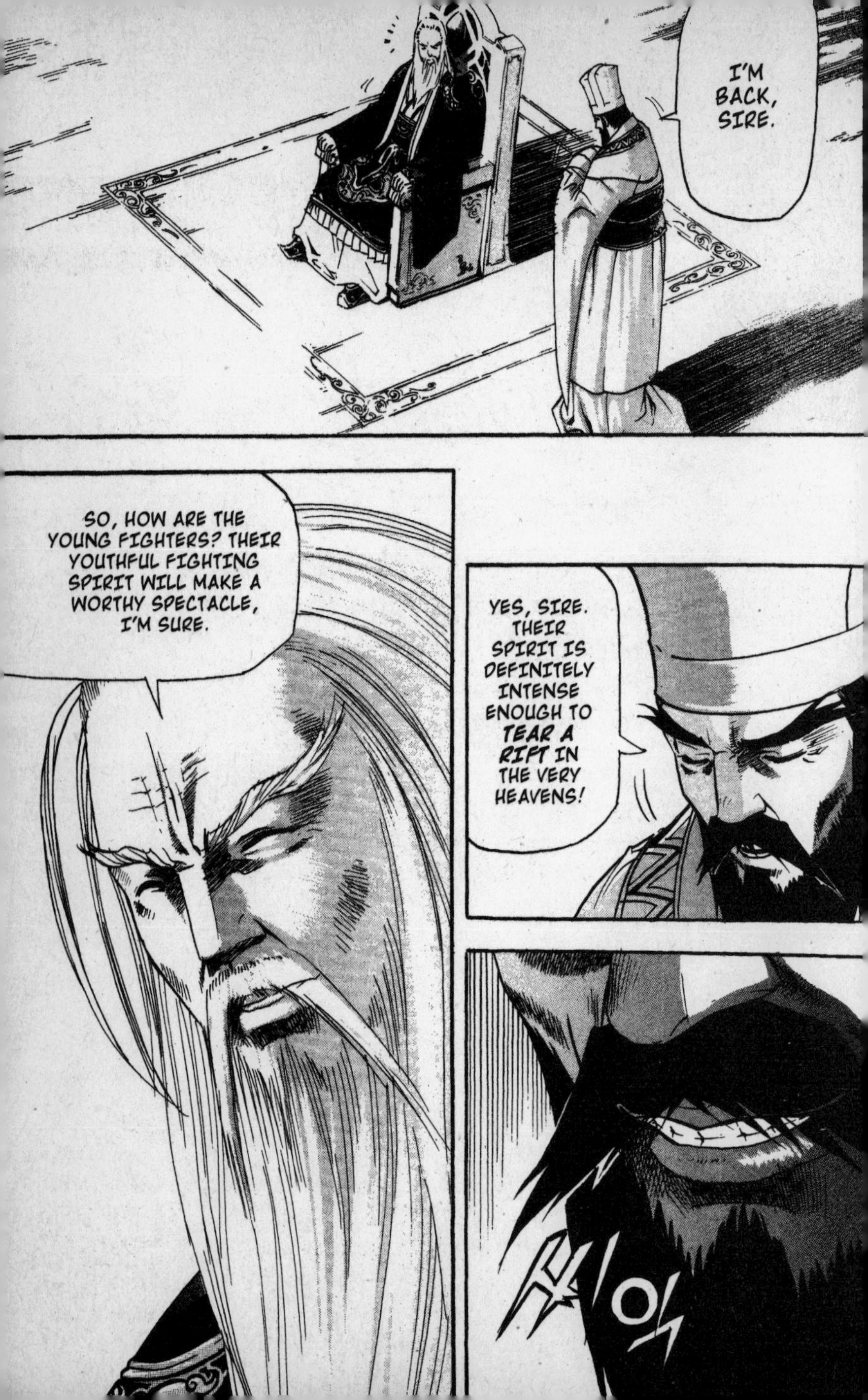
I'M BACK, SIRE.
SO, HOW ARE THE YOUNG FIGHTERS? THEIR YOUTHFUL FIGHTING SPIRIT WILL MAKE A WORTHY SPECTACLE, I'M SURE.
YES, SIRE. THEIR SPIRIT IS DEFINITELY INTENSE ENOUGH TO *TEAR A RIFT* IN THE VERY HEAVENS!

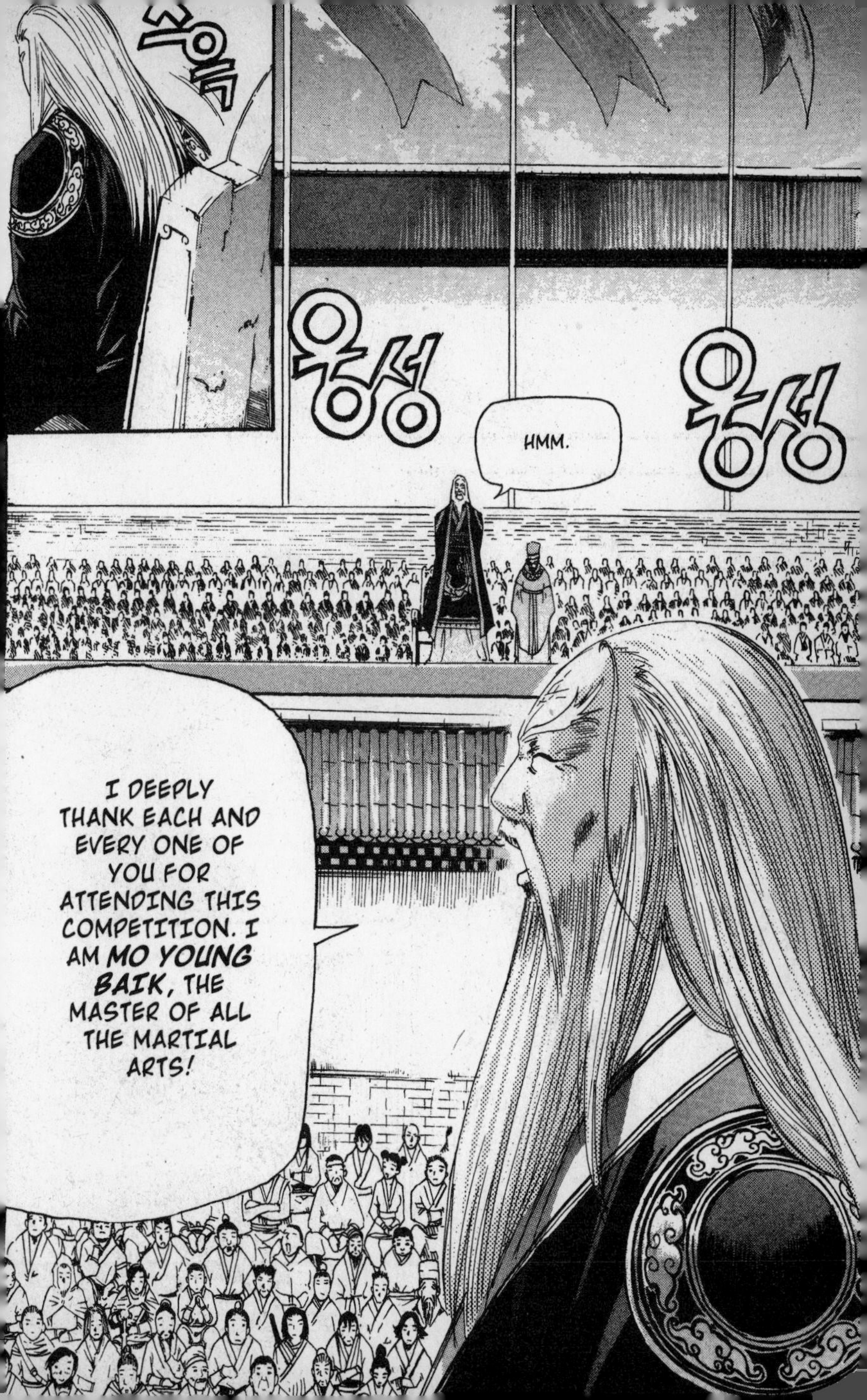
웅성
HMM.
웅성
I DEEPLY THANK EACH AND EVERY ONE OF YOU FOR ATTENDING THIS COMPETITION. I AM ***MO YOUNG BAIK***, THE MASTER OF ALL THE MARTIAL ARTS!

WE WILL NOW BEGIN PHASE ONE OF THE MARTIAL ARTS CHAMPION COMPETITION!!
I HOPE YOU ALL ENJOY THE YOUNG DRAGONS AS THEY DISPLAY THEIR SKILLS!

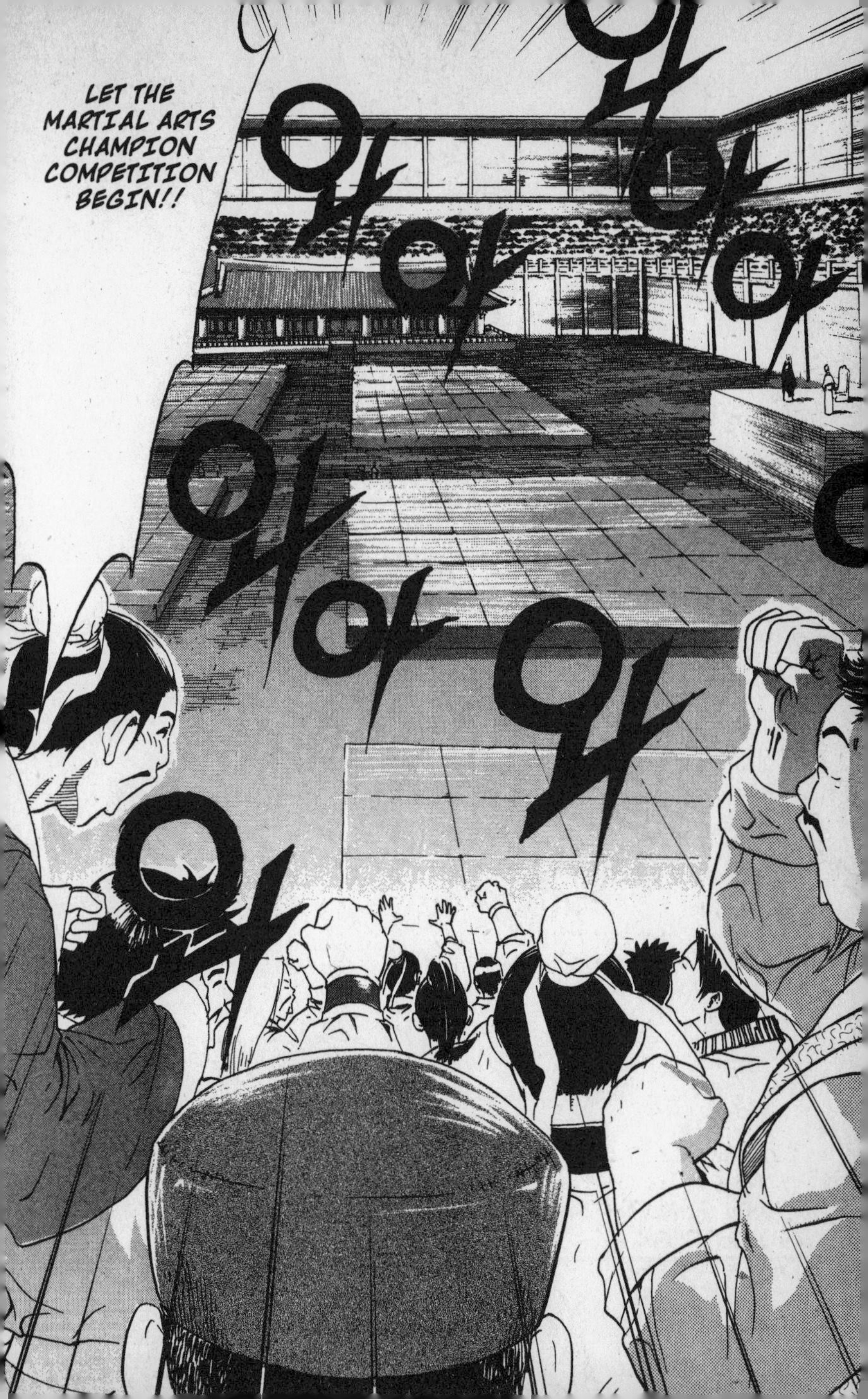
LET THE MARTIAL ARTS CHAMPION COMPETITION BEGIN!!

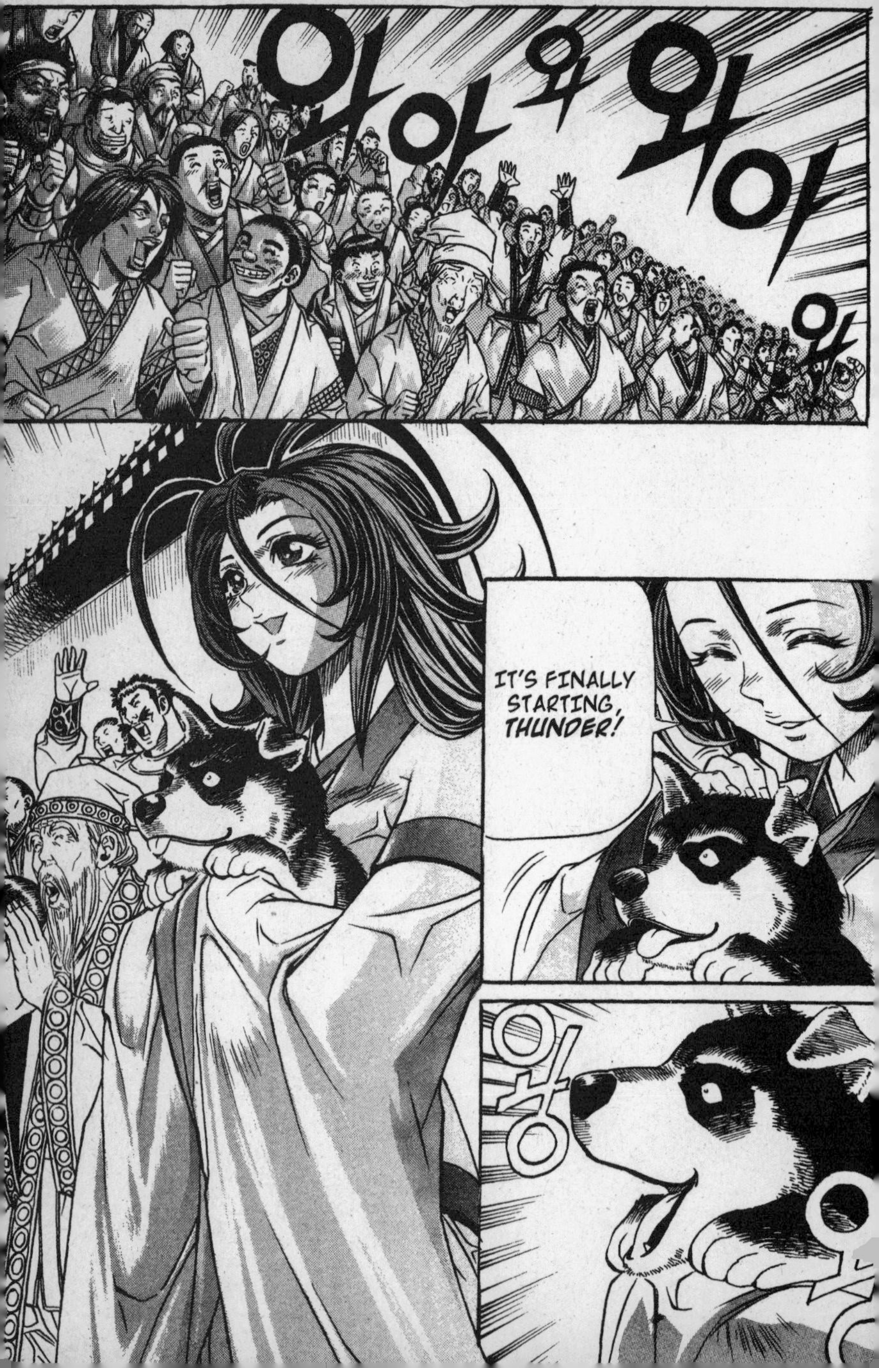
와아 와 와아 와
IT'S FINALLY STARTING, THUNDER!
왕

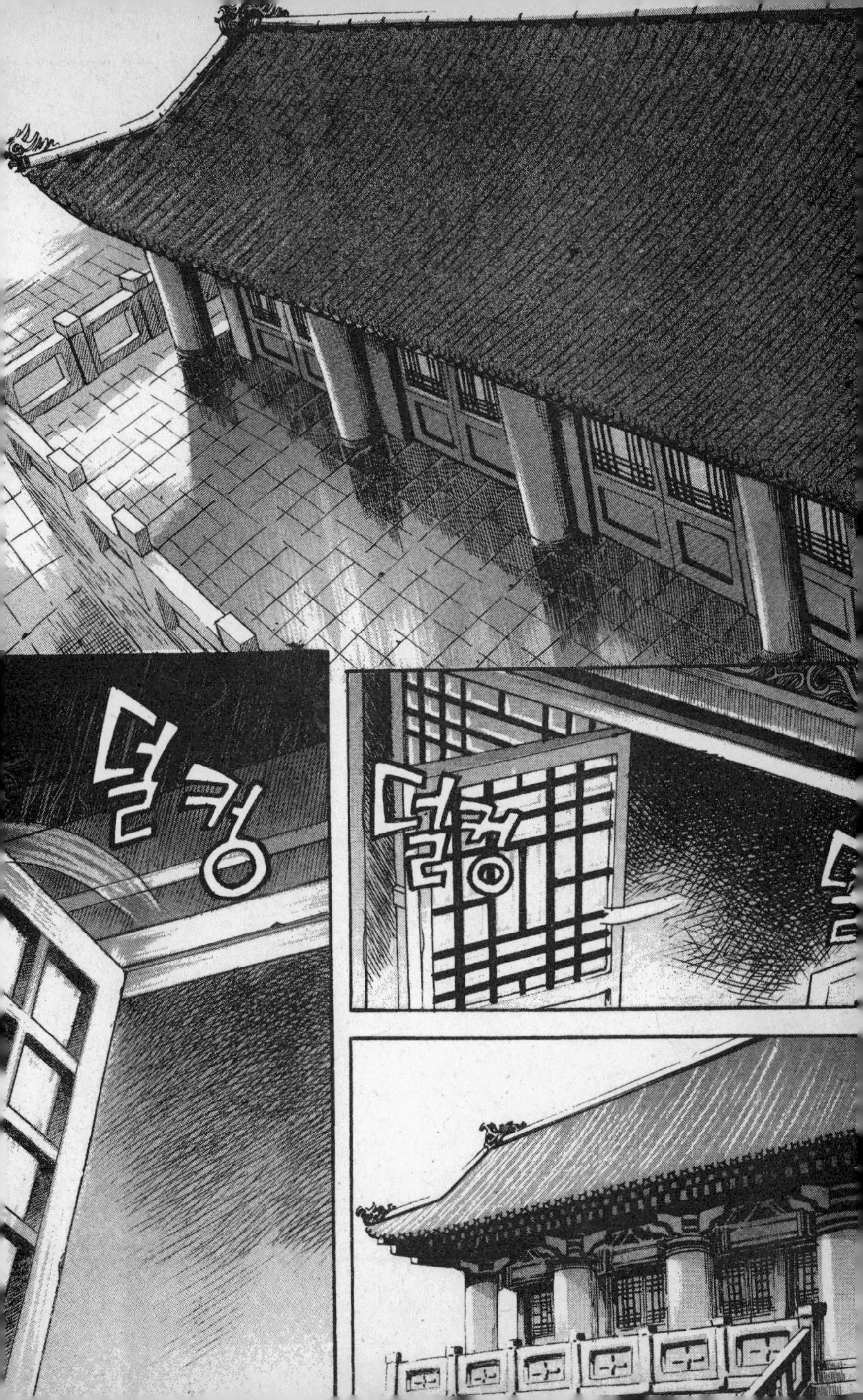
덜컹
덜컹

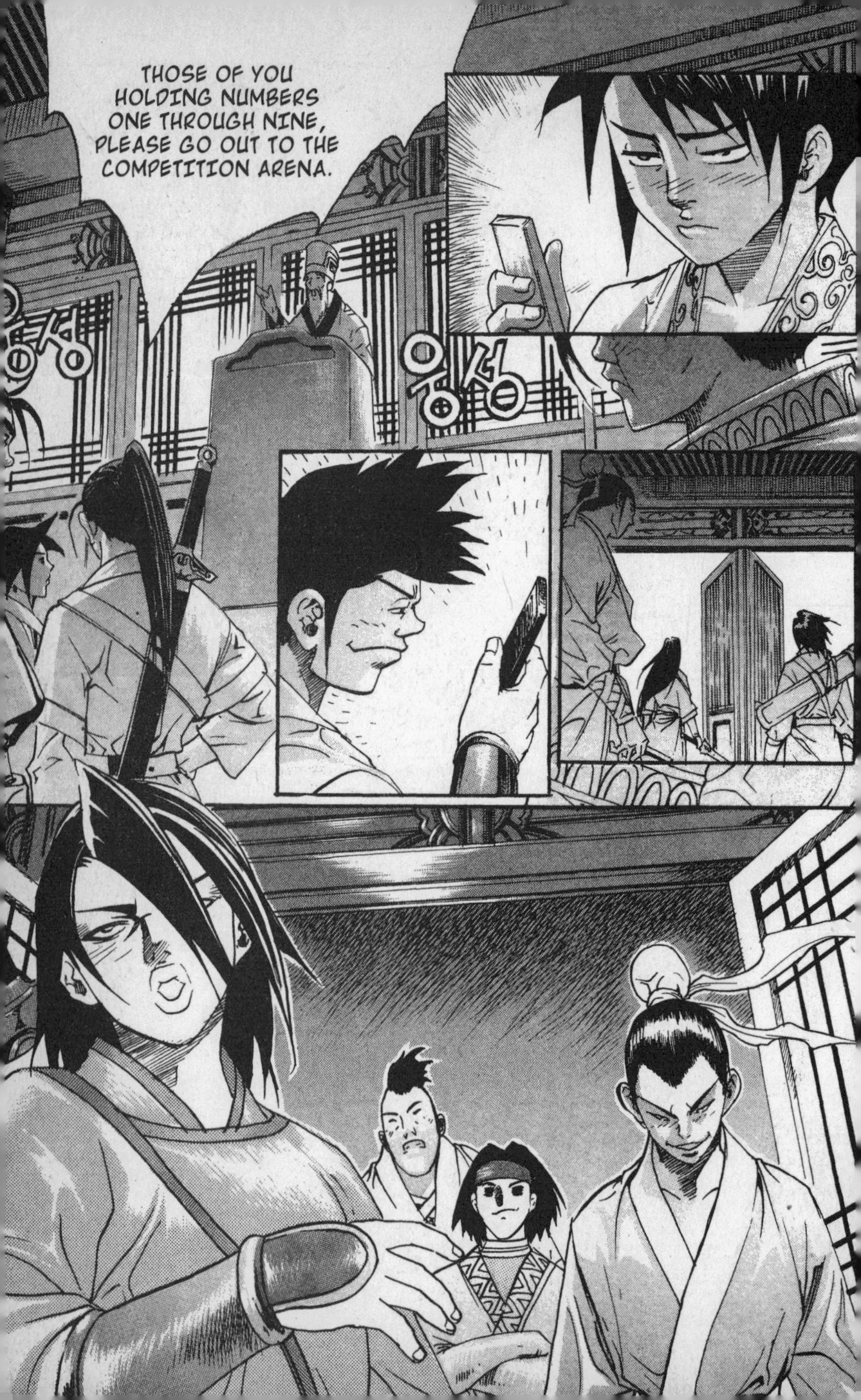
THOSE OF YOU HOLDING NUMBERS ONE THROUGH NINE, PLEASE GO OUT TO THE COMPETITION ARENA.
웅성
웅성

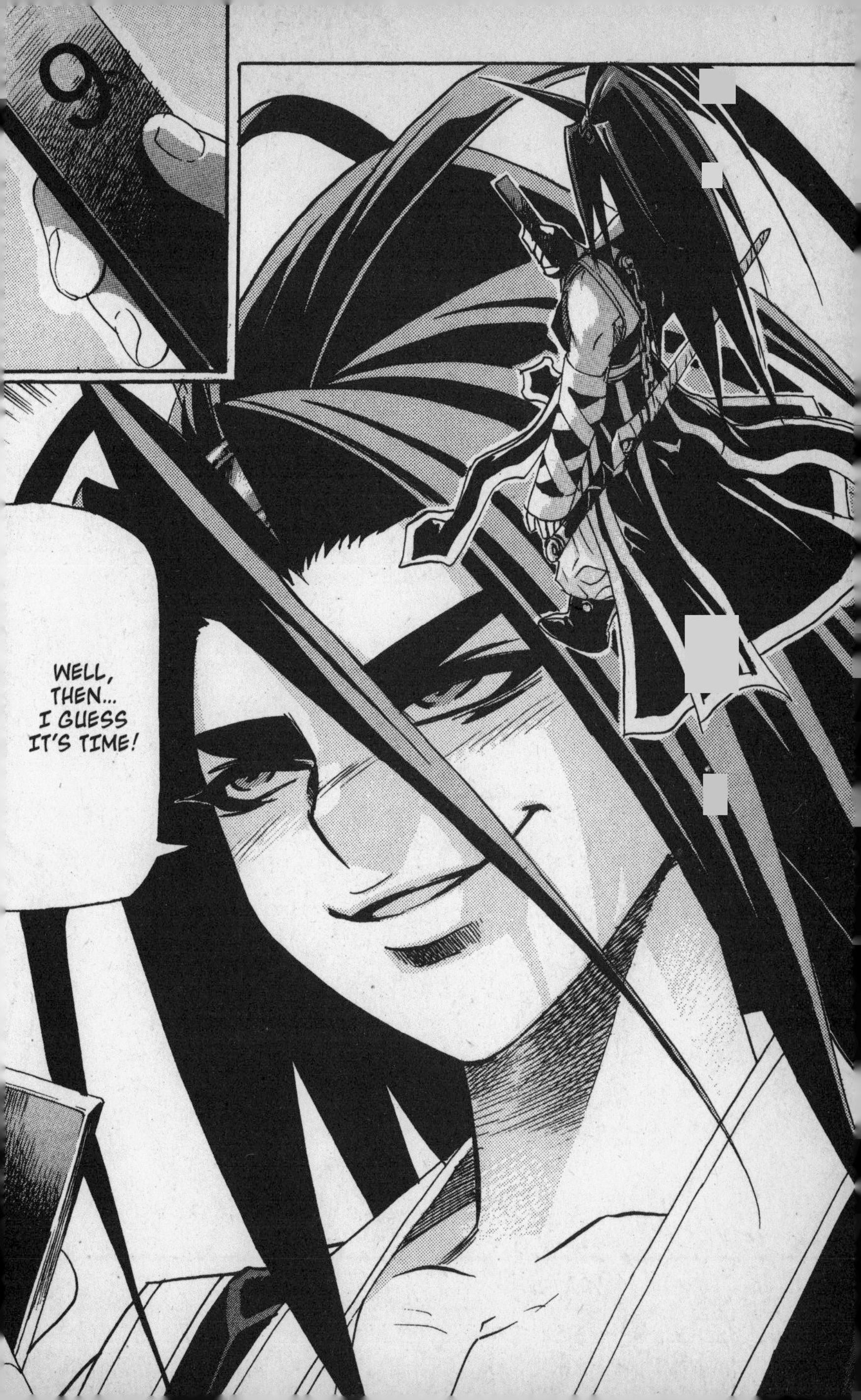
WELL, THEN... I GUESS IT'S TIME!
9

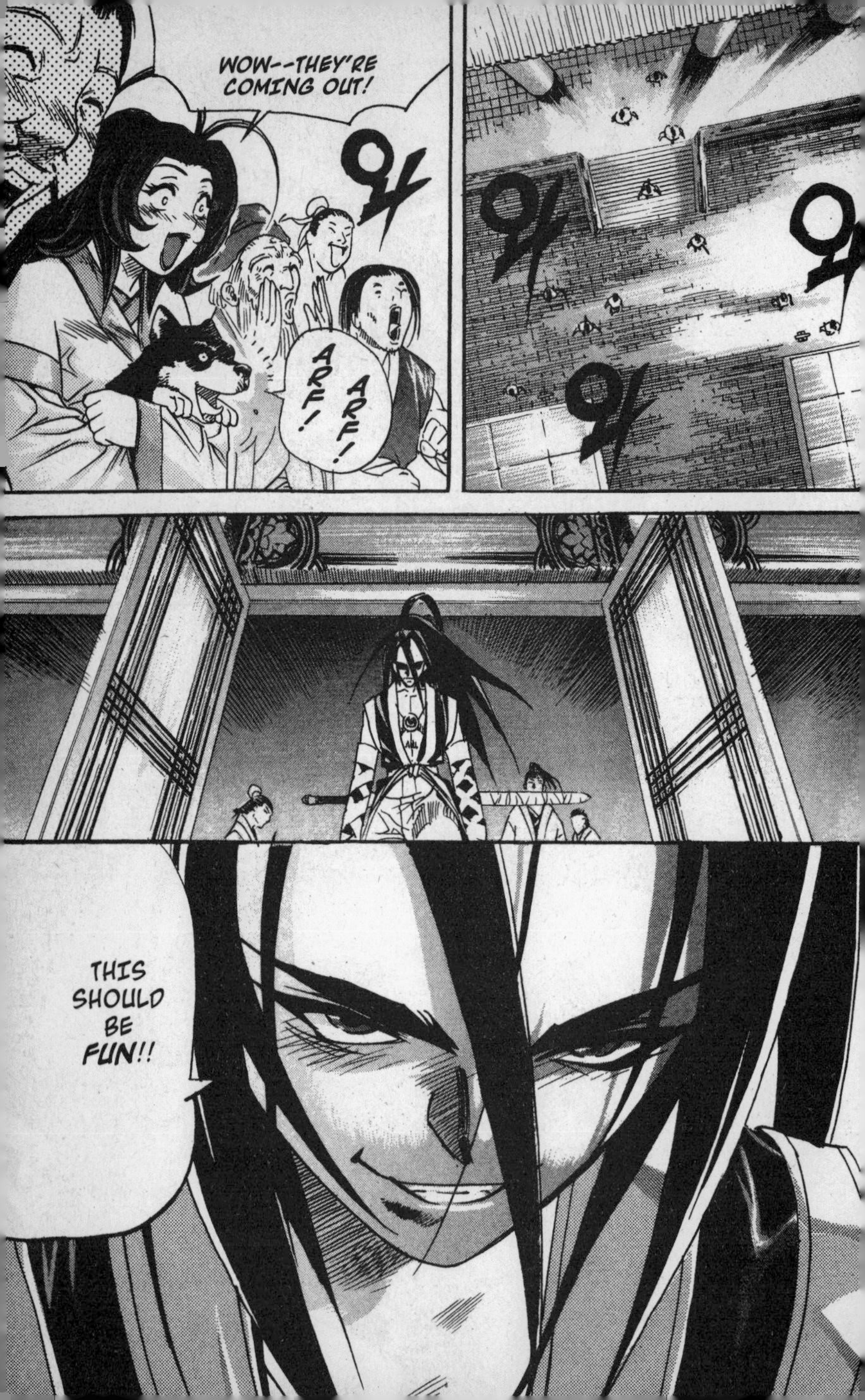
WOW--THEY'RE COMING OUT!
ARF! ARF!
THIS SHOULD BE FUN!!

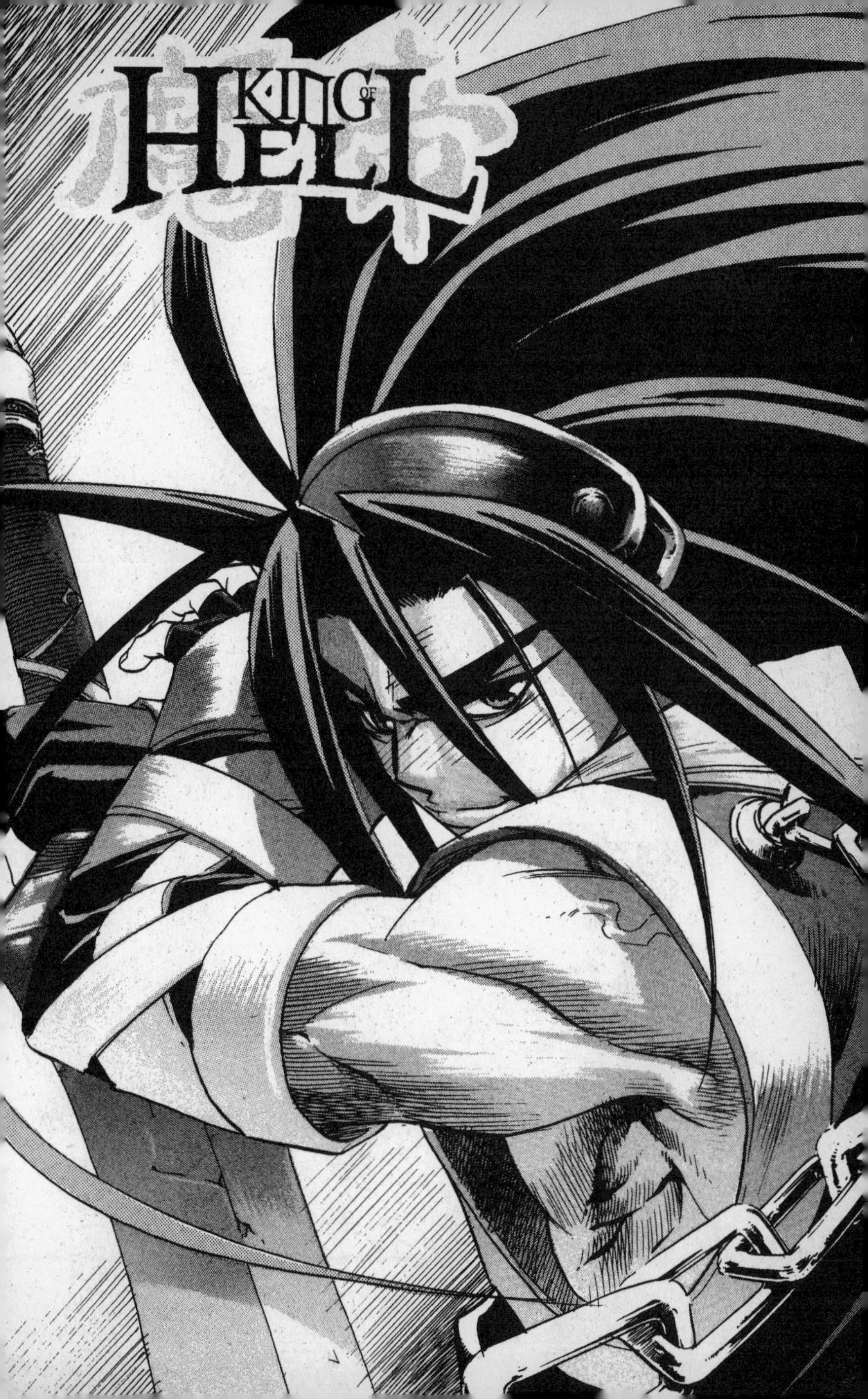
KING OF HELL

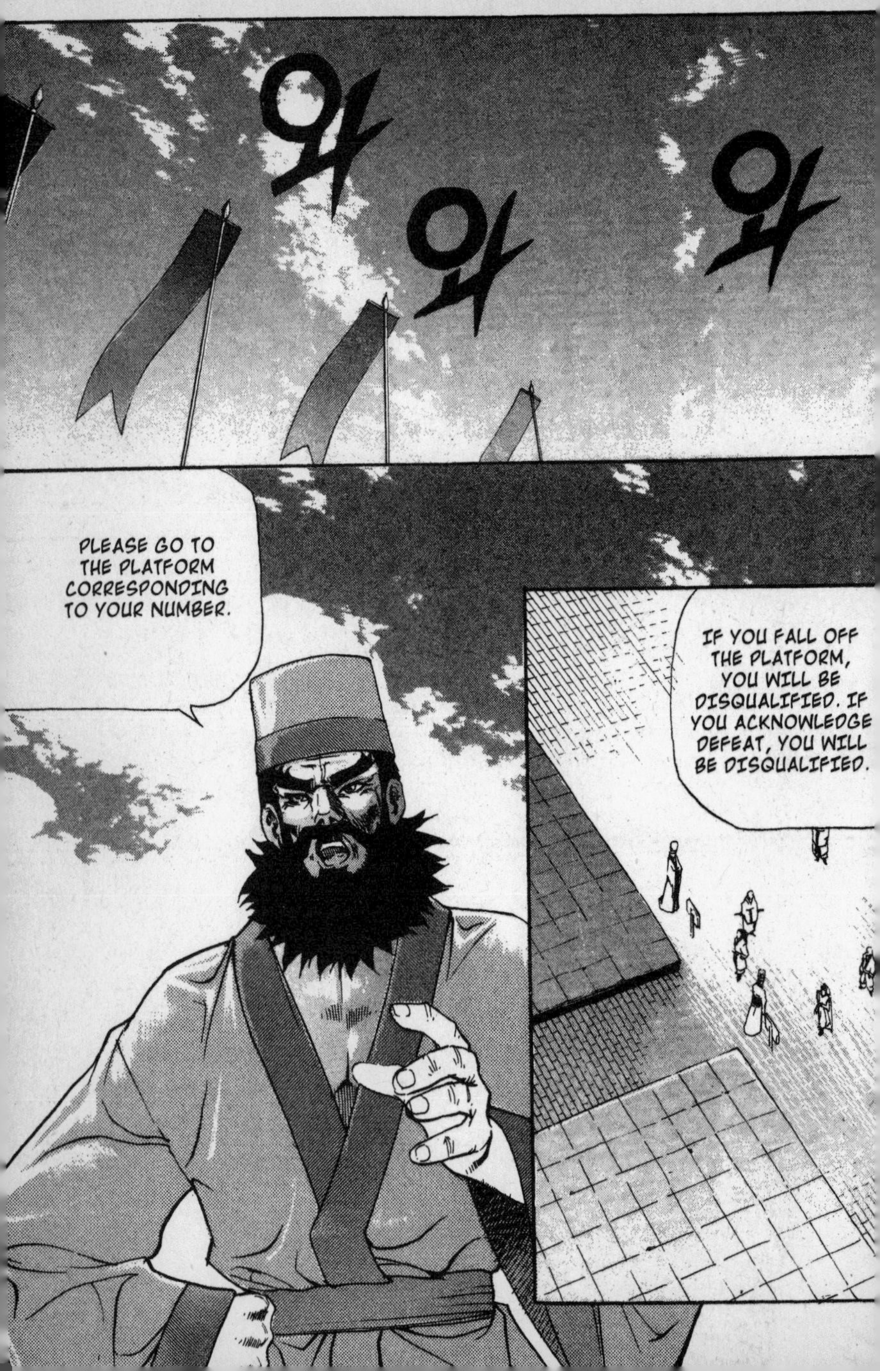
와
와
와
PLEASE GO TO THE PLATFORM CORRESPONDING TO YOUR NUMBER.
IF YOU FALL OFF THE PLATFORM, YOU WILL BE DISQUALIFIED. IF YOU ACKNOWLEDGE DEFEAT, YOU WILL BE DISQUALIFIED.

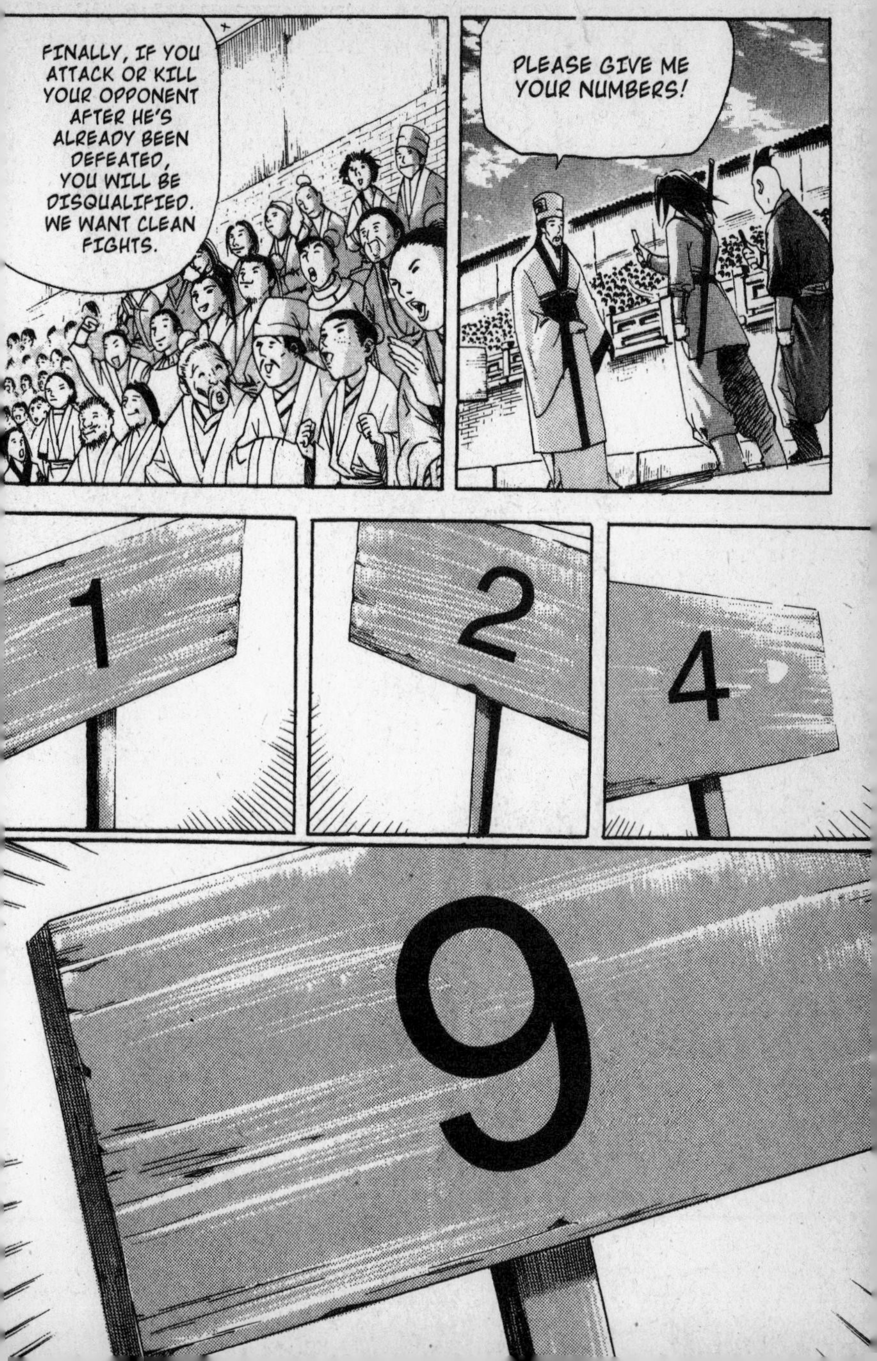
FINALLY, IF YOU ATTACK OR KILL YOUR OPPONENT AFTER HE'S ALREADY BEEN DEFEATED, YOU WILL BE DISQUALIFIED. WE WANT CLEAN FIGHTS.
PLEASE GIVE ME YOUR NUMBERS!
1
2
4
9

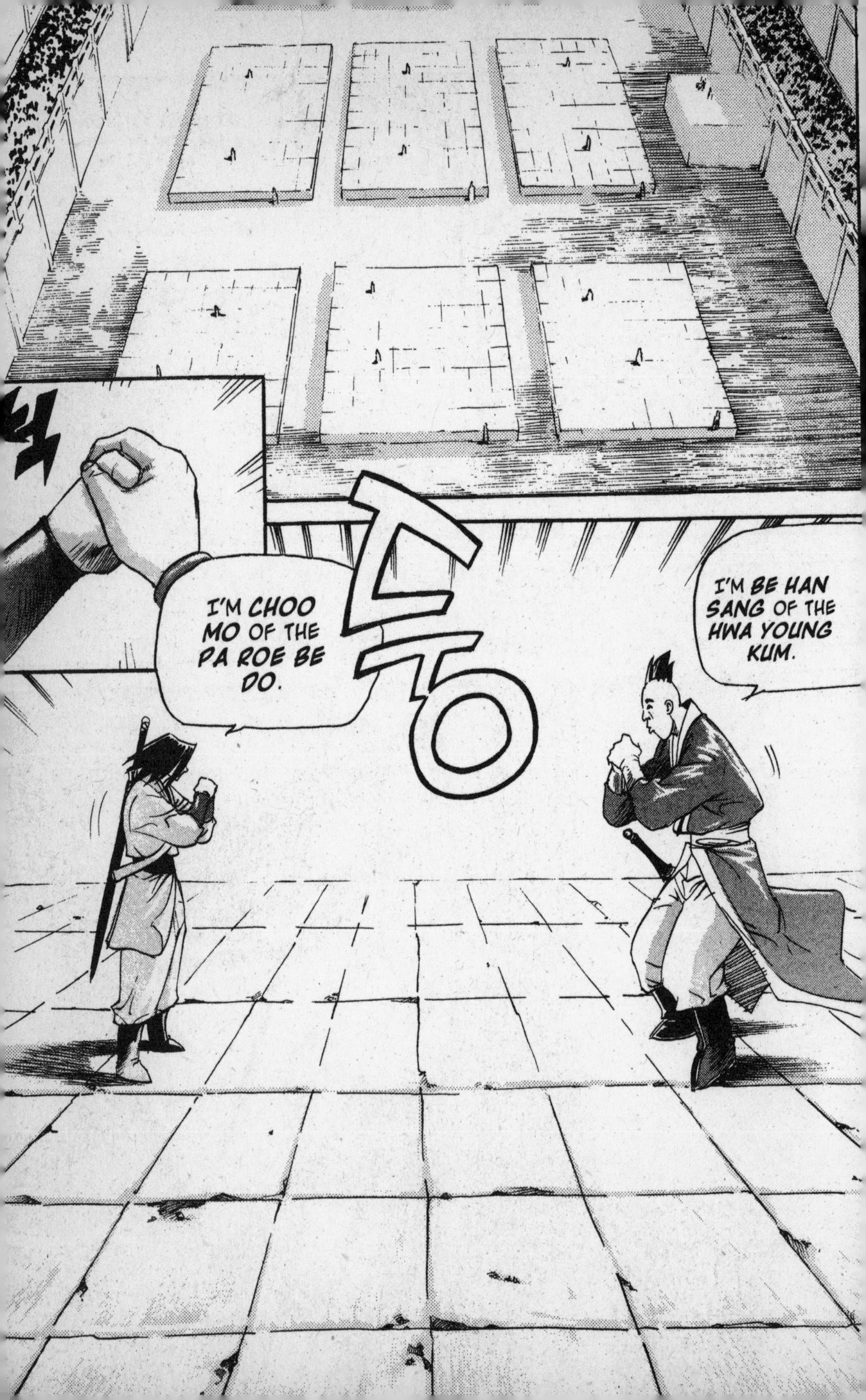
I'M BE HAN SANG OF THE HWA YOUNG KUM.
I'M CHOO MO OF THE PA ROE BE DO.

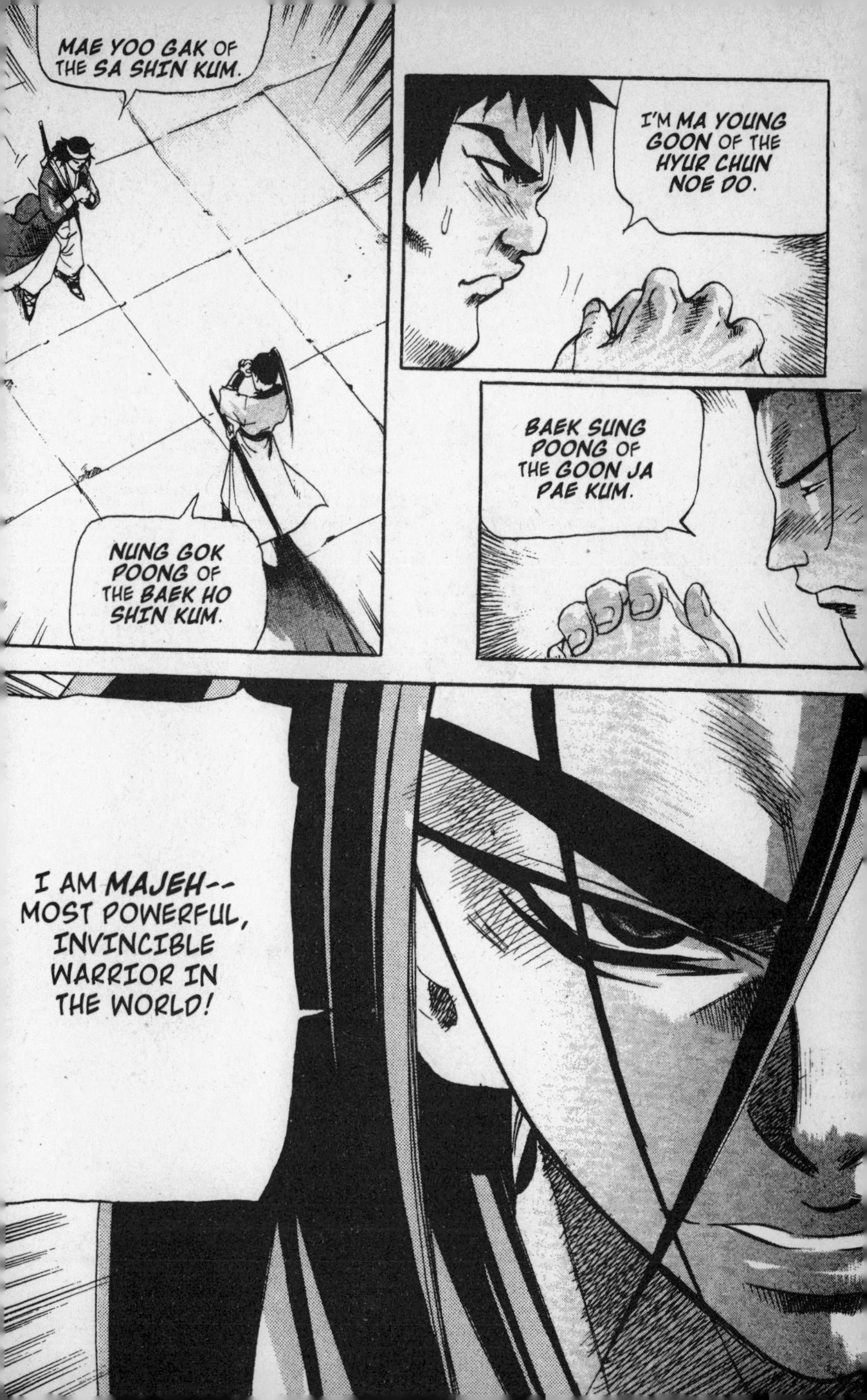
MAE YOO GAK OF THE SA SHIN KUM.
NUNG GOK POONG OF THE BAEK HO SHIN KUM.
I'M MA YOUNG GOON OF THE HYUR CHUN NOE DO.
BAEK SUNG POONG OF THE GOON JA PAE KUM.
I AM MAJEH--MOST POWERFUL, INVINCIBLE WARRIOR IN THE WORLD!

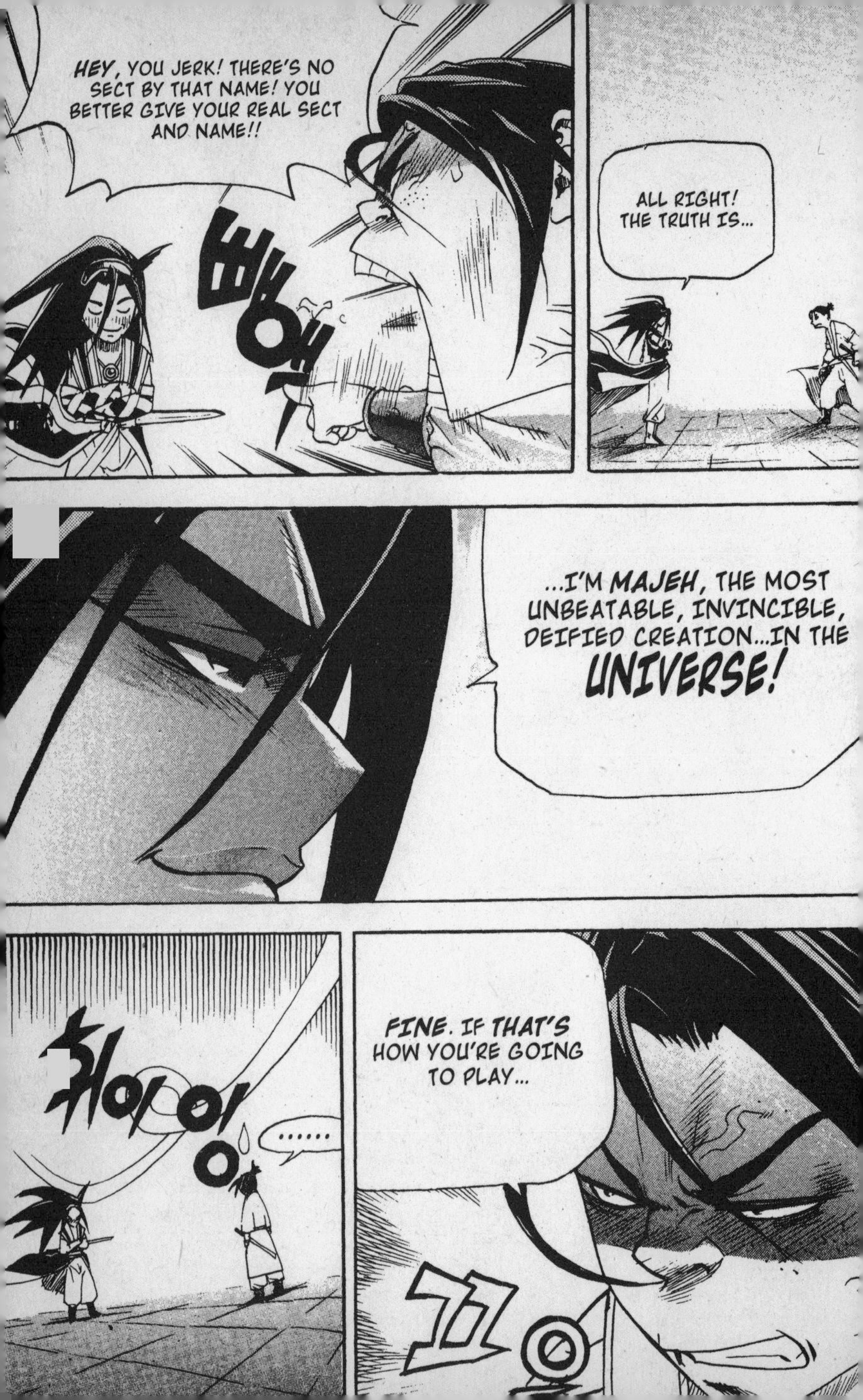
HEY, YOU JERK! THERE'S NO SECT BY THAT NAME! YOU BETTER GIVE YOUR REAL SECT AND NAME!!
ALL RIGHT! THE TRUTH IS...
...I'M MAJEH, THE MOST UNBEATABLE, INVINCIBLE, DEIFIED CREATION...IN THE UNIVERSE!
......
FINE. IF THAT'S HOW YOU'RE GOING TO PLAY...

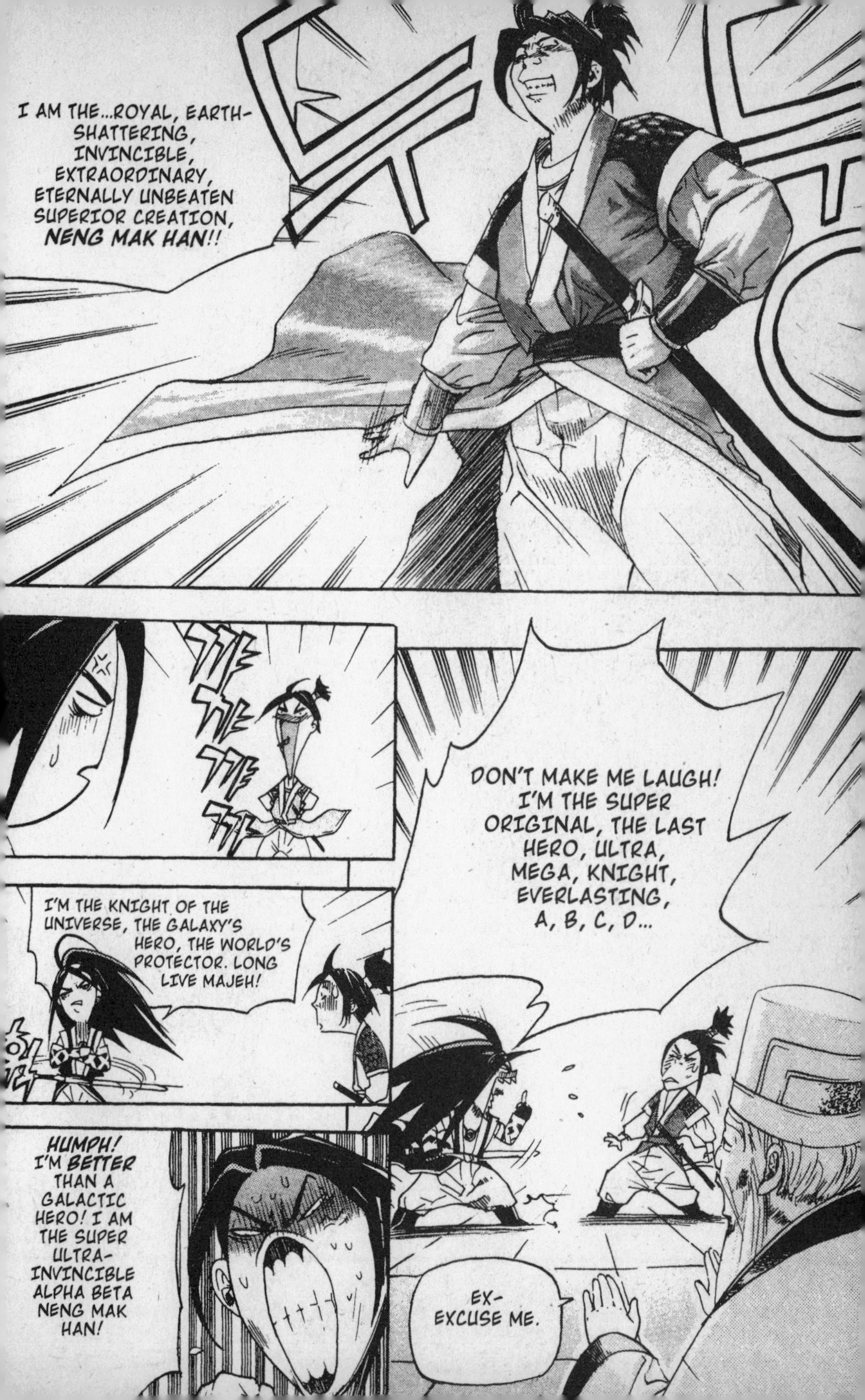

I AM THE...ROYAL, EARTH-SHATTERING, INVINCIBLE, EXTRAORDINARY, ETERNALLY UNBEATEN SUPERIOR CREATION, NENG MAK HAN!!
I'M THE KNIGHT OF THE UNIVERSE, THE GALAXY'S HERO, THE WORLD'S PROTECTOR. LONG LIVE MAJEH!
HUMPH! I'M BETTER THAN A GALACTIC HERO! I AM THE SUPER ULTRA-INVINCIBLE ALPHA BETA NENG MAK HAN!
DON'T MAKE ME LAUGH! I'M THE SUPER ORIGINAL, THE LAST HERO, ULTRA, MEGA, KNIGHT, EVERLASTING, A, B, C, D...
EX-EXCUSE ME.

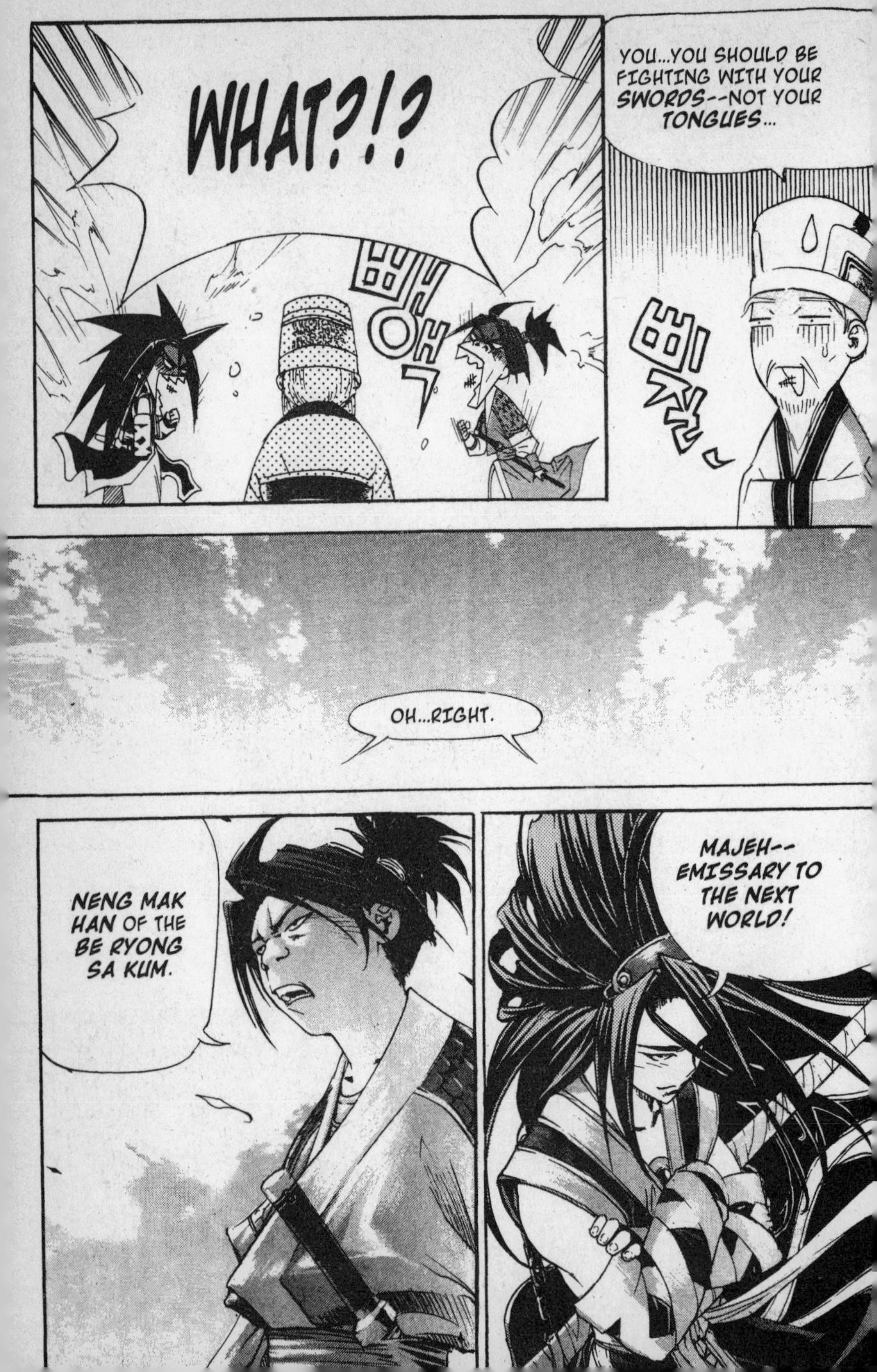
WHAT?!?
YOU...YOU SHOULD BE FIGHTING WITH YOUR SWORDS--NOT YOUR TONGUES...
OH...RIGHT.
NENG MAK HAN OF THE BE RYONG SA KUM.
MAJEH--EMISSARY TO THE NEXT WORLD!

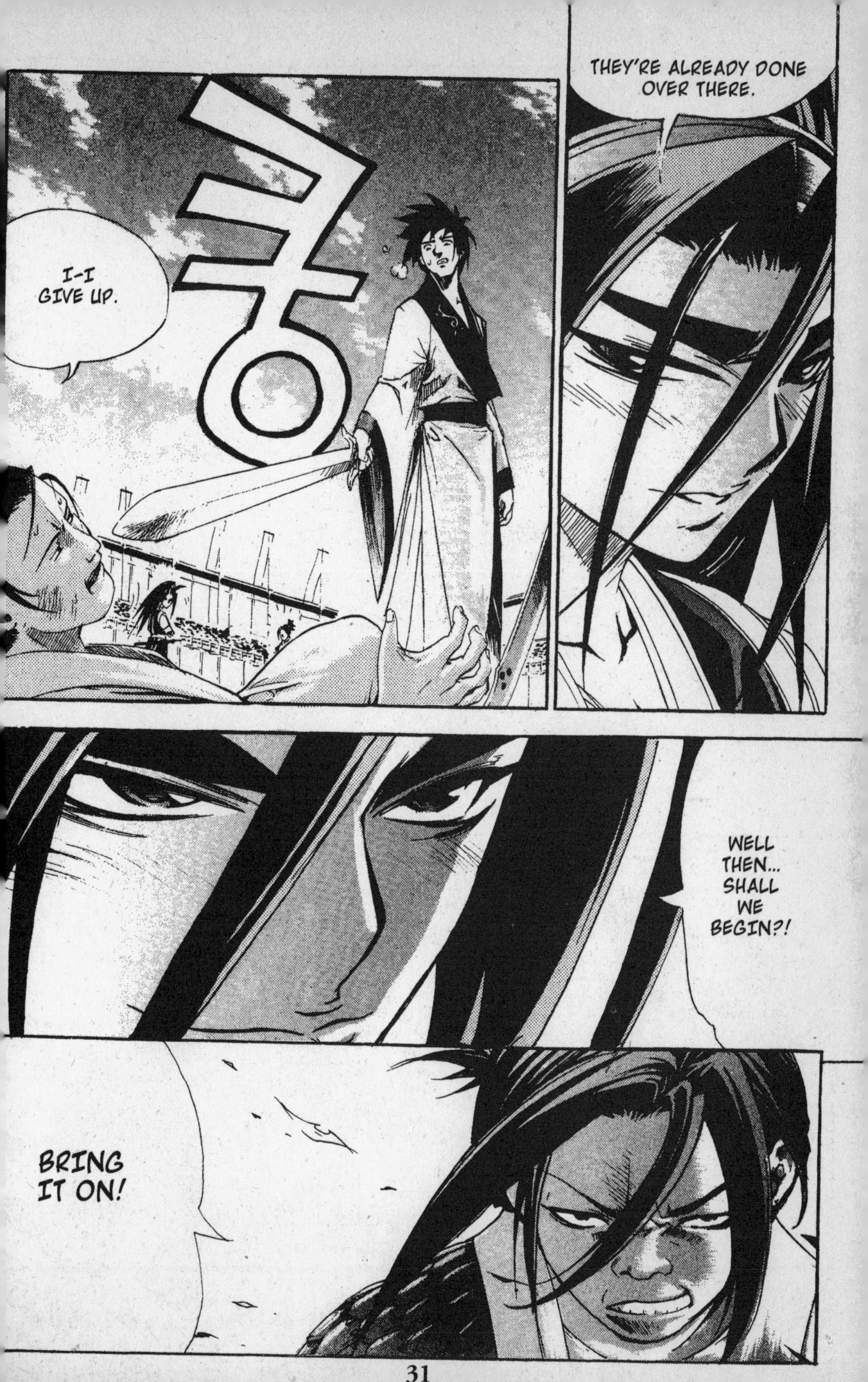
I-I GIVE UP.
THEY'RE ALREADY DONE OVER THERE.
WELL THEN... SHALL WE BEGIN?!
BRING IT ON!

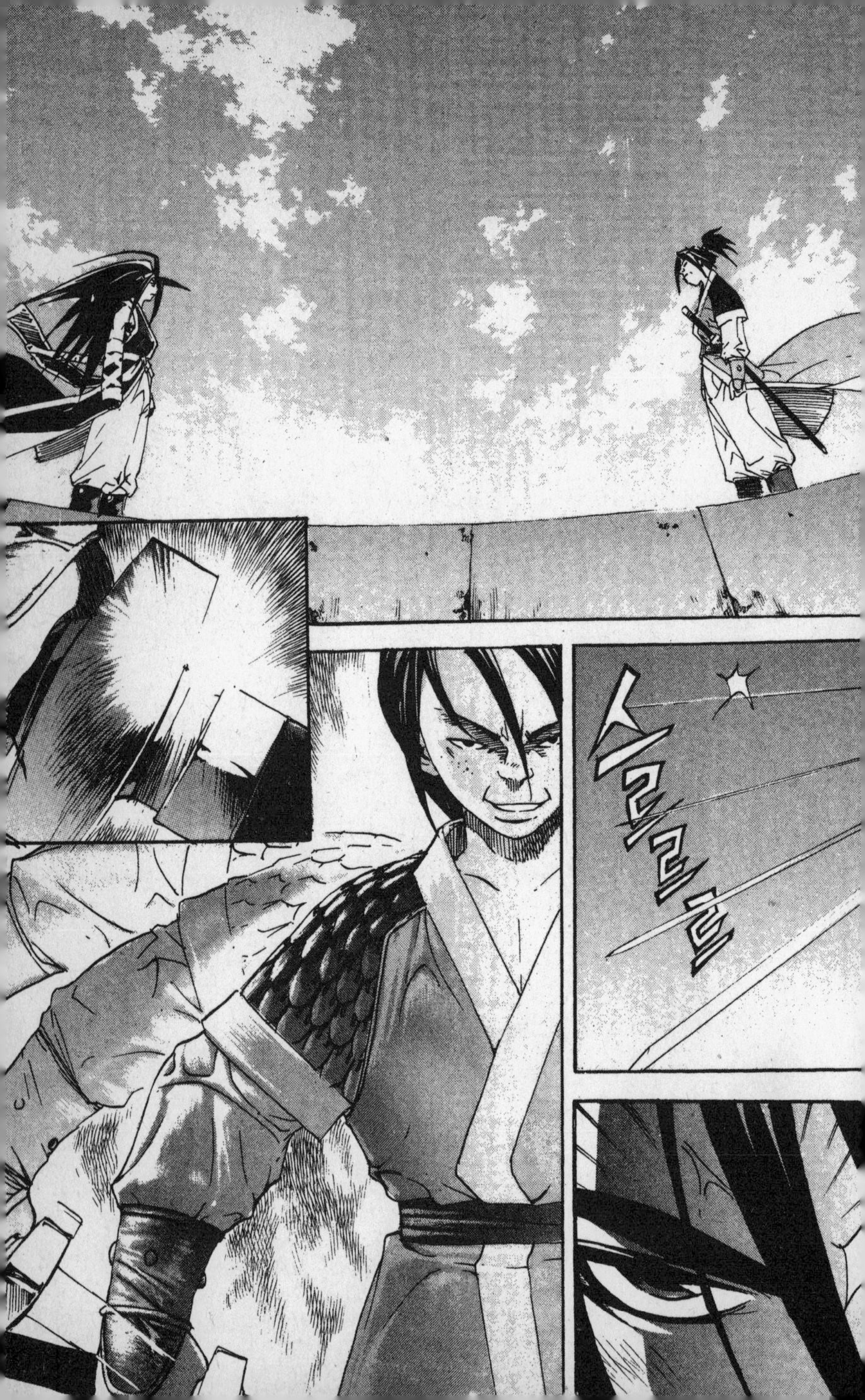

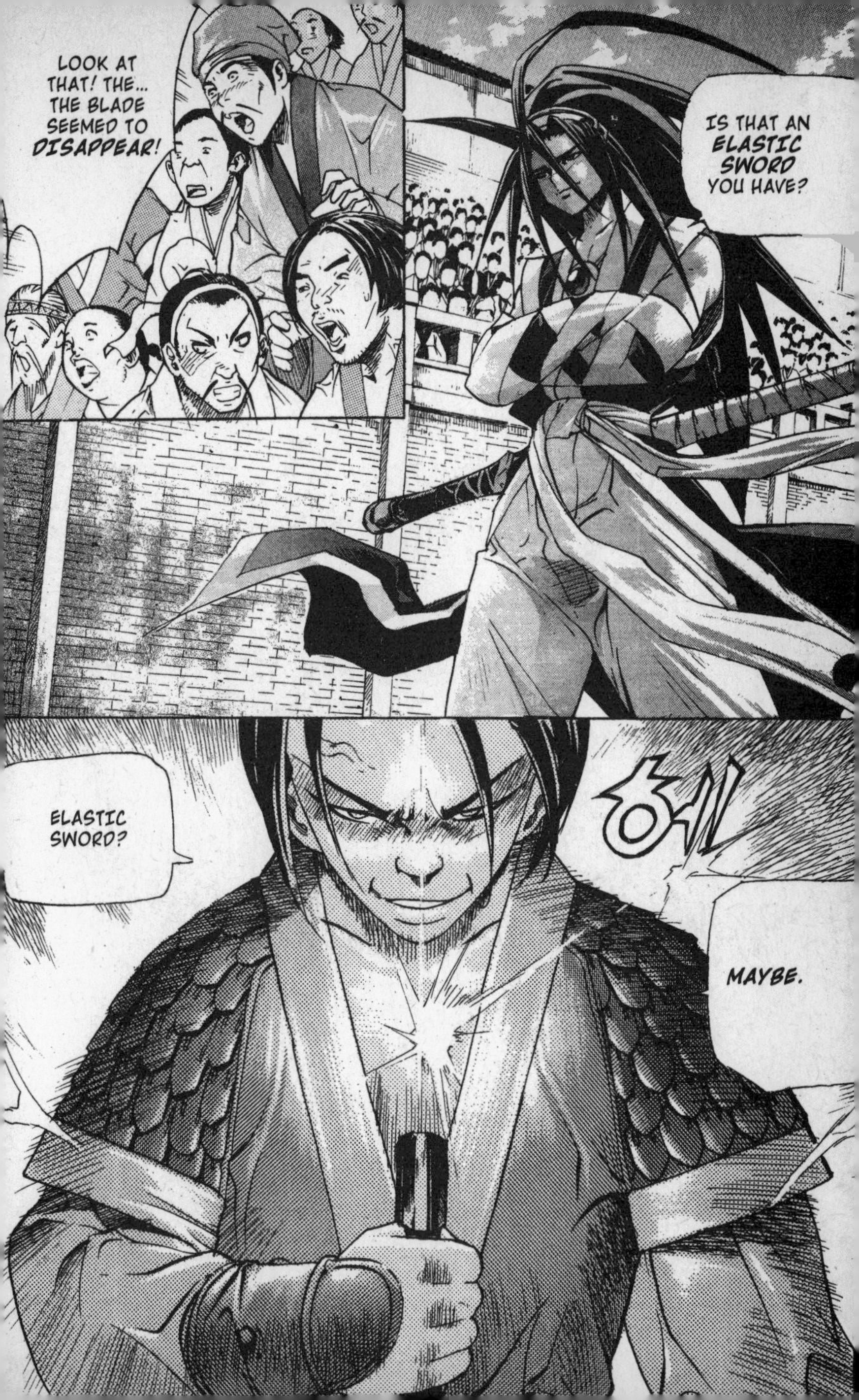
IS THAT AN ELASTIC SWORD YOU HAVE?
LOOK AT THAT! THE... THE BLADE SEEMED TO DISAPPEAR!
MAYBE.
ELASTIC SWORD?

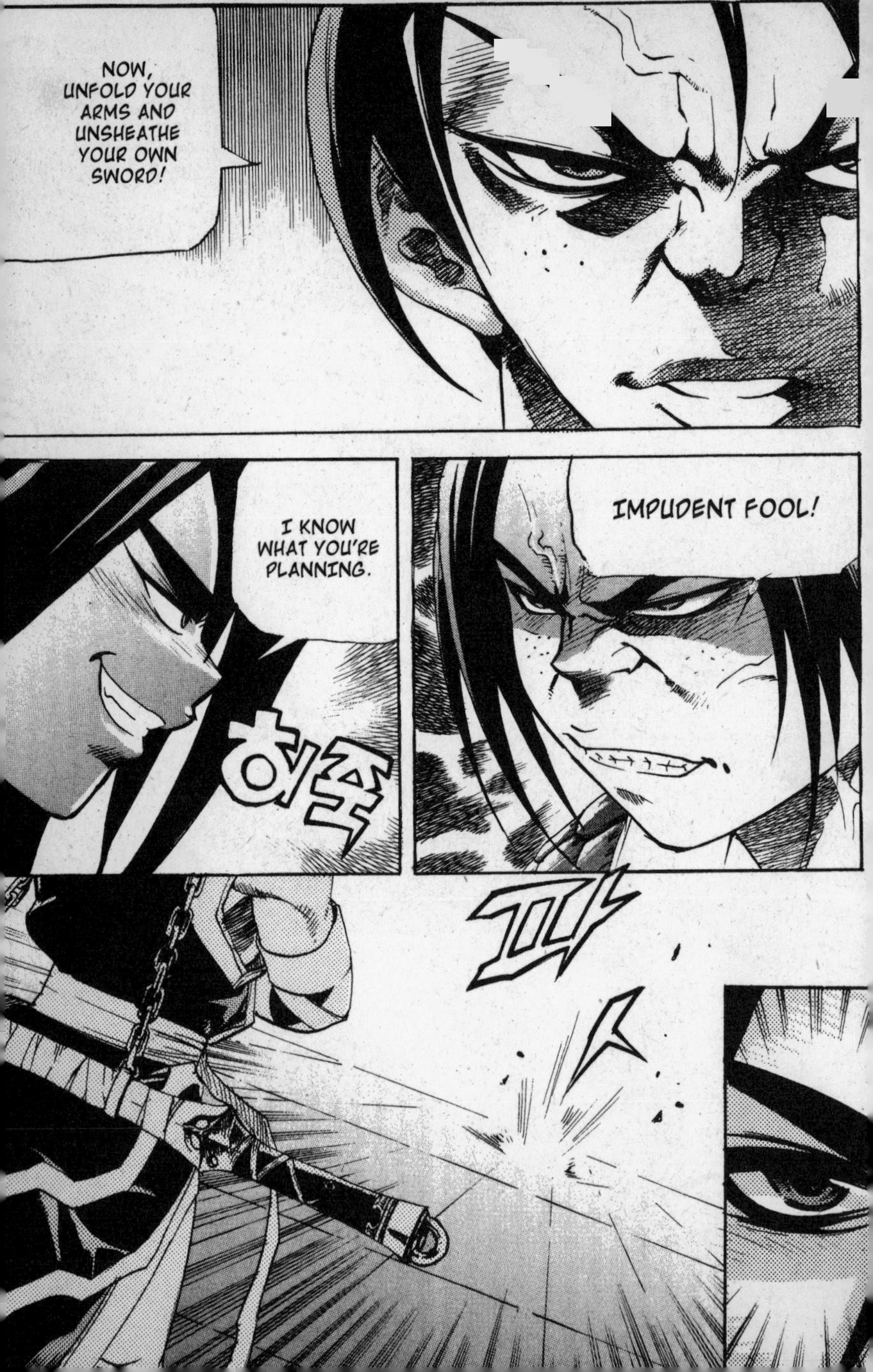
NOW, UNFOLD YOUR ARMS AND UNSHEATHE YOUR OWN SWORD!
IMPUDENT FOOL!
I KNOW WHAT YOU'RE PLANNING.
히죽

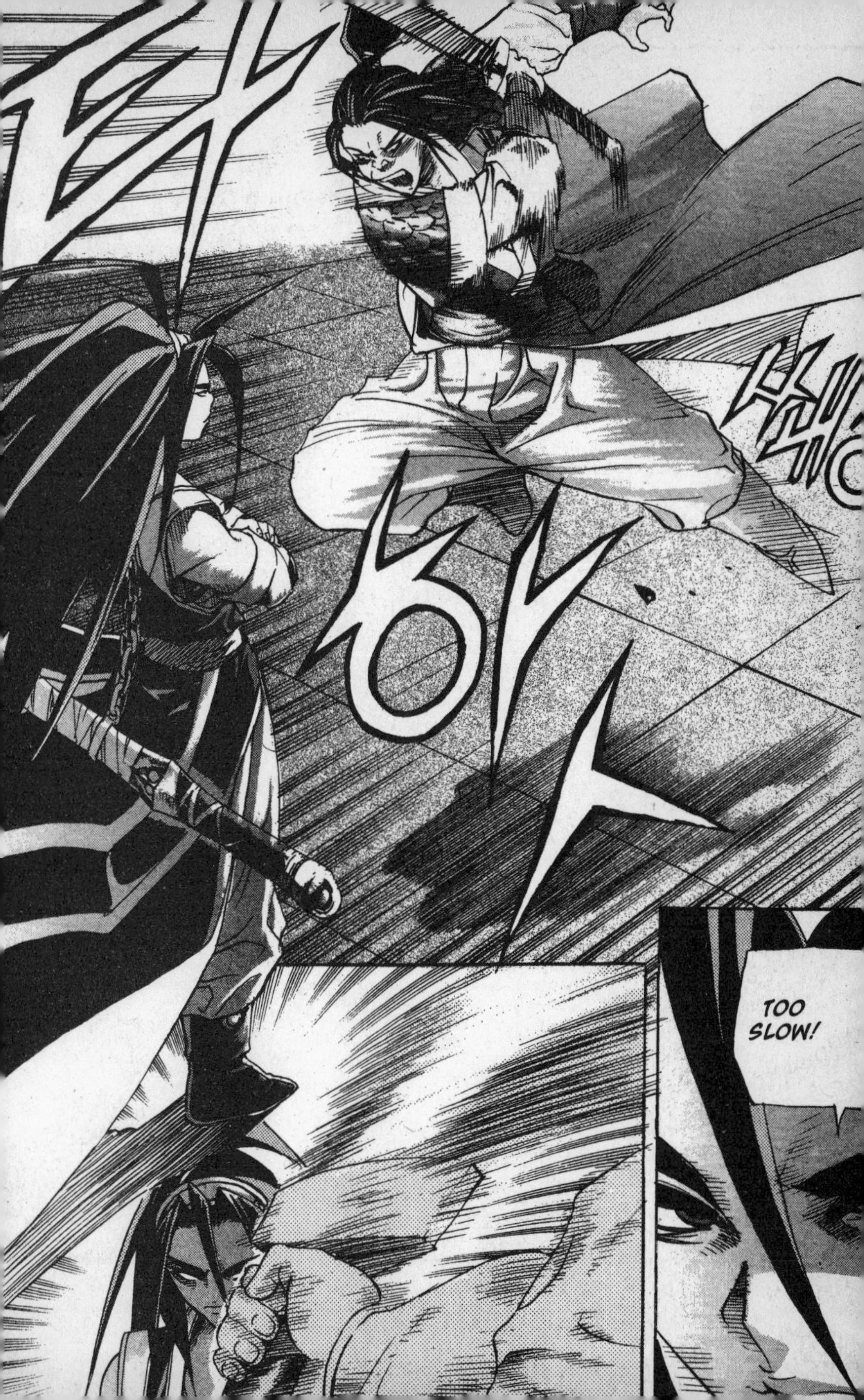
TOO SLOW!

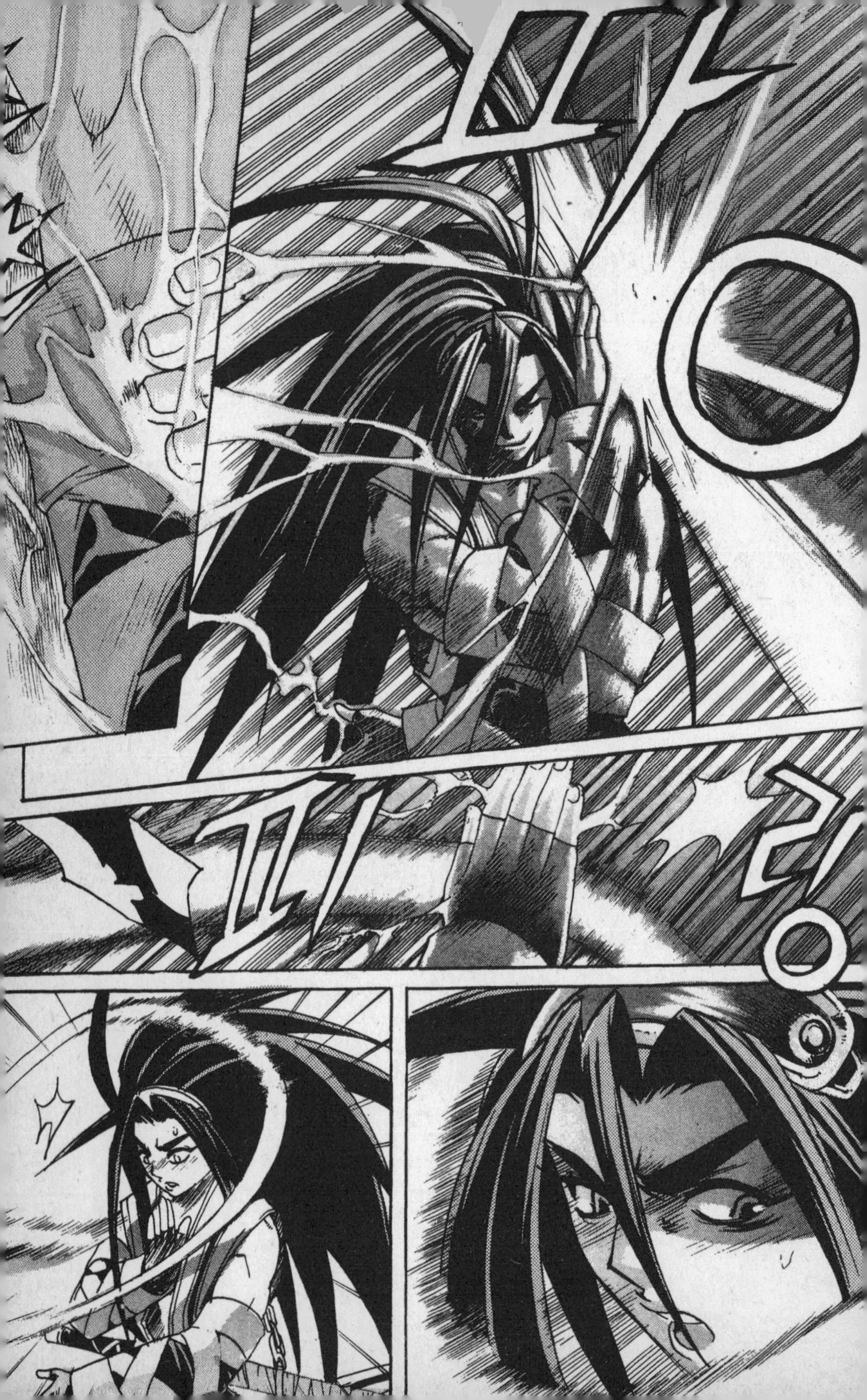

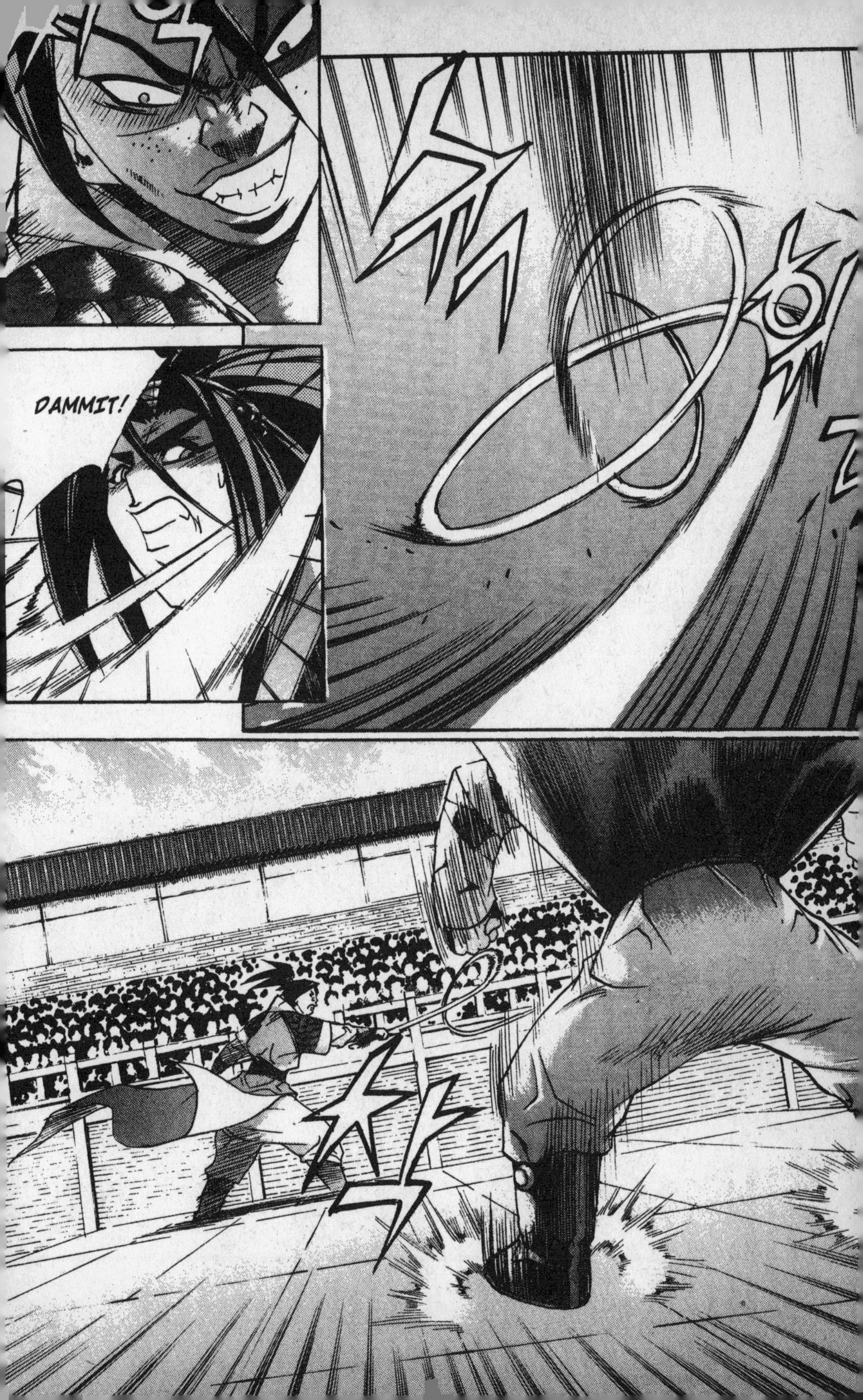
DAMMIT!

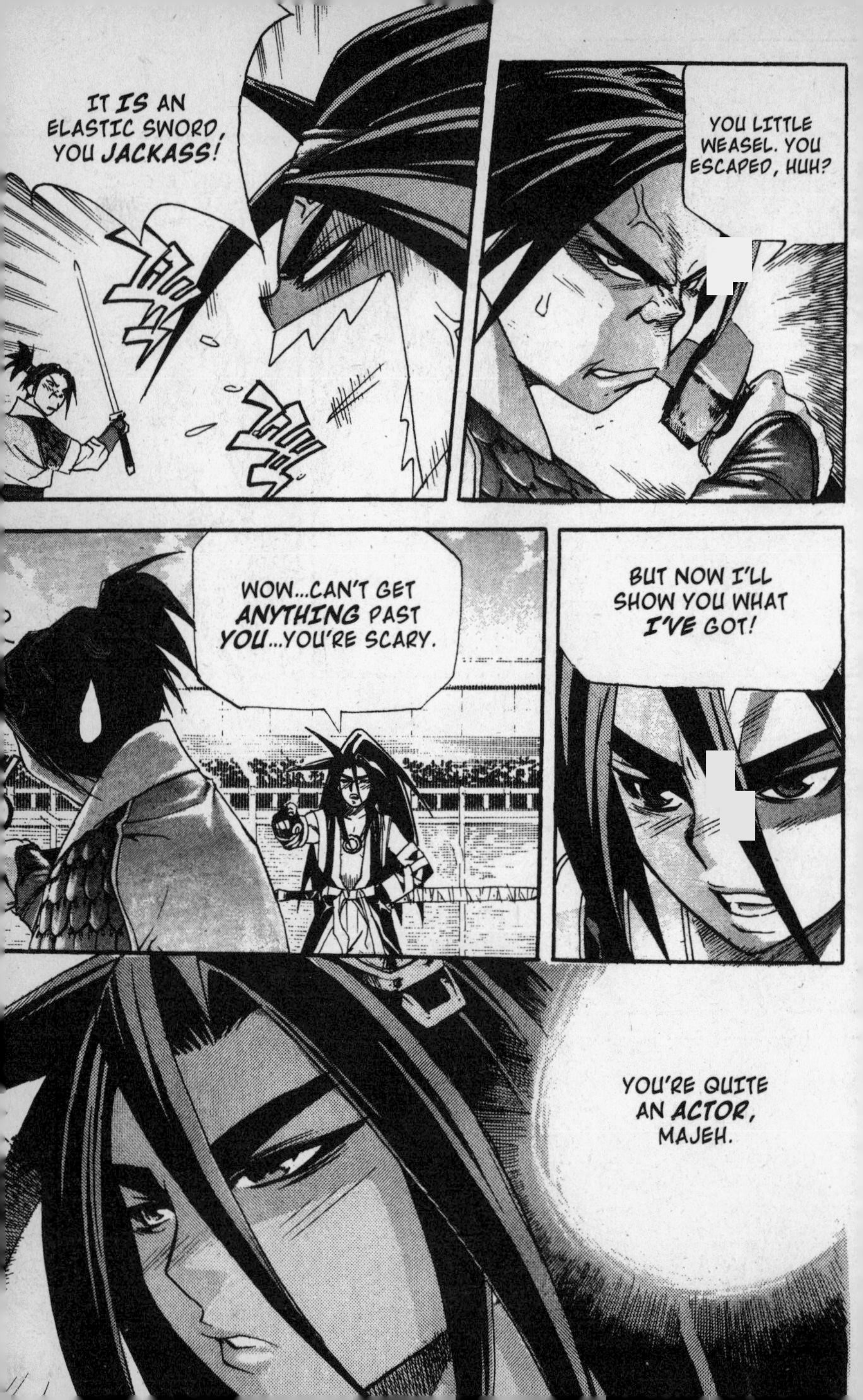
IT IS AN ELASTIC SWORD, YOU JACKASS!
YOU LITTLE WEASEL. YOU ESCAPED, HUH?
WOW...CAN'T GET ANYTHING PAST YOU...YOU'RE SCARY.
BUT NOW I'LL SHOW YOU WHAT I'VE GOT!
YOU'RE QUITE AN ACTOR, MAJEH.

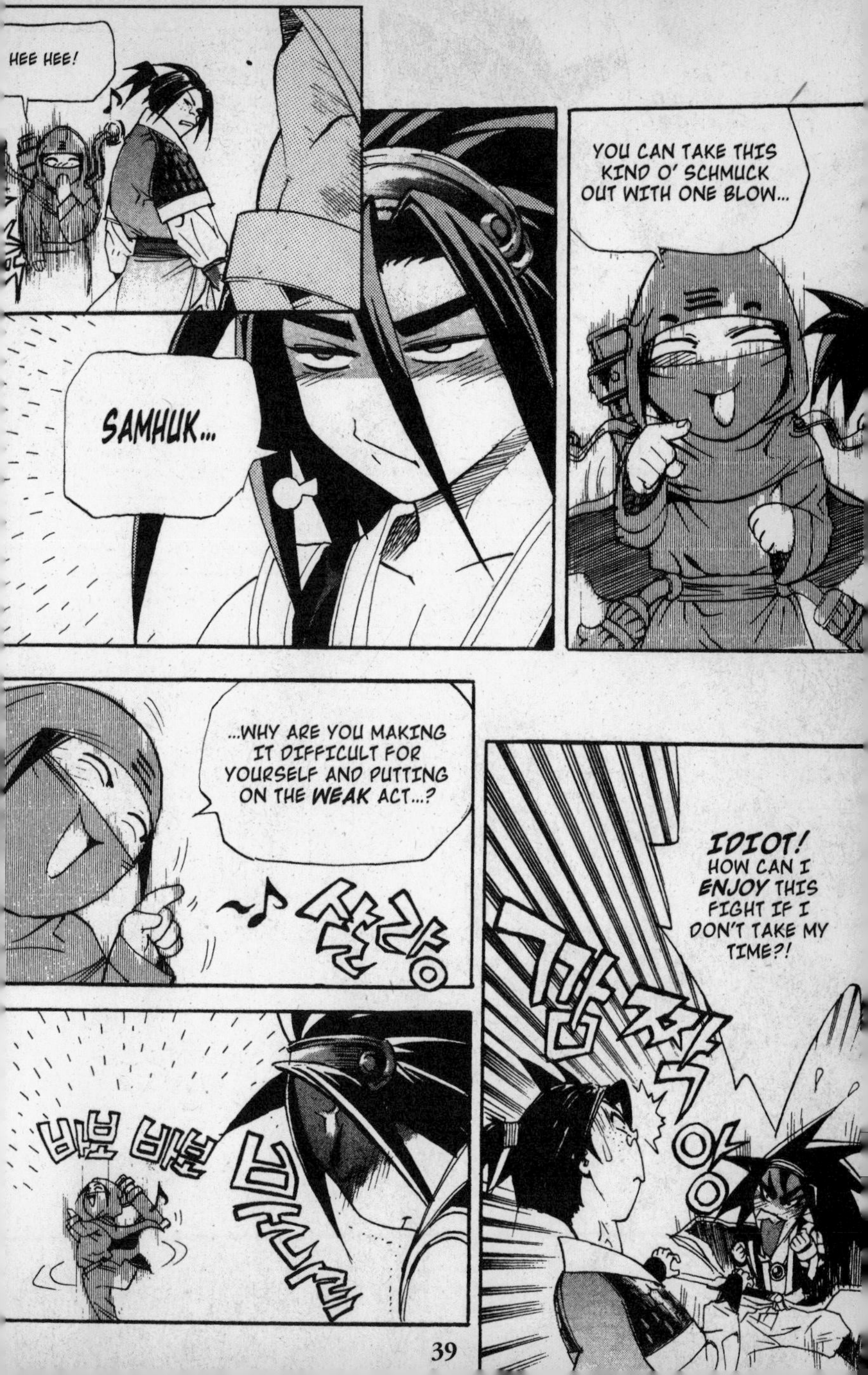
HEE HEE!
SAMHUK...
YOU CAN TAKE THIS KIND O' SCHMUCK OUT WITH ONE BLOW...
...WHY ARE YOU MAKING IT DIFFICULT FOR YOURSELF AND PUTTING ON THE WEAK ACT...?
~♪
바보 바보
IDIOT! HOW CAN I ENJOY THIS FIGHT IF I DON'T TAKE MY TIME?!

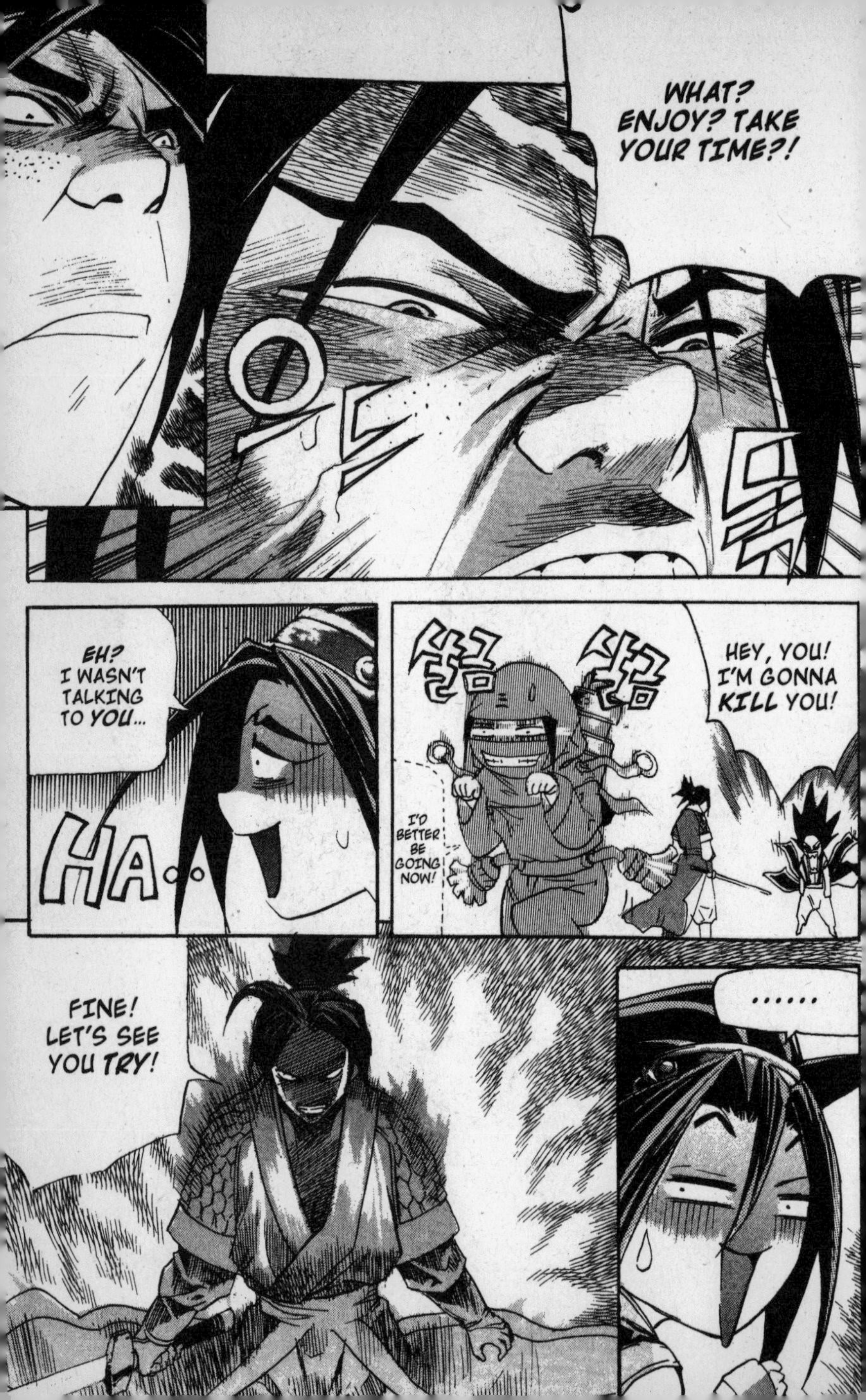
WHAT? ENJOY? TAKE YOUR TIME?!
EH? I WASN'T TALKING TO YOU...
HA..
HEY, YOU! I'M GONNA KILL YOU!
I'D BETTER BE GOING NOW!
FINE! LET'S SEE YOU TRY!
......

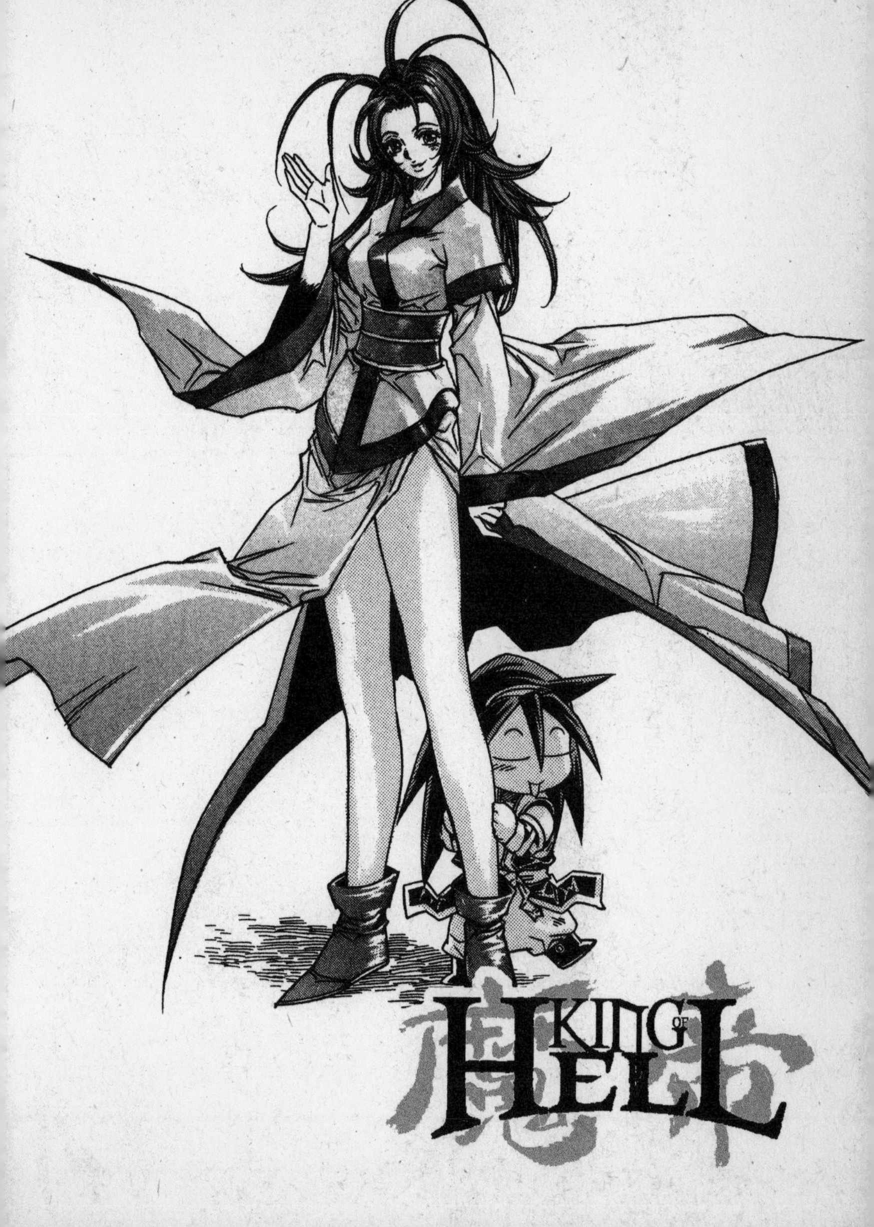
KING OF HELL

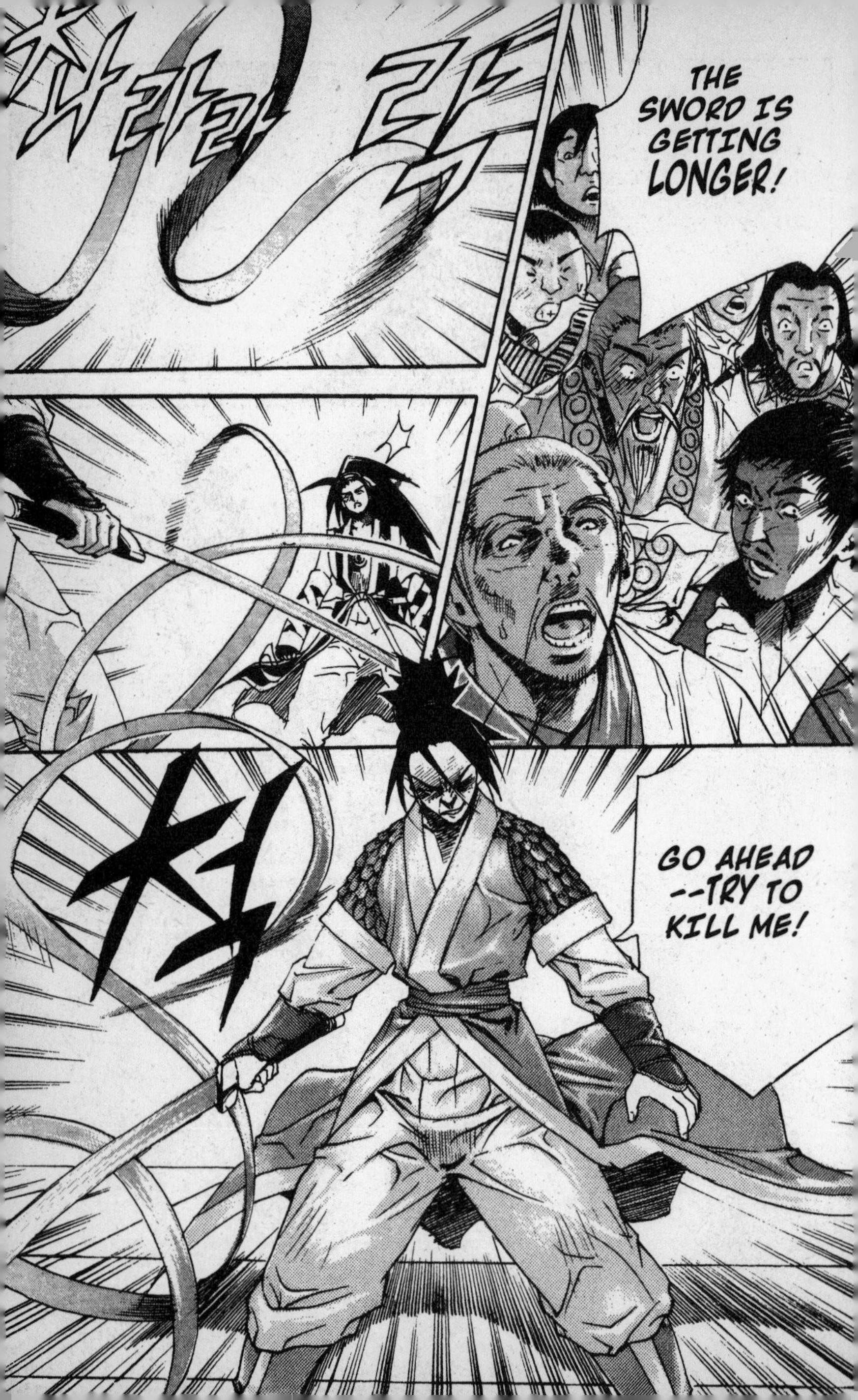
THE SWORD IS GETTING LONGER!
GO AHEAD --TRY TO KILL ME!

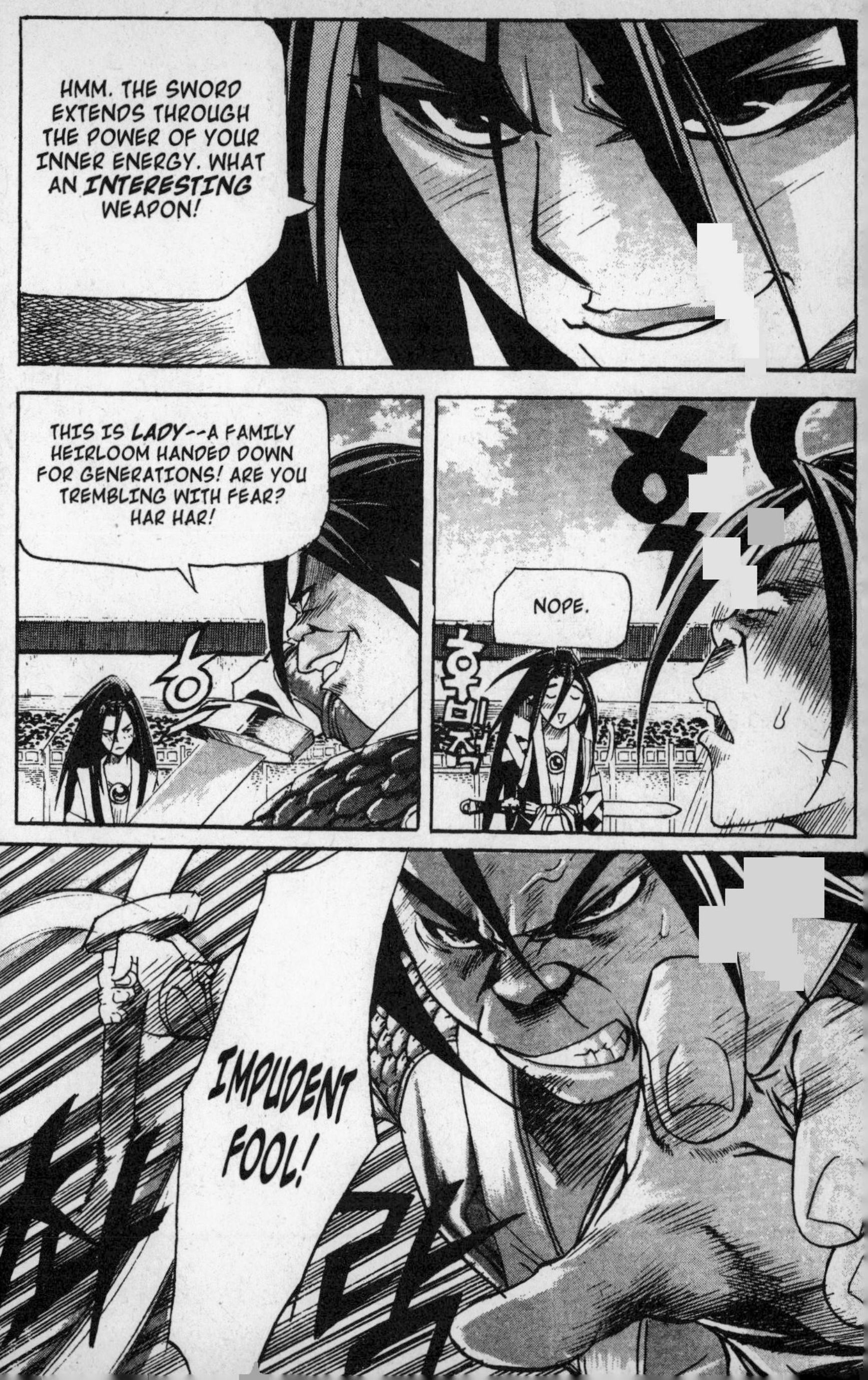
HMM. THE SWORD EXTENDS THROUGH THE POWER OF YOUR INNER ENERGY. WHAT AN INTERESTING WEAPON!
THIS IS LADY--A FAMILY HEIRLOOM HANDED DOWN FOR GENERATIONS! ARE YOU TREMBLING WITH FEAR? HAR HAR!
NOPE.
IMPUDENT FOOL!

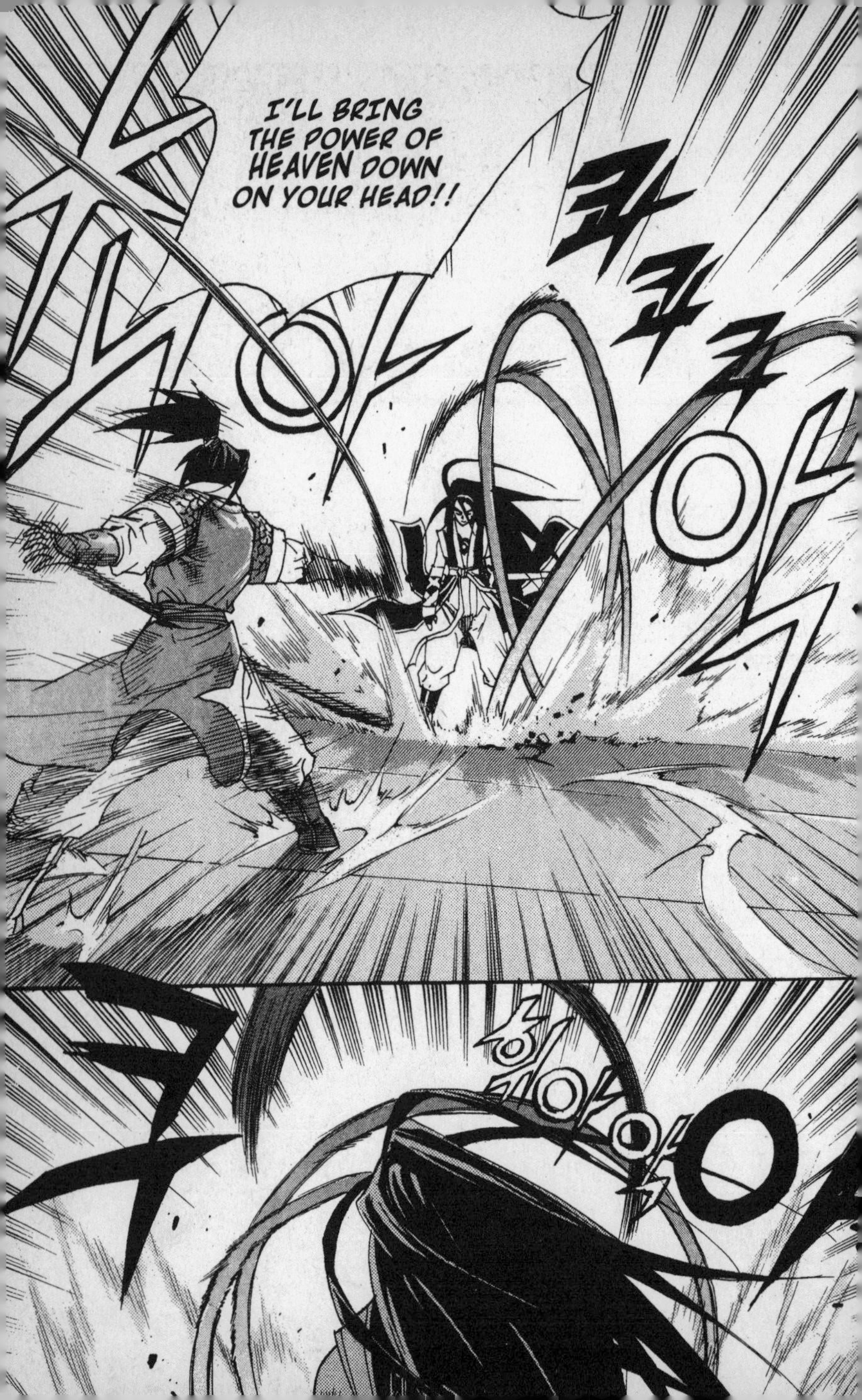
I'LL BRING THE POWER OF HEAVEN DOWN ON YOUR HEAD!!

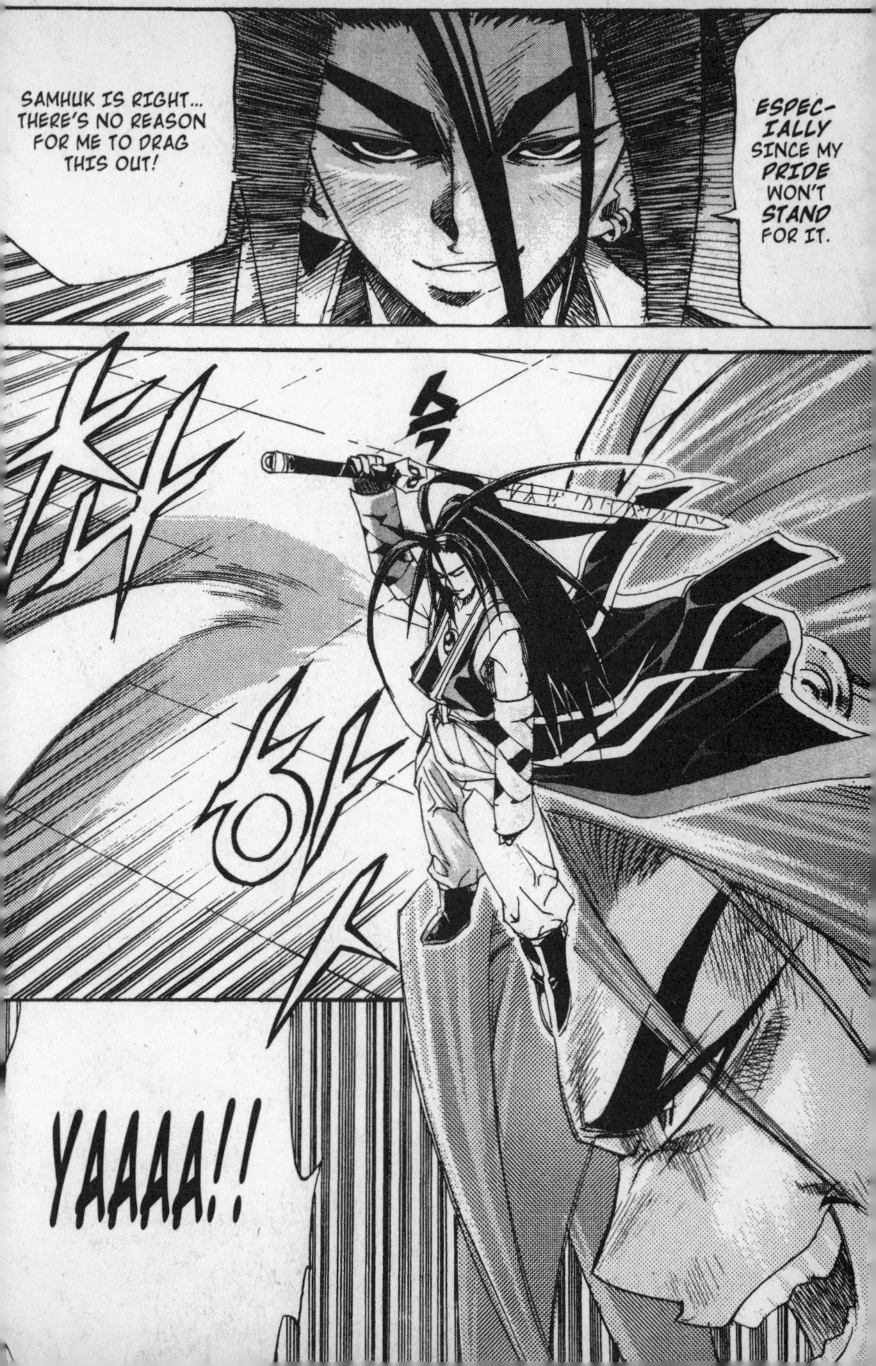
ESPEC-IALLY SINCE MY PRIDE WON'T STAND FOR IT.
SAMHUK IS RIGHT... THERE'S NO REASON FOR ME TO DRAG THIS OUT!
YAAAA!!

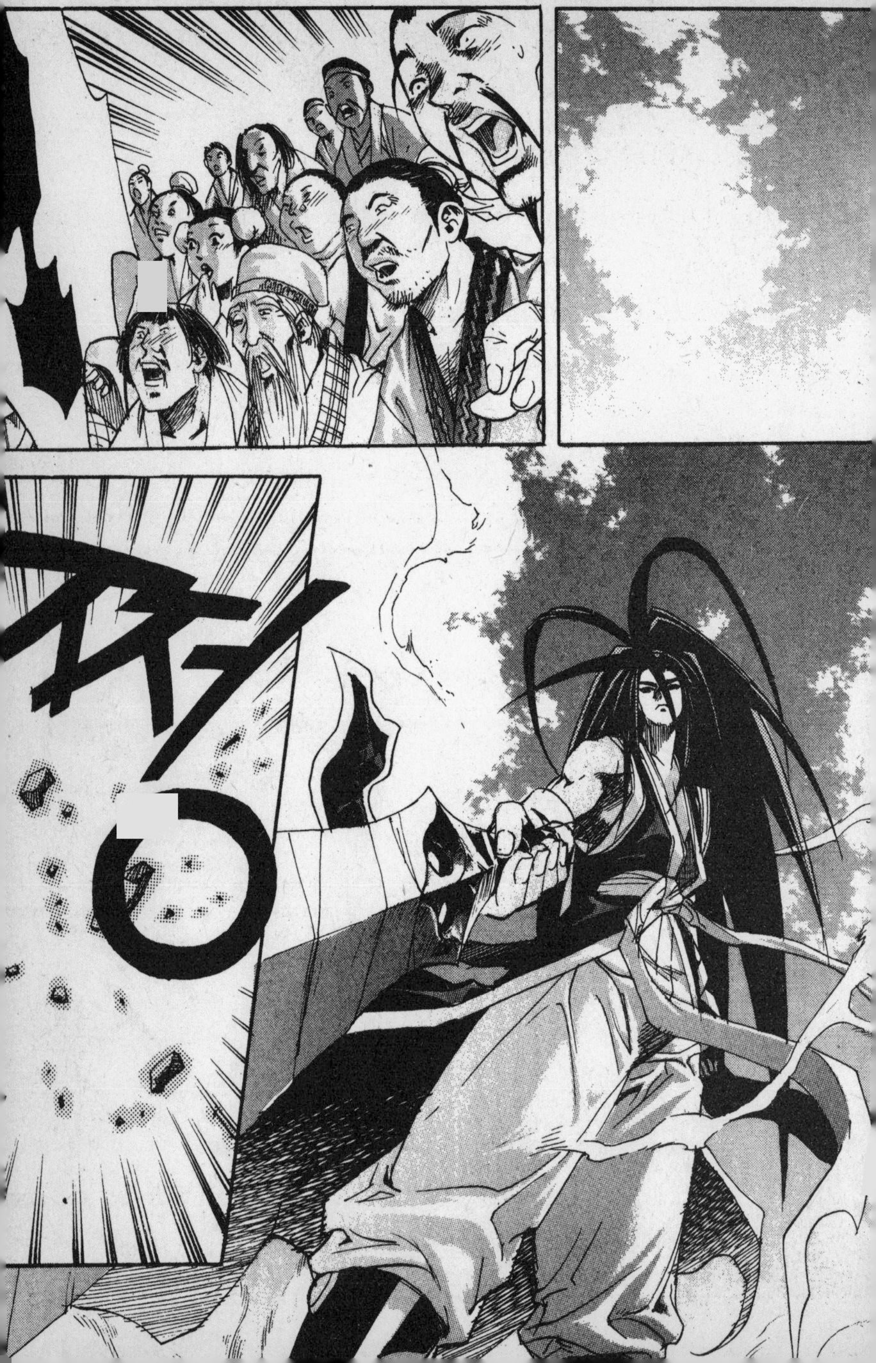

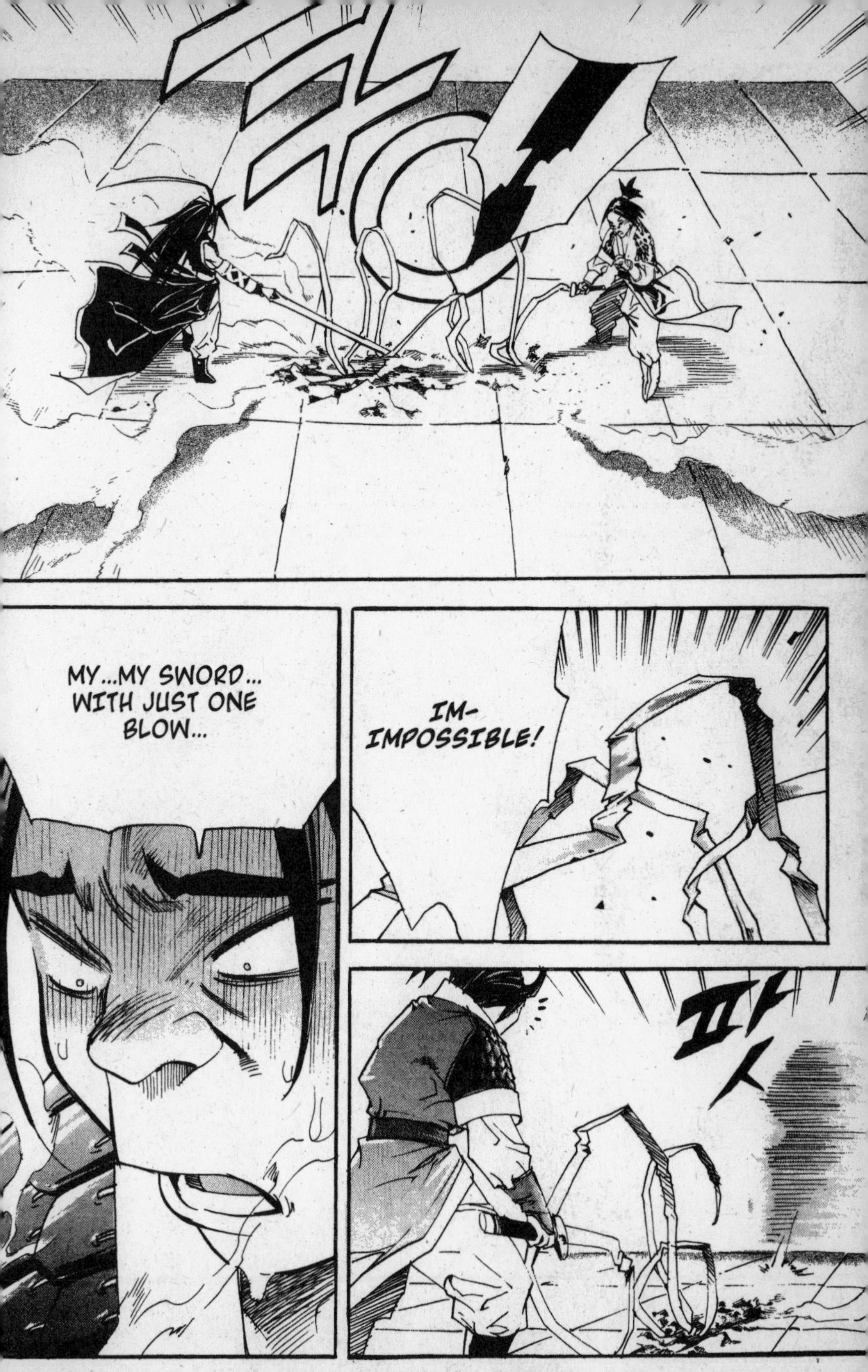
IM-
IMPOSSIBLE!
MY...MY SWORD...
WITH JUST ONE
BLOW...

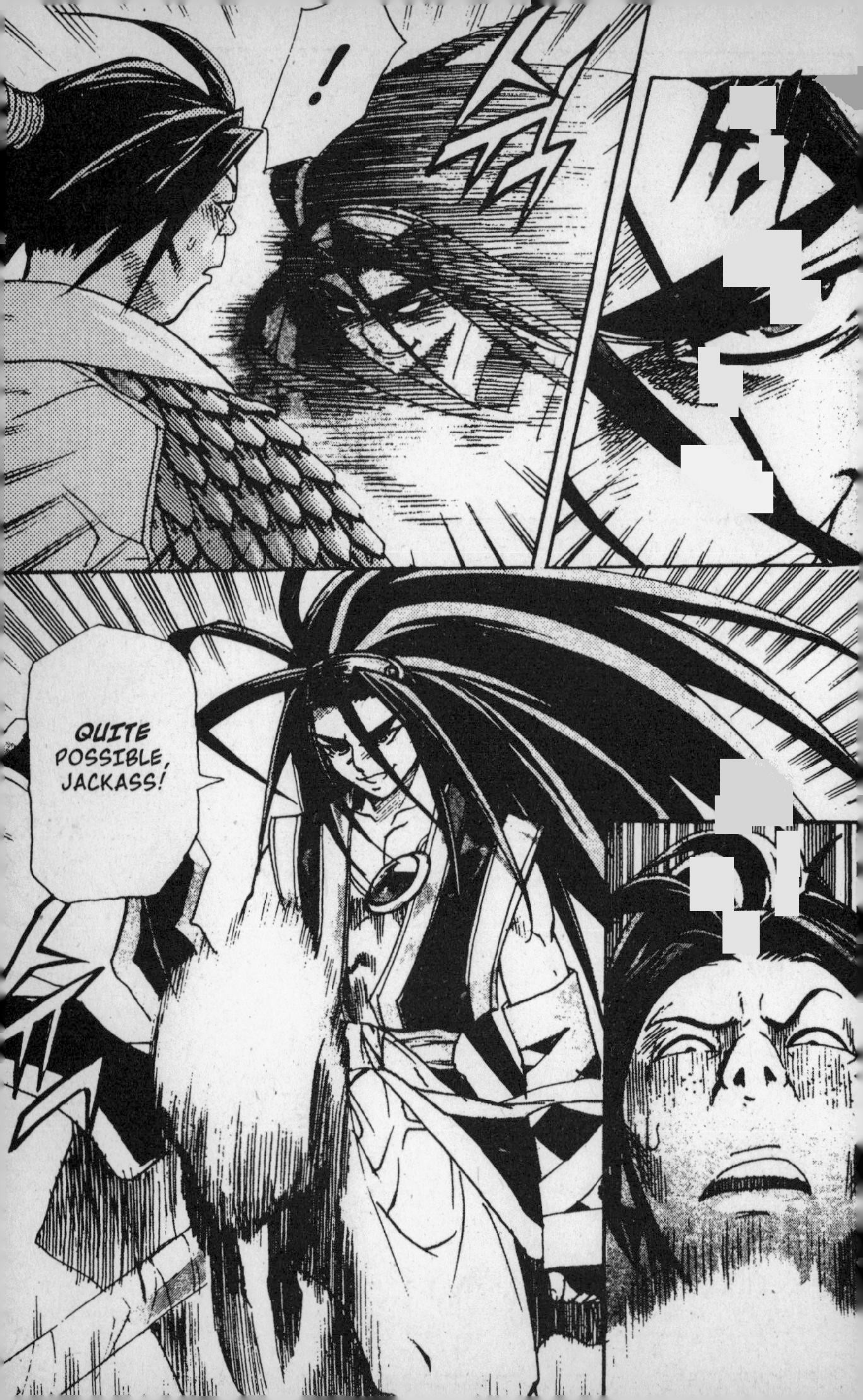
!
QUITE POSSIBLE, JACKASS!

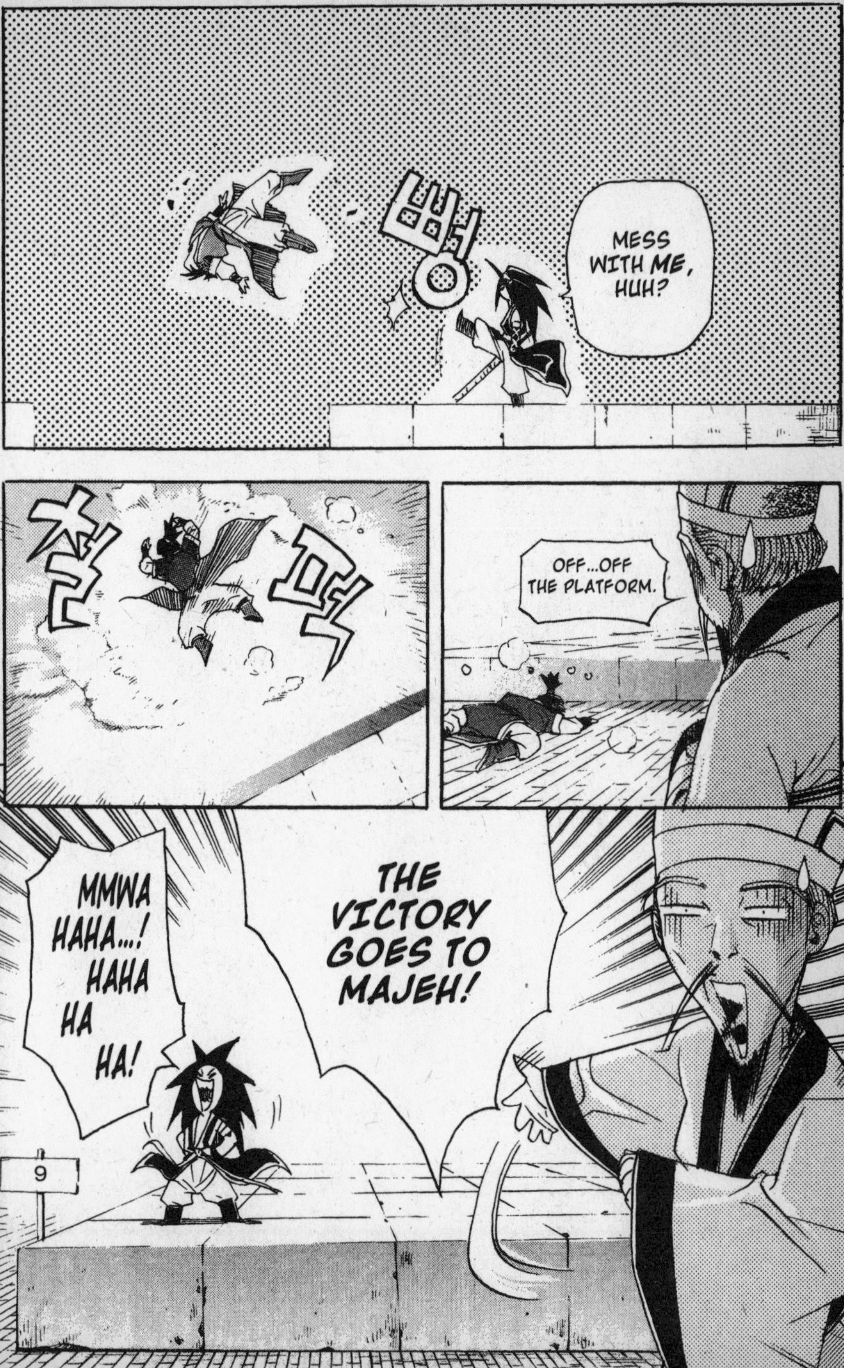
MESS WITH ME, HUH?
OFF...OFF THE PLATFORM.
MMWA HAHA...! HAHA HA HA!
THE VICTORY GOES TO MAJEH!
9

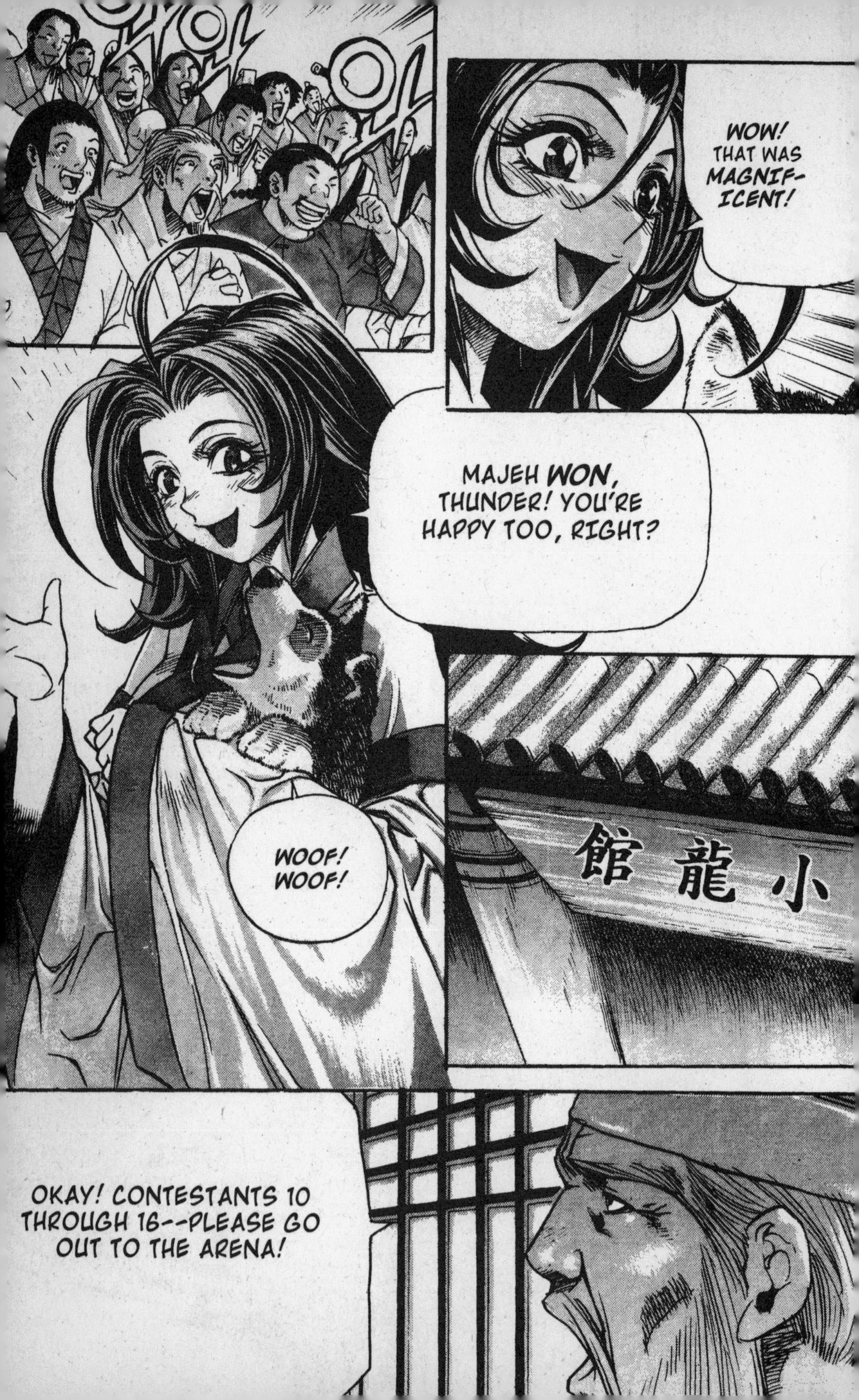
WOW! THAT WAS MAGNIFICENT!
MAJEH WON, THUNDER! YOU'RE HAPPY TOO, RIGHT?
WOOF! WOOF!
小龍館
OKAY! CONTESTANTS 10 THROUGH 16--PLEASE GO OUT TO THE ARENA!

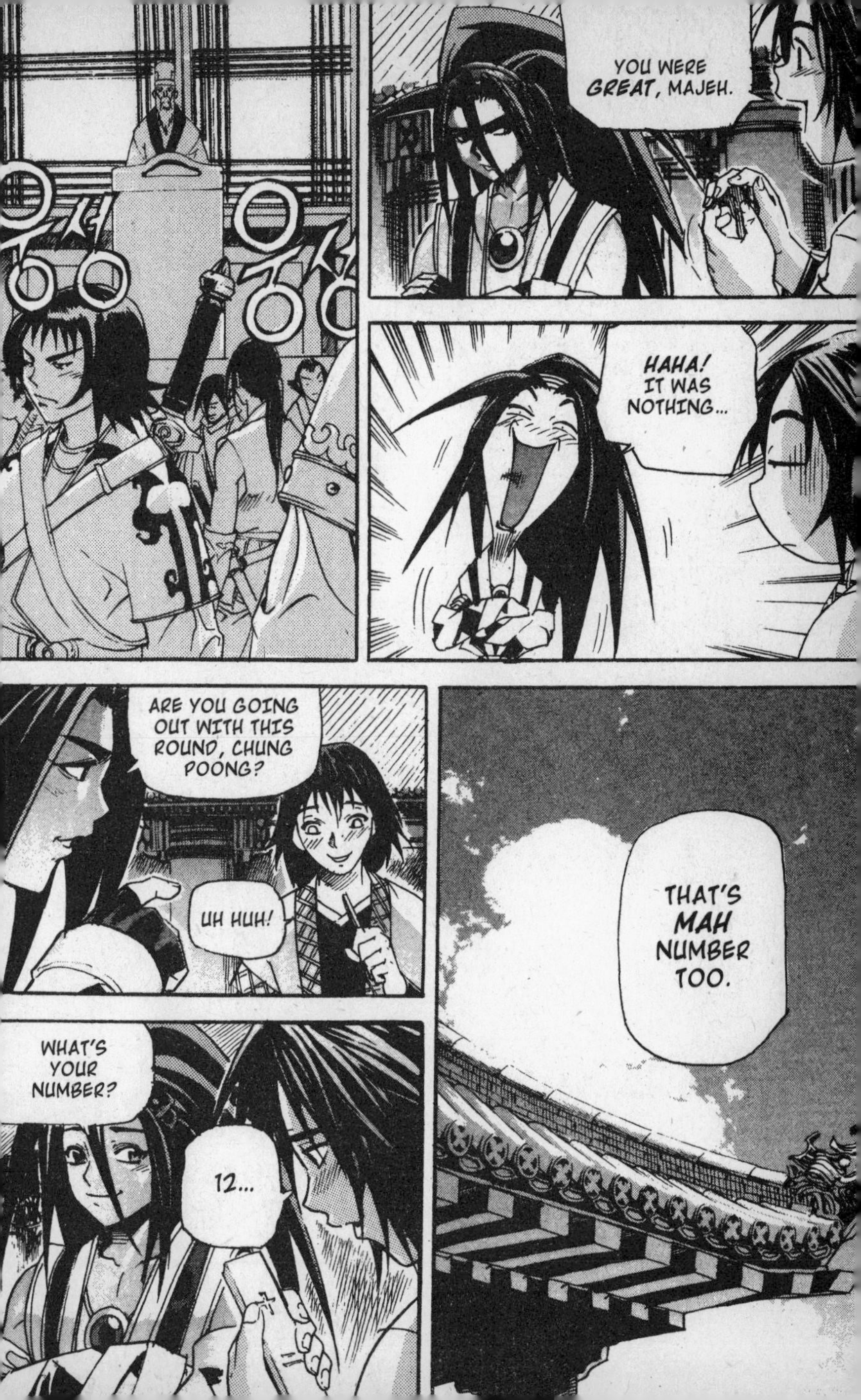
YOU WERE GREAT, MAJEH.
HAHA! IT WAS NOTHING...
ARE YOU GOING OUT WITH THIS ROUND, CHUNG POONG?
UH HUH!
WHAT'S YOUR NUMBER?
12...
THAT'S MAH NUMBER TOO.

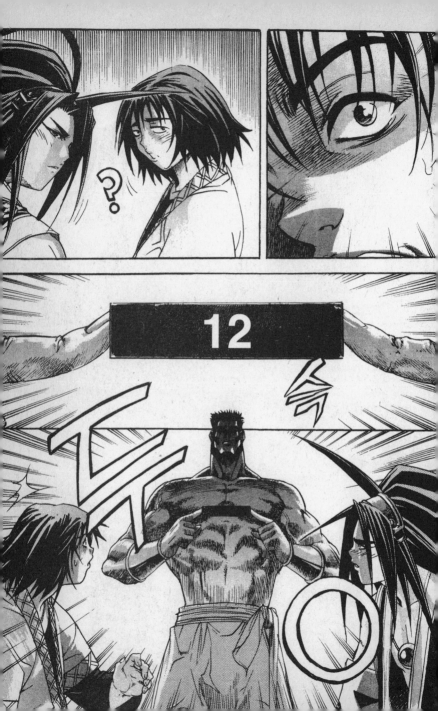

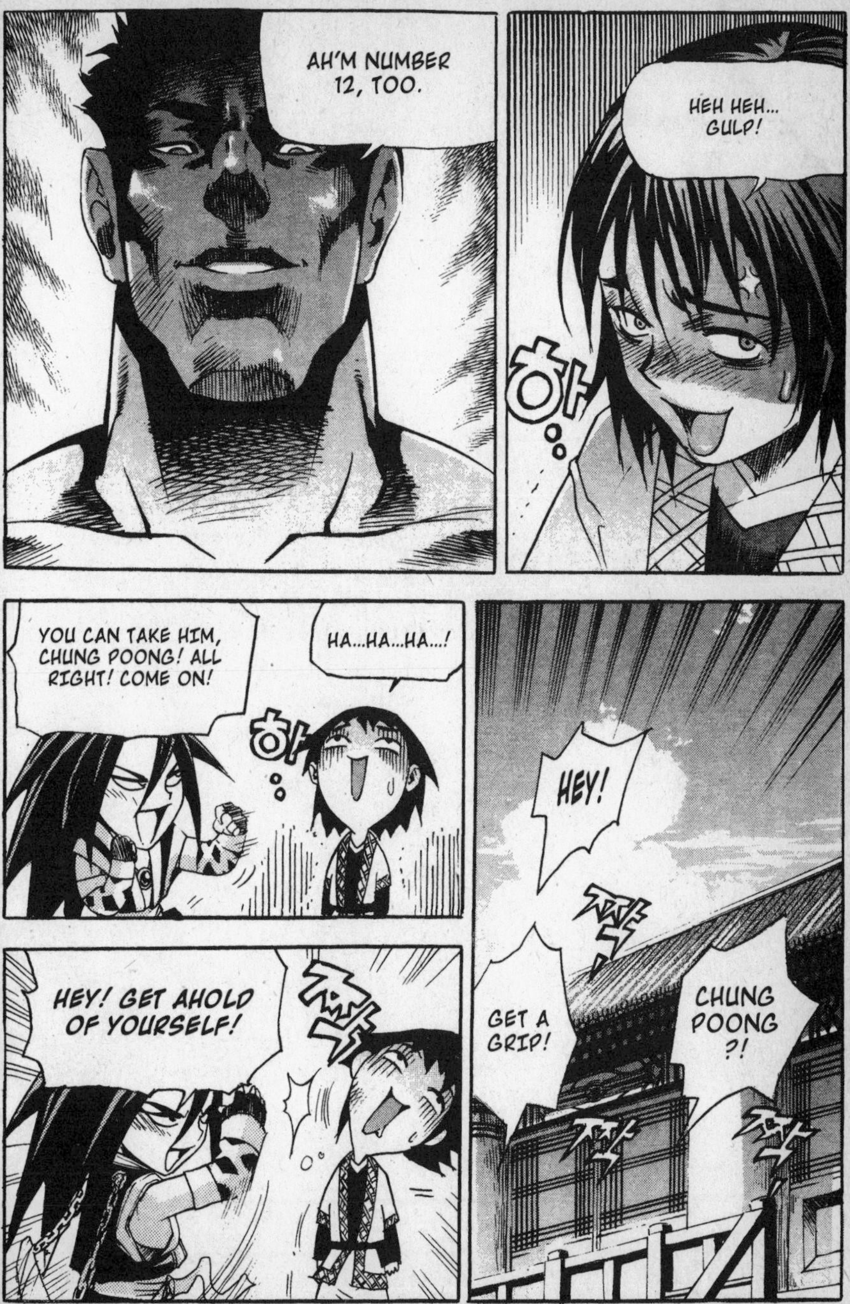
AH'M NUMBER 12, TOO.
HEH HEH... GULP!
하
YOU CAN TAKE HIM, CHUNG POONG! ALL RIGHT! COME ON!
HA...HA...HA...!
하
HEY! GET AHOLD OF YOURSELF!
HEY!
GET A GRIP!
CHUNG POONG ?!

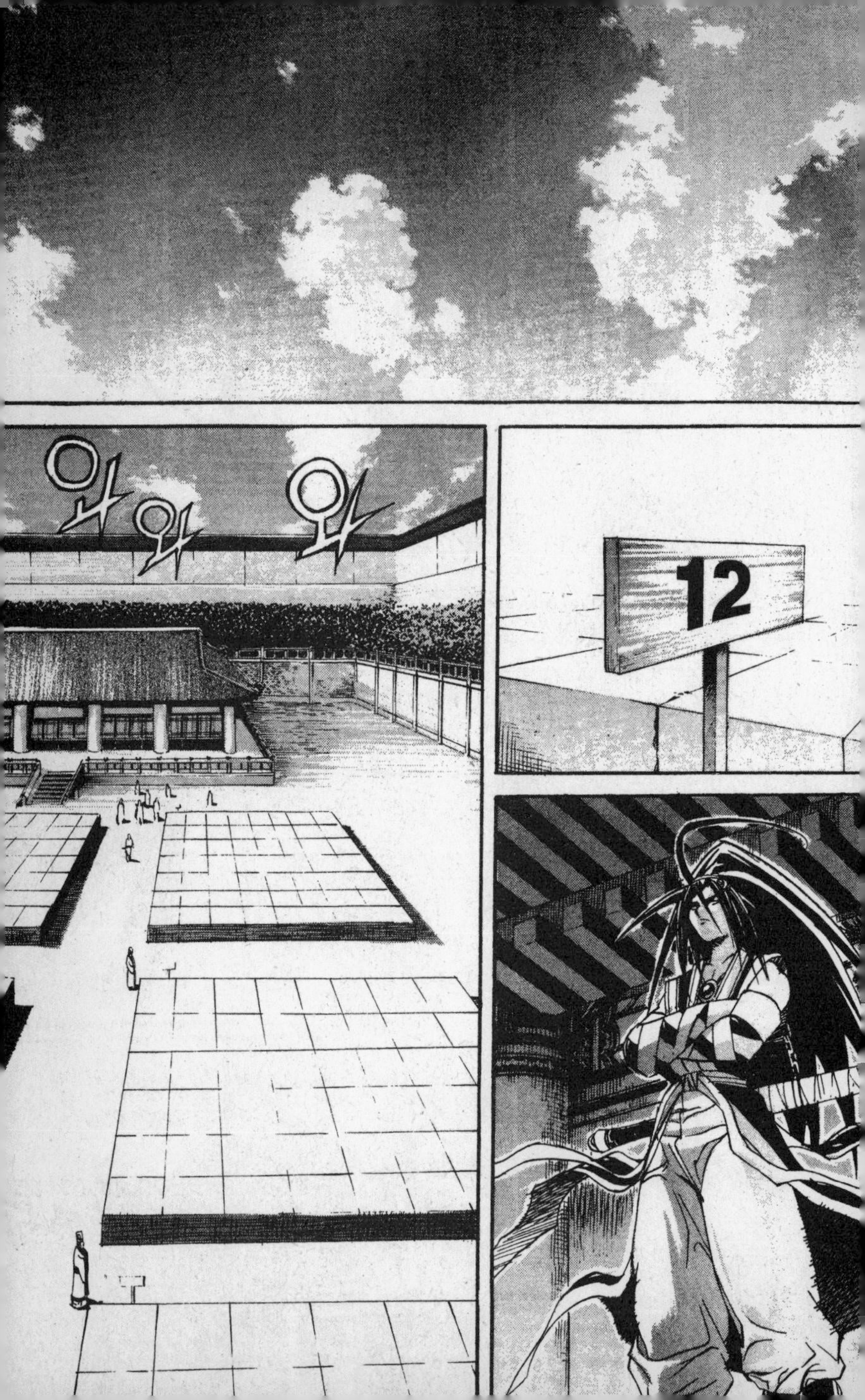
12
와 와 와

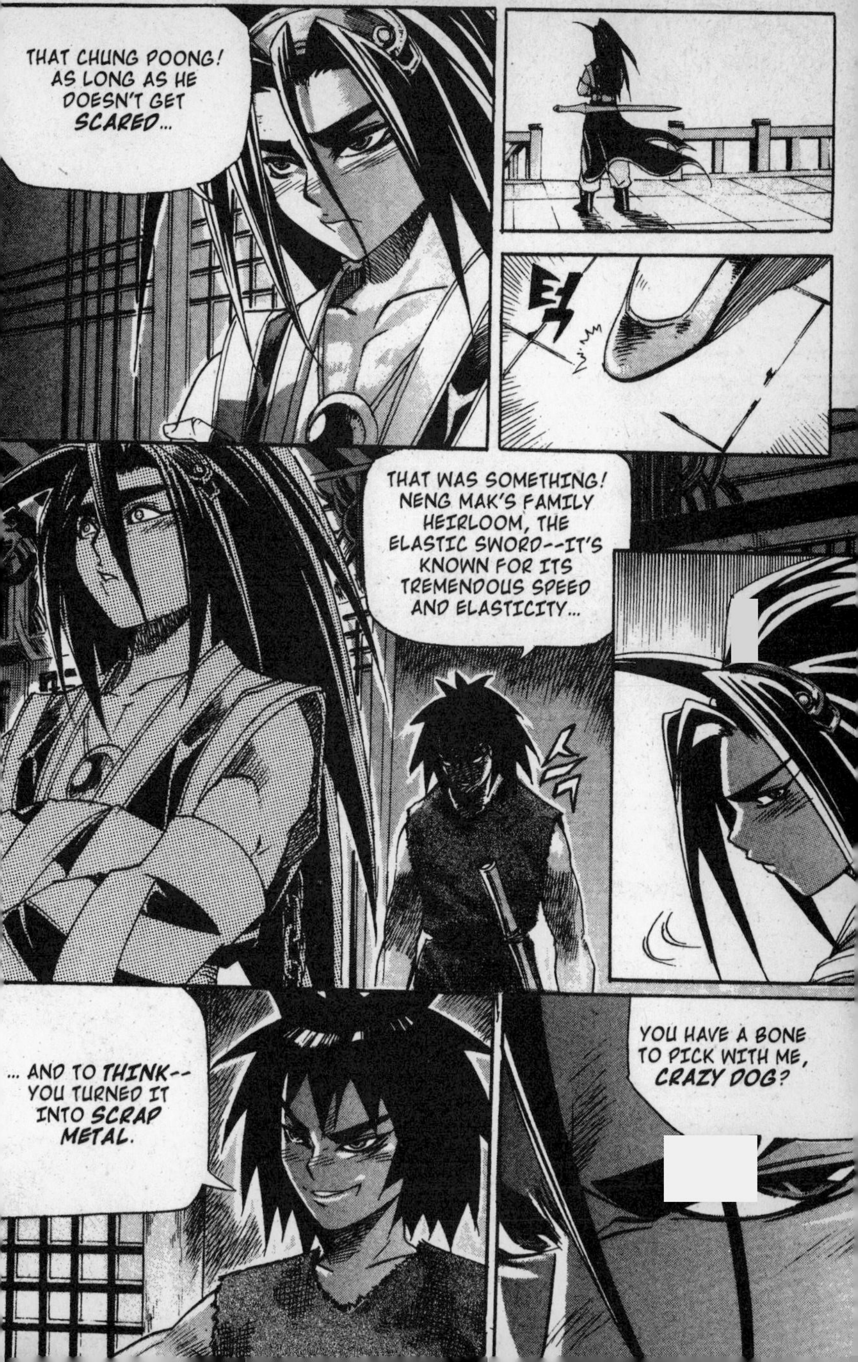
THAT CHUNG POONG! AS LONG AS HE DOESN'T GET SCARED...
THAT WAS SOMETHING! NENG MAK'S FAMILY HEIRLOOM, THE ELASTIC SWORD--IT'S KNOWN FOR ITS TREMENDOUS SPEED AND ELASTICITY...
... AND TO THINK-- YOU TURNED IT INTO SCRAP METAL.
YOU HAVE A BONE TO PICK WITH ME, CRAZY DOG?

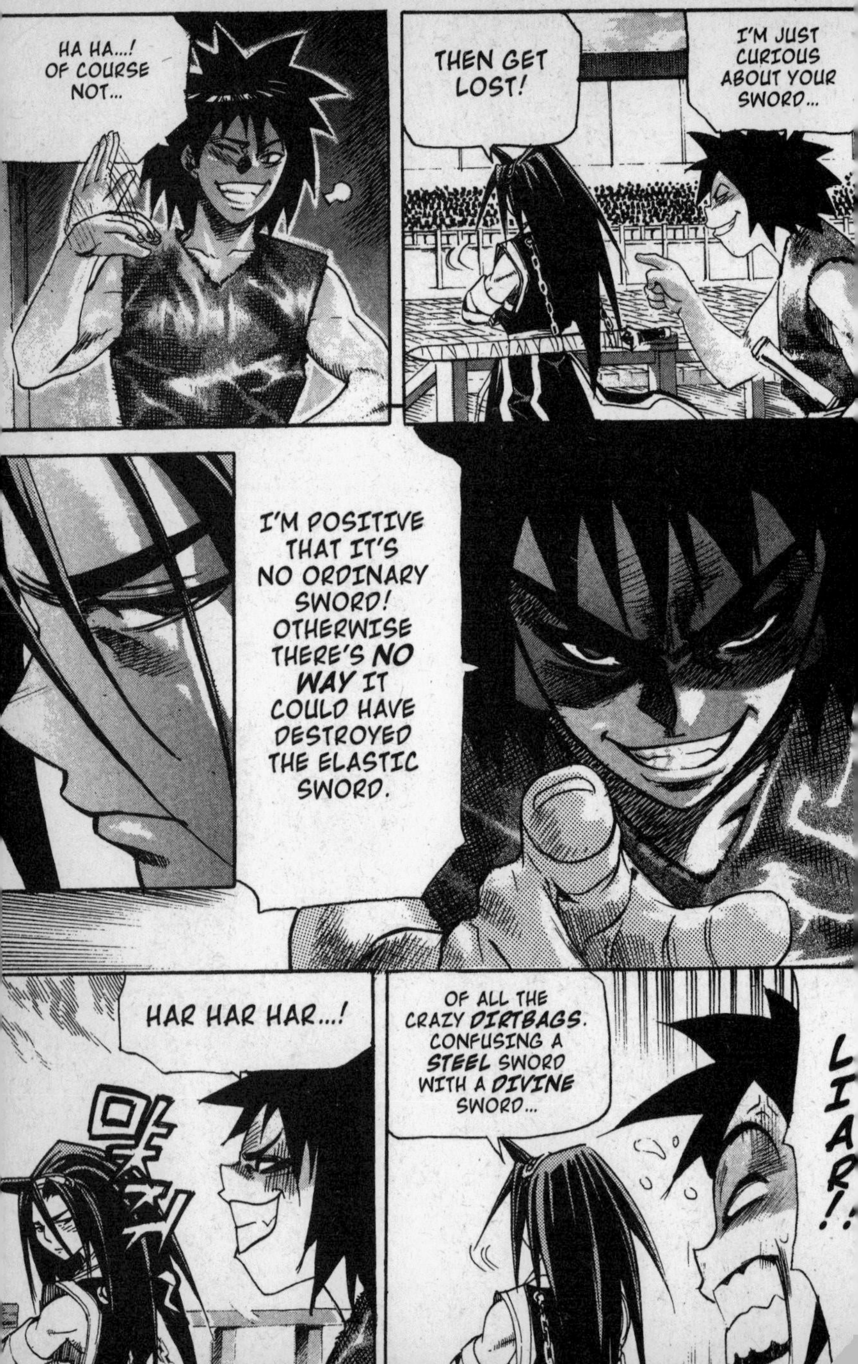
I'M JUST CURIOUS ABOUT YOUR SWORD...
THEN GET LOST!
HA HA...! OF COURSE NOT...
I'M POSITIVE THAT IT'S NO ORDINARY SWORD! OTHERWISE THERE'S NO WAY IT COULD HAVE DESTROYED THE ELASTIC SWORD.
LIAR!!
OF ALL THE CRAZY DIRTBAGS. CONFUSING A STEEL SWORD WITH A DIVINE SWORD...
HAR HAR HAR...!

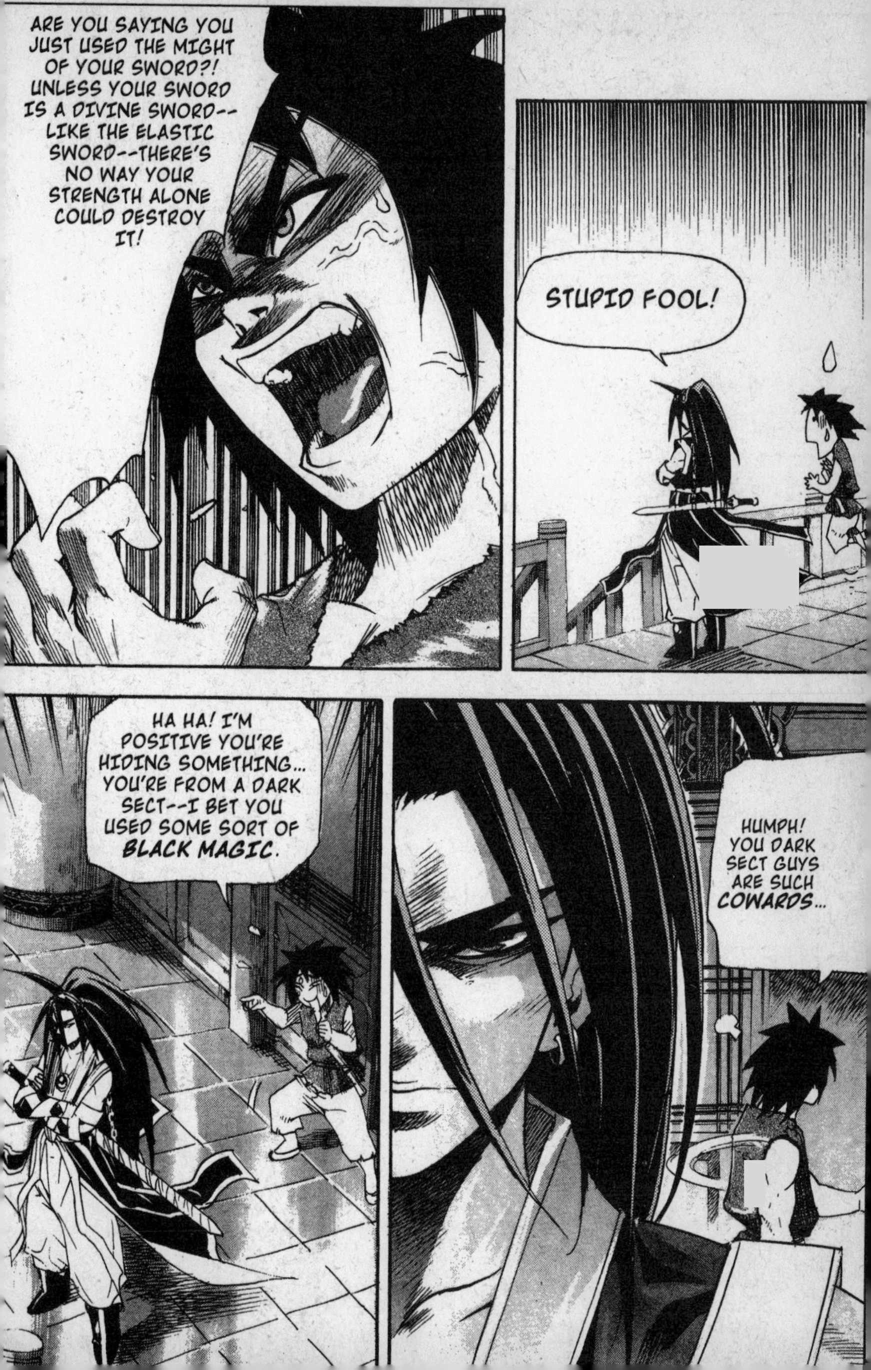
ARE YOU SAYING YOU JUST USED THE MIGHT OF YOUR SWORD?! UNLESS YOUR SWORD IS A DIVINE SWORD--LIKE THE ELASTIC SWORD--THERE'S NO WAY YOUR STRENGTH ALONE COULD DESTROY IT!
STUPID FOOL!
HA HA! I'M POSITIVE YOU'RE HIDING SOMETHING... YOU'RE FROM A DARK SECT--I BET YOU USED SOME SORT OF **BLACK MAGIC**.
HUMPH! YOU DARK SECT GUYS ARE SUCH **COWARDS**...

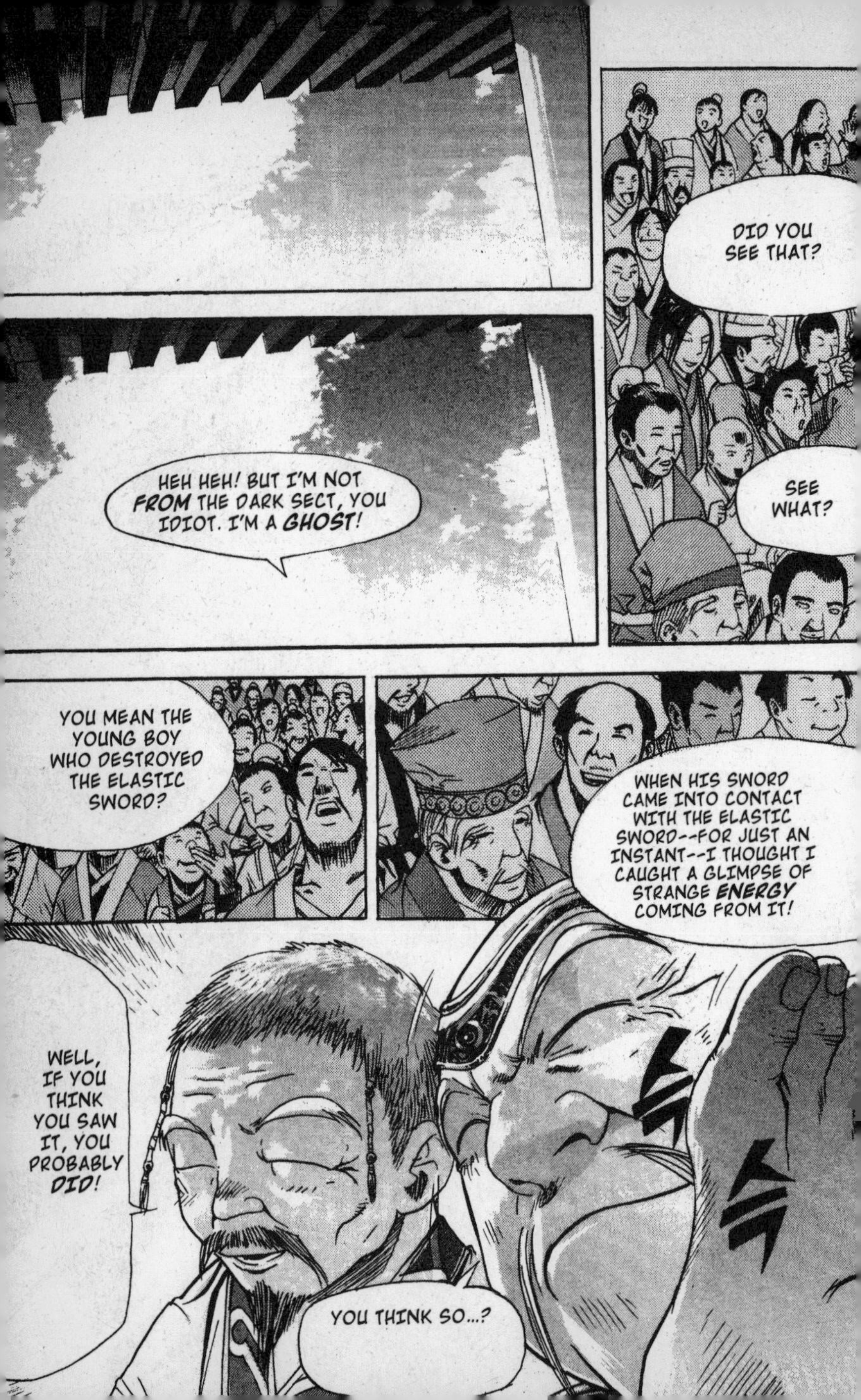
HEH HEH! BUT I'M NOT FROM THE DARK SECT, YOU IDIOT. I'M A GHOST!
DID YOU SEE THAT?
SEE WHAT?
YOU MEAN THE YOUNG BOY WHO DESTROYED THE ELASTIC SWORD?
WHEN HIS SWORD CAME INTO CONTACT WITH THE ELASTIC SWORD--FOR JUST AN INSTANT--I THOUGHT I CAUGHT A GLIMPSE OF STRANGE ENERGY COMING FROM IT!
WELL, IF YOU THINK YOU SAW IT, YOU PROBABLY DID!
YOU THINK SO...?

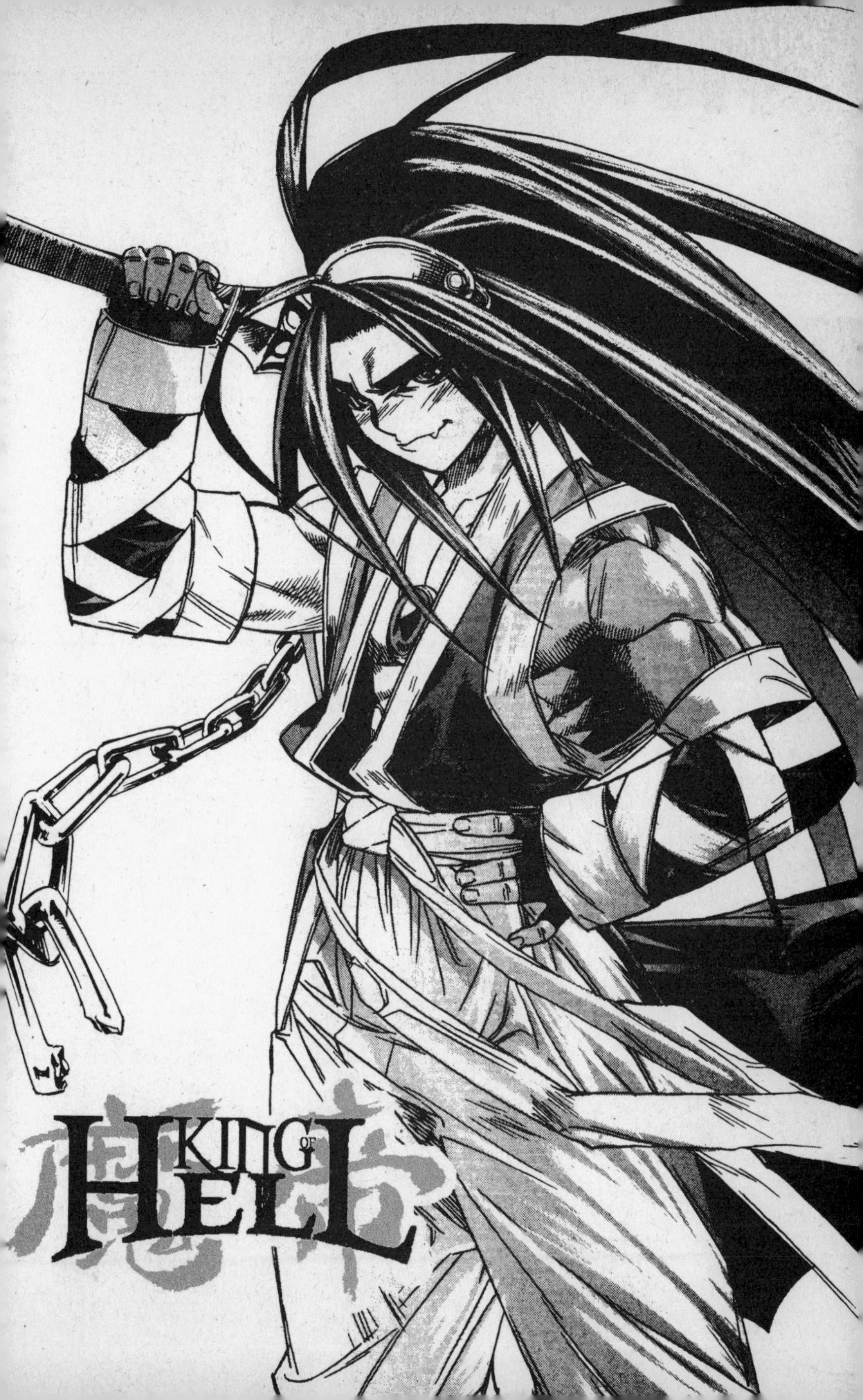
KING OF HELL

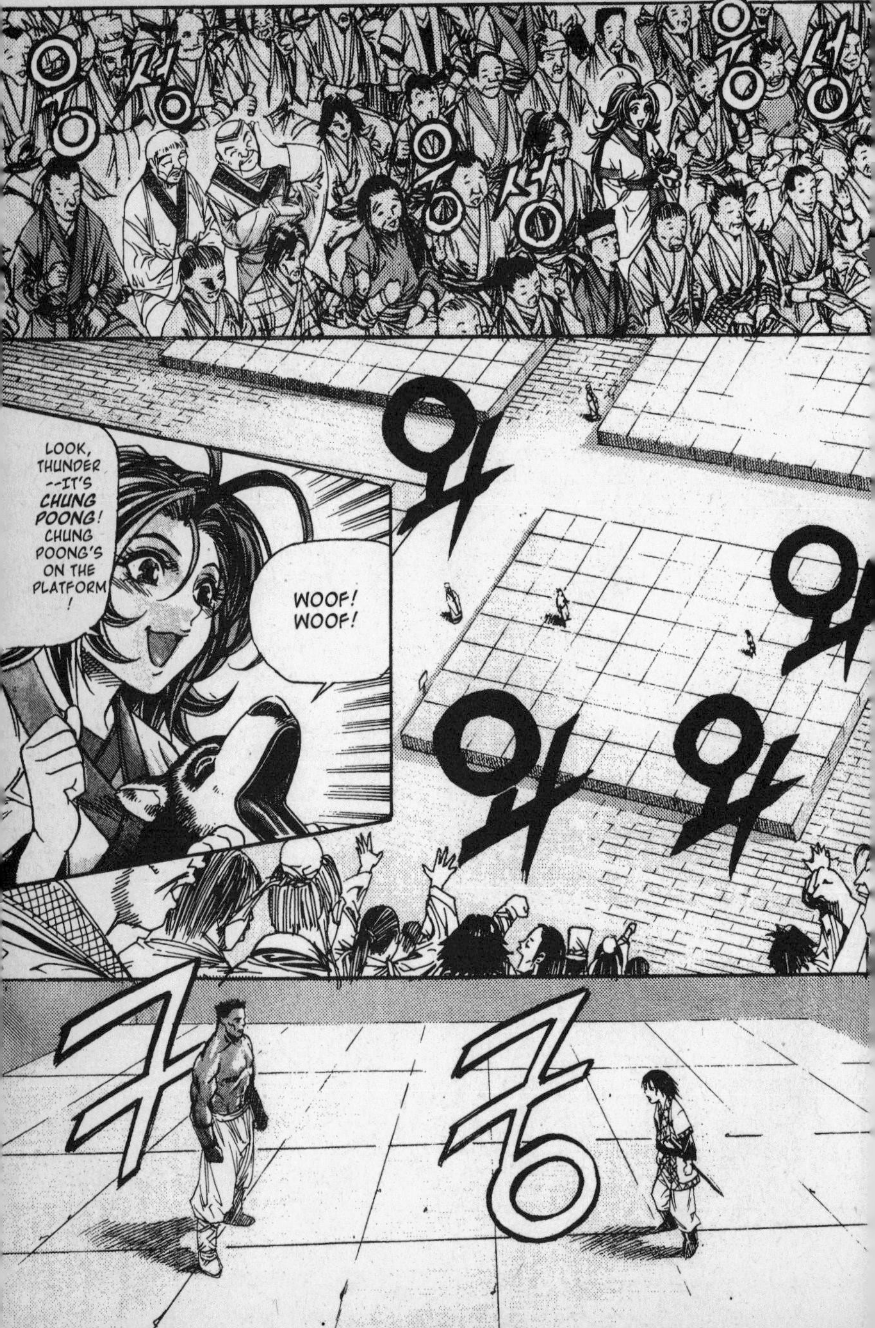
LOOK, THUNDER --IT'S CHUNG POONG! CHUNG POONG'S ON THE PLATFORM!
WOOF! WOOF!

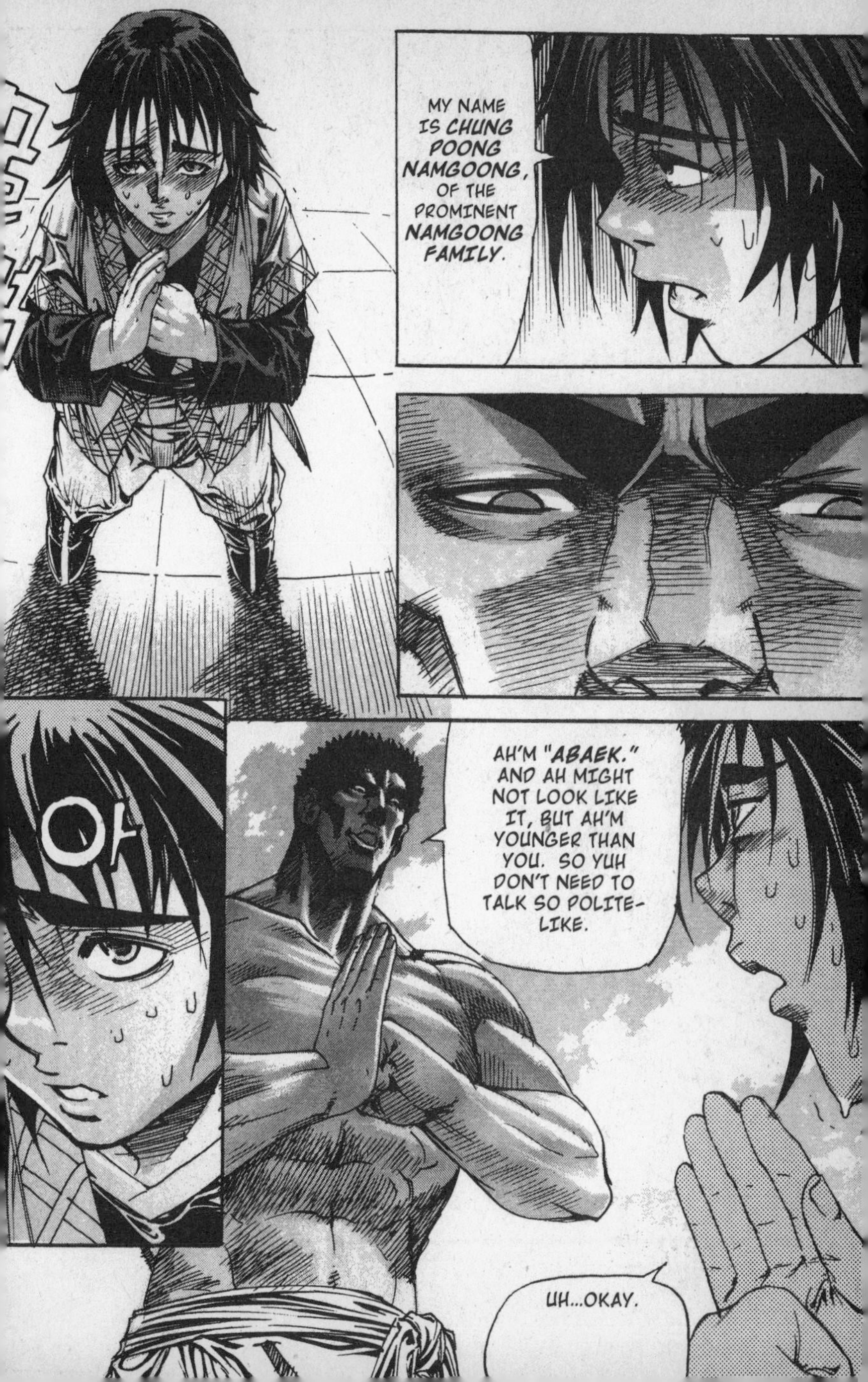
MY NAME IS CHUNG POONG NAMGOONG, OF THE PROMINENT NAMGOONG FAMILY.
AH'M "ABAEK." AND AH MIGHT NOT LOOK LIKE IT, BUT AH'M YOUNGER THAN YOU. SO YUH DON'T NEED TO TALK SO POLITE-LIKE.
UH...OKAY.

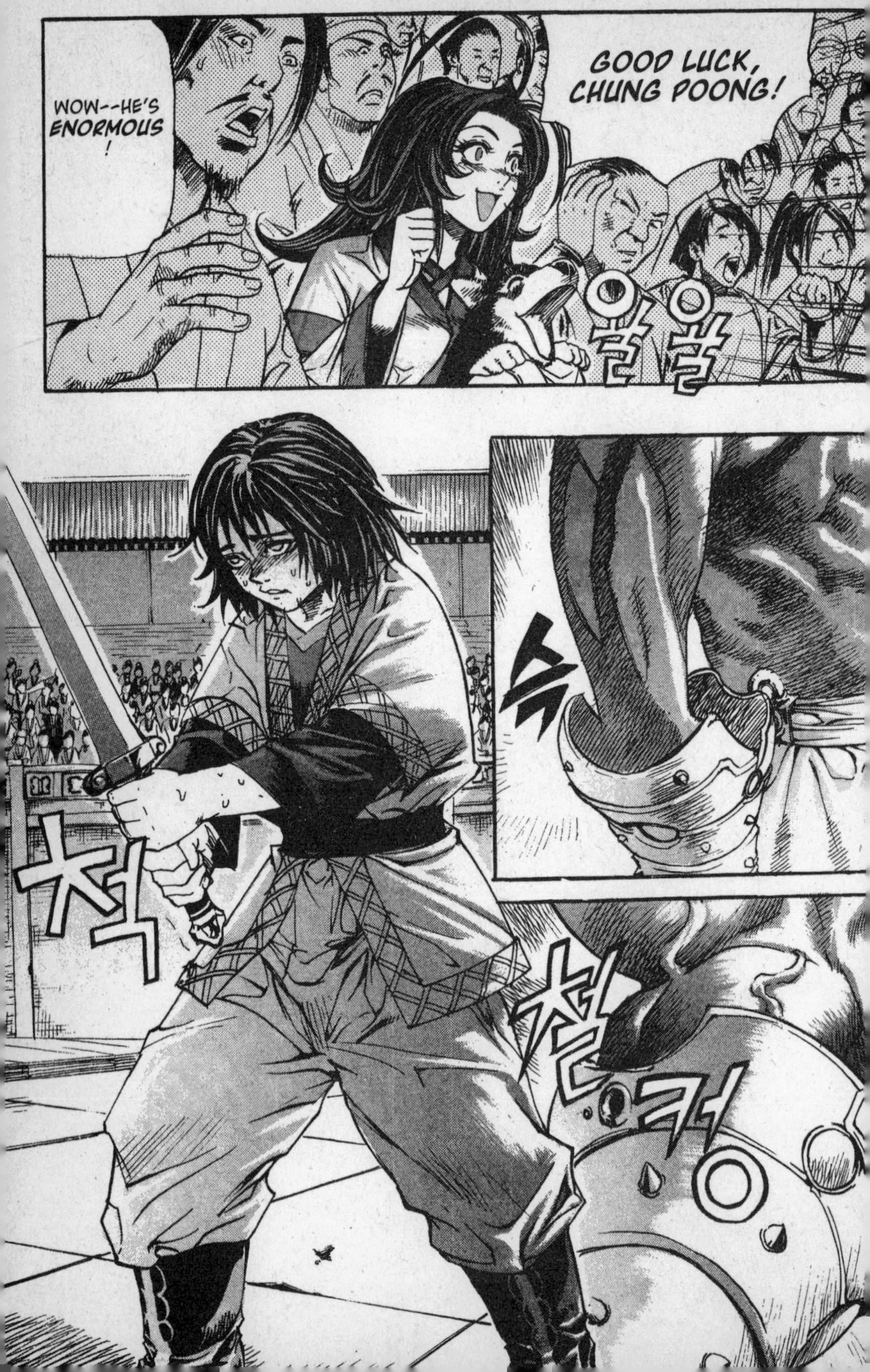
WOW--HE'S ENORMOUS!
GOOD LUCK, CHUNG POONG!
척
슥

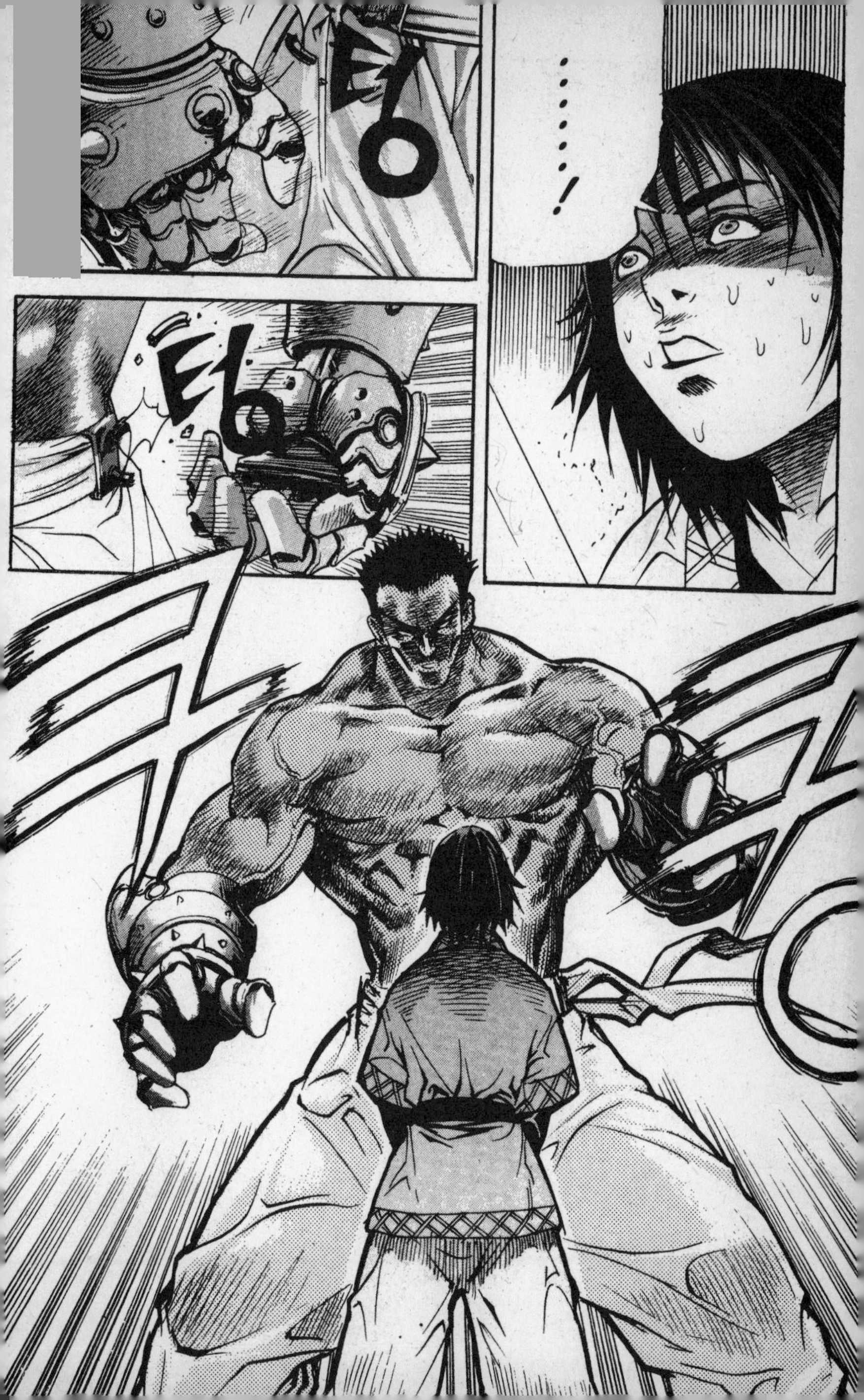

……!

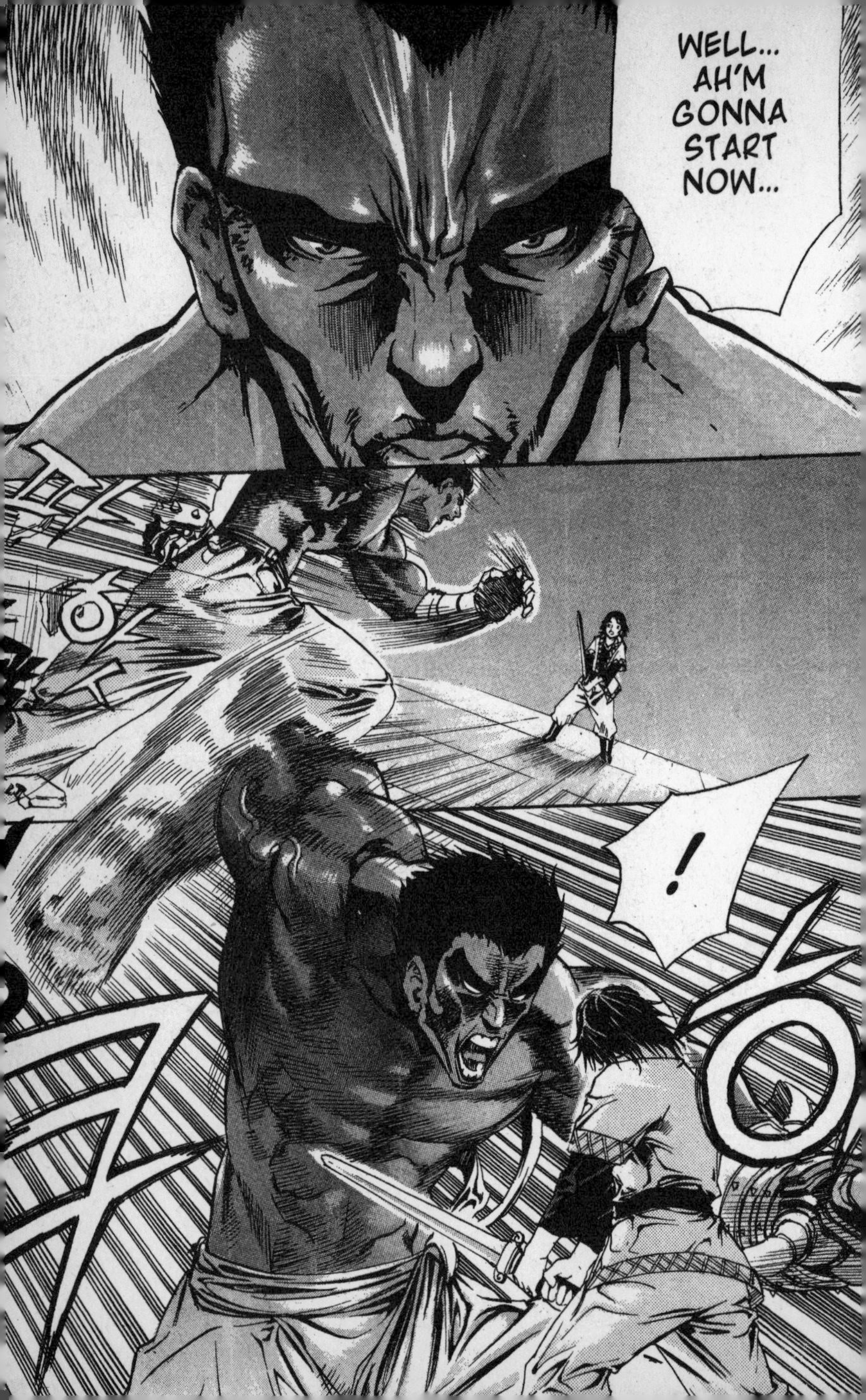
WELL... AH'M GONNA START NOW...
!

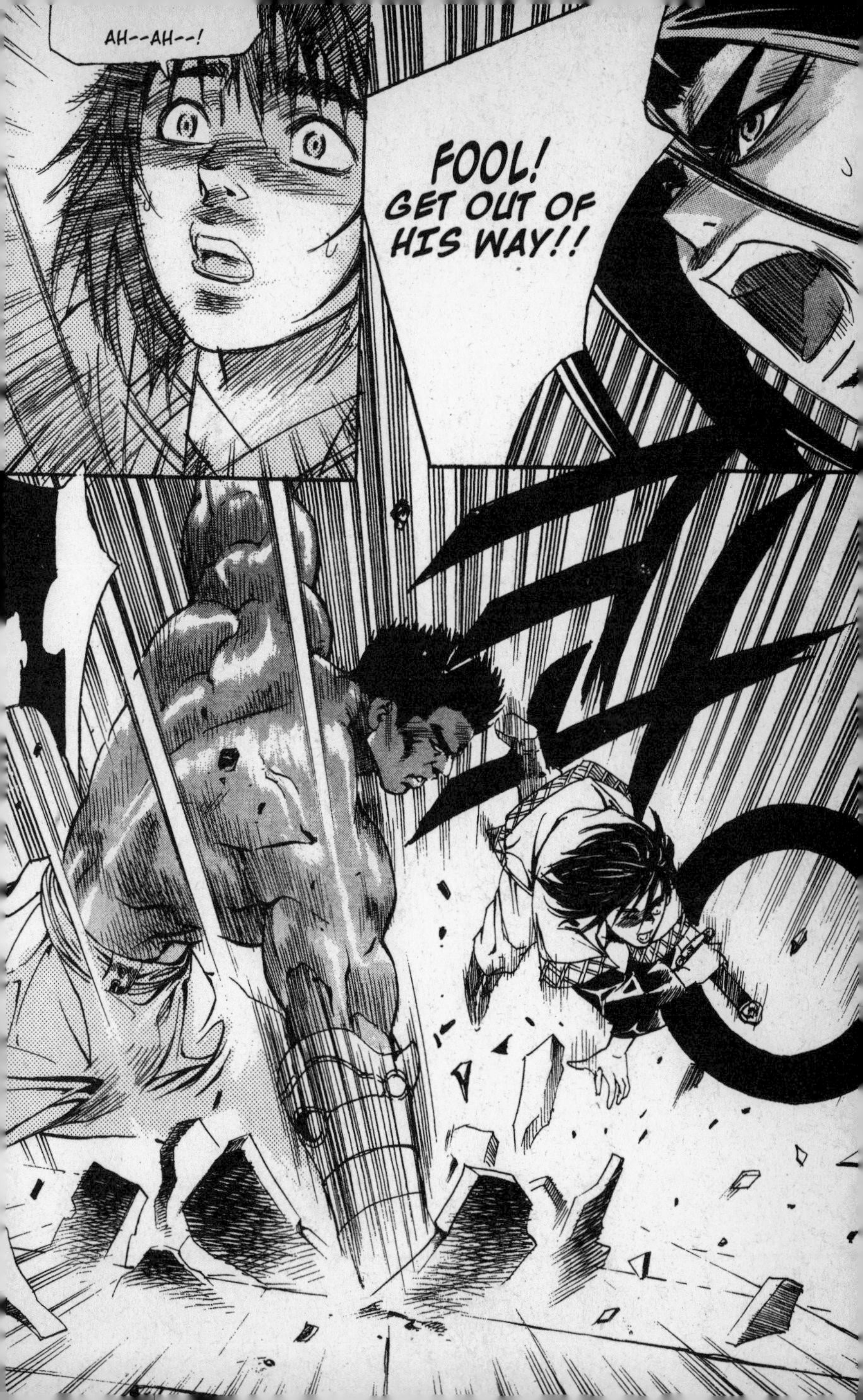
AH--AH--!
FOOL! GET OUT OF HIS WAY!!

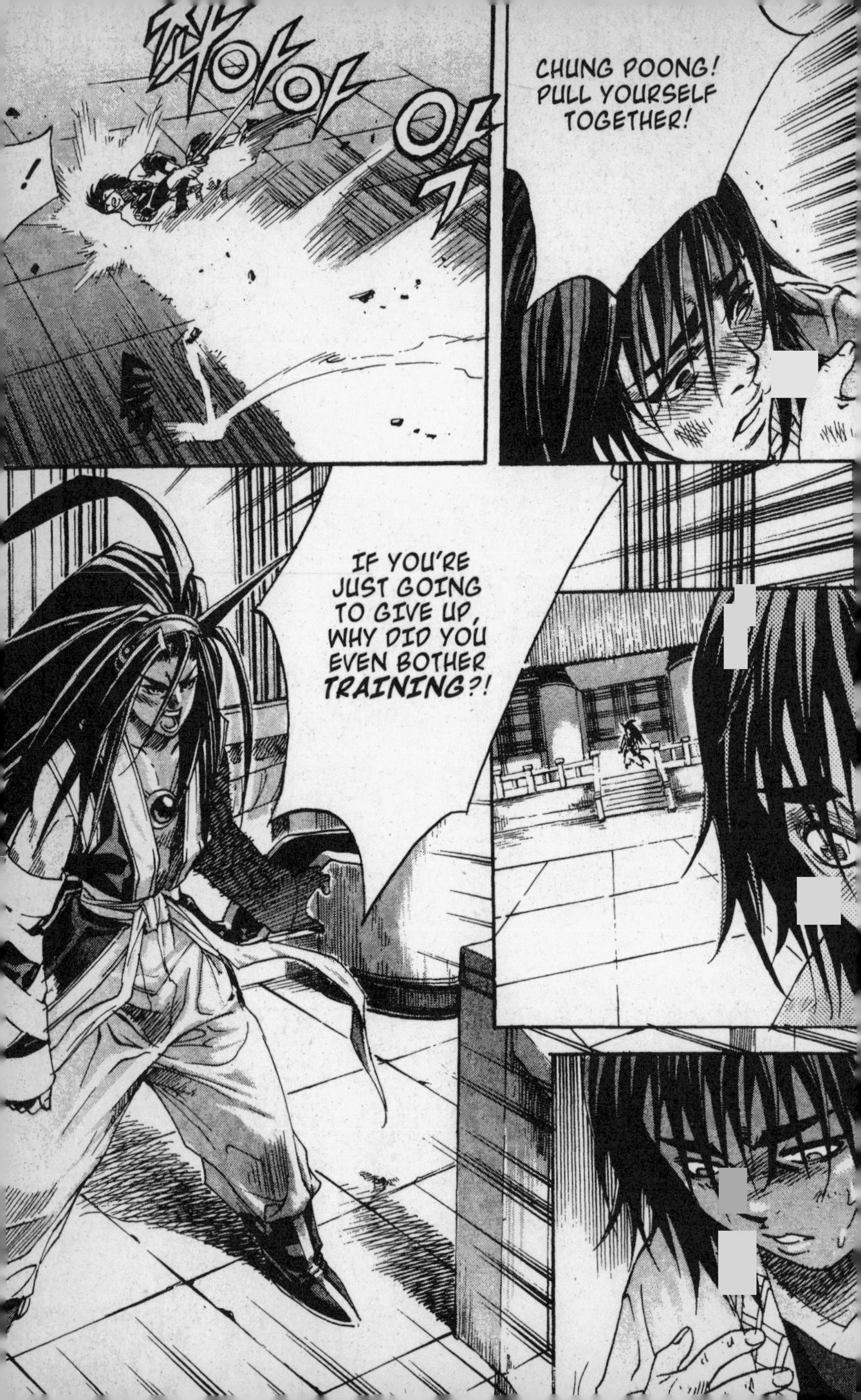
!
CHUNG POONG! PULL YOURSELF TOGETHER!
IF YOU'RE JUST GOING TO GIVE UP, WHY DID YOU EVEN BOTHER TRAINING?!

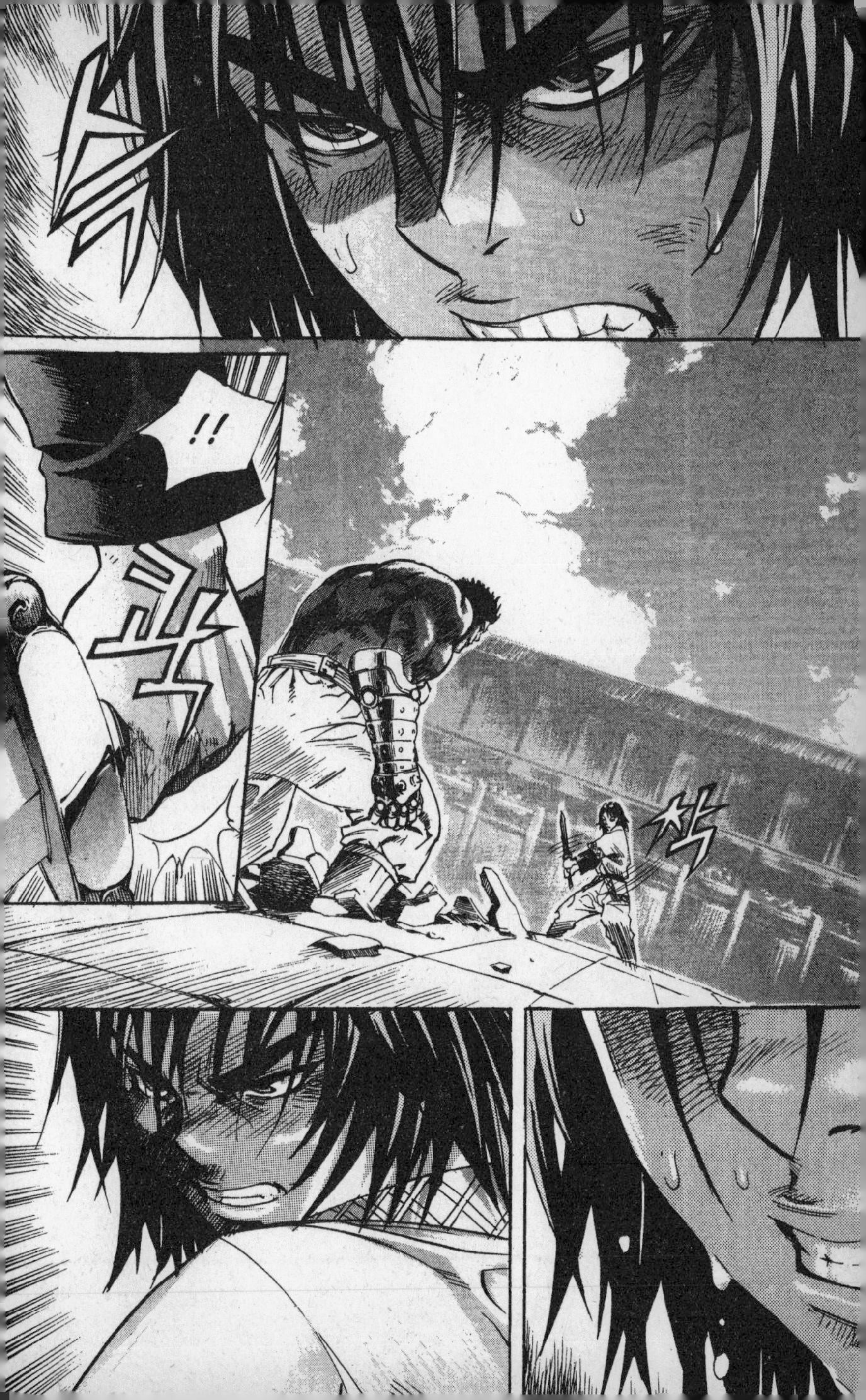
!!

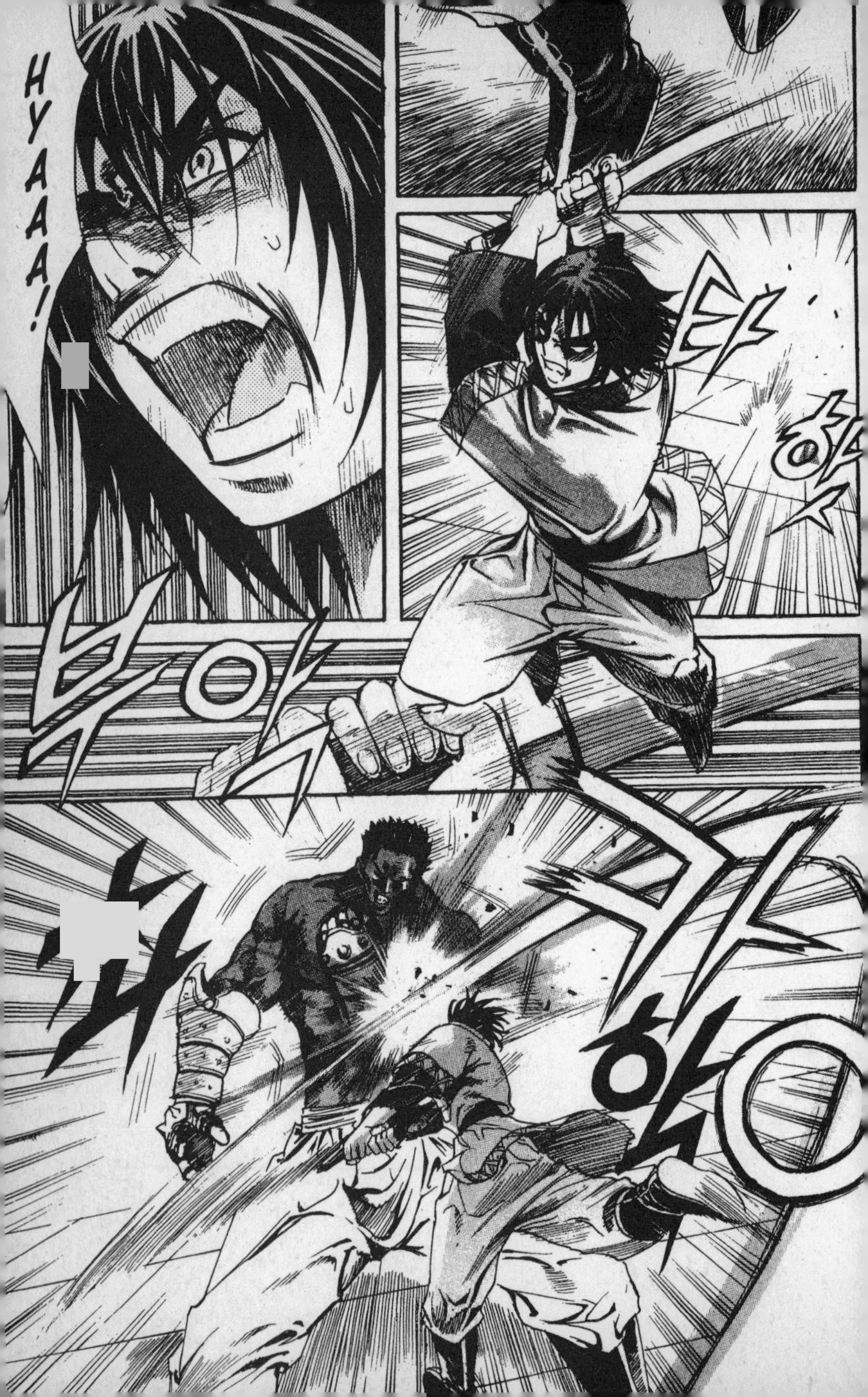
HYAAAA!!

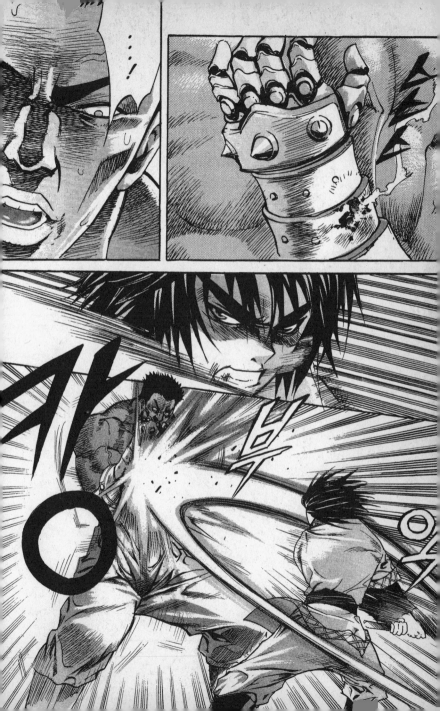

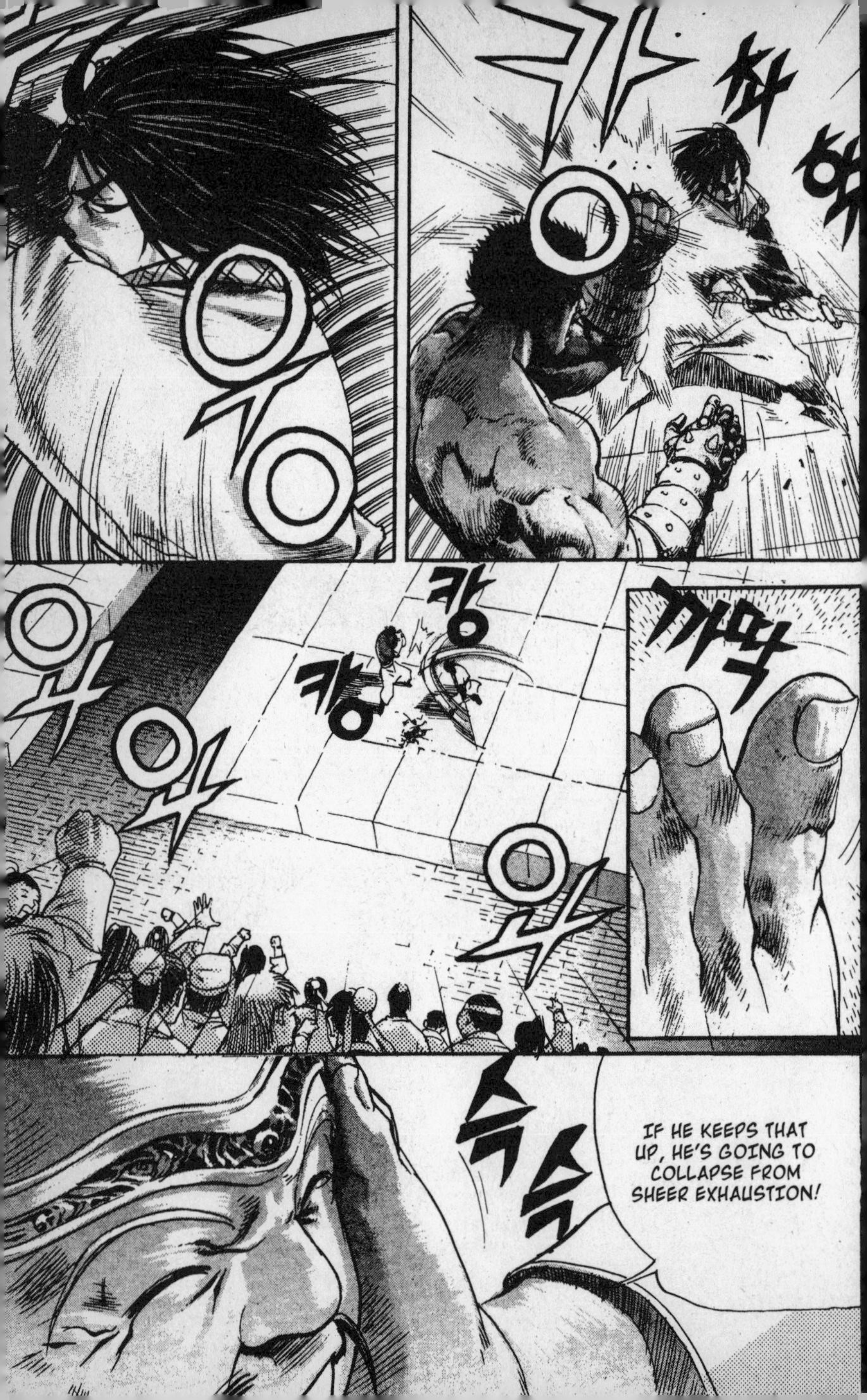
IF HE KEEPS THAT UP, HE'S GOING TO COLLAPSE FROM SHEER EXHAUSTION!

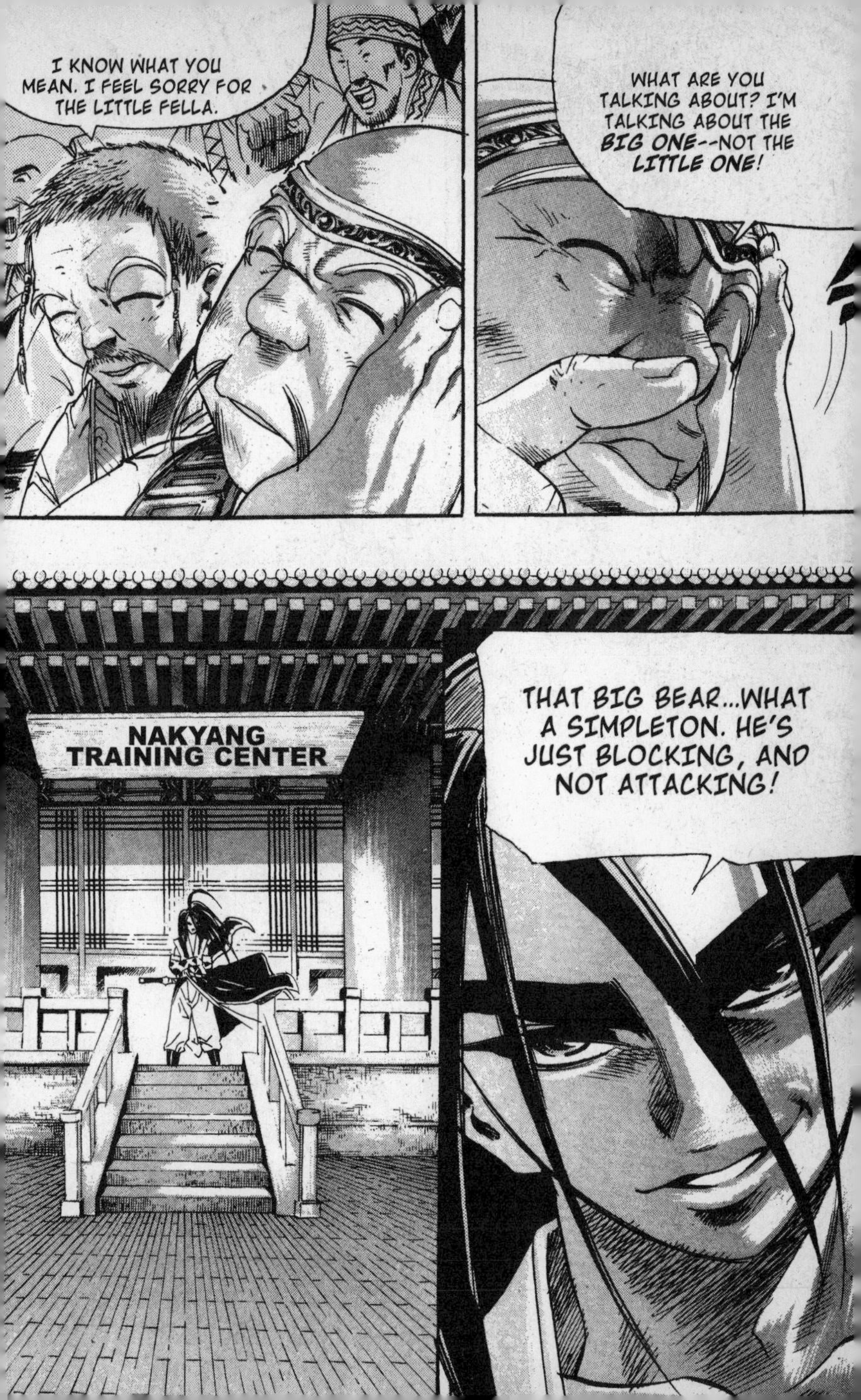
I KNOW WHAT YOU MEAN. I FEEL SORRY FOR THE LITTLE FELLA.
WHAT ARE YOU TALKING ABOUT? I'M TALKING ABOUT THE BIG ONE--NOT THE LITTLE ONE!
NAKYANG TRAINING CENTER
THAT BIG BEAR...WHAT A SIMPLETON. HE'S JUST BLOCKING, AND NOT ATTACKING!

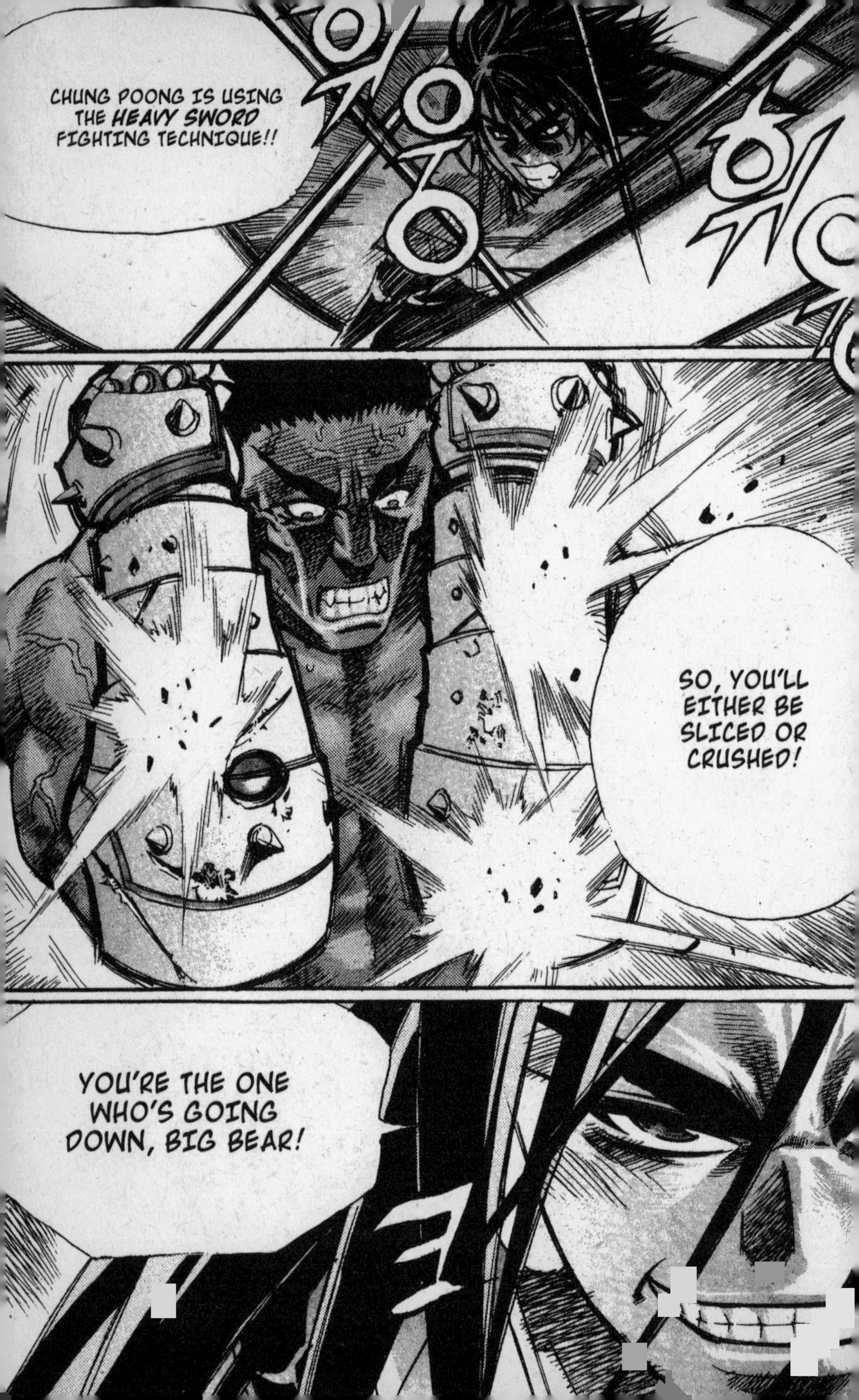
CHUNG POONG IS USING THE HEAVY SWORD FIGHTING TECHNIQUE!!
SO, YOU'LL EITHER BE SLICED OR CRUSHED!
YOU'RE THE ONE WHO'S GOING DOWN, BIG BEAR!

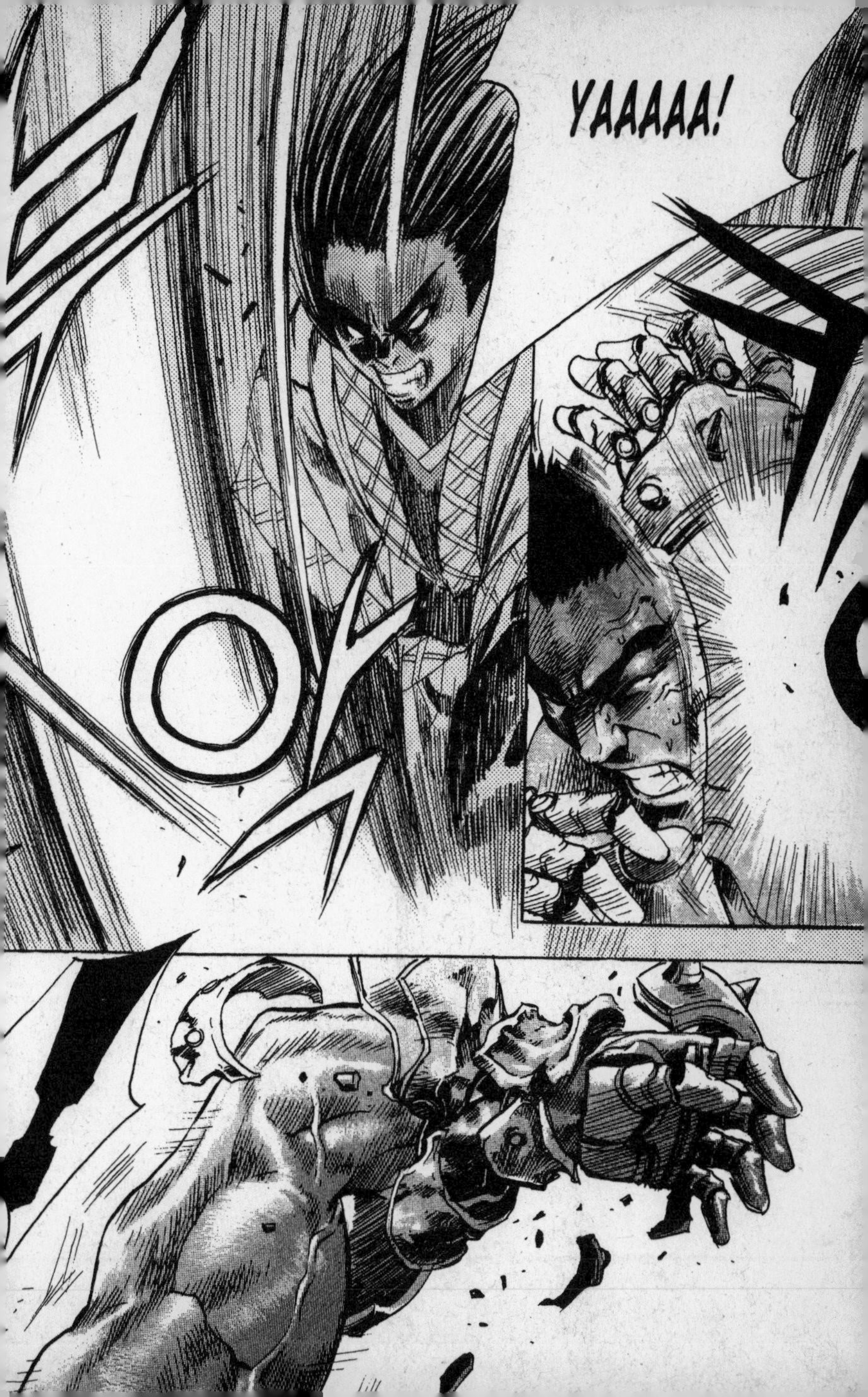
YAAAAA!

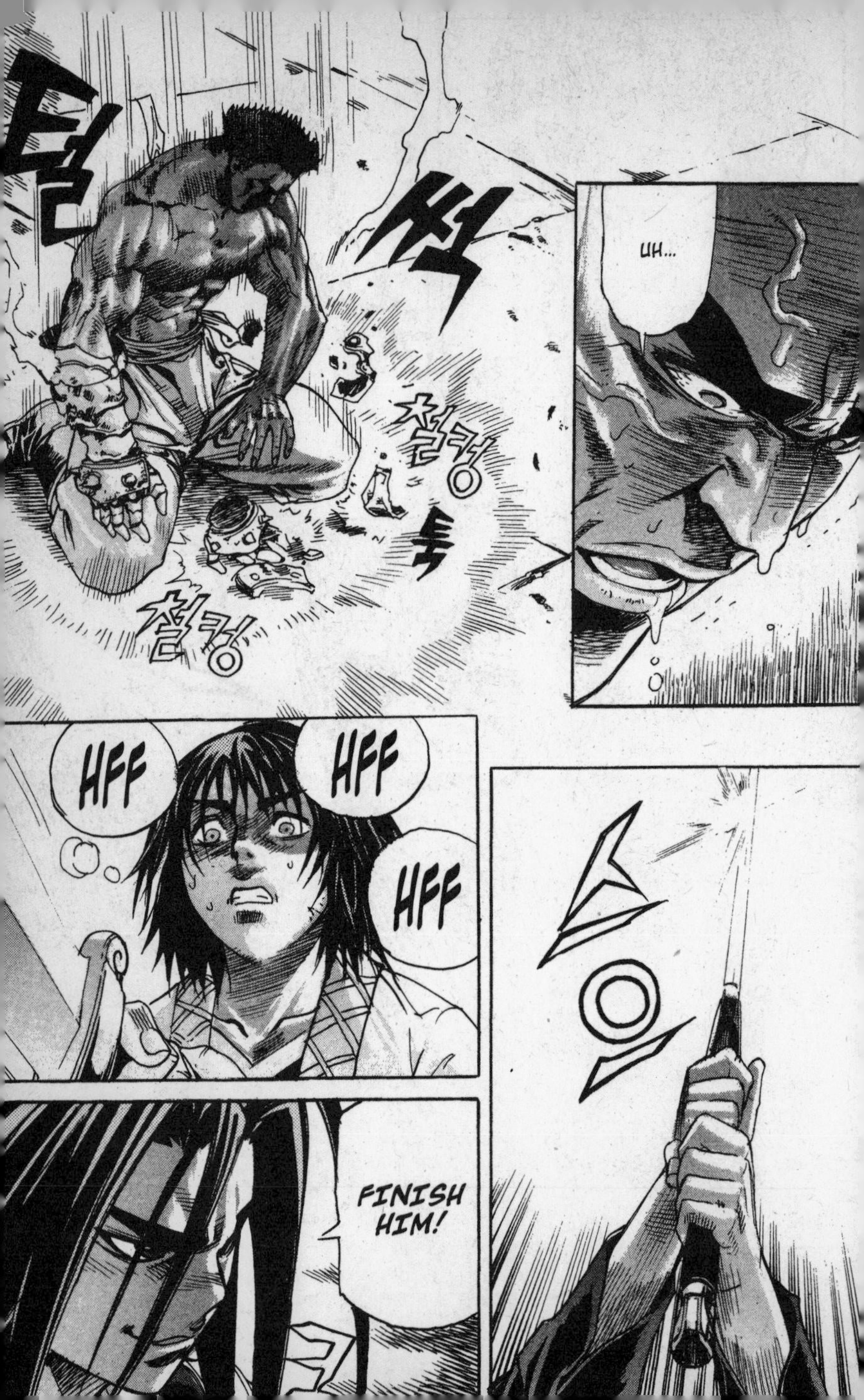
털썩
철컹
툭
철컹
UH...
HFF
HFF
HFF
FINISH HIM!

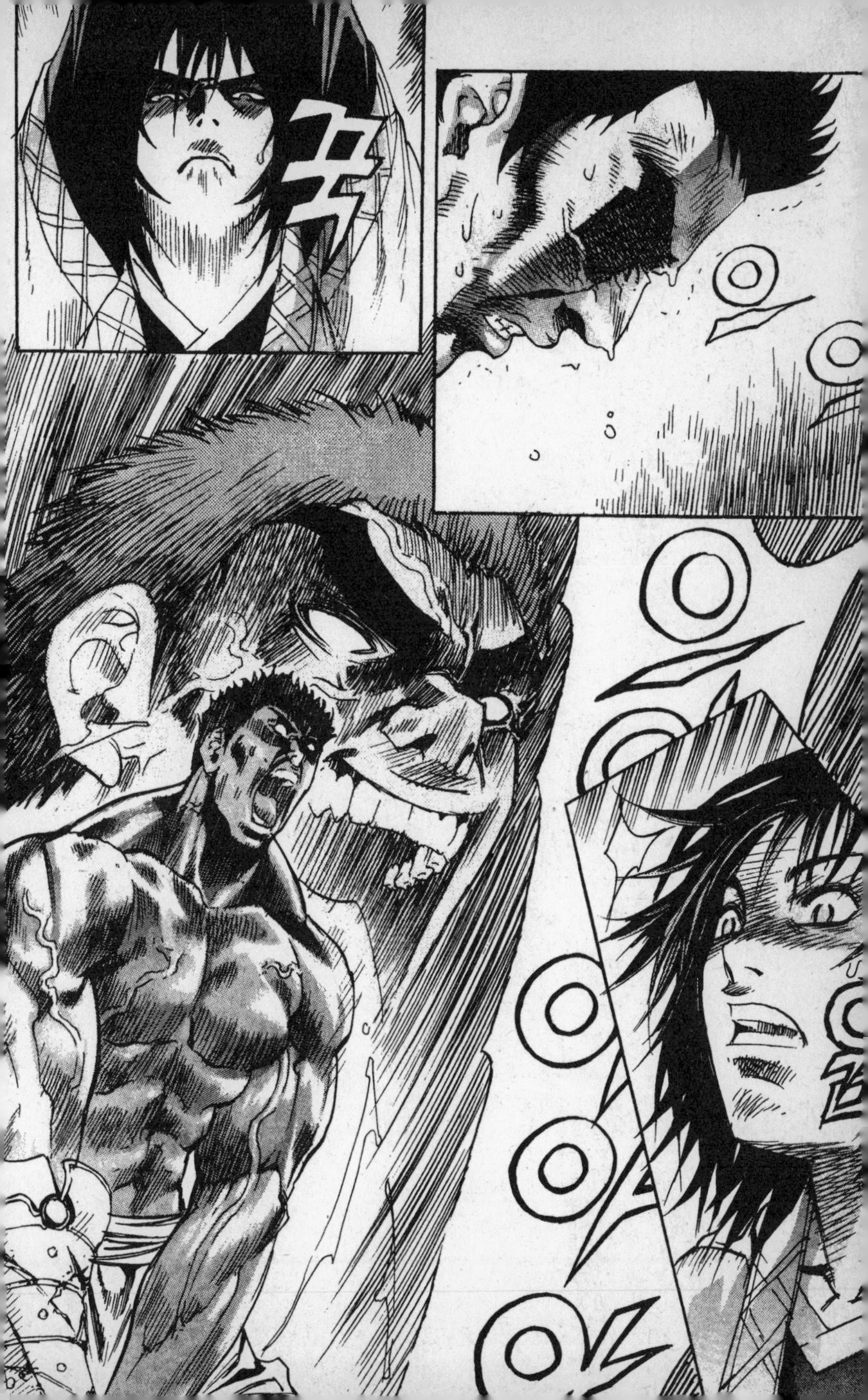

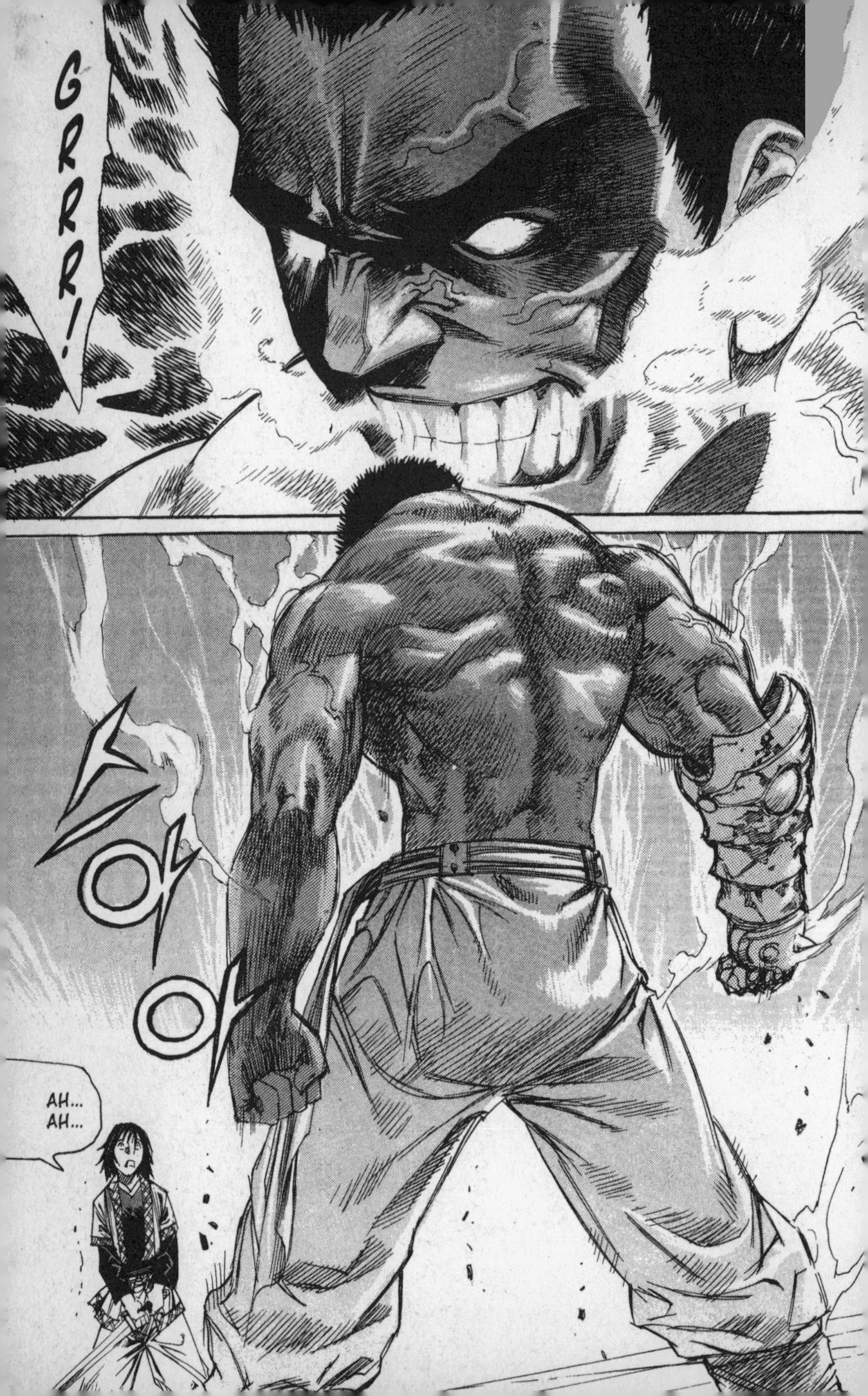
GRRR!
AH... AH...

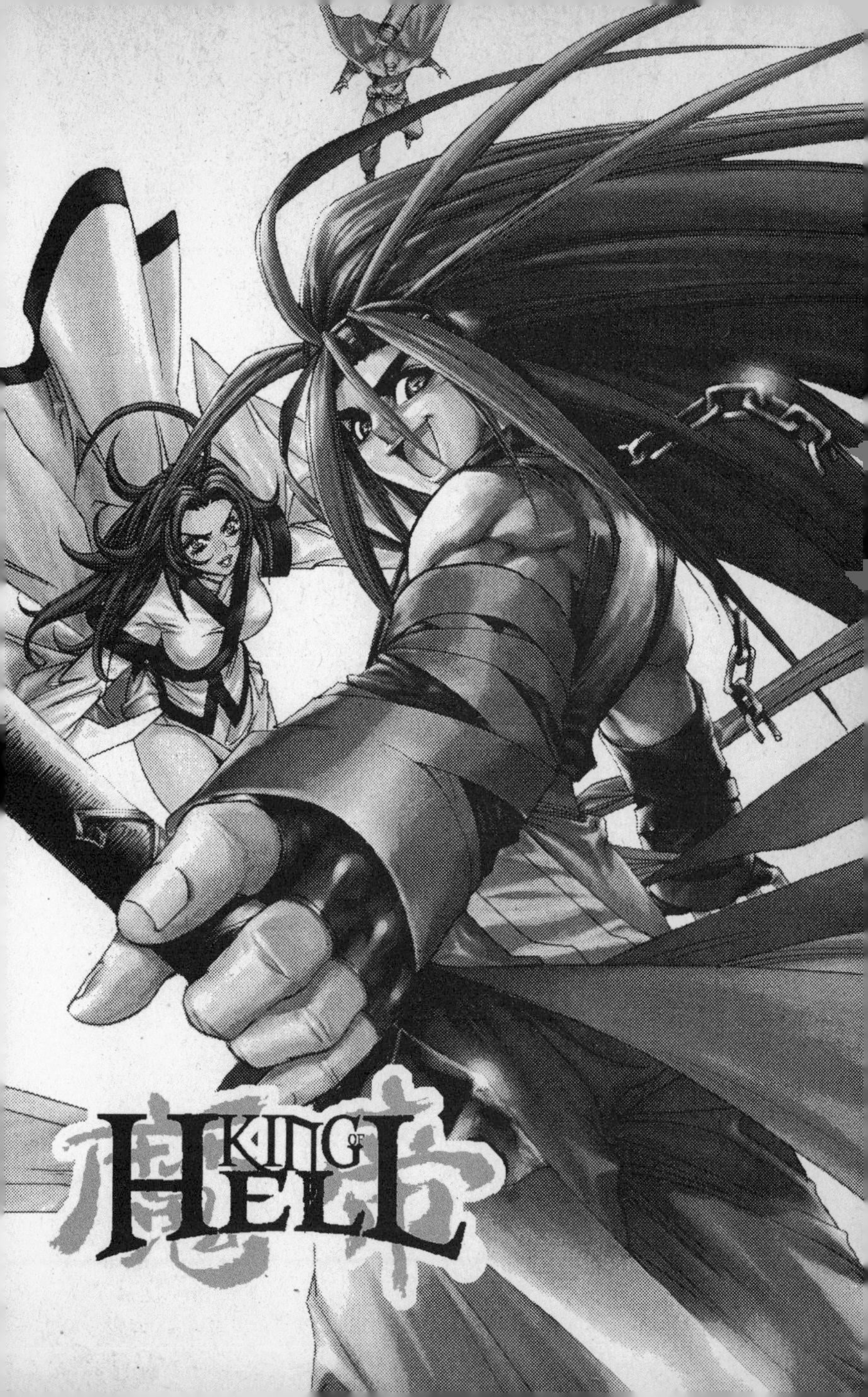
KING OF HELL

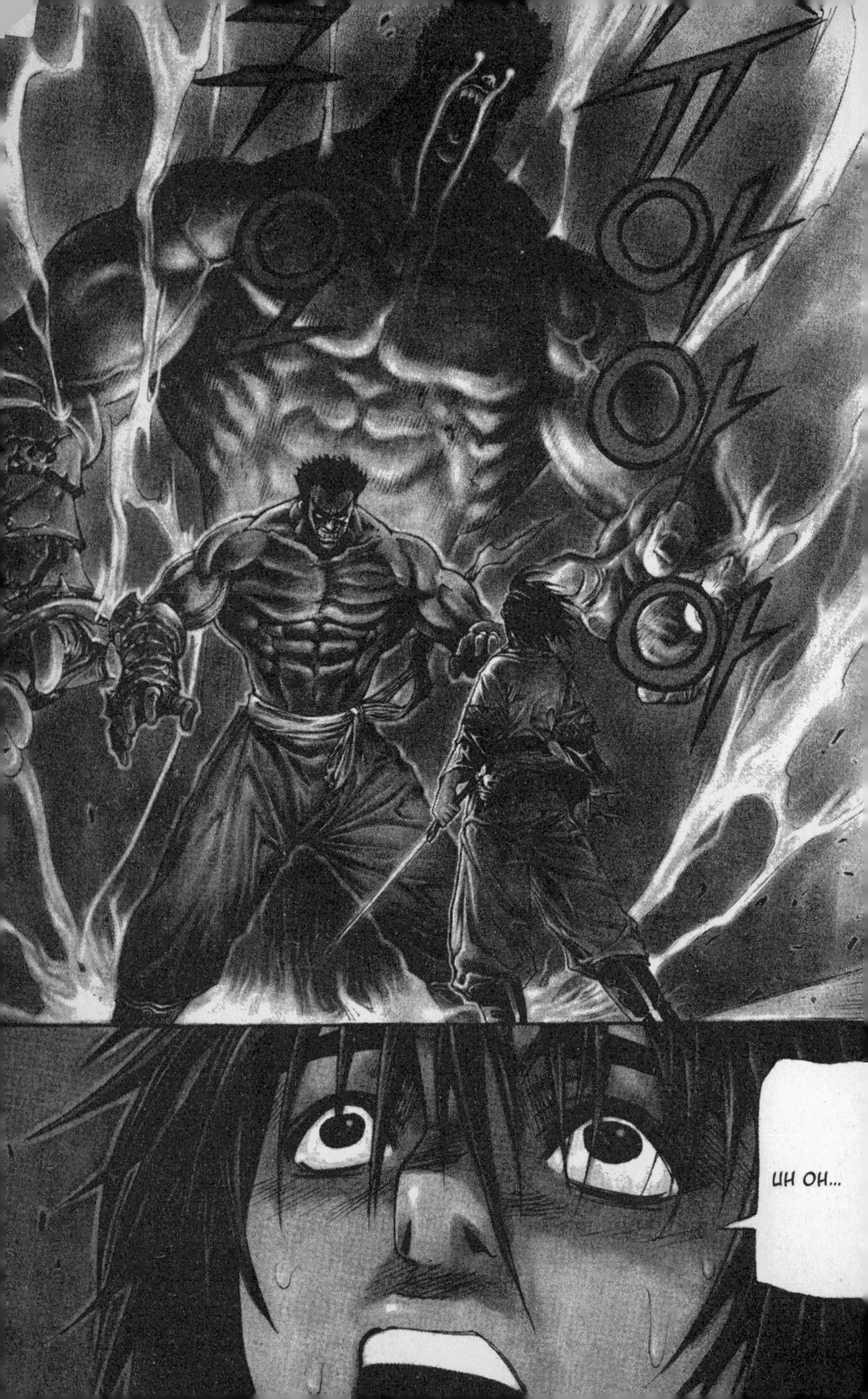
UH OH...

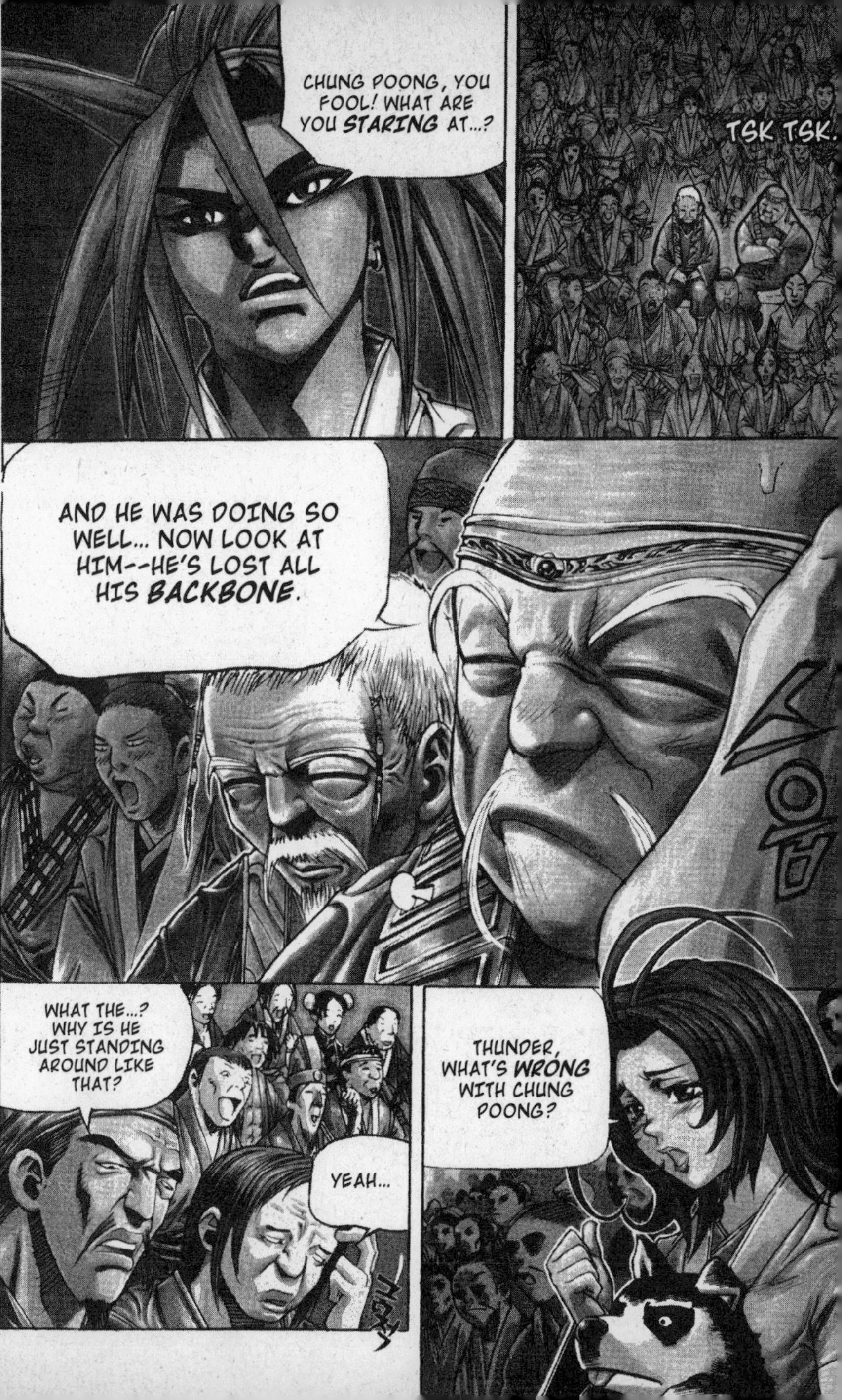
CHUNG POONG, YOU FOOL! WHAT ARE YOU STARING AT...?
TSK TSK.
AND HE WAS DOING SO WELL... NOW LOOK AT HIM--HE'S LOST ALL HIS BACKBONE.
WHAT THE...? WHY IS HE JUST STANDING AROUND LIKE THAT?
YEAH...
THUNDER, WHAT'S WRONG WITH CHUNG POONG?

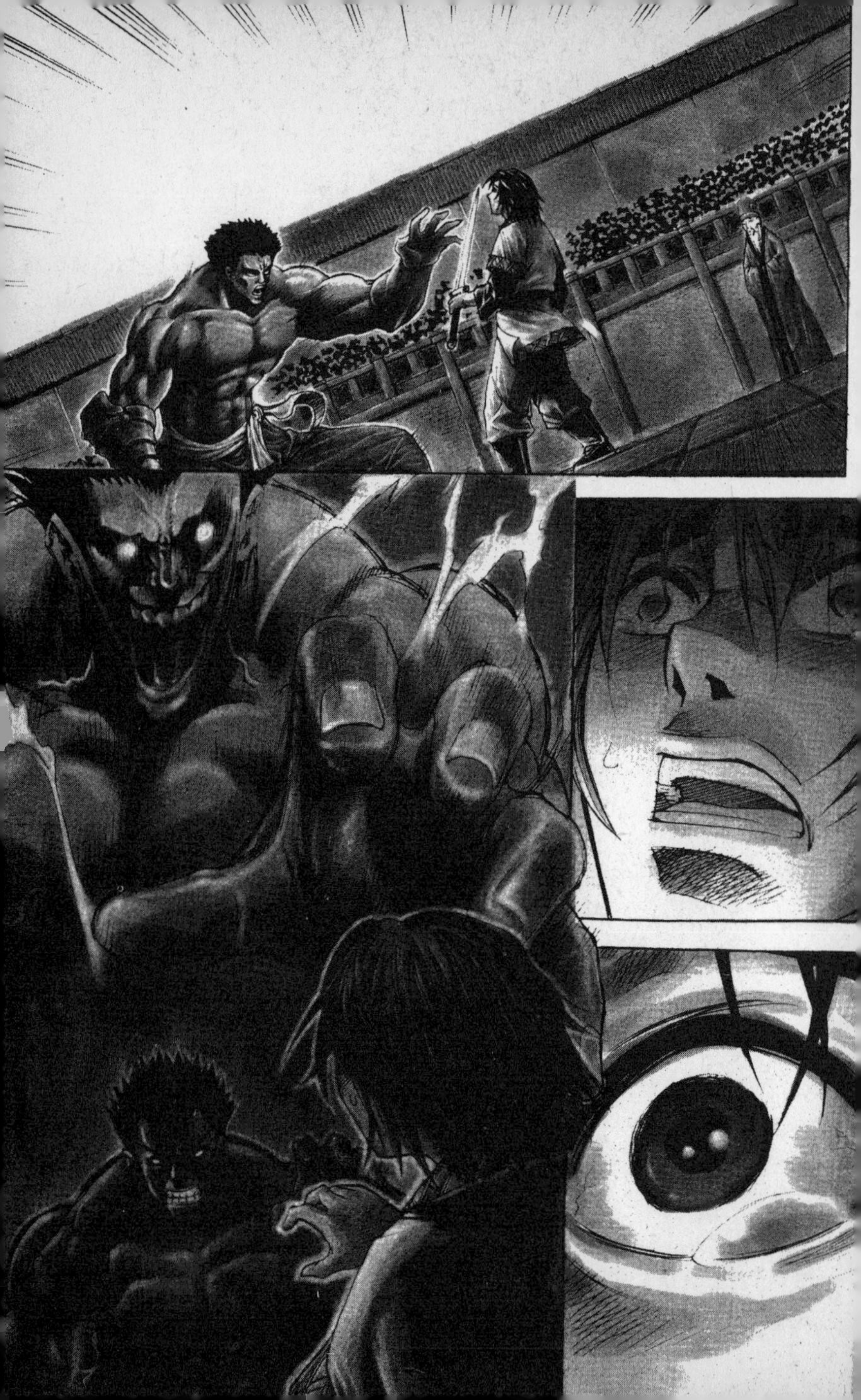

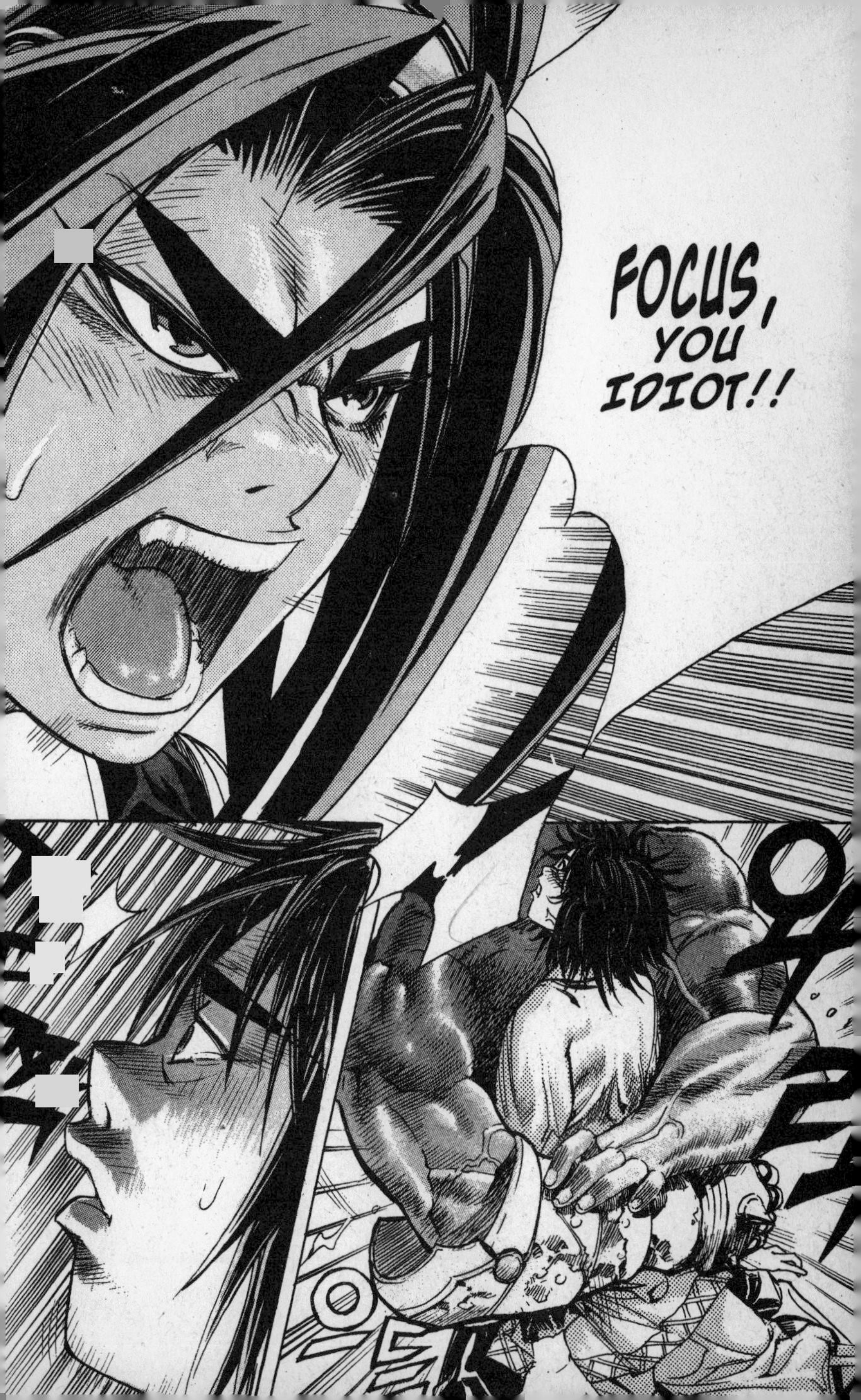
FOCUS, YOU IDIOT!!

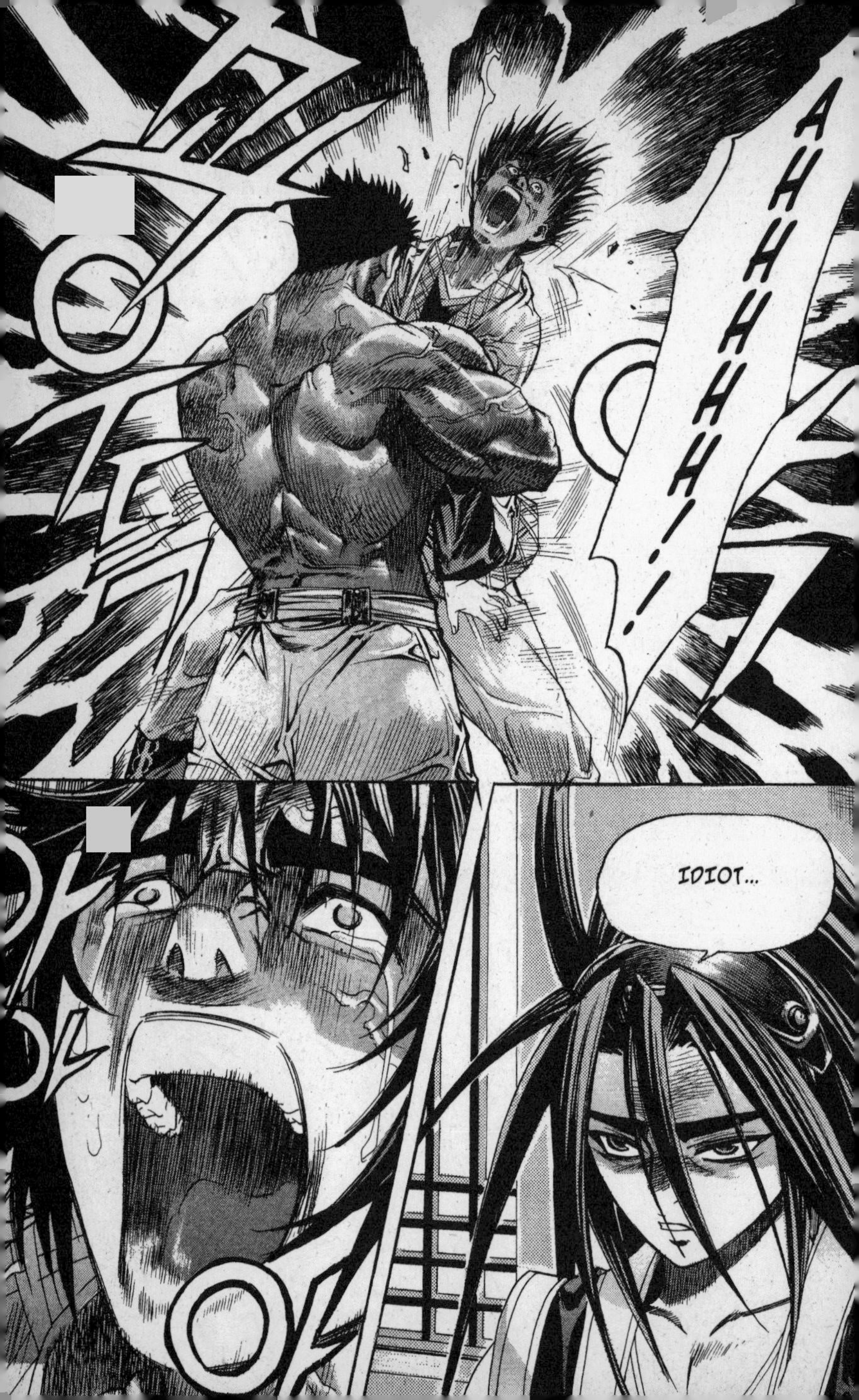
AHHHHHH!!!
IDIOT...

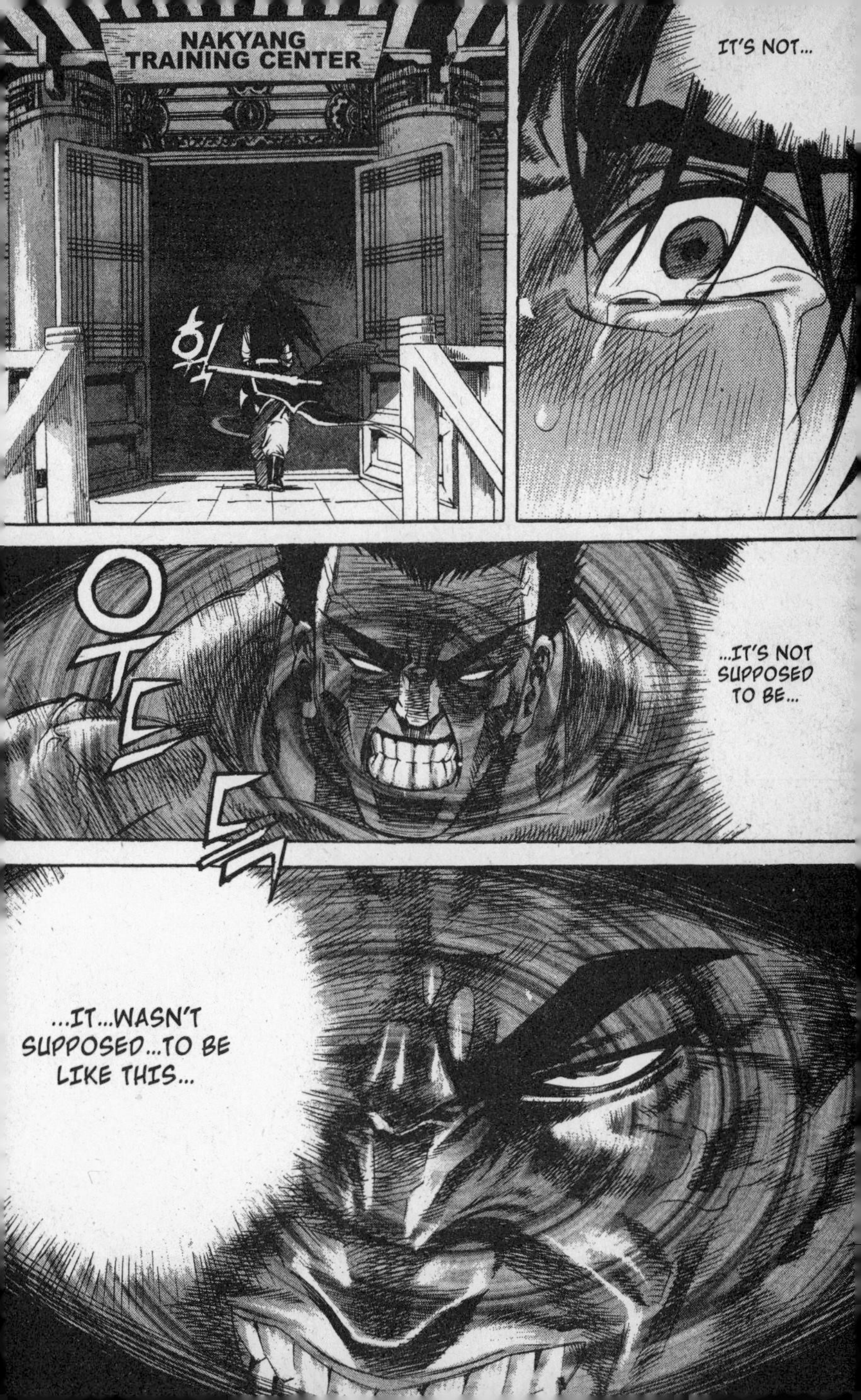
NAKYANG TRAINING CENTER
IT'S NOT...
...IT'S NOT SUPPOSED TO BE...
...IT...WASN'T SUPPOSED...TO BE LIKE THIS...

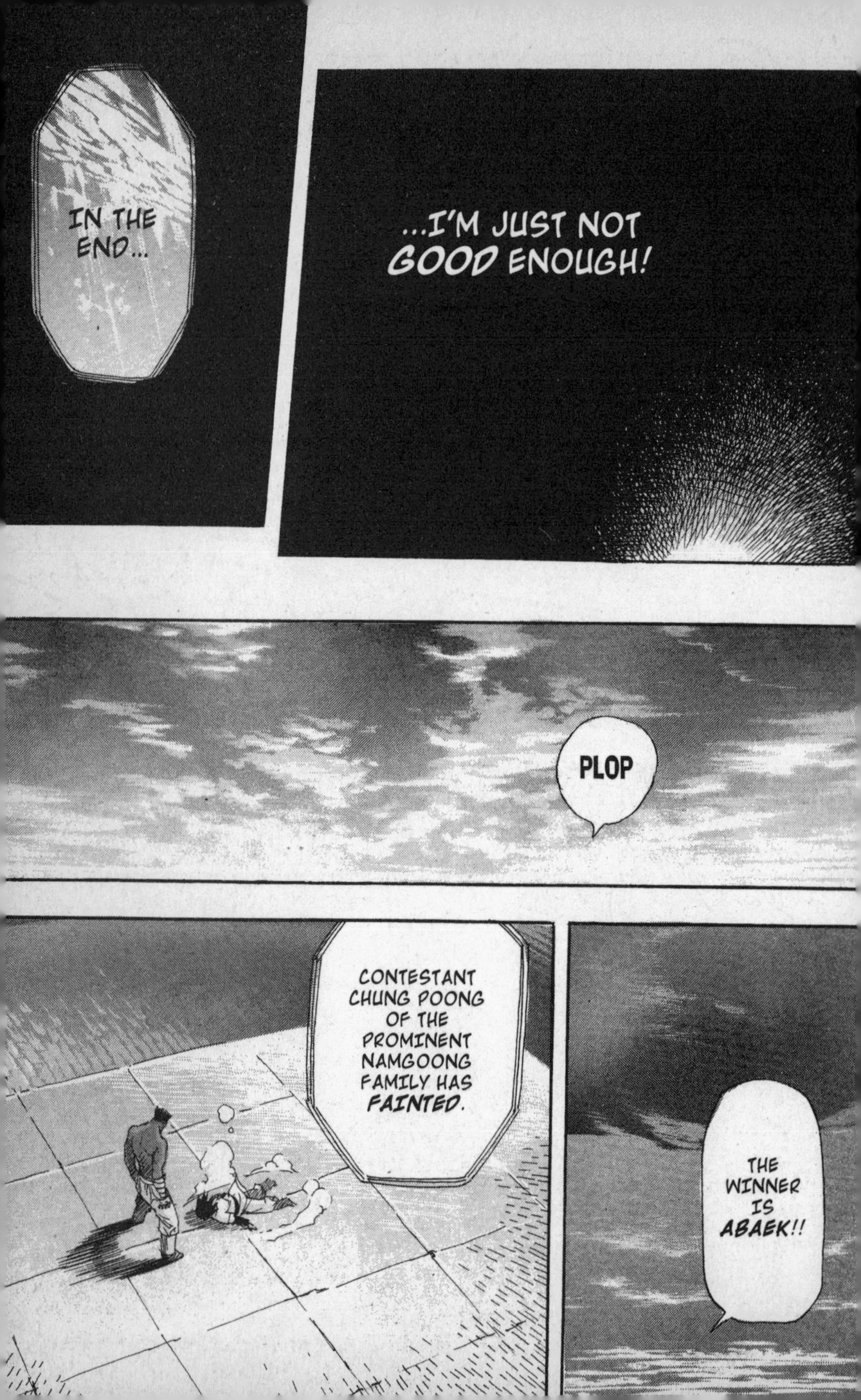
IN THE END...
...I'M JUST NOT GOOD ENOUGH!
PLOP
CONTESTANT CHUNG POONG OF THE PROMINENT NAMGOONG FAMILY HAS FAINTED.
THE WINNER IS ABAEK!!

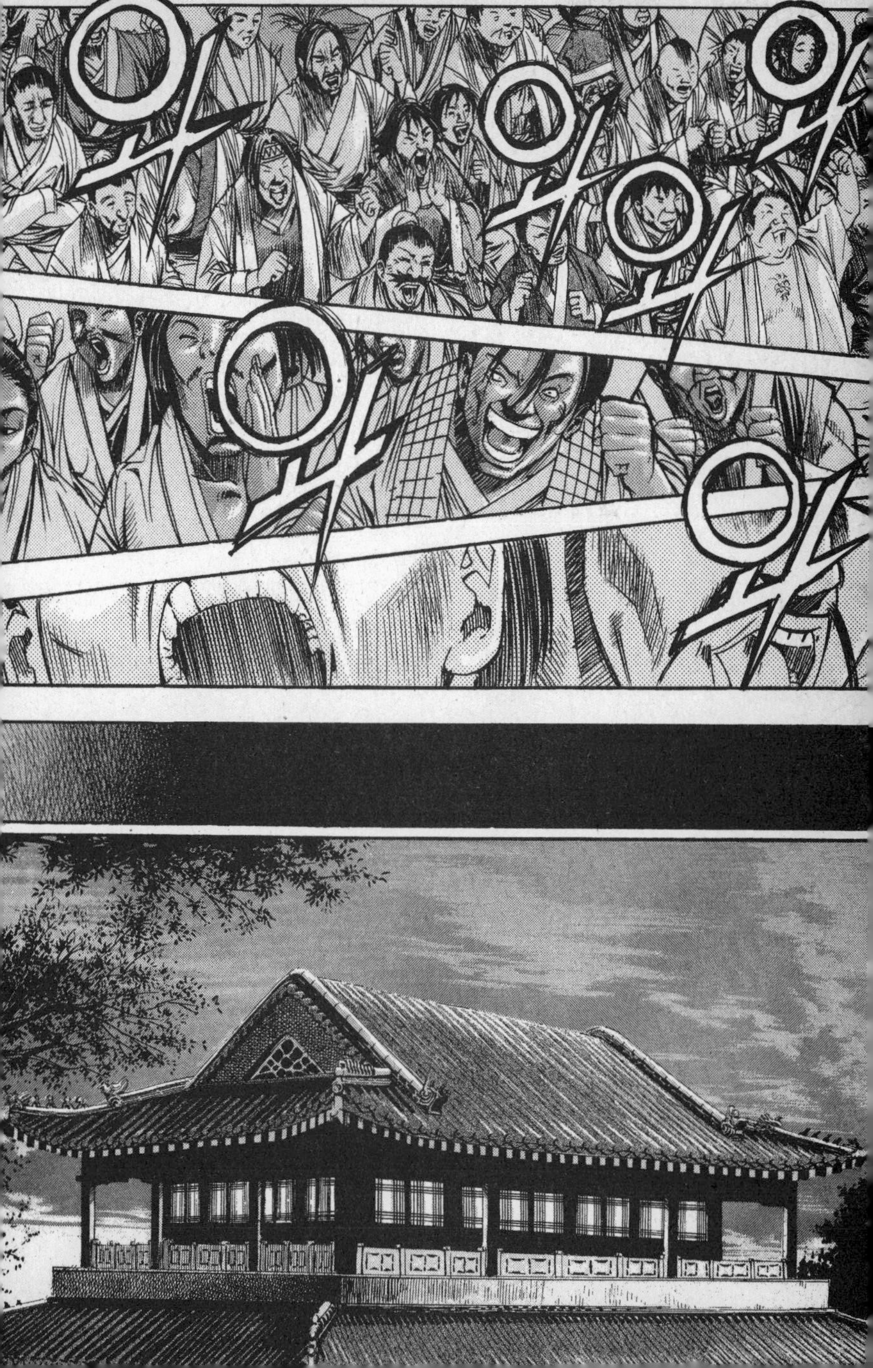

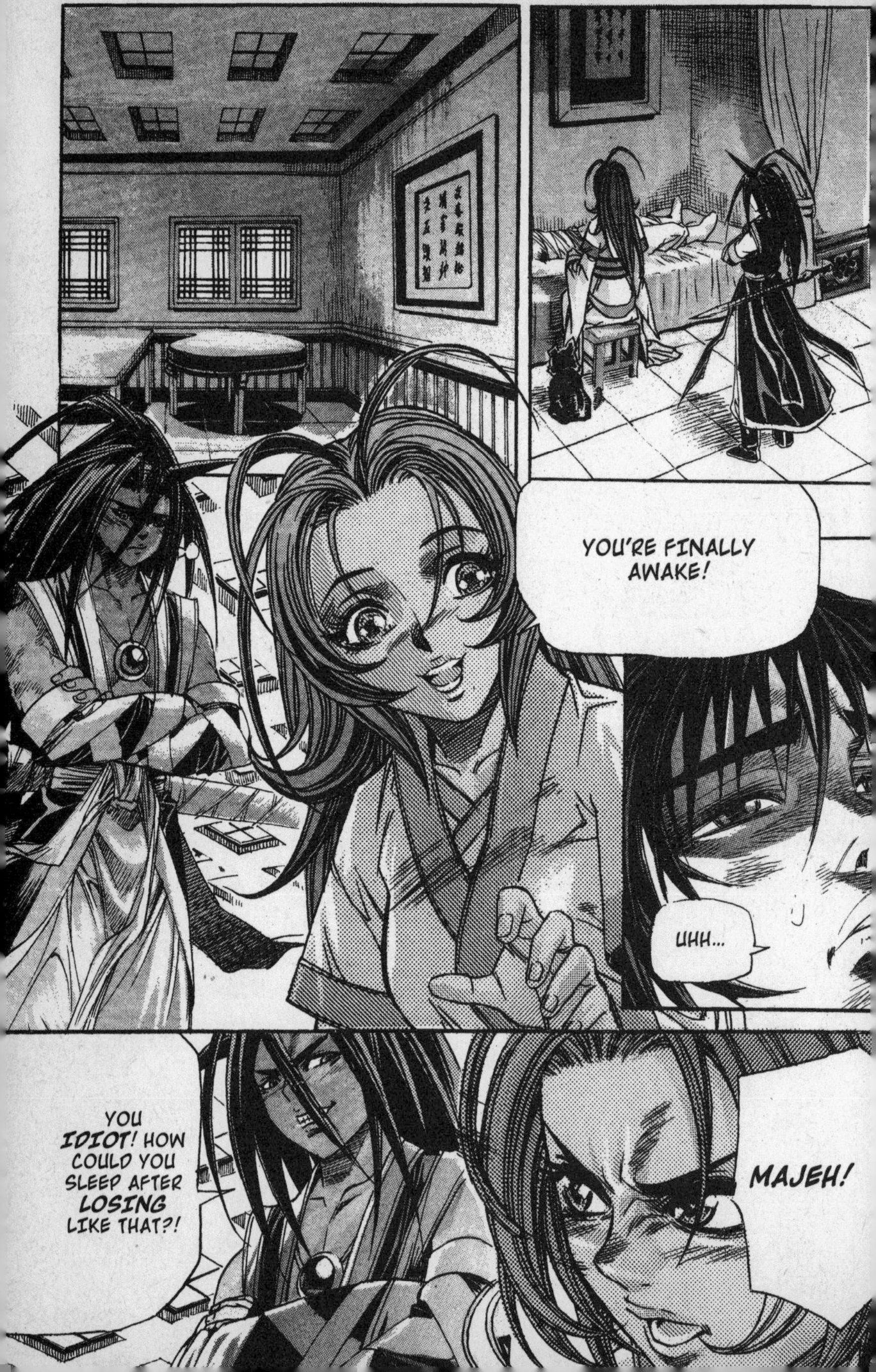
YOU'RE FINALLY AWAKE!
UHH...
MAJEH!
YOU IDIOT! HOW COULD YOU SLEEP AFTER LOSING LIKE THAT?!

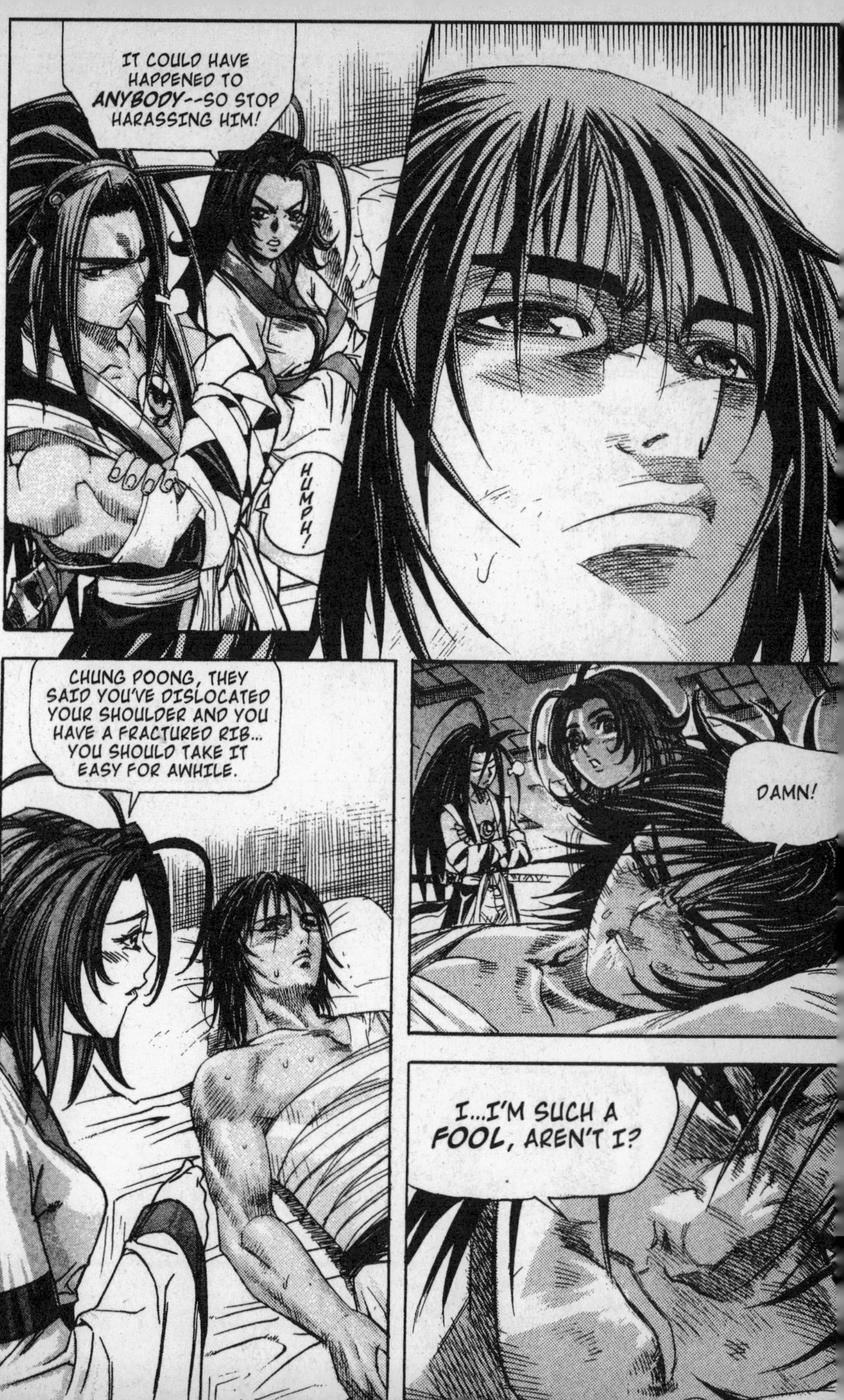
IT COULD HAVE HAPPENED TO ANYBODY--SO STOP HARASSING HIM!
HUMPH!
CHUNG POONG, THEY SAID YOU'VE DISLOCATED YOUR SHOULDER AND YOU HAVE A FRACTURED RIB... YOU SHOULD TAKE IT EASY FOR AWHILE.
DAMN!
I...I'M SUCH A FOOL, AREN'T I?

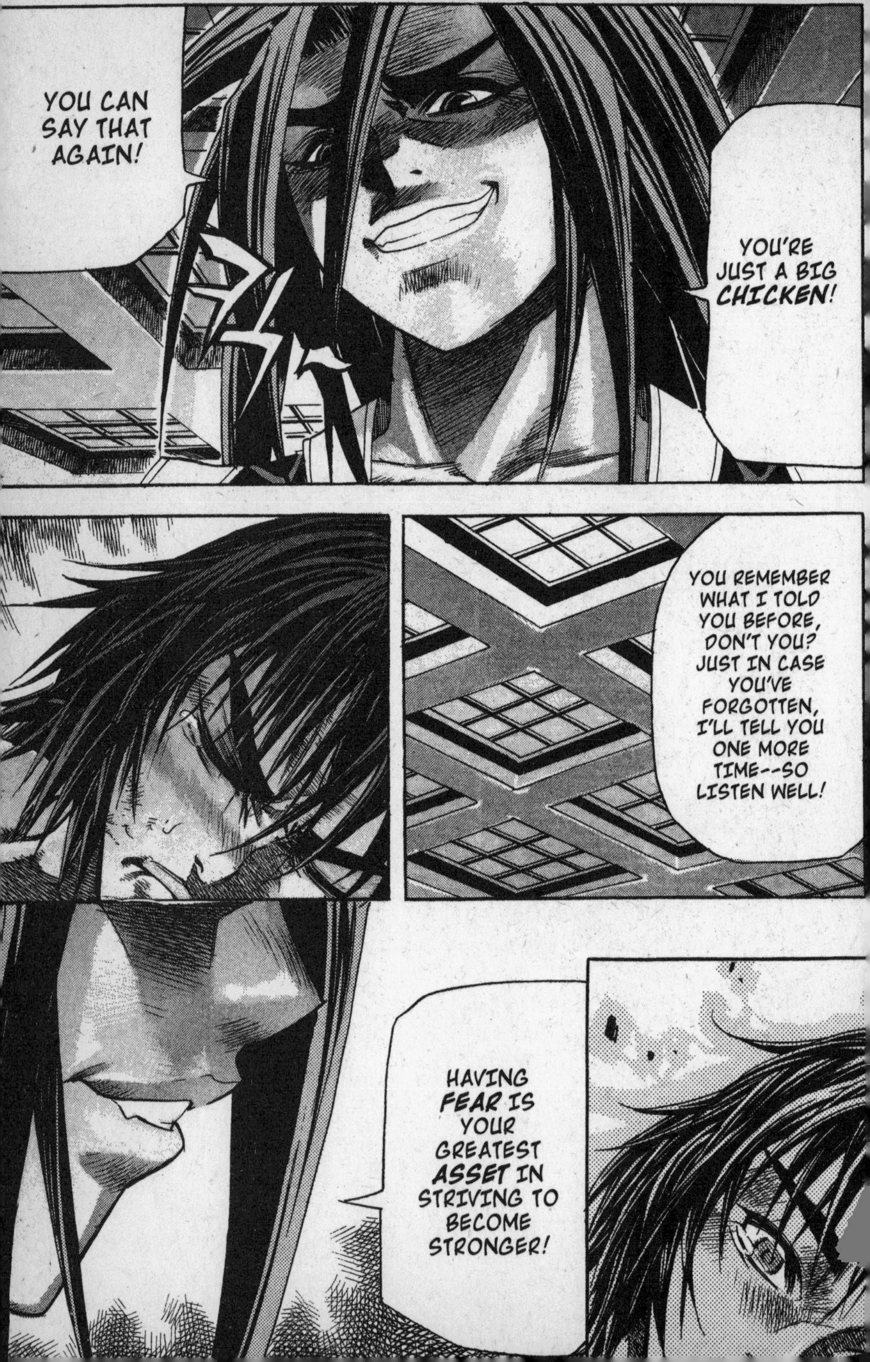
YOU'RE JUST A BIG CHICKEN!
YOU CAN SAY THAT AGAIN!
YOU REMEMBER WHAT I TOLD YOU BEFORE, DON'T YOU? JUST IN CASE YOU'VE FORGOTTEN, I'LL TELL YOU ONE MORE TIME--SO LISTEN WELL!
HAVING FEAR IS YOUR GREATEST ASSET IN STRIVING TO BECOME STRONGER!

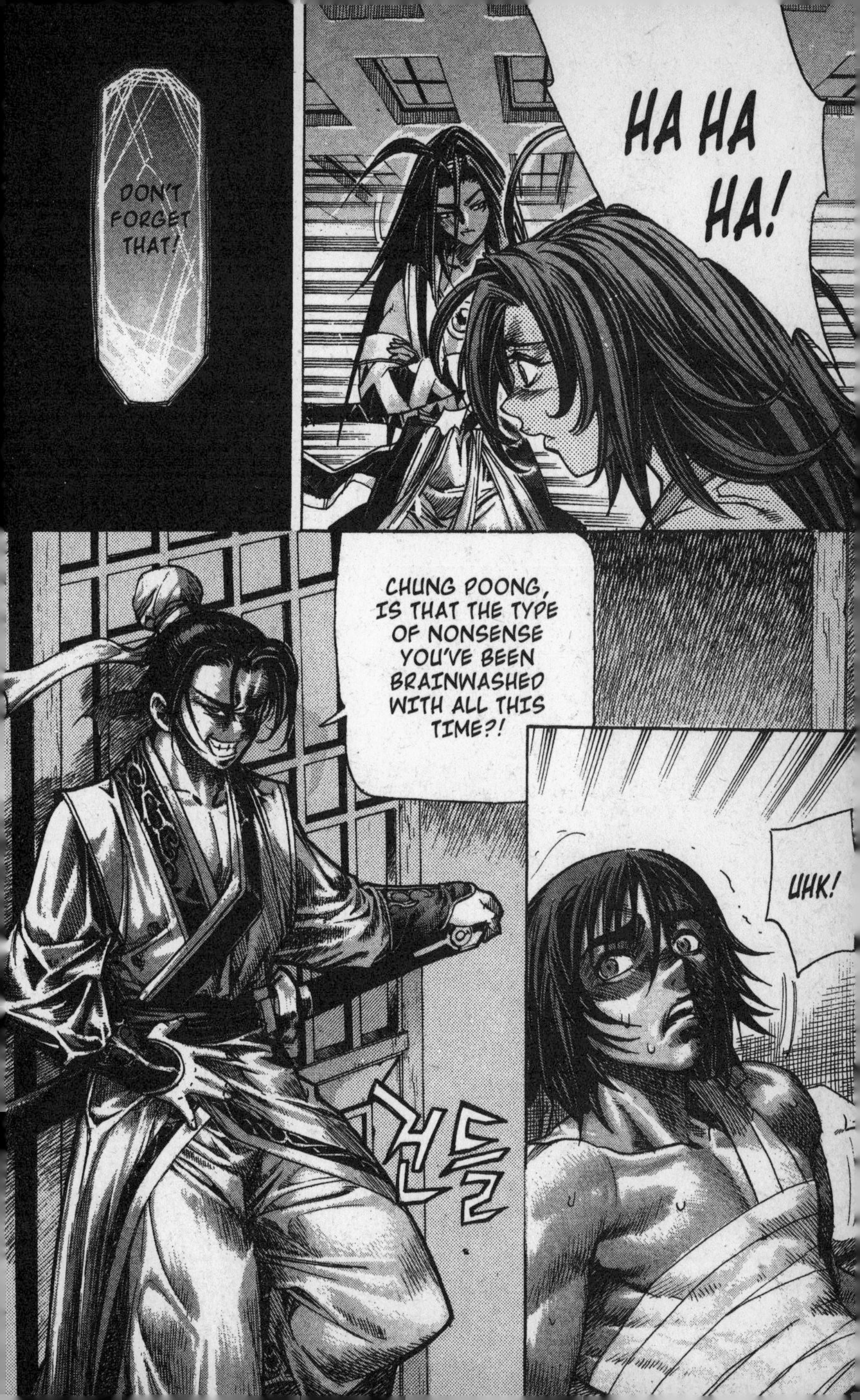
DON'T FORGET THAT!
HA HA HA!
CHUNG POONG, IS THAT THE TYPE OF NONSENSE YOU'VE BEEN BRAINWASHED WITH ALL THIS TIME?!
UHK!

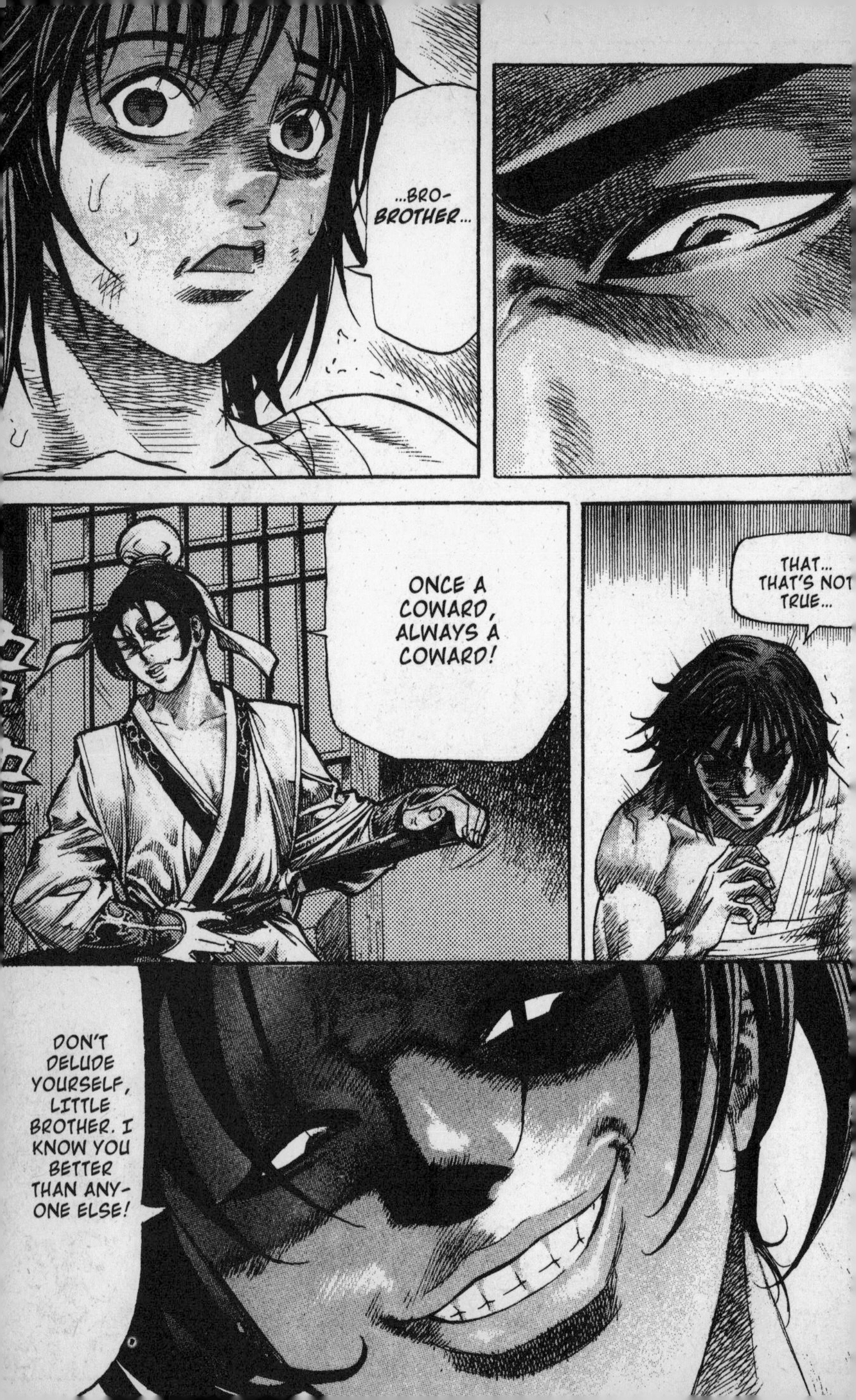
...BRO-
BROTHER...
THAT... THAT'S NOT TRUE...
ONCE A COWARD, ALWAYS A COWARD!
DON'T DELUDE YOURSELF, LITTLE BROTHER. I KNOW YOU BETTER THAN ANY-ONE ELSE!

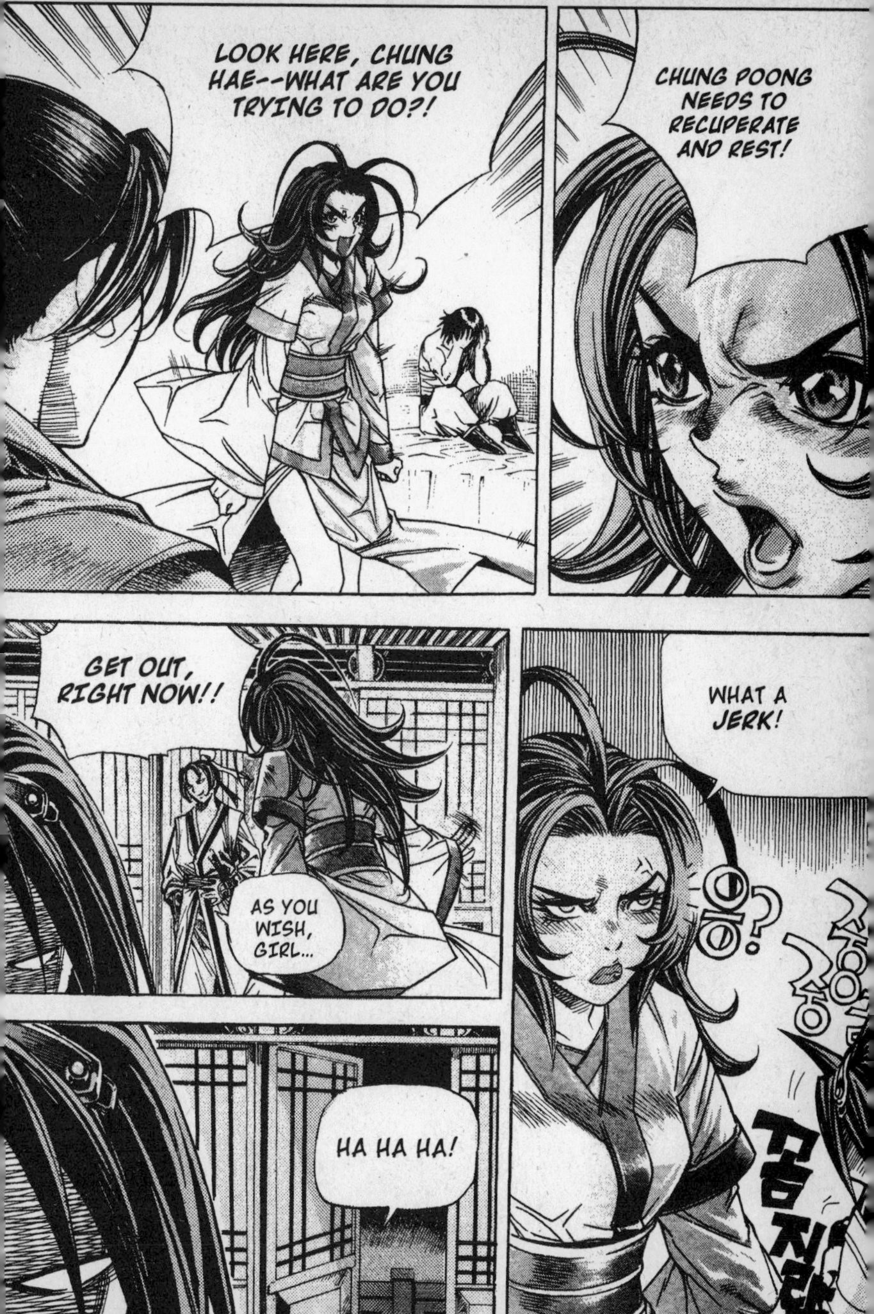
LOOK HERE, CHUNG HAE--WHAT ARE YOU TRYING TO DO?!
CHUNG POONG NEEDS TO RECUPERATE AND REST!
GET OUT, RIGHT NOW!!
AS YOU WISH, GIRL...
HA HA HA!
WHAT A JERK!

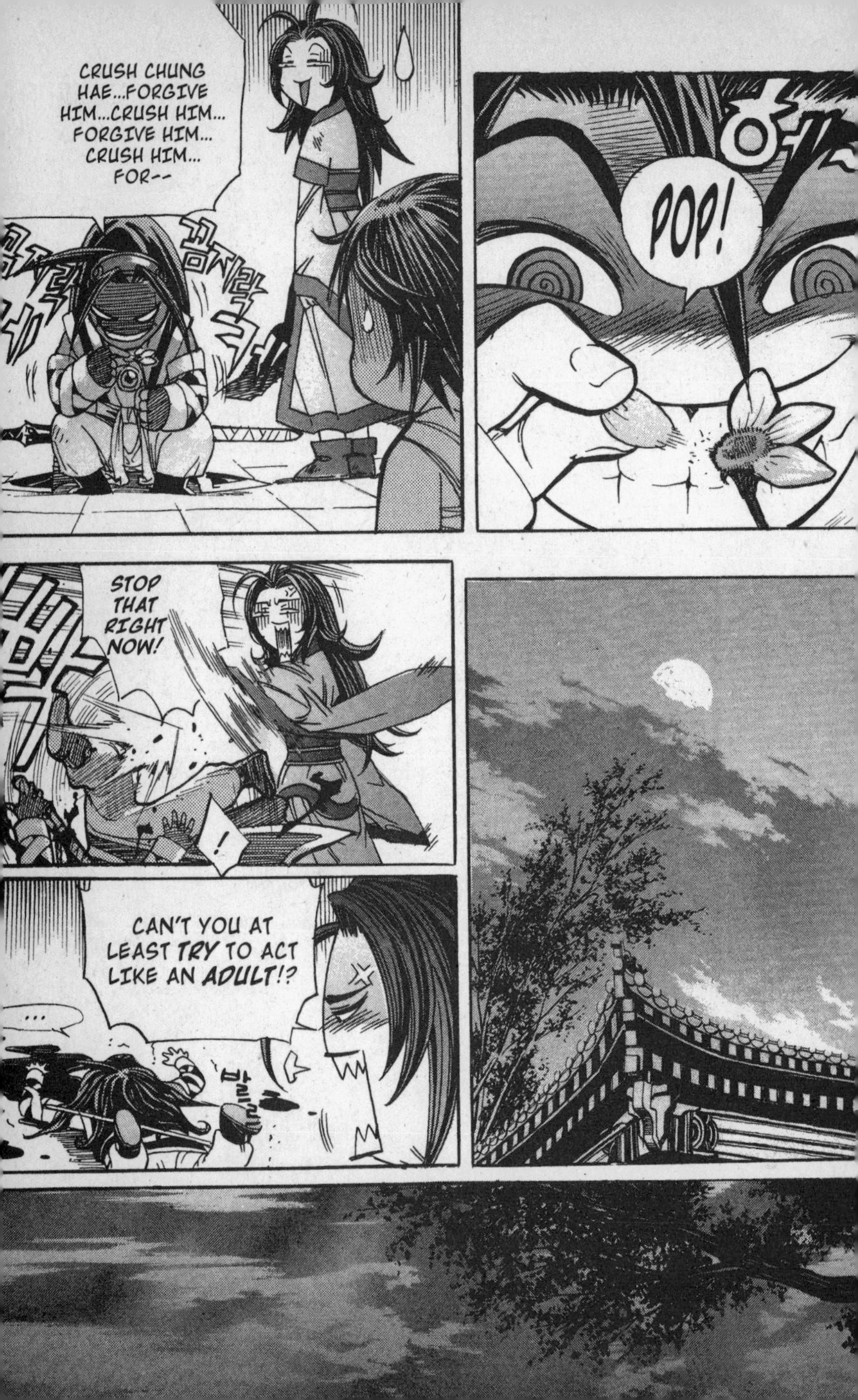
CRUSH CHUNG HAE...FORGIVE HIM...CRUSH HIM... FORGIVE HIM... CRUSH HIM... FOR--
POP!
STOP THAT RIGHT NOW!
!
CAN'T YOU AT LEAST TRY TO ACT LIKE AN ADULT!?
...

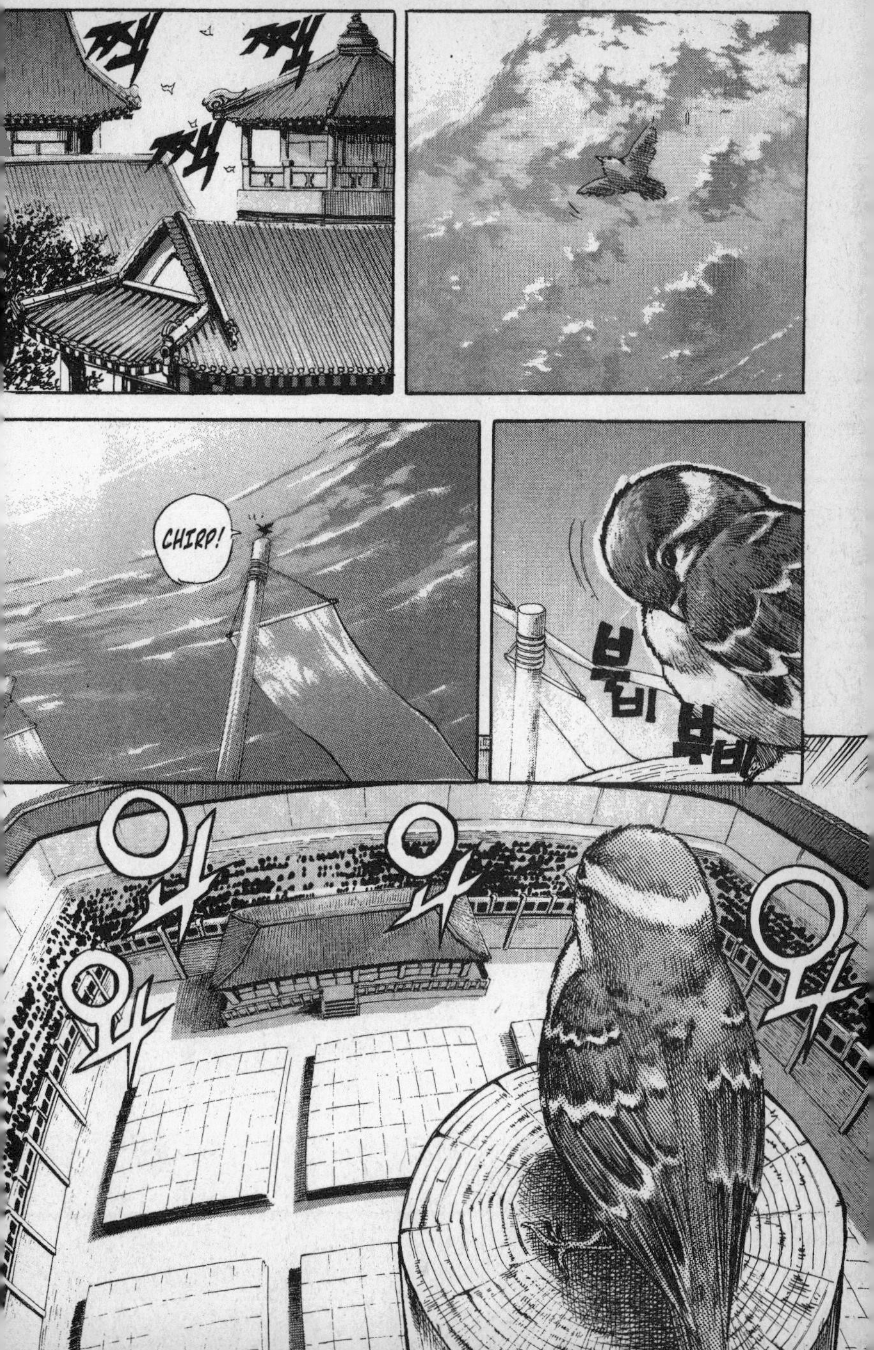
짹
짹
짹
CHIRP!
부비 부비
와
와
와
와

WE WANT TO EXPRESS OUR DEEPEST GRATITUDE TO ALL THE ATTENDEES FOR JOINING US AGAIN TODAY!
AT THIS VERY MOMENT...THE 16 WINNERS OF YESTERDAY'S MATCHES HAVE ALREADY DRAWN LOTS AND ARE NOW ENTERING THE ARENA.

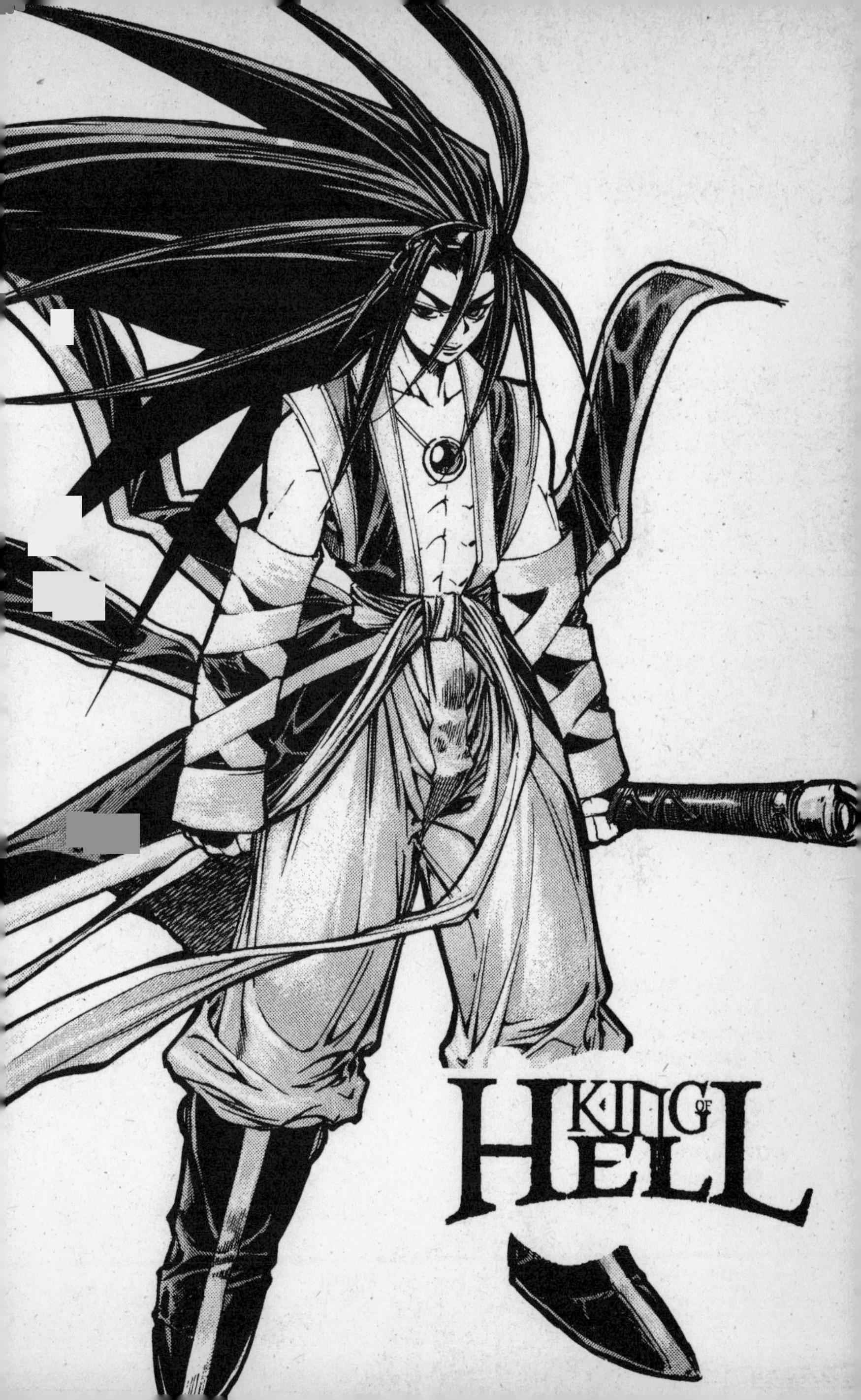
KING OF HELL

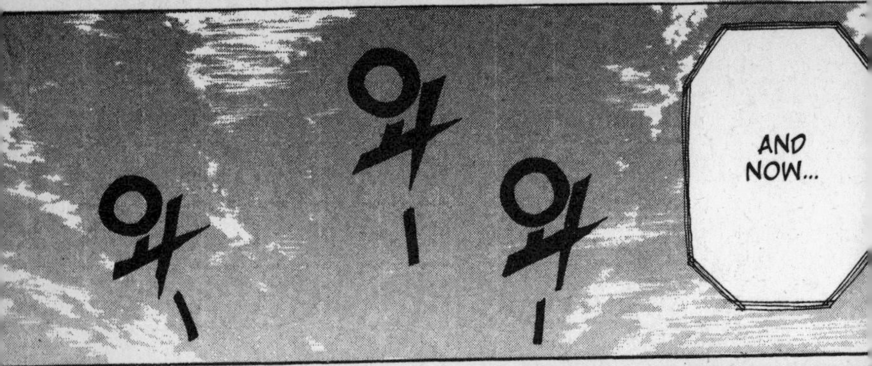
AND NOW...
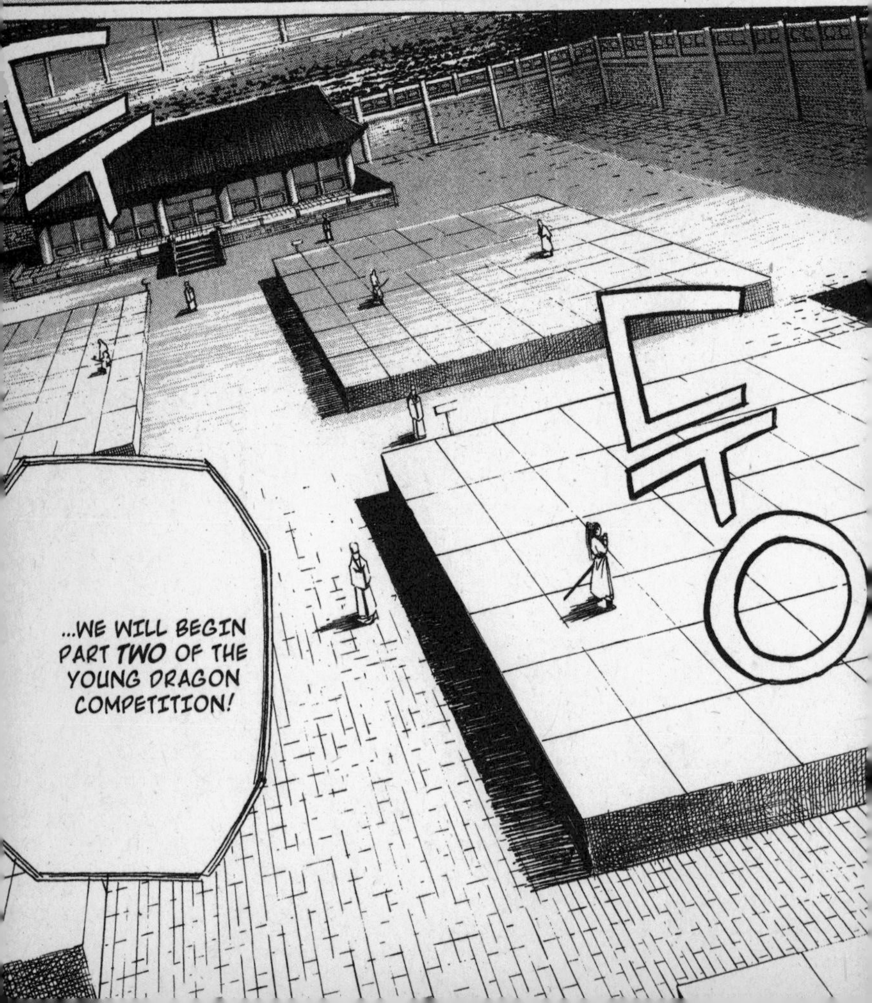
...WE WILL BEGIN PART TWO OF THE YOUNG DRAGON COMPETITION!

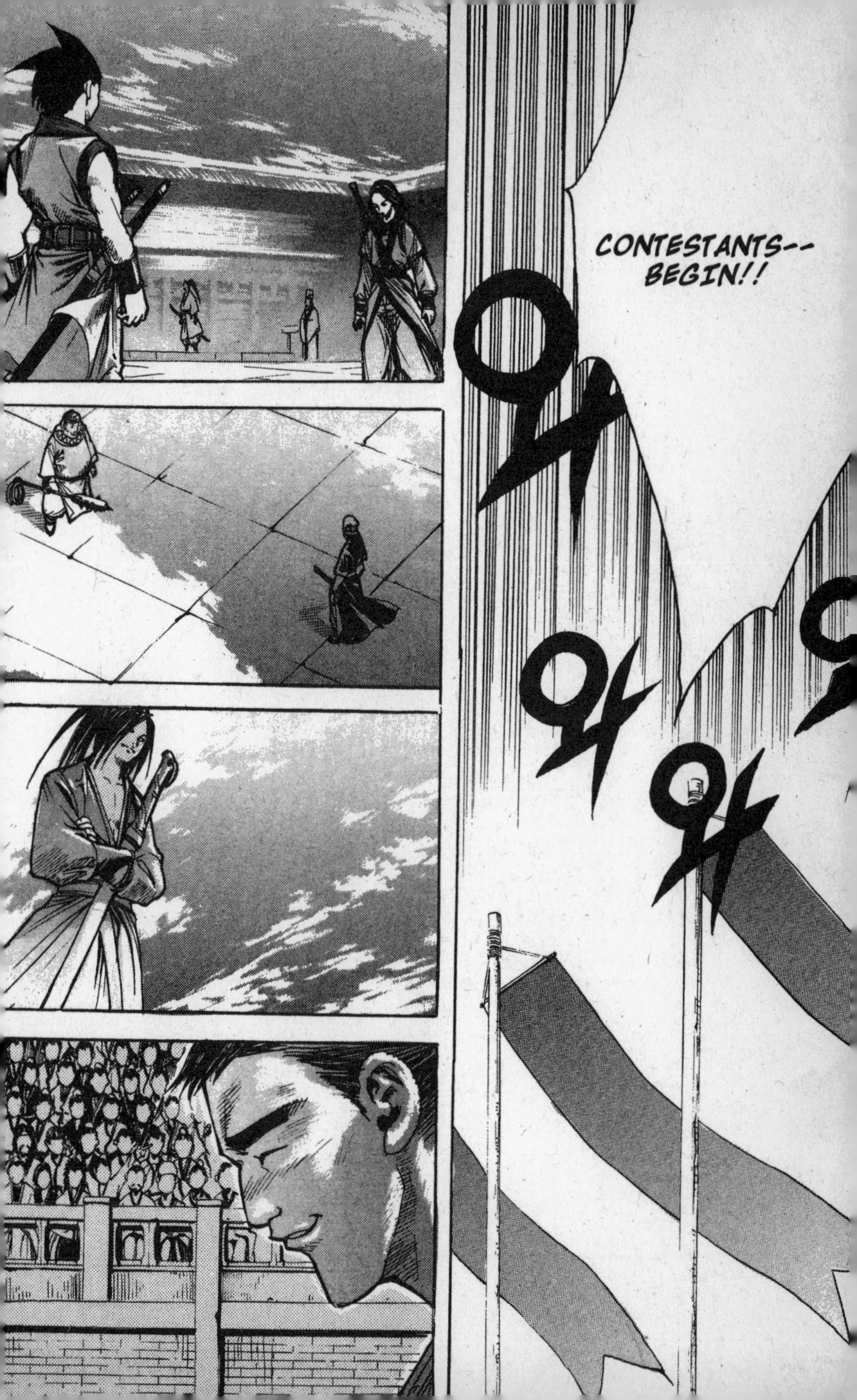
CONTESTANTS--
BEGIN!!

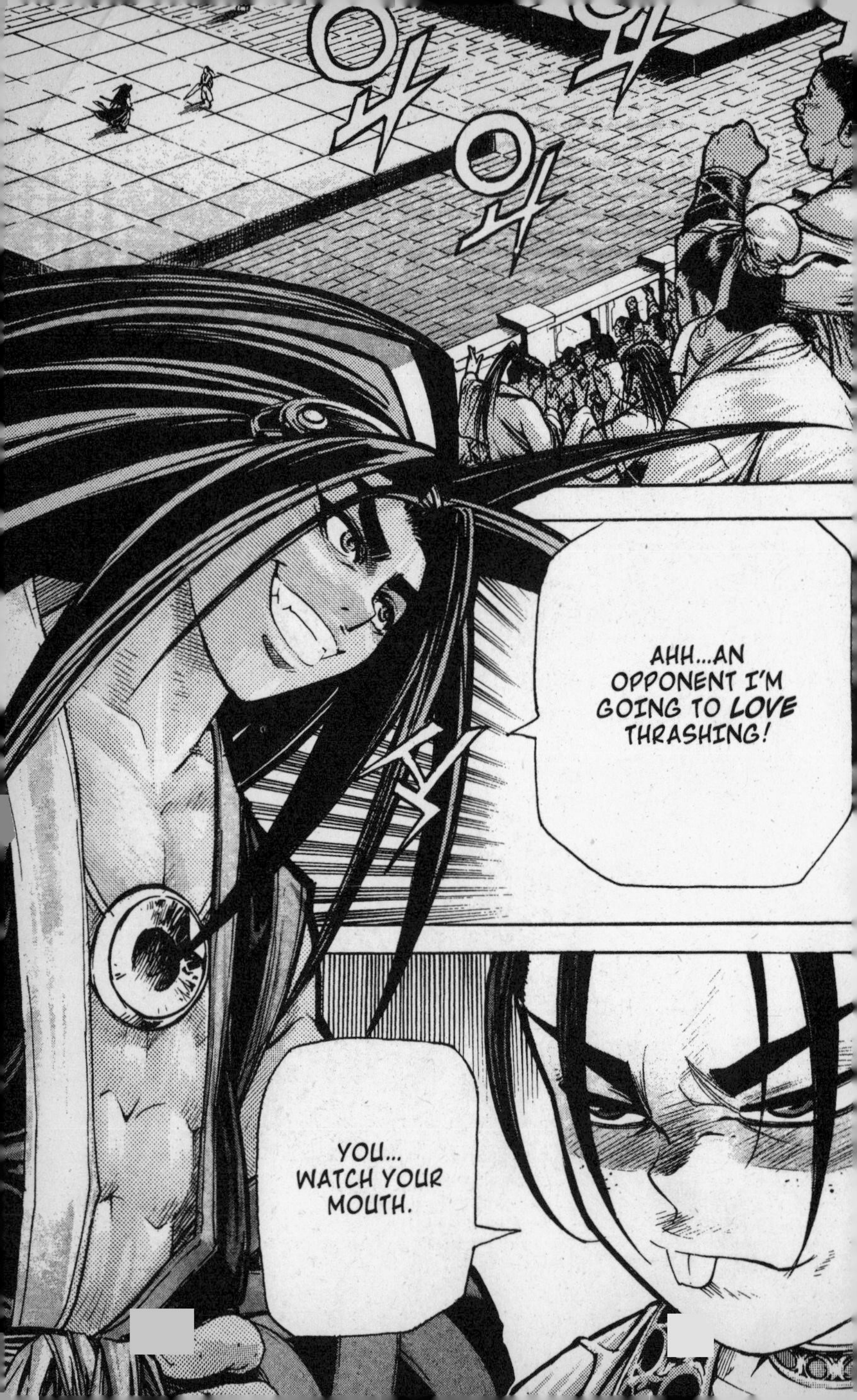
AHH...AN OPPONENT I'M GOING TO *LOVE* THRASHING!
YOU... WATCH YOUR MOUTH.

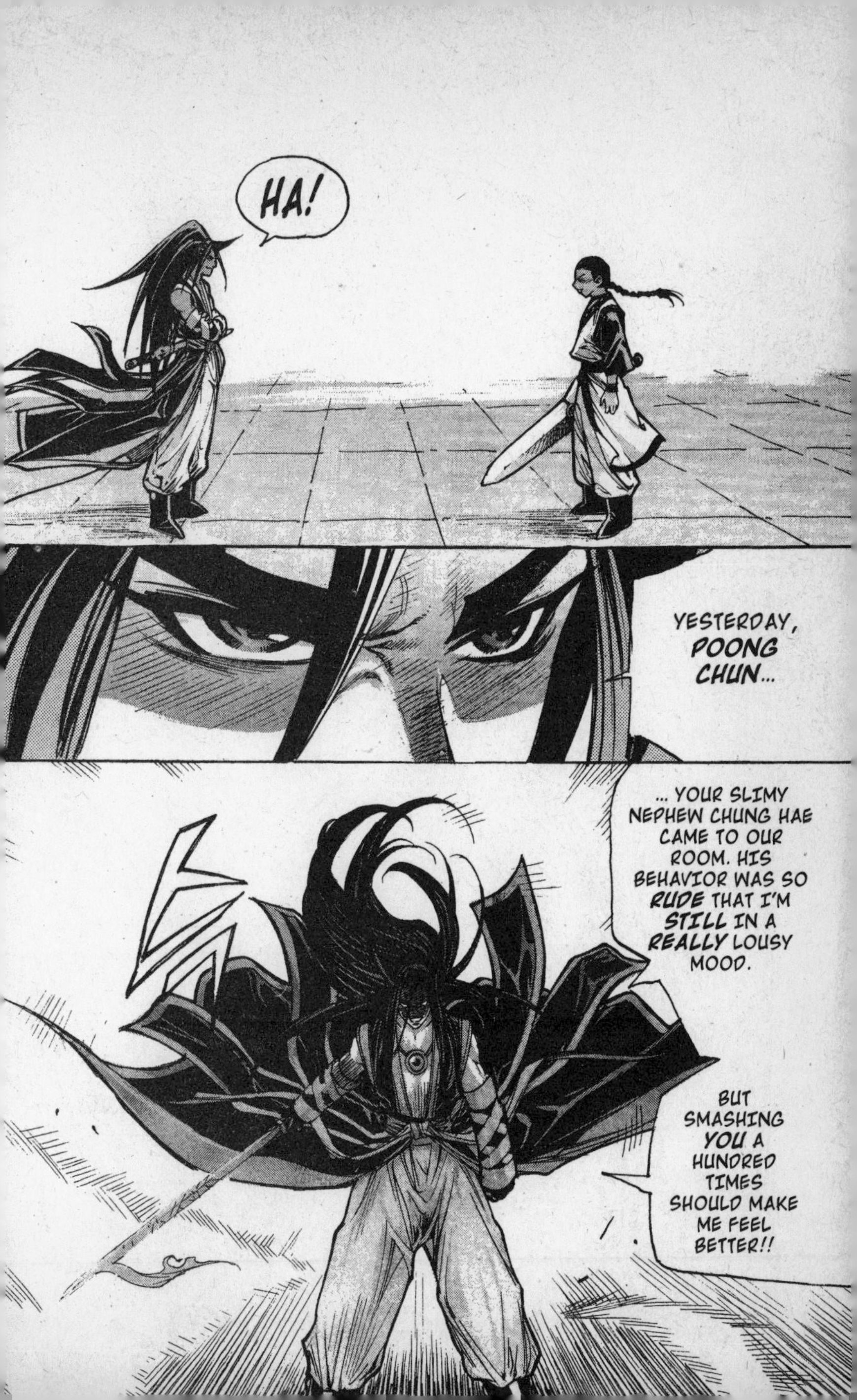
HA!
YESTERDAY, POONG CHUN...
... YOUR SLIMY NEPHEW CHUNG HAE CAME TO OUR ROOM. HIS BEHAVIOR WAS SO RUDE THAT I'M STILL IN A REALLY LOUSY MOOD.
BUT SMASHING YOU A HUNDRED TIMES SHOULD MAKE ME FEEL BETTER!!

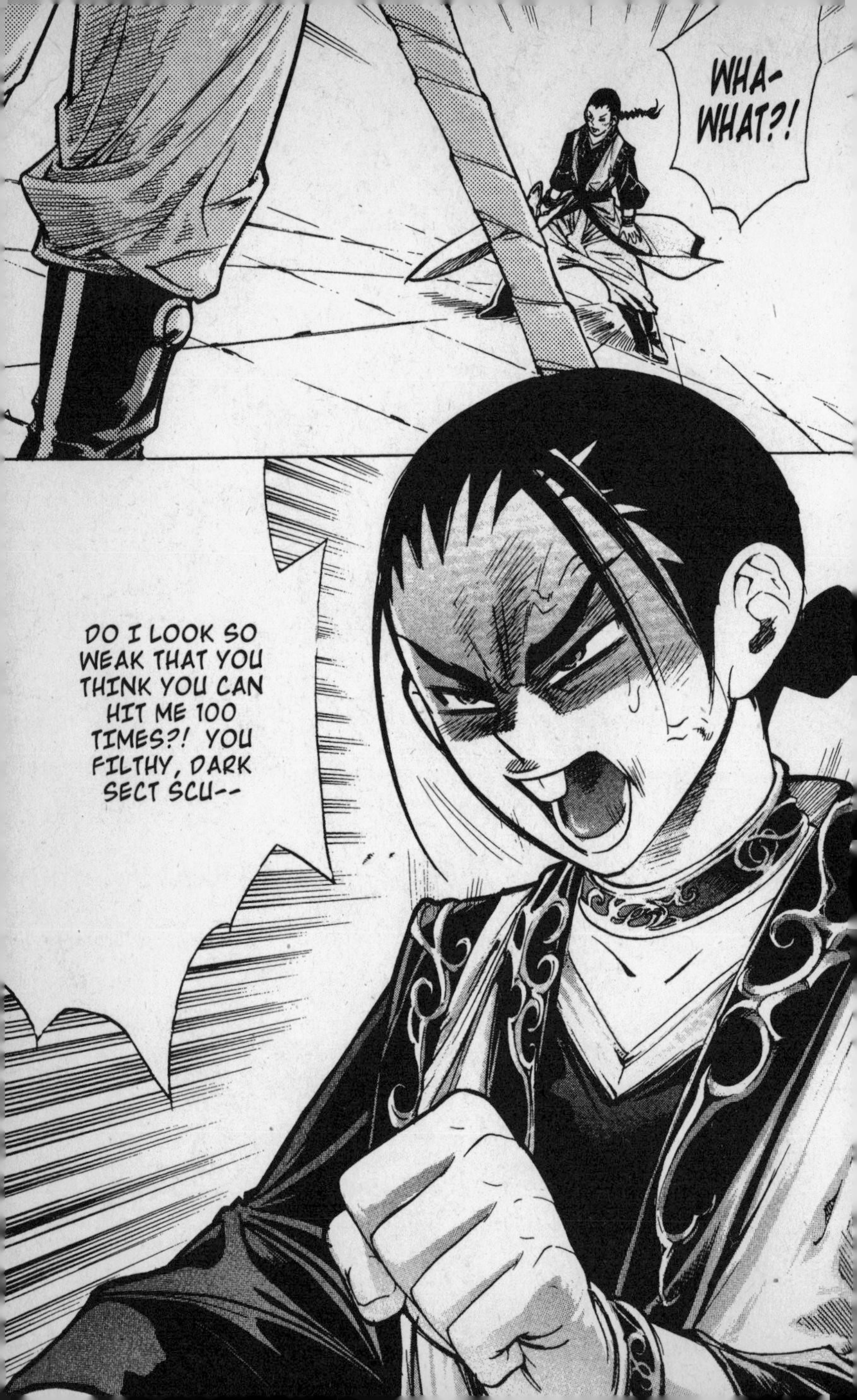
WHA-WHAT?!
DO I LOOK SO WEAK THAT YOU THINK YOU CAN HIT ME 100 TIMES?! YOU FILTHY, DARK SECT SCU--

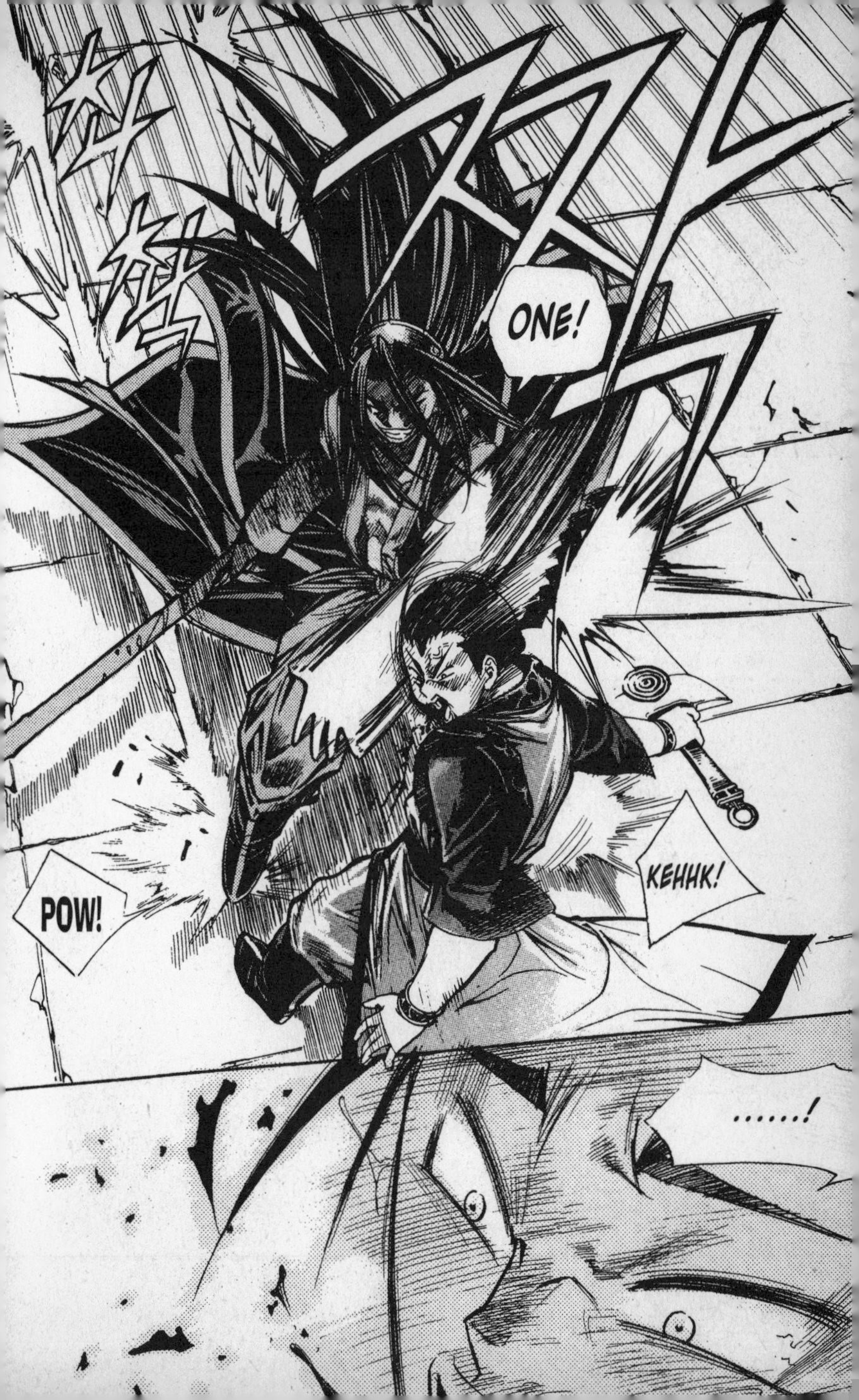
ONE!
KEHHK!
POW!
......!

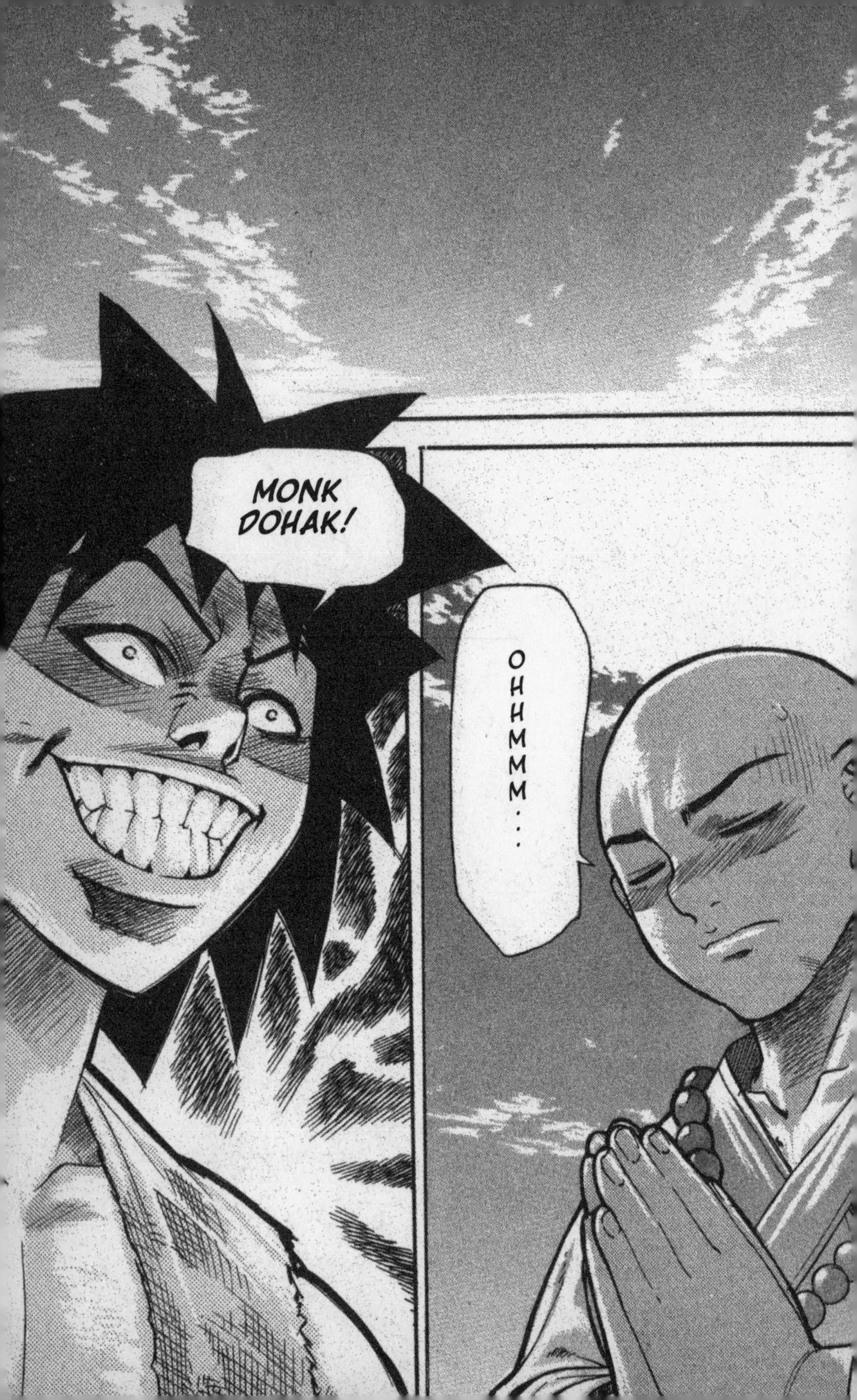
MONK DOHAK!
OHHMMM...

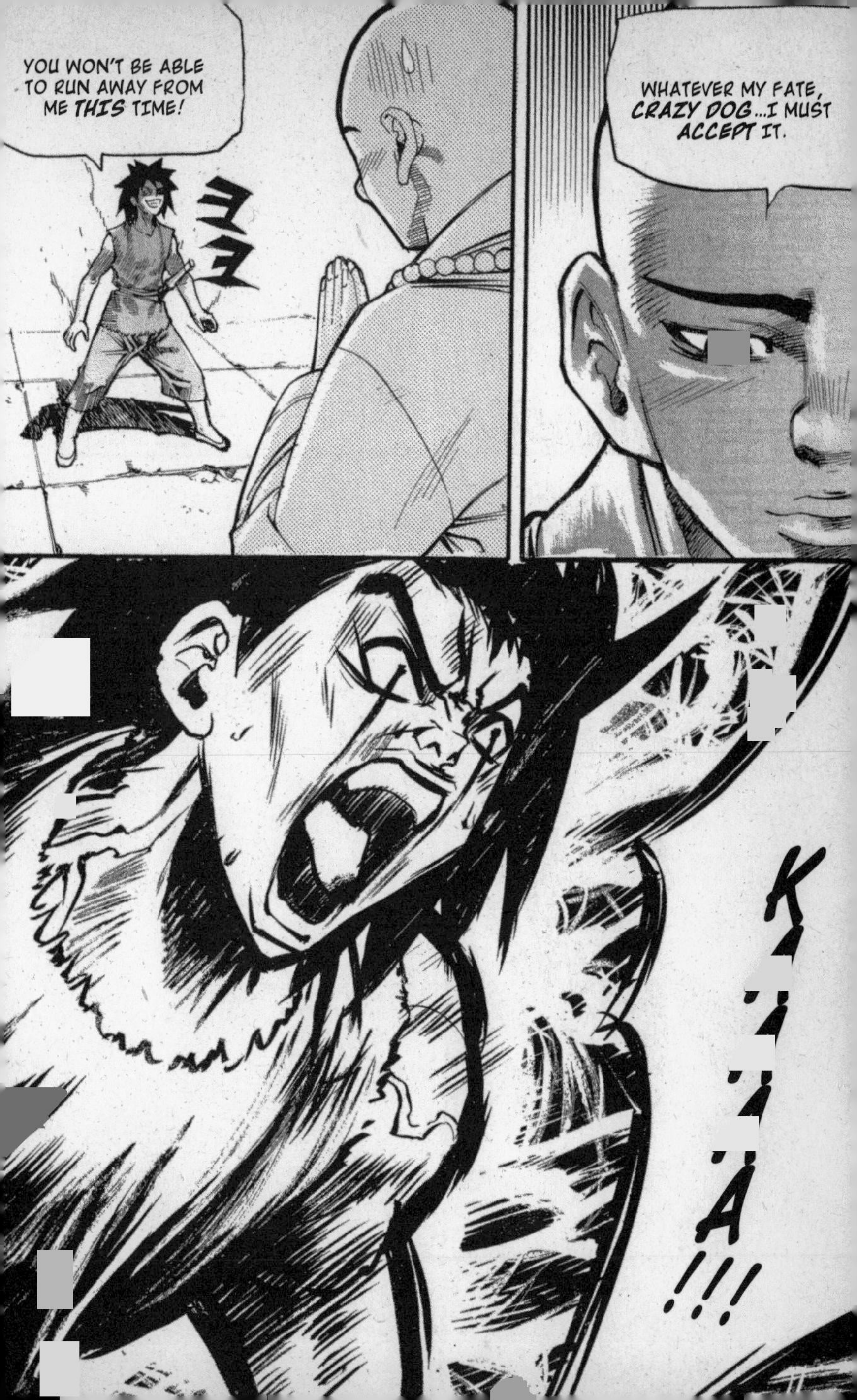
YOU WON'T BE ABLE TO RUN AWAY FROM ME THIS TIME!
ㅋㅋ
WHATEVER MY FATE, CRAZY DOG...I MUST ACCEPT IT.

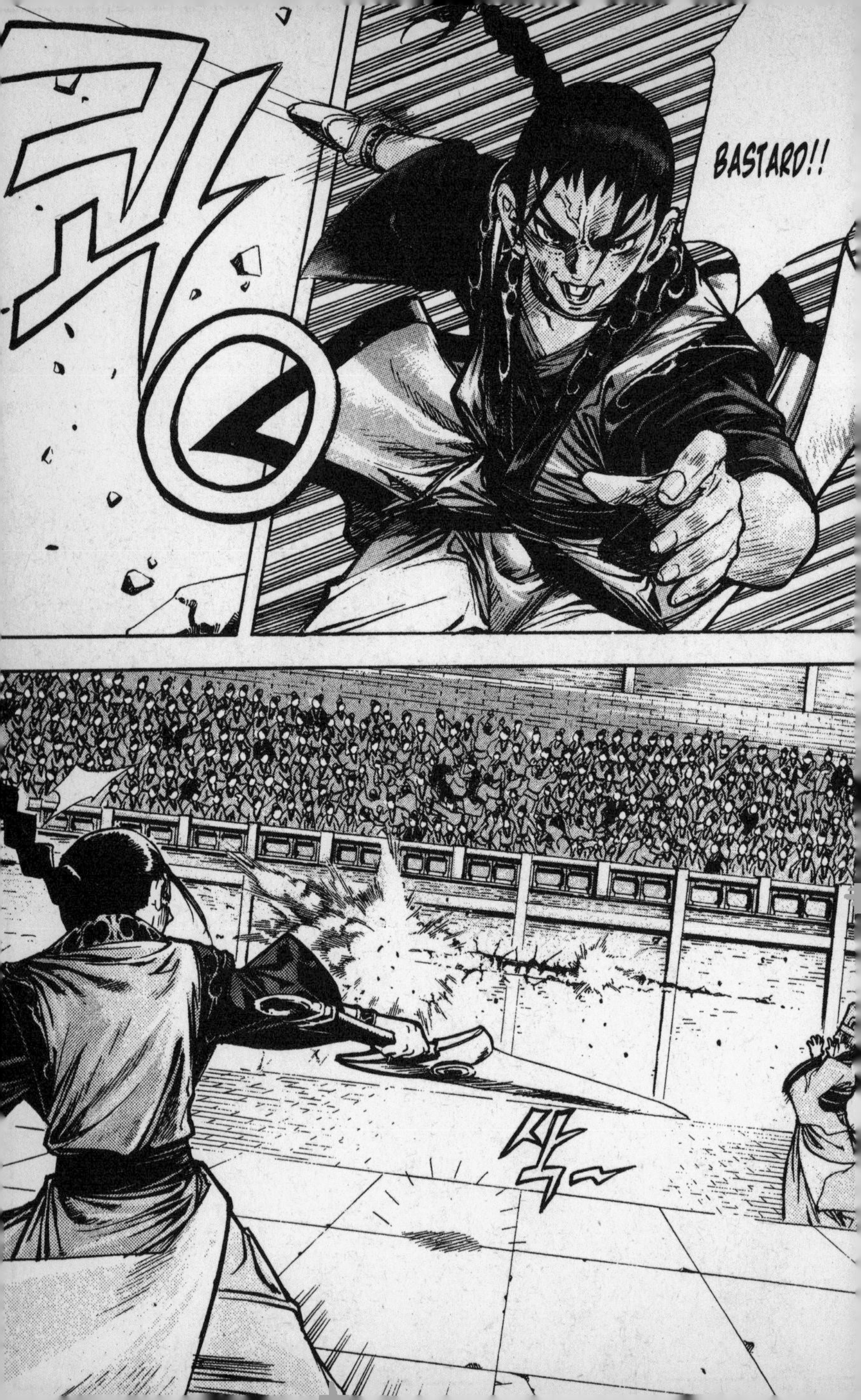
BASTARD!!

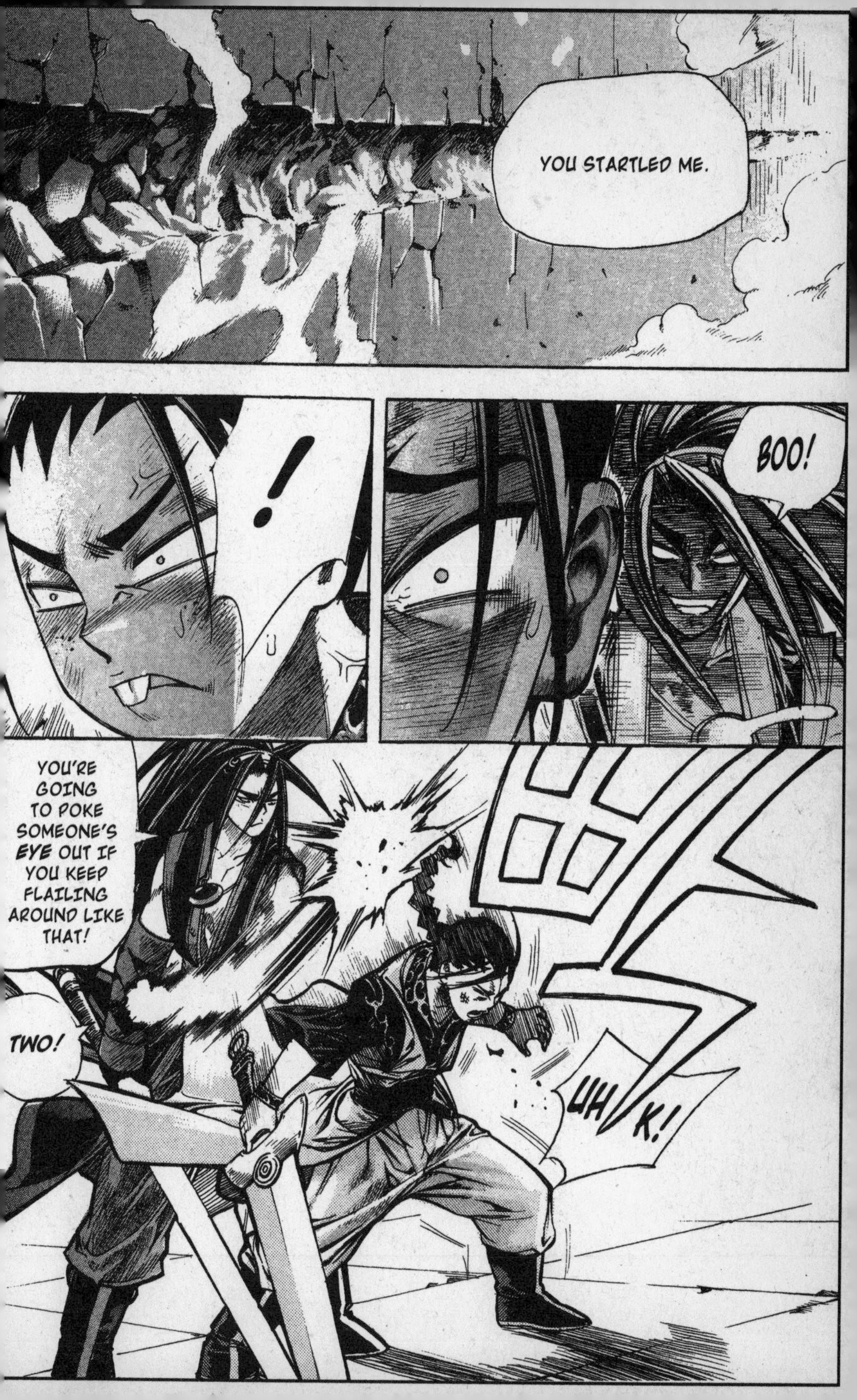
YOU STARTLED ME.
BOO!
!
UHK!
YOU'RE GOING TO POKE SOMEONE'S EYE OUT IF YOU KEEP FLAILING AROUND LIKE THAT!
TWO!

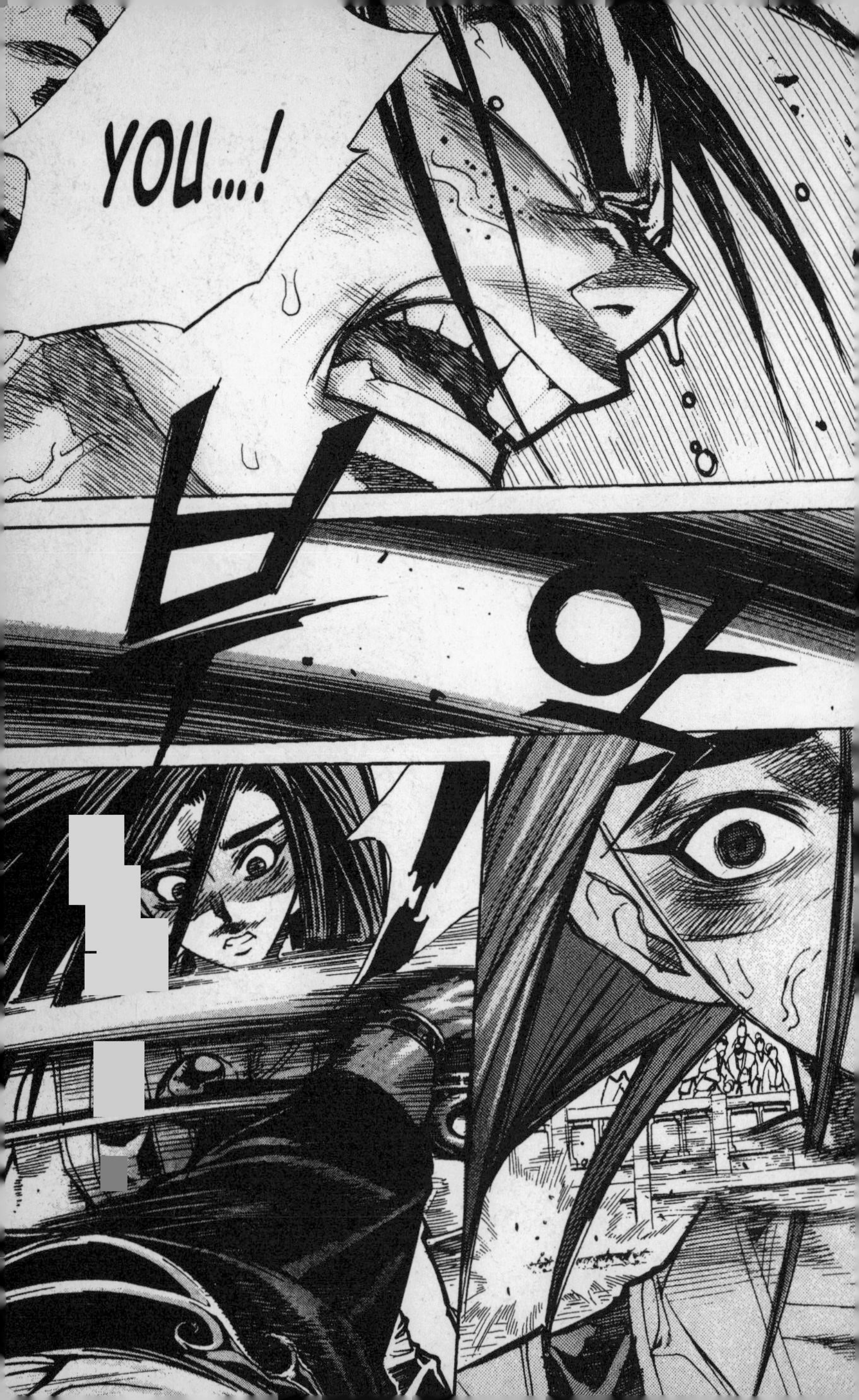
YOU...!

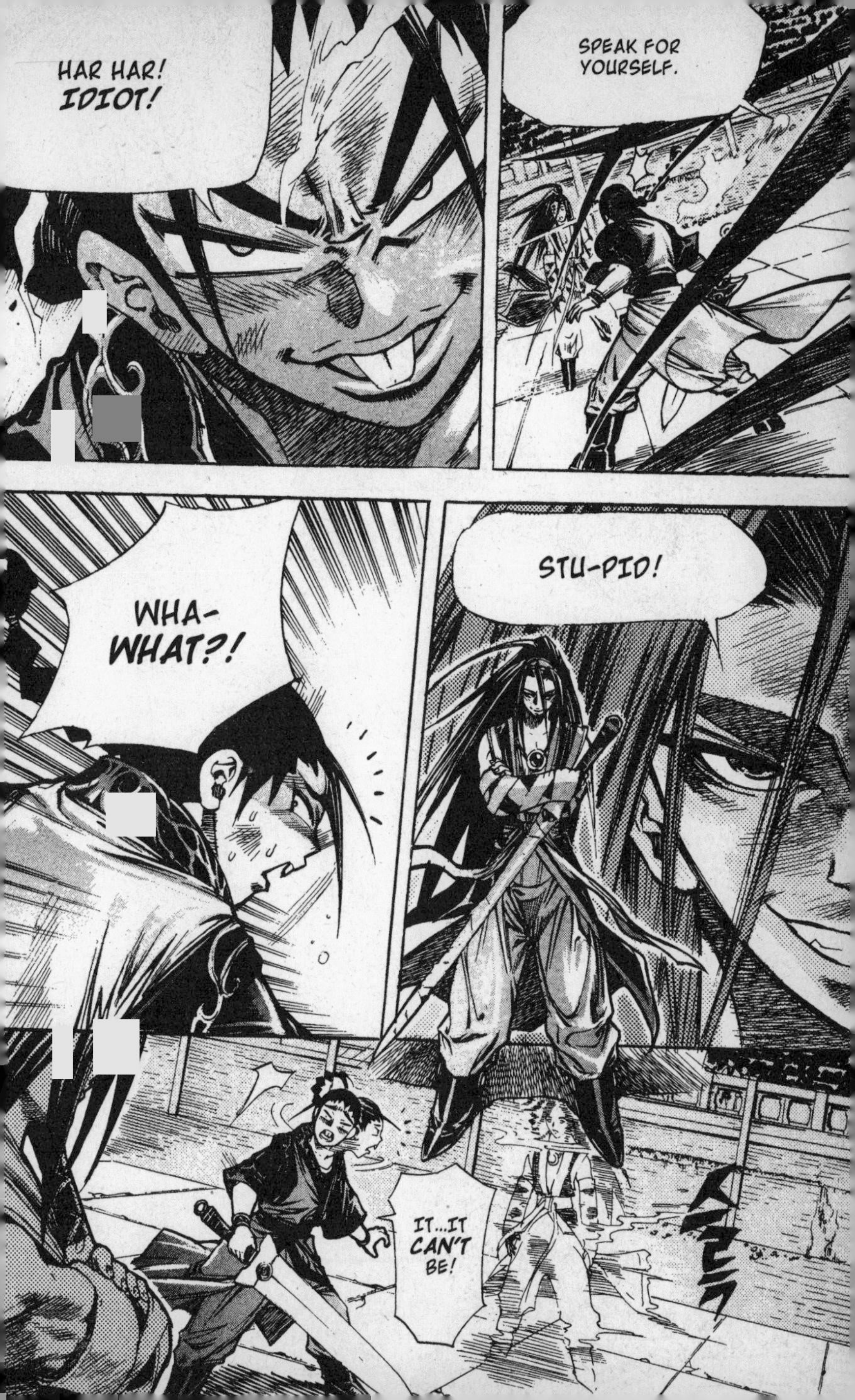
HAR HAR! IDIOT!
SPEAK FOR YOURSELF.
WHA-WHAT?!
STU-PID!
IT...IT CAN'T BE!

INSTEAD OF TALKING ALL THE TIME--WHY DON'T YOU TRY USING YOUR SWORD?!
WHAT?! BUT HE WAS--! I CUT--!
IM-IMPOSSIBLE! I'M THE MOST HIGHLY REGARDED FIGHTER FROM THE SHAMAN SECT...HOW COULD I HAVE MISJUDGED WHERE HE WAS...?

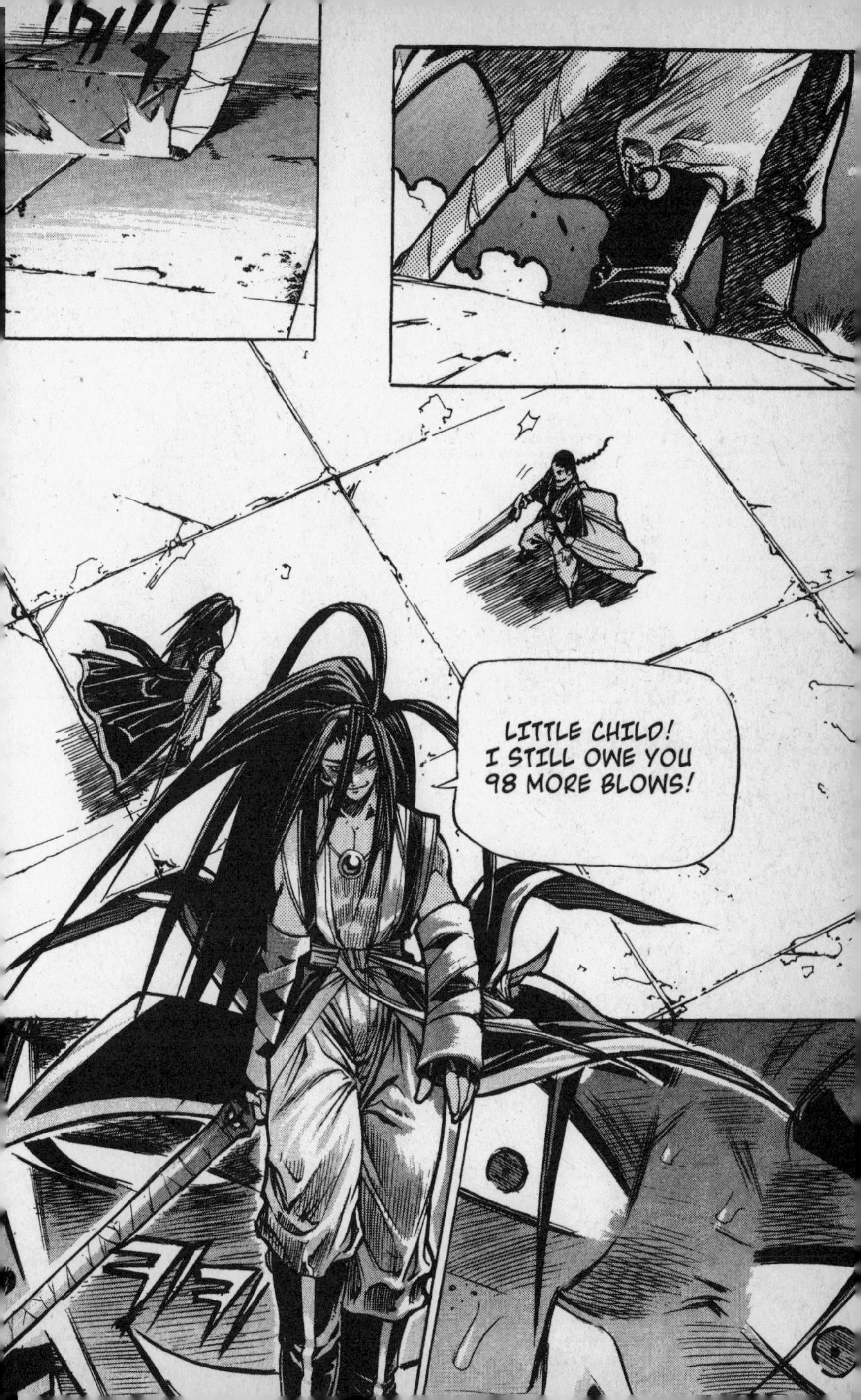
LITTLE CHILD! I STILL OWE YOU 98 MORE BLOWS!

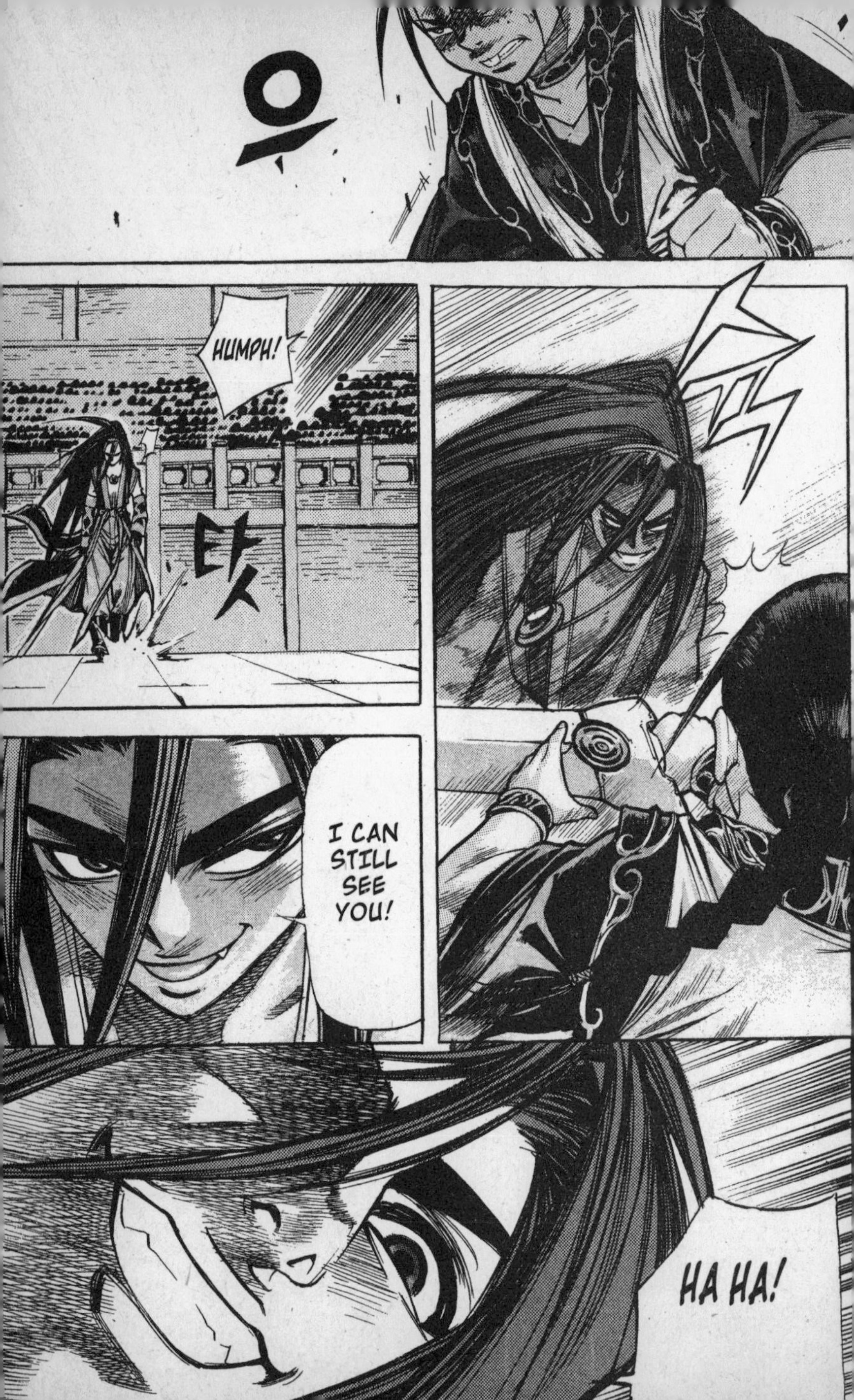
HUMPH!
탓
I CAN STILL SEE YOU!
HA HA!

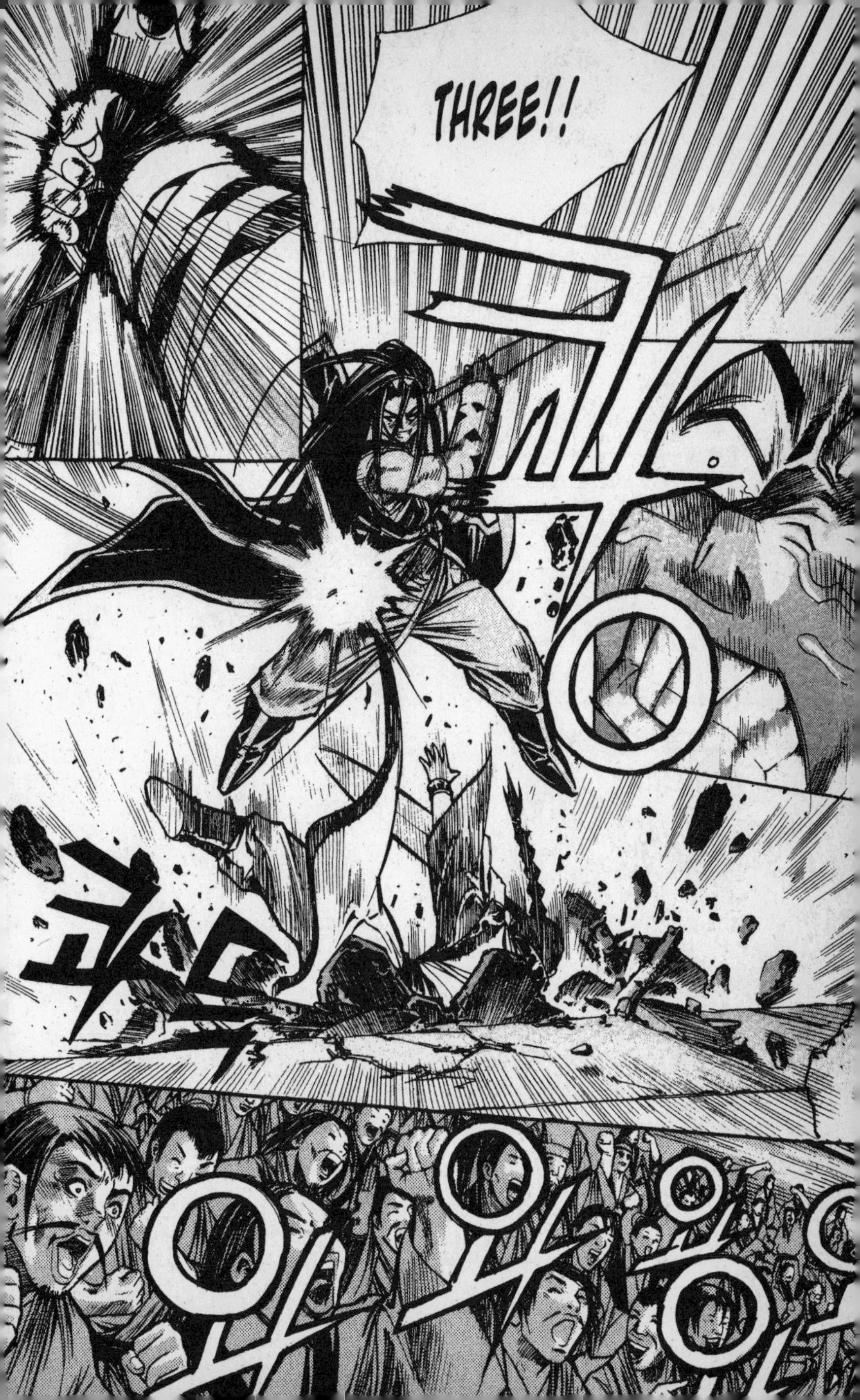
THREE!!

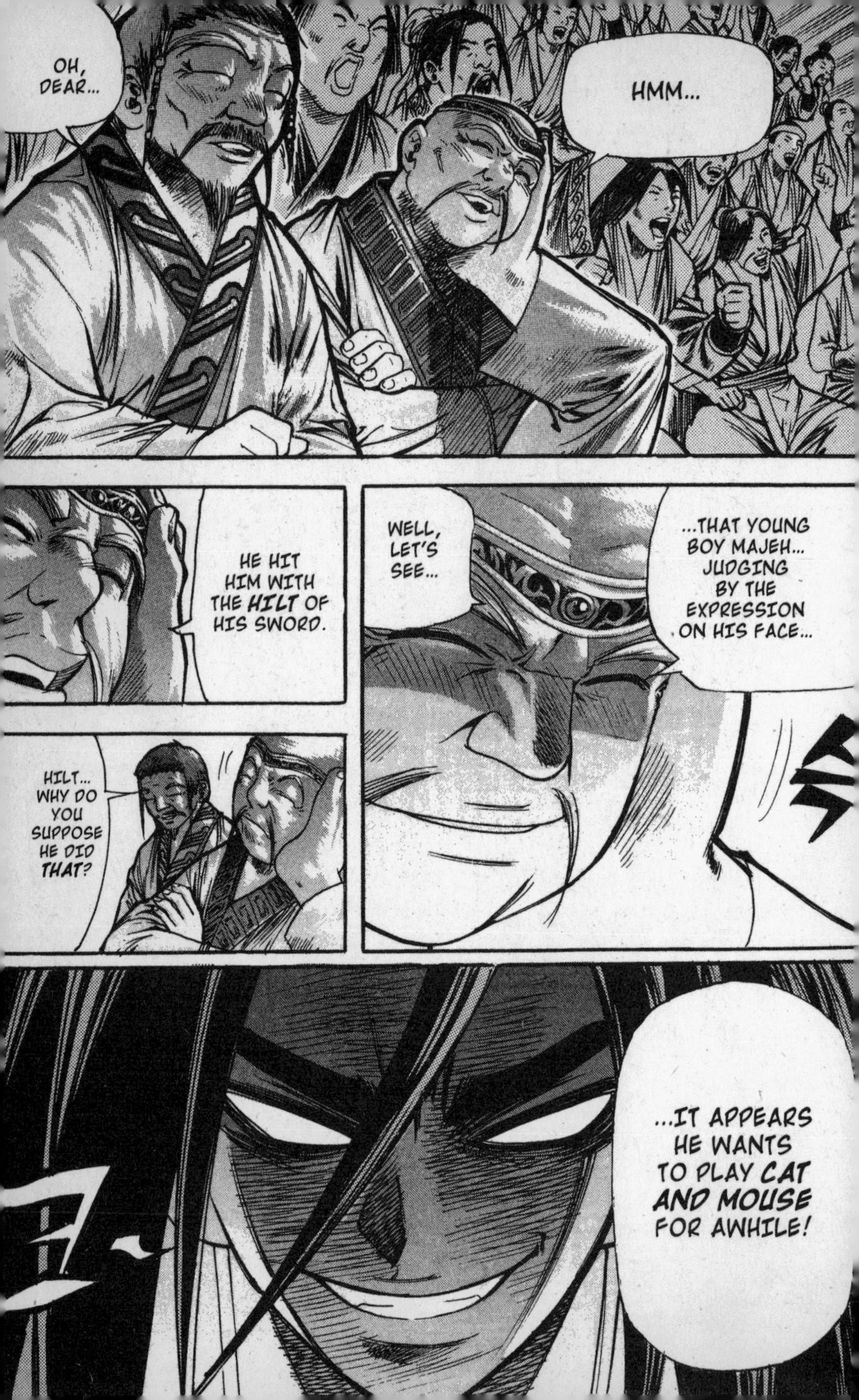
OH, DEAR...
HMM...
HE HIT HIM WITH THE HILT OF HIS SWORD.
HILT... WHY DO YOU SUPPOSE HE DID THAT?
WELL, LET'S SEE...
...THAT YOUNG BOY MAJEH... JUDGING BY THE EXPRESSION ON HIS FACE...
...IT APPEARS HE WANTS TO PLAY CAT AND MOUSE FOR AWHILE!

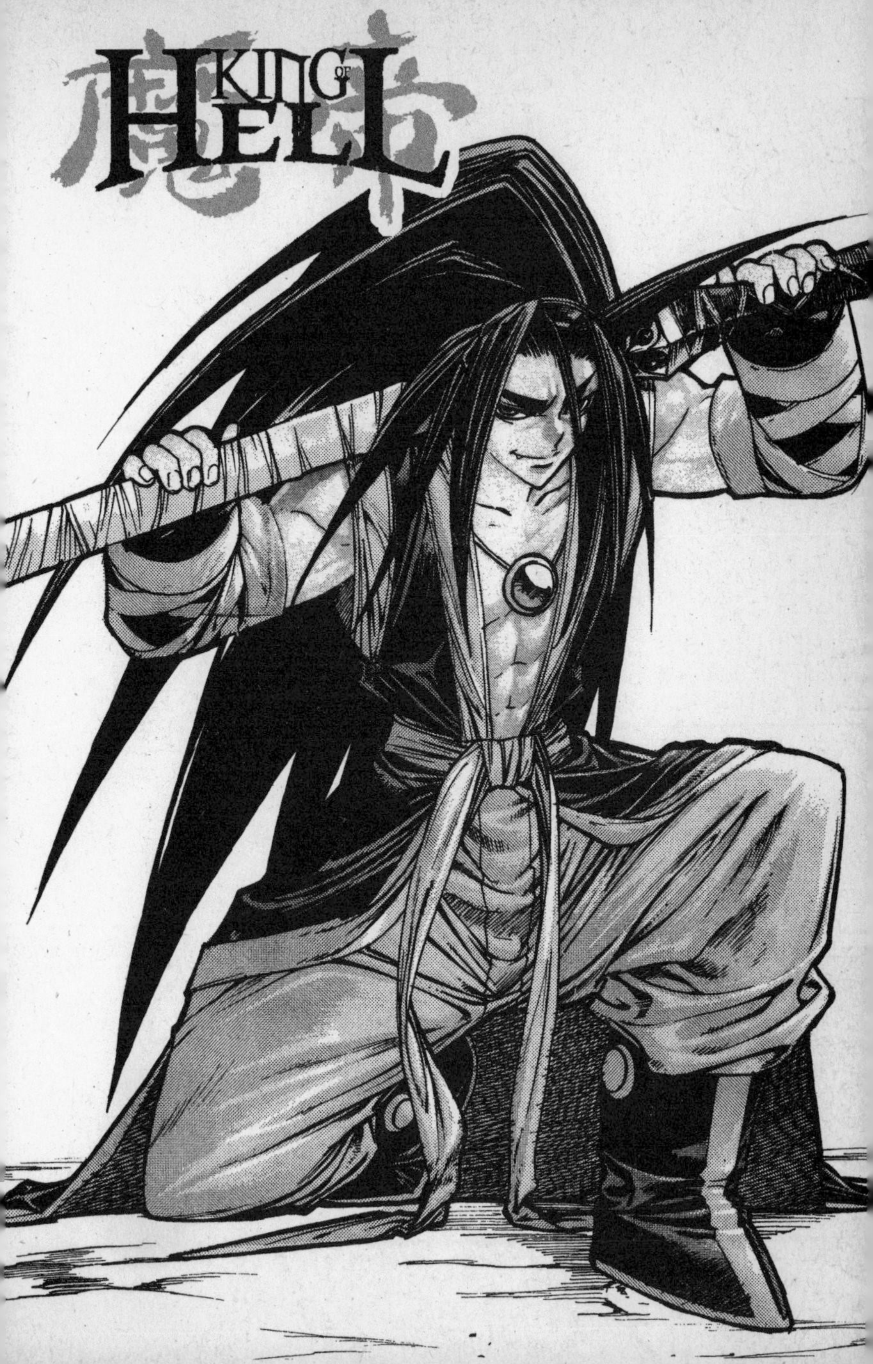
KING OF HELL

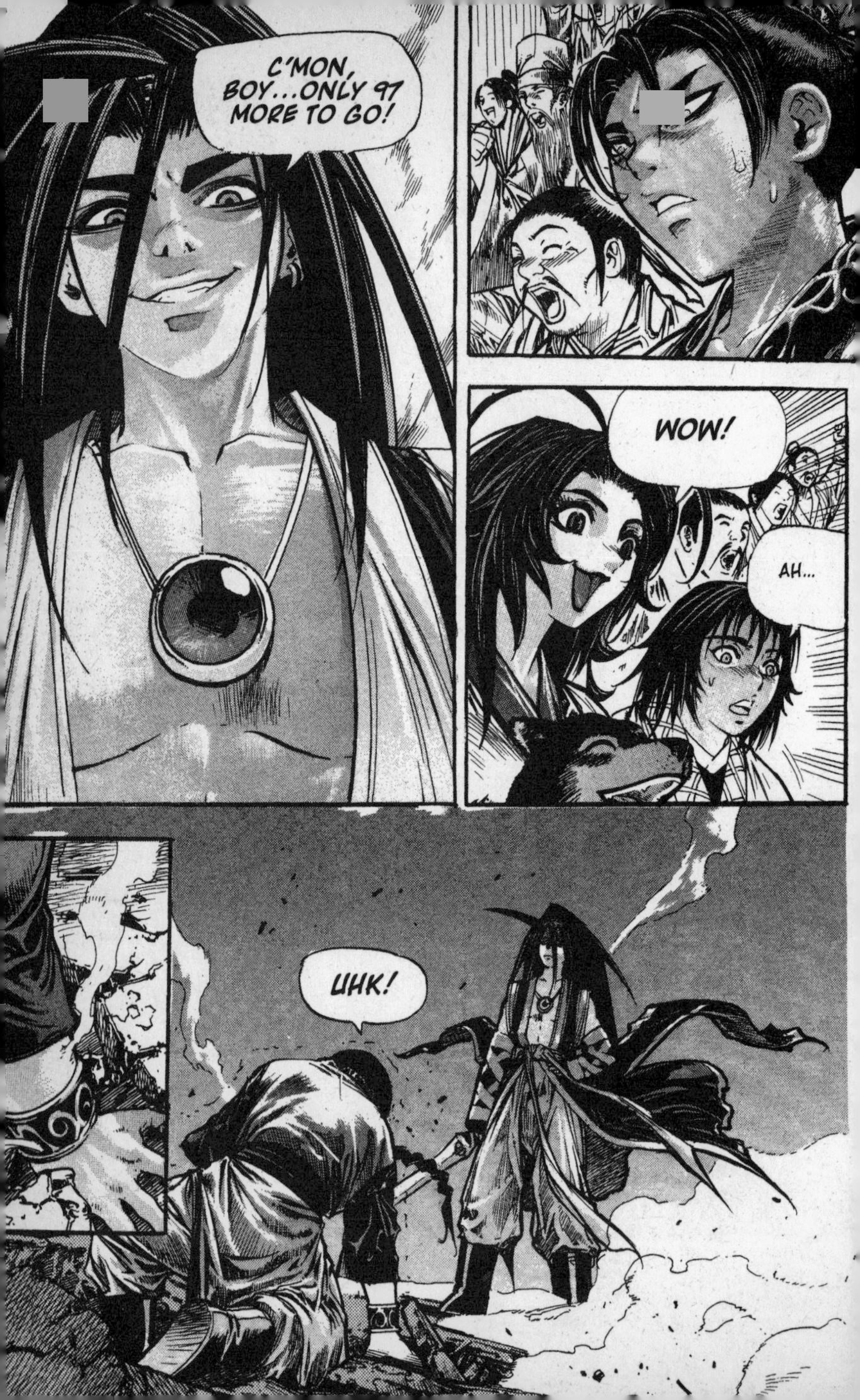
WOW!
AH...
C'MON, BOY...ONLY 97 MORE TO GO!
UHK!

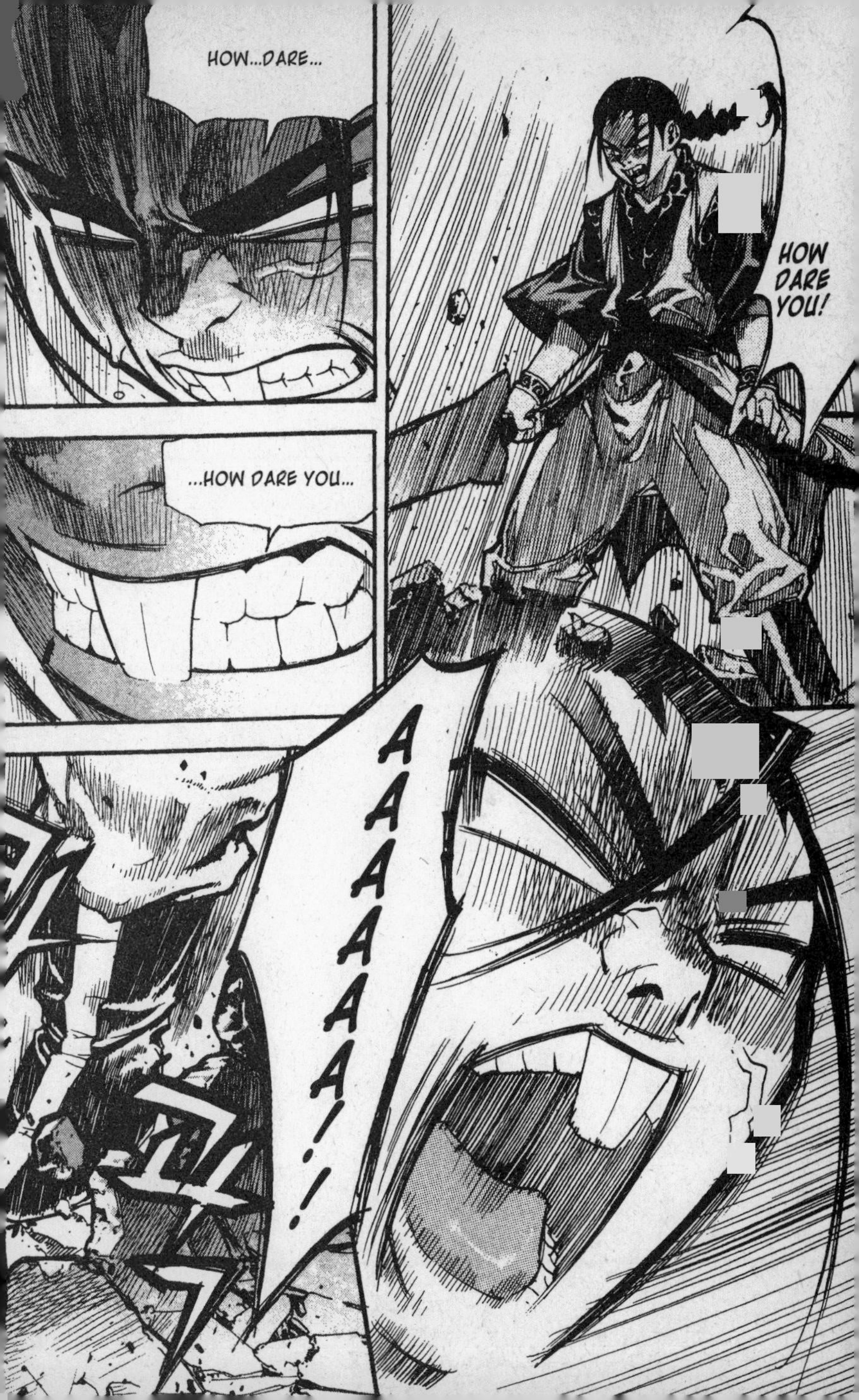
HOW DARE YOU!
HOW...DARE...
...HOW DARE YOU...
AAAAAAAAA!!!

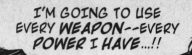

I'M GOING TO USE
EVERY **WEAPON**--EVERY
POWER I HAVE...!!

......!

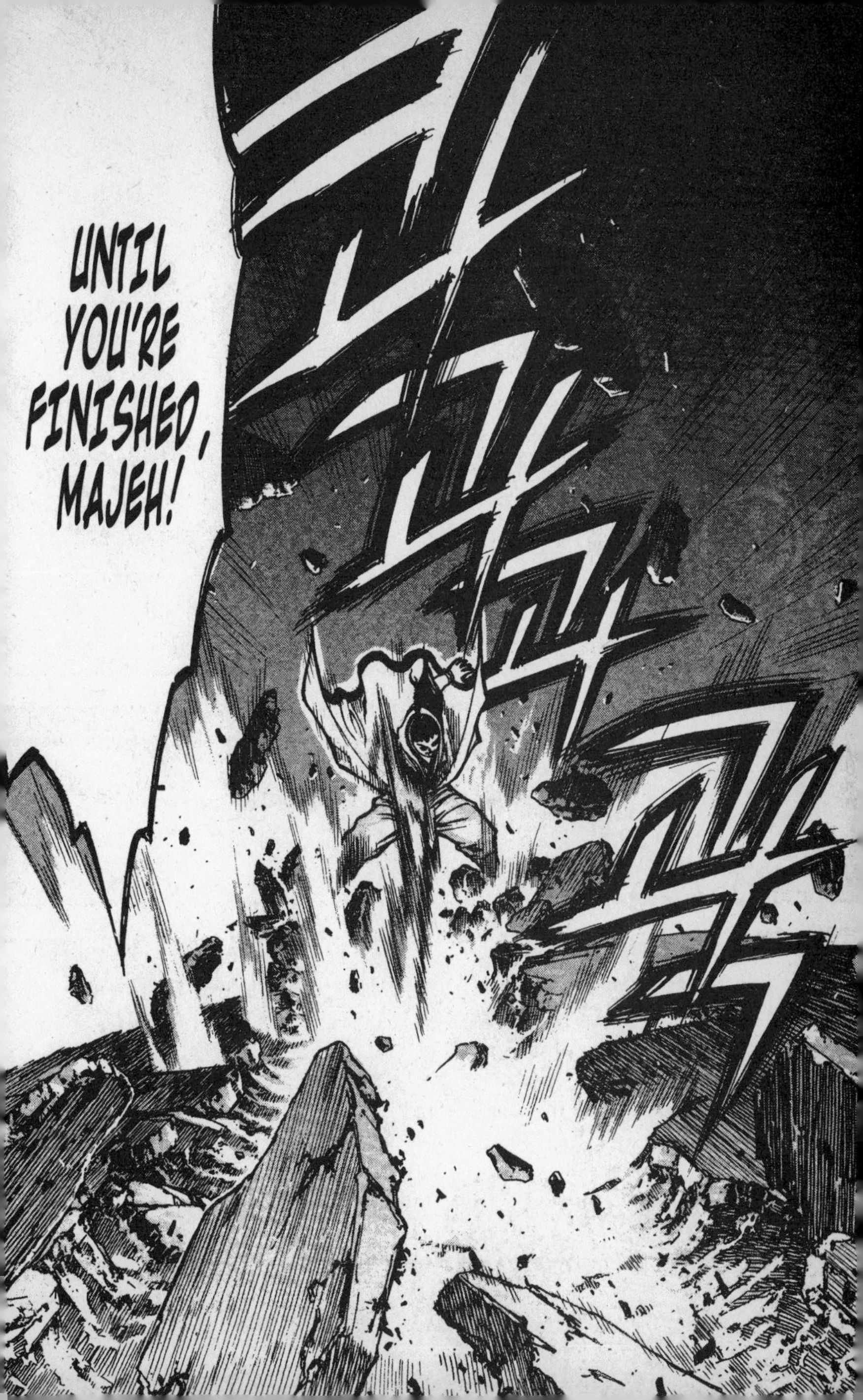
UNTIL YOU'RE FINISHED, MAJEH!

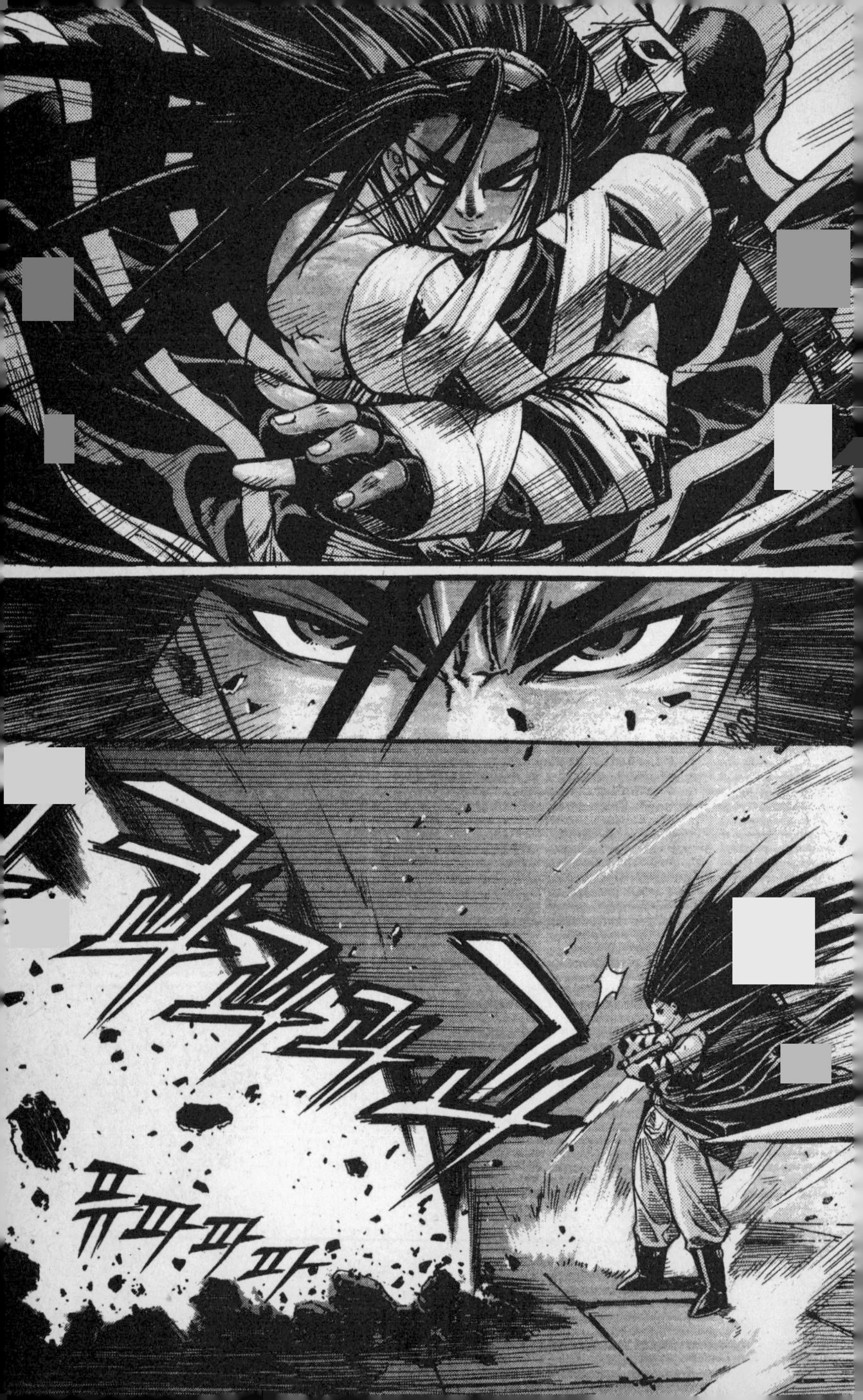

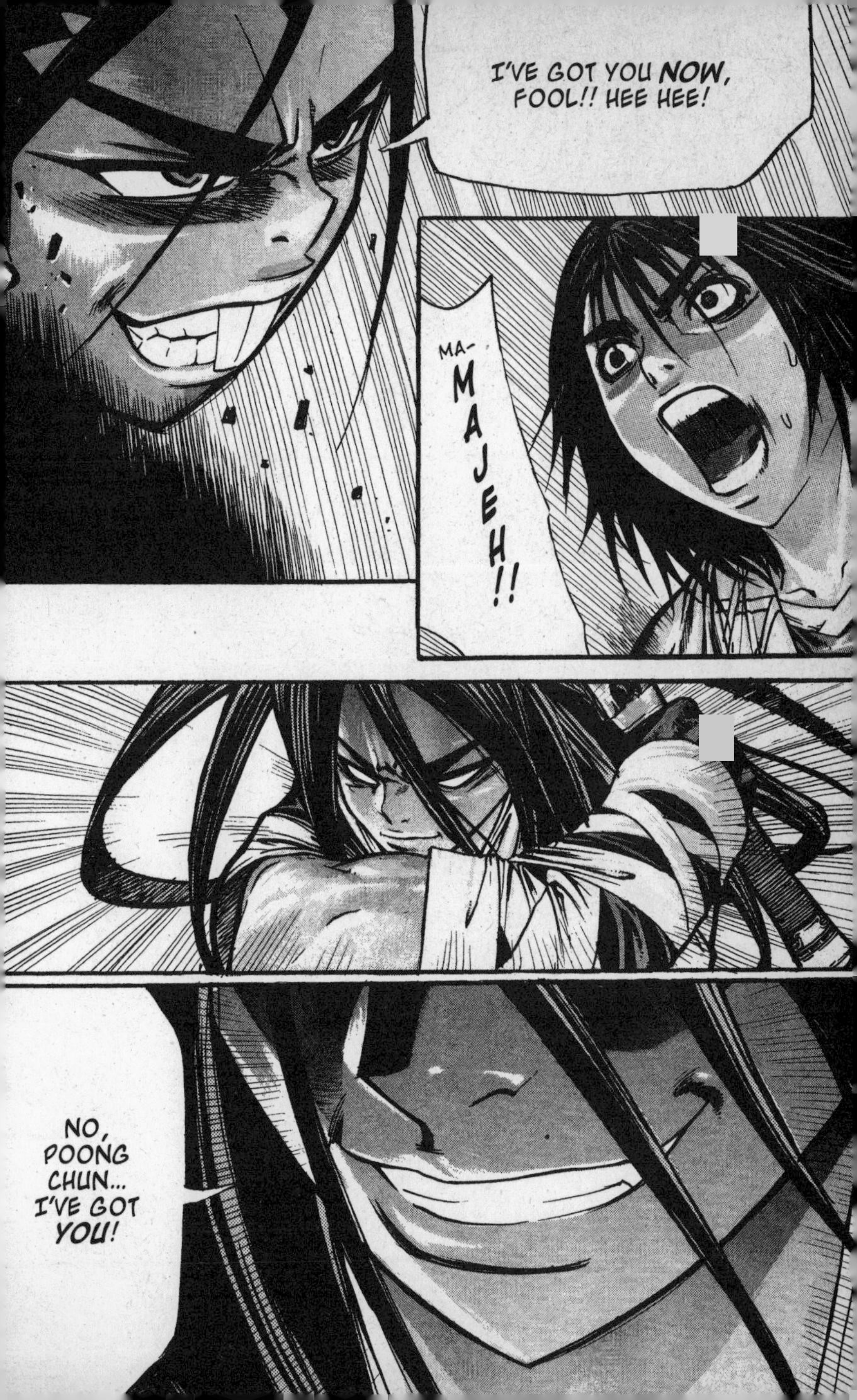
I'VE GOT YOU NOW, FOOL!! HEE HEE!
MA-MAJEH!!
NO, POONG CHUN... I'VE GOT YOU!

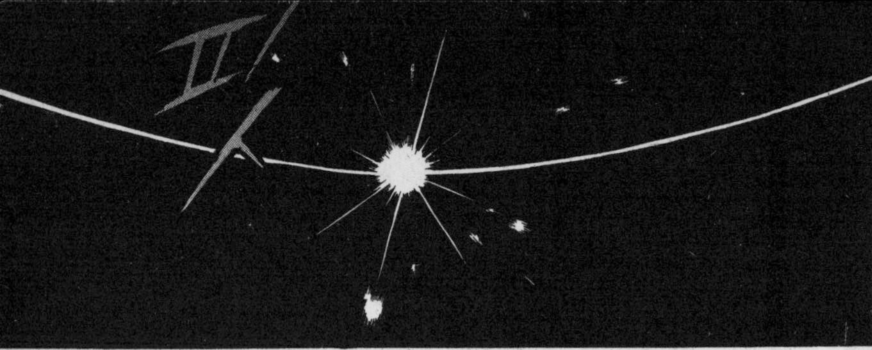
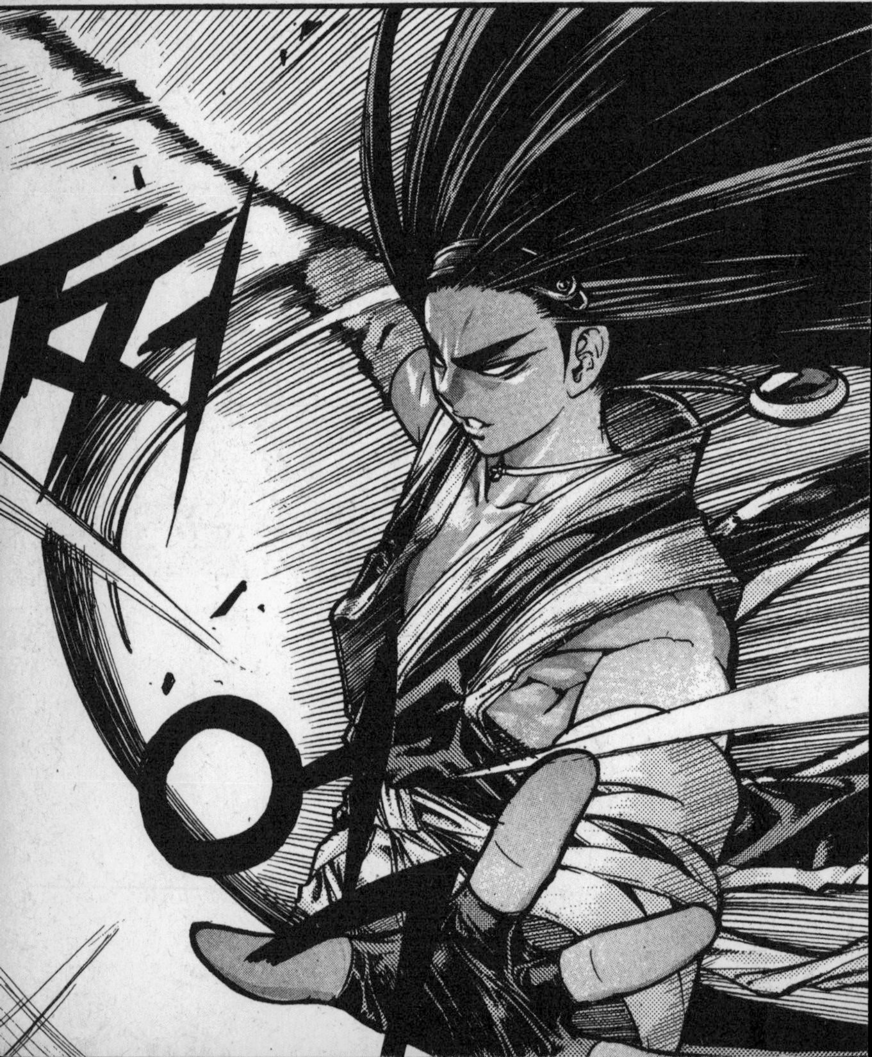

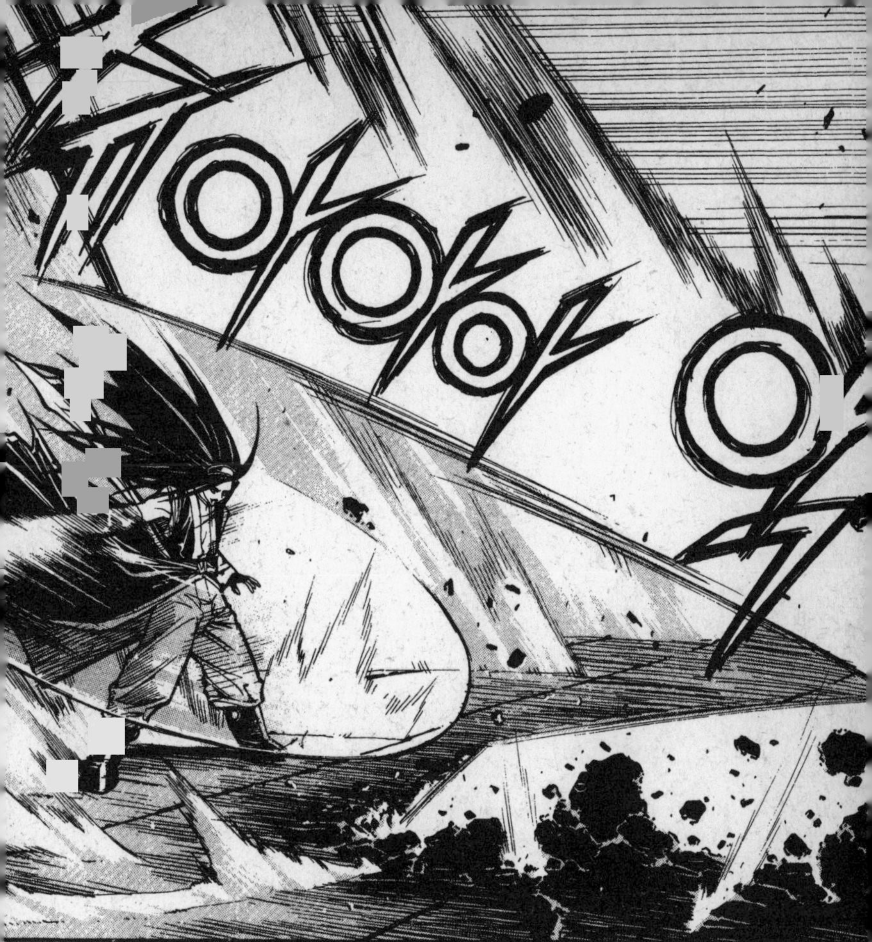

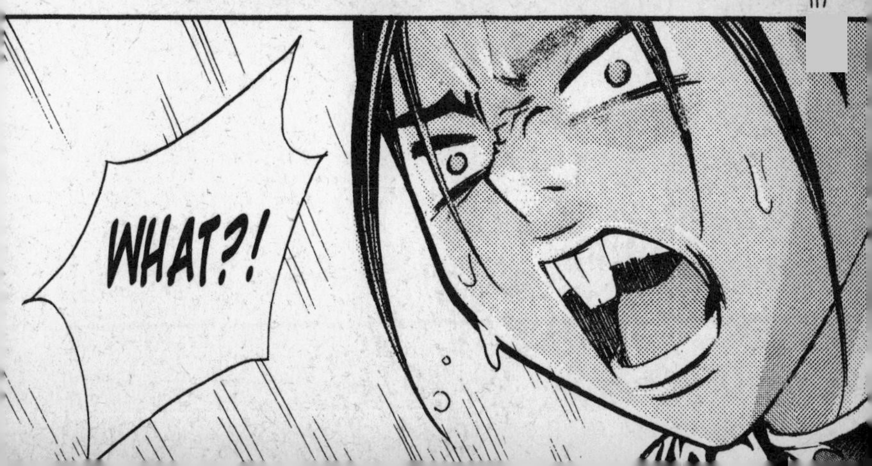
WHAT?!

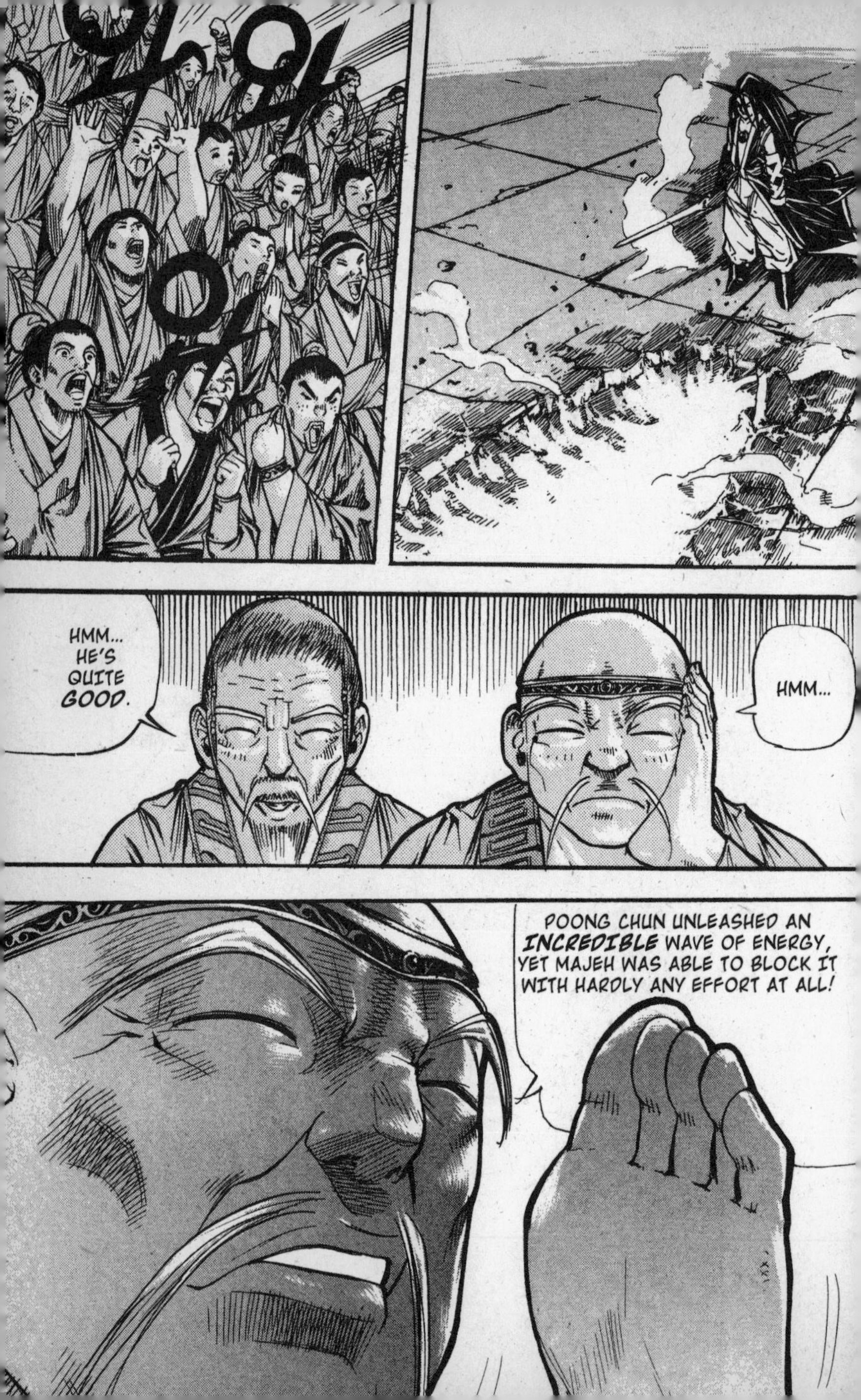
HMM...
HMM... HE'S QUITE GOOD.
POONG CHUN UNLEASHED AN INCREDIBLE WAVE OF ENERGY, YET MAJEH WAS ABLE TO BLOCK IT WITH HARDLY ANY EFFORT AT ALL!

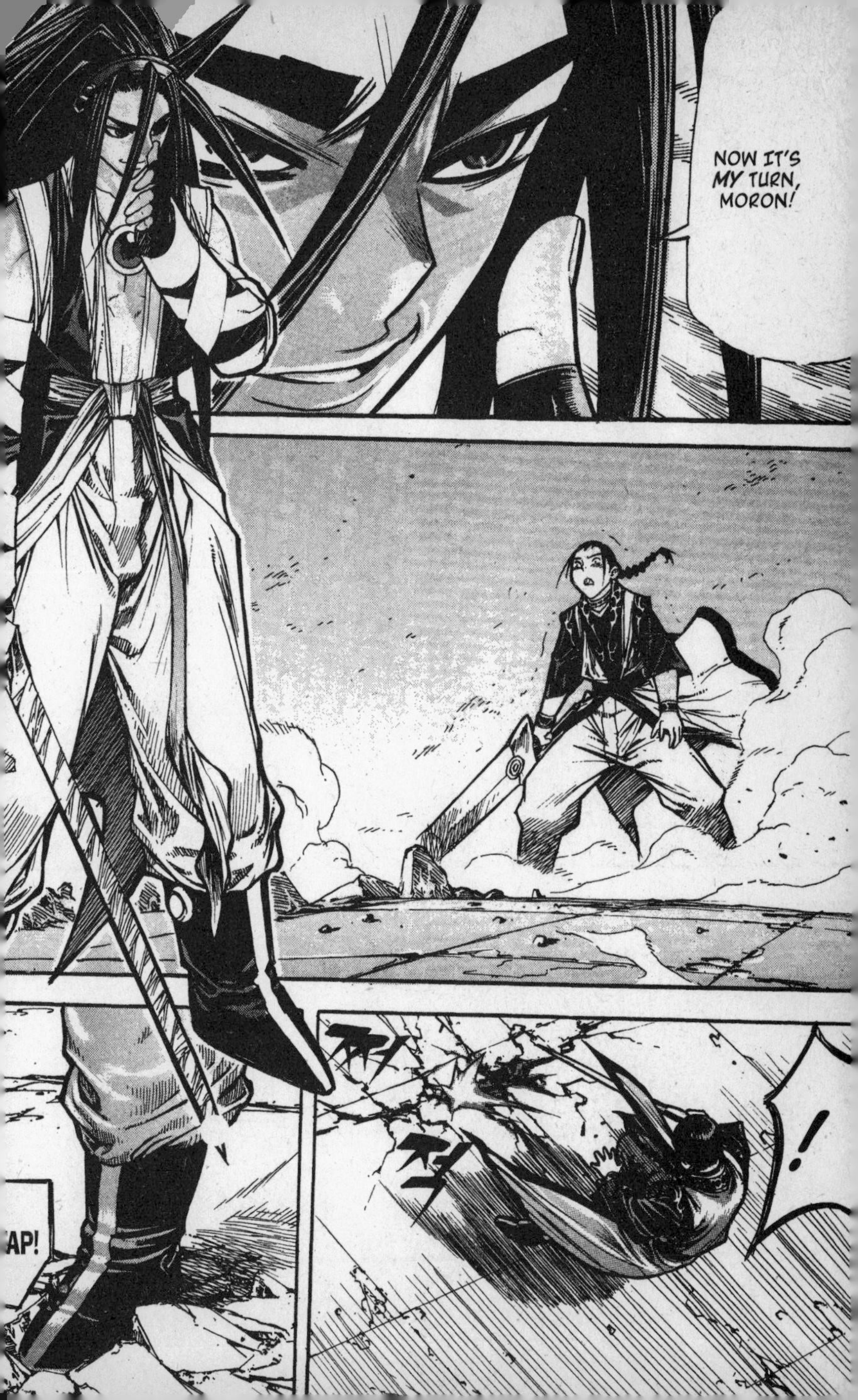
NOW IT'S MY TURN, MORON!
AP!
!

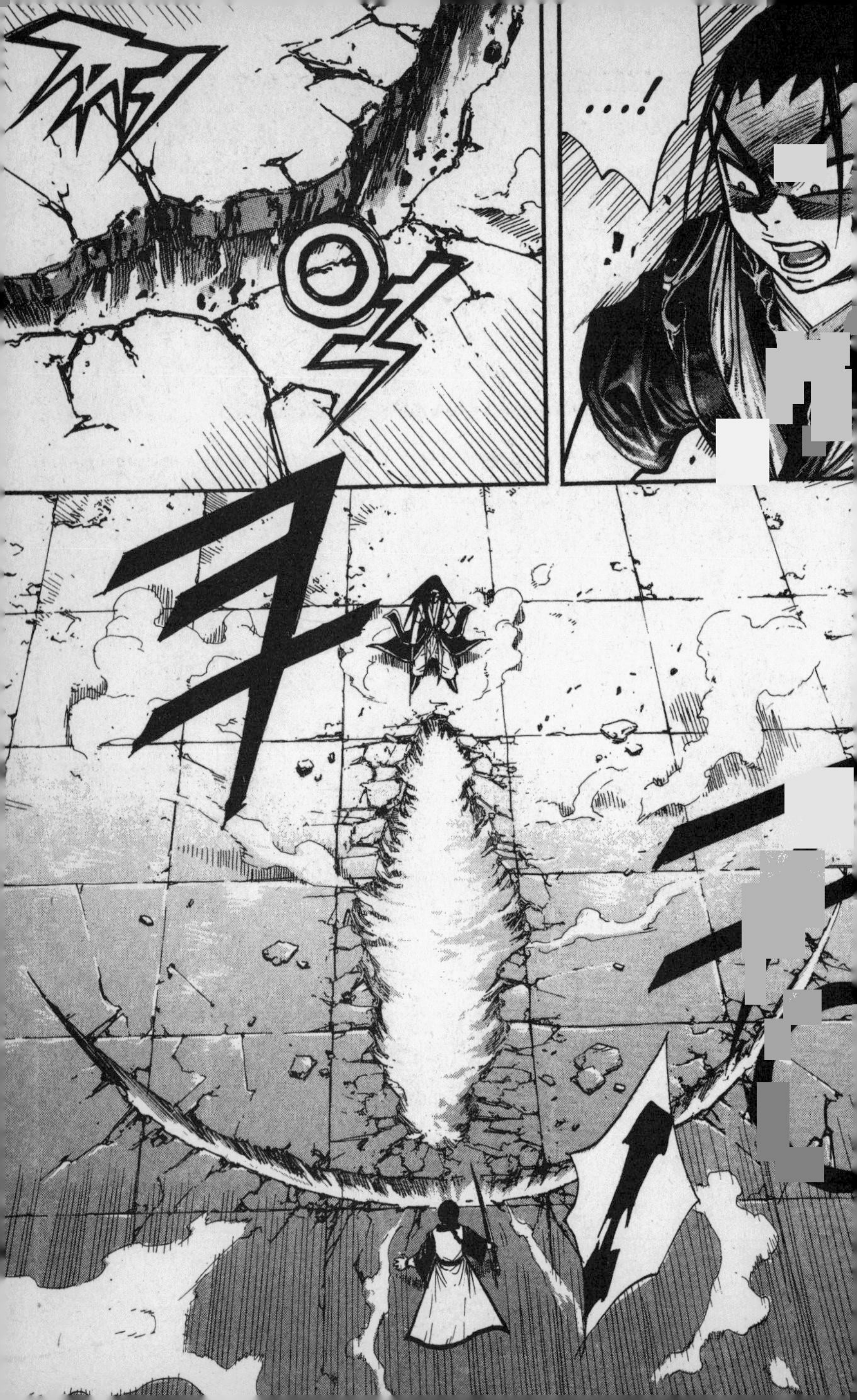
...!

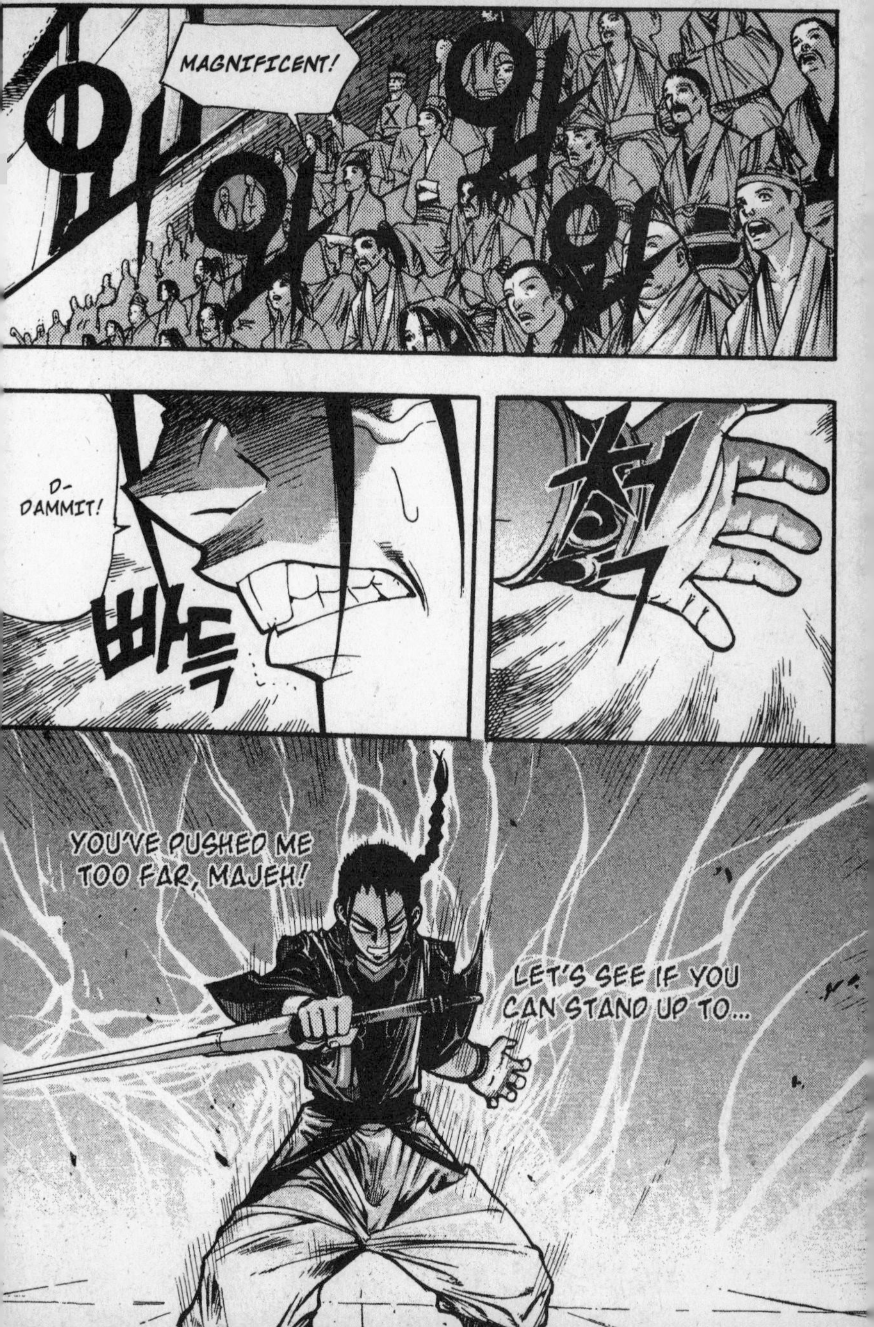
MAGNIFICENT!
D-DAMMIT!
YOU'VE PUSHED ME TOO FAR, MAJEH!
LET'S SEE IF YOU CAN STAND UP TO...

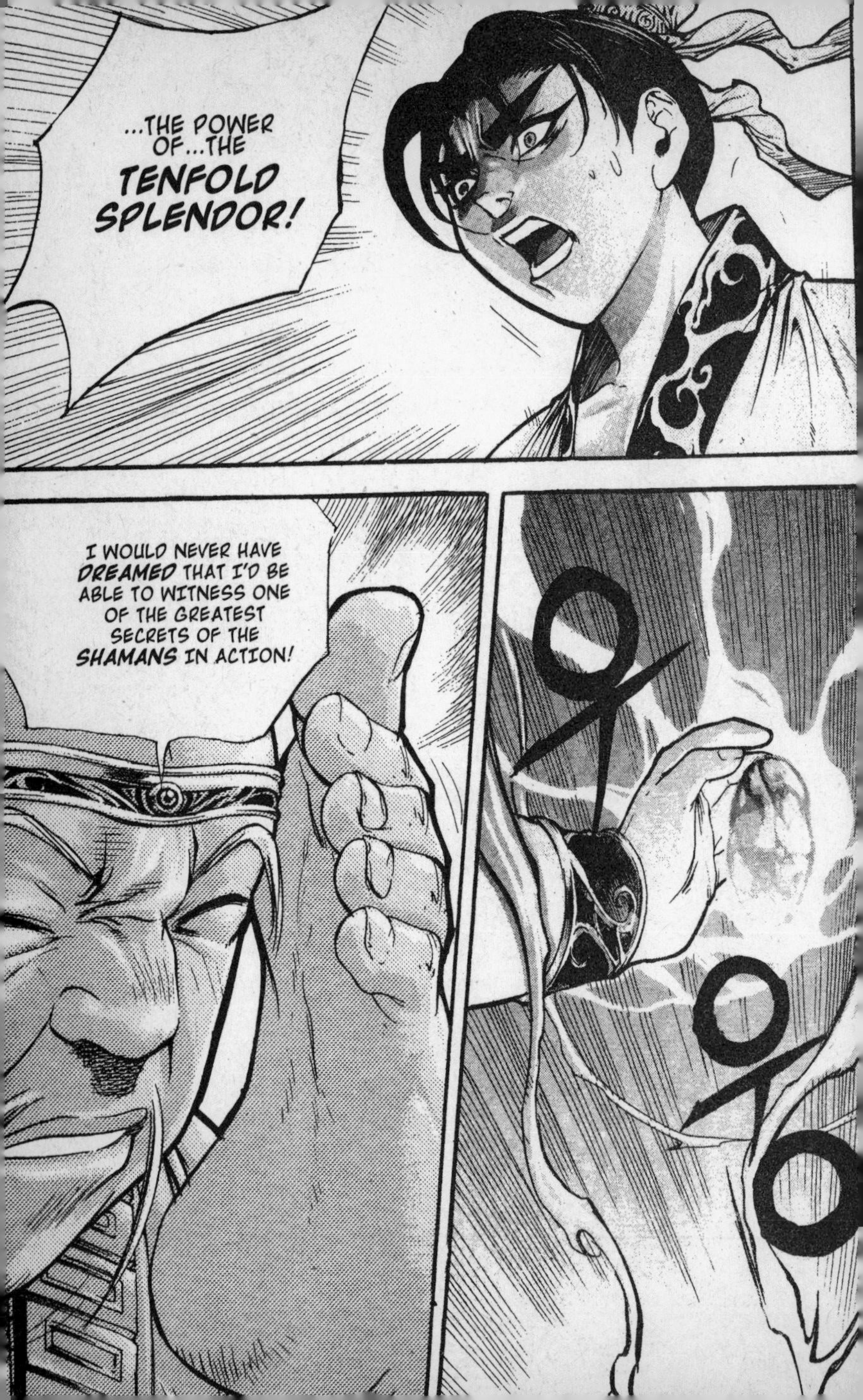
...THE POWER OF...THE TENFOLD SPLENDOR!
I WOULD NEVER HAVE DREAMED THAT I'D BE ABLE TO WITNESS ONE OF THE GREATEST SECRETS OF THE SHAMANS IN ACTION!

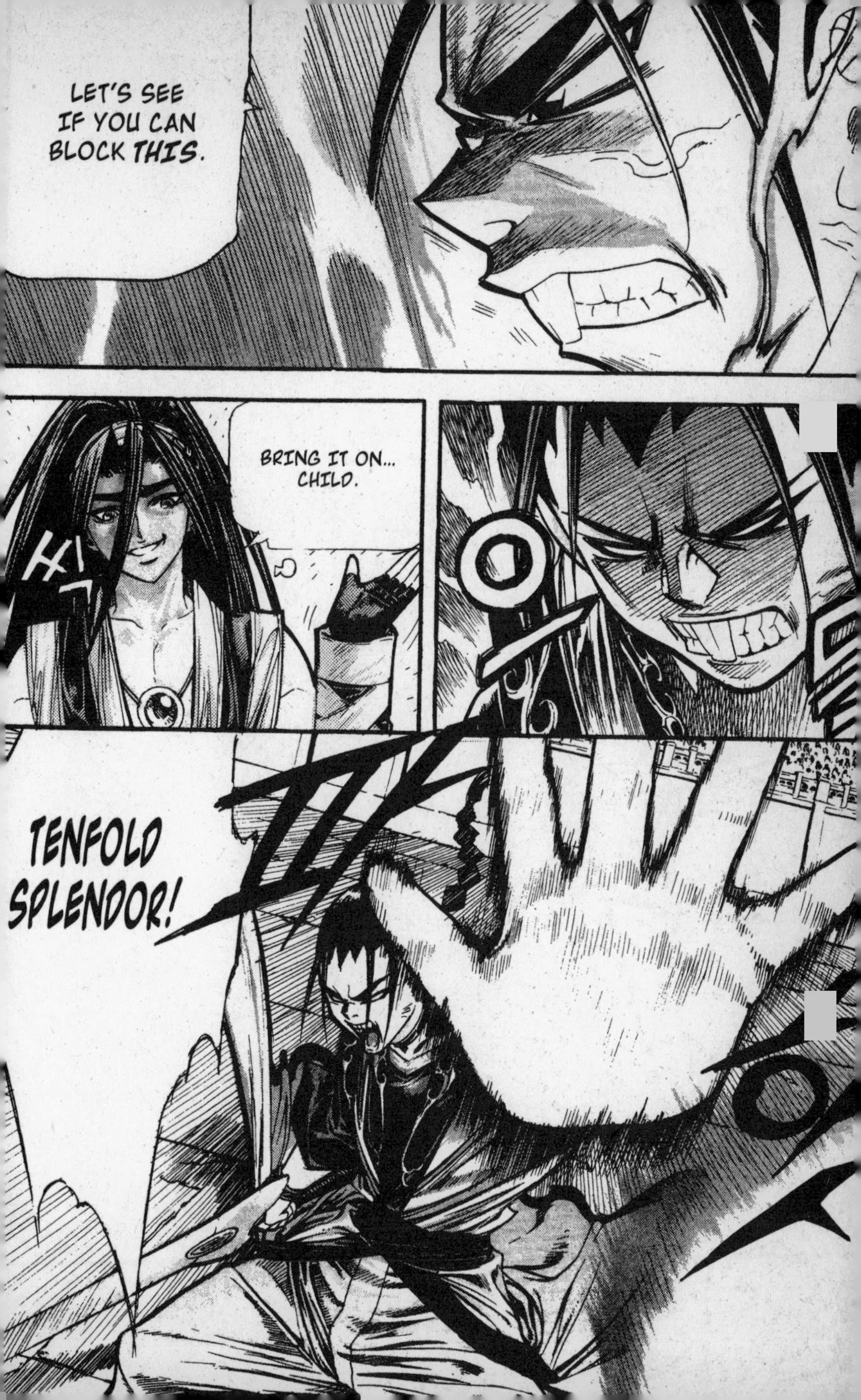
LET'S SEE IF YOU CAN BLOCK THIS.
BRING IT ON... CHILD.
TENFOLD SPLENDOR!

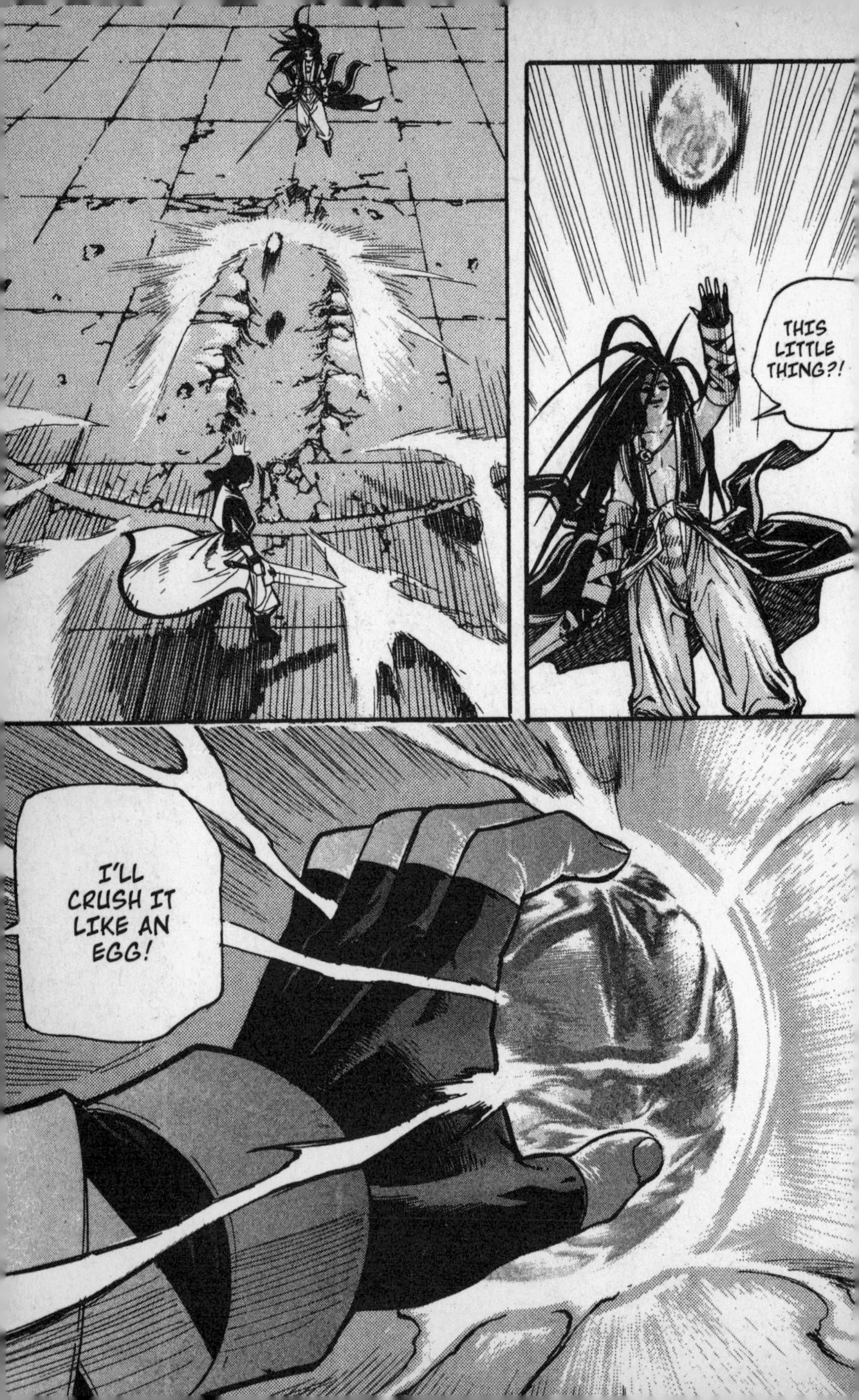
THIS LITTLE THING?!
I'LL CRUSH IT LIKE AN EGG!

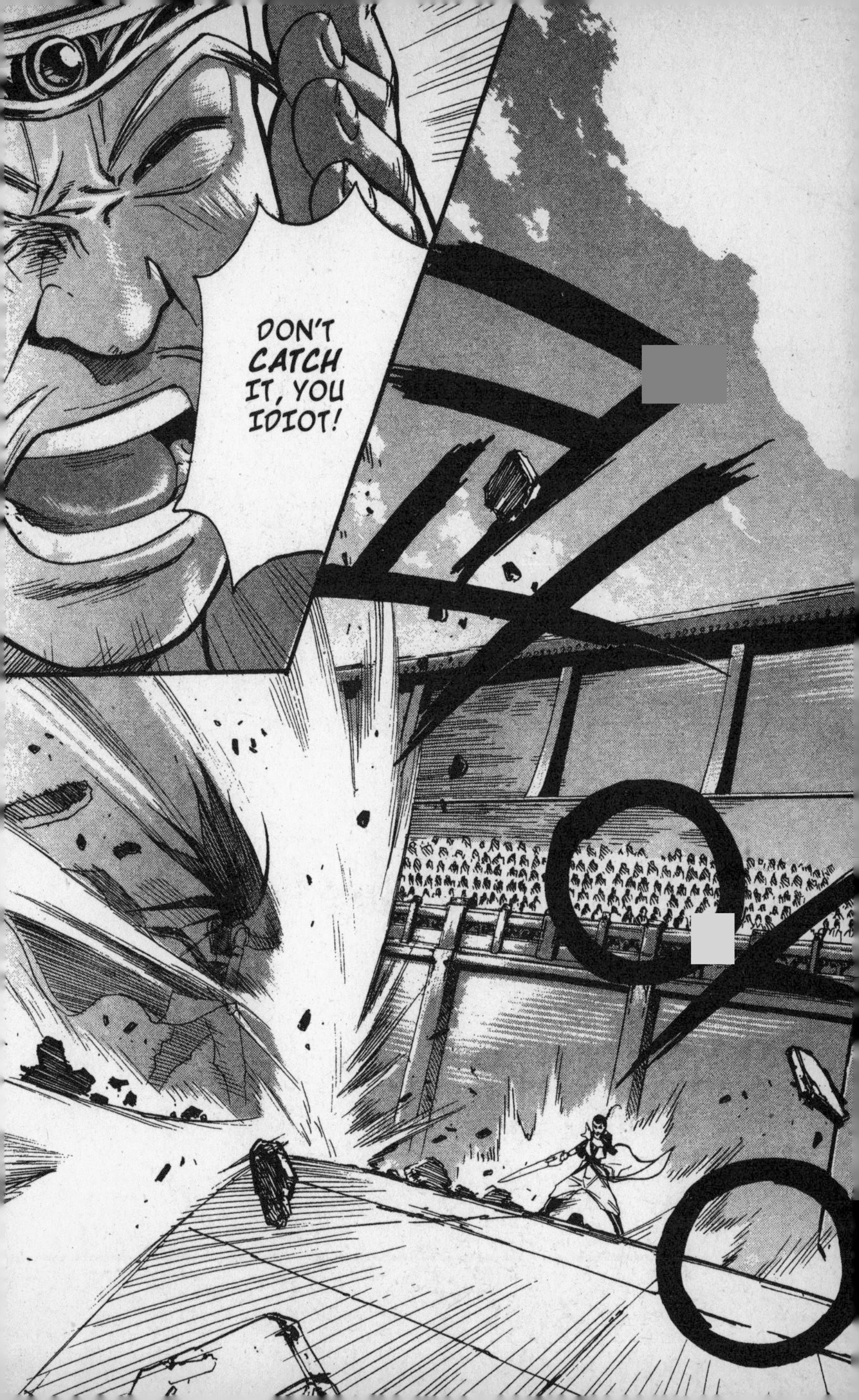
DON'T CATCH IT, YOU IDIOT!

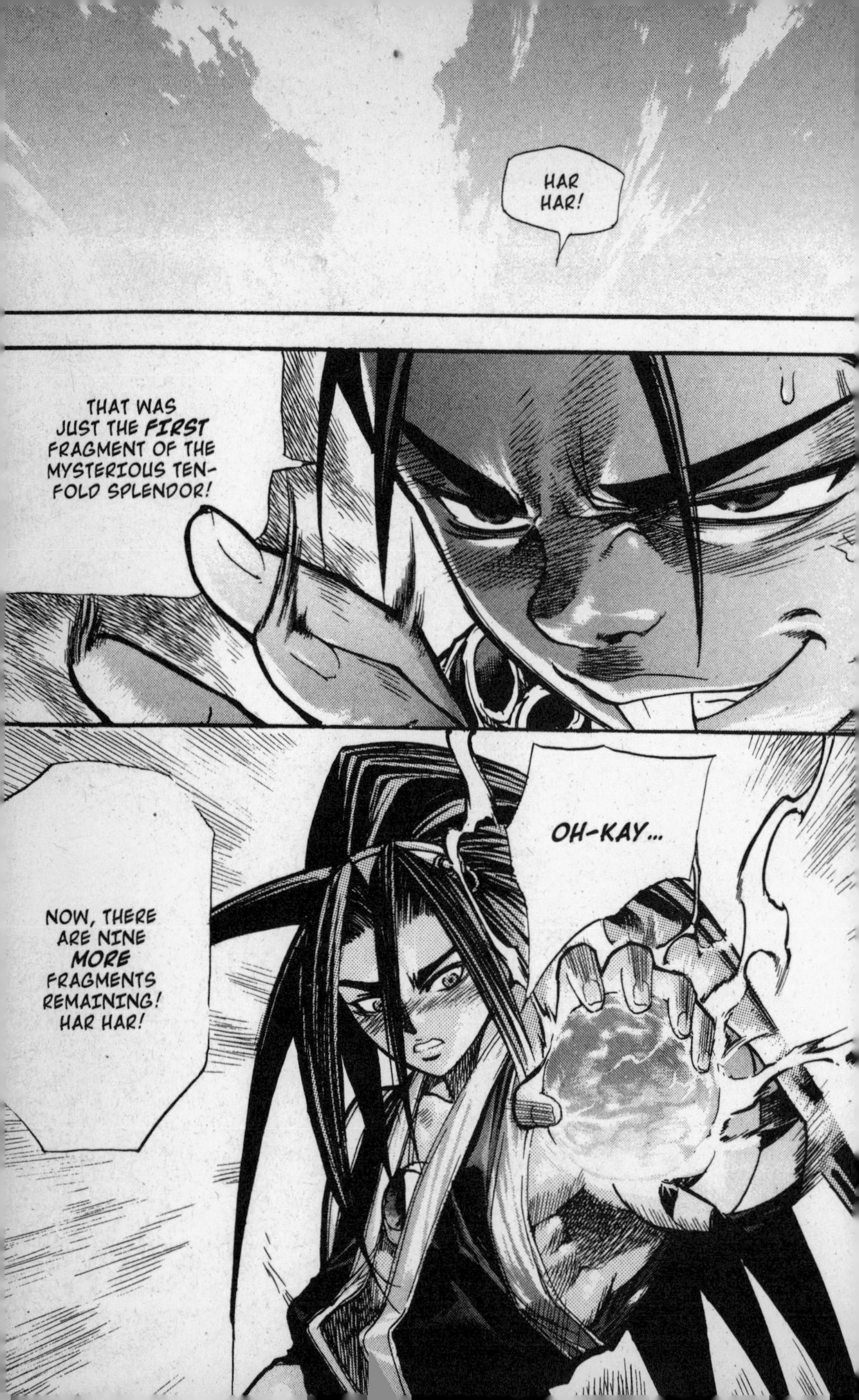
HAR HAR!
THAT WAS JUST THE *FIRST* FRAGMENT OF THE MYSTERIOUS TEN-FOLD SPLENDOR!
OH-KAY...
NOW, THERE ARE NINE *MORE* FRAGMENTS REMAINING! HAR HAR!

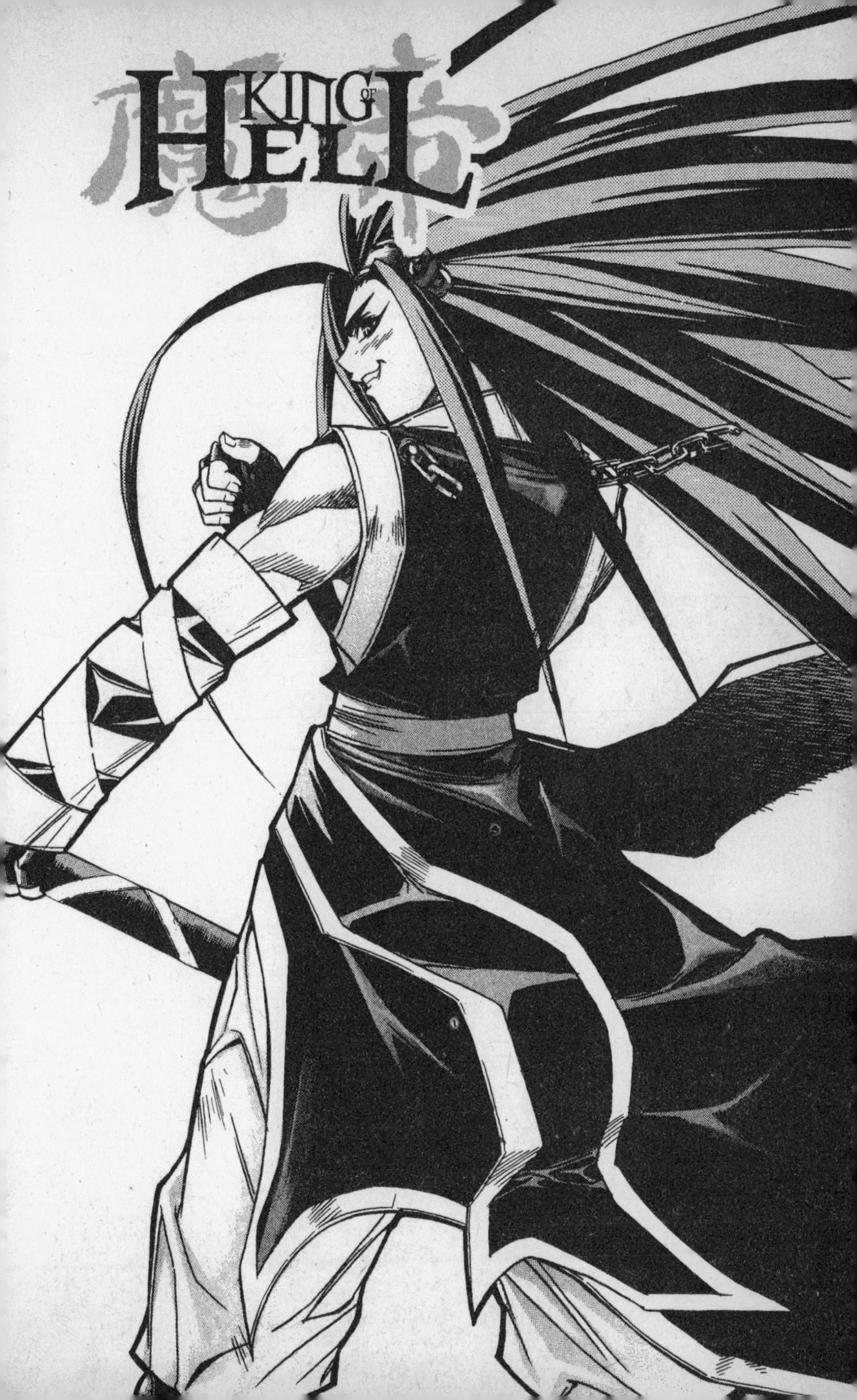
KING OF HELL

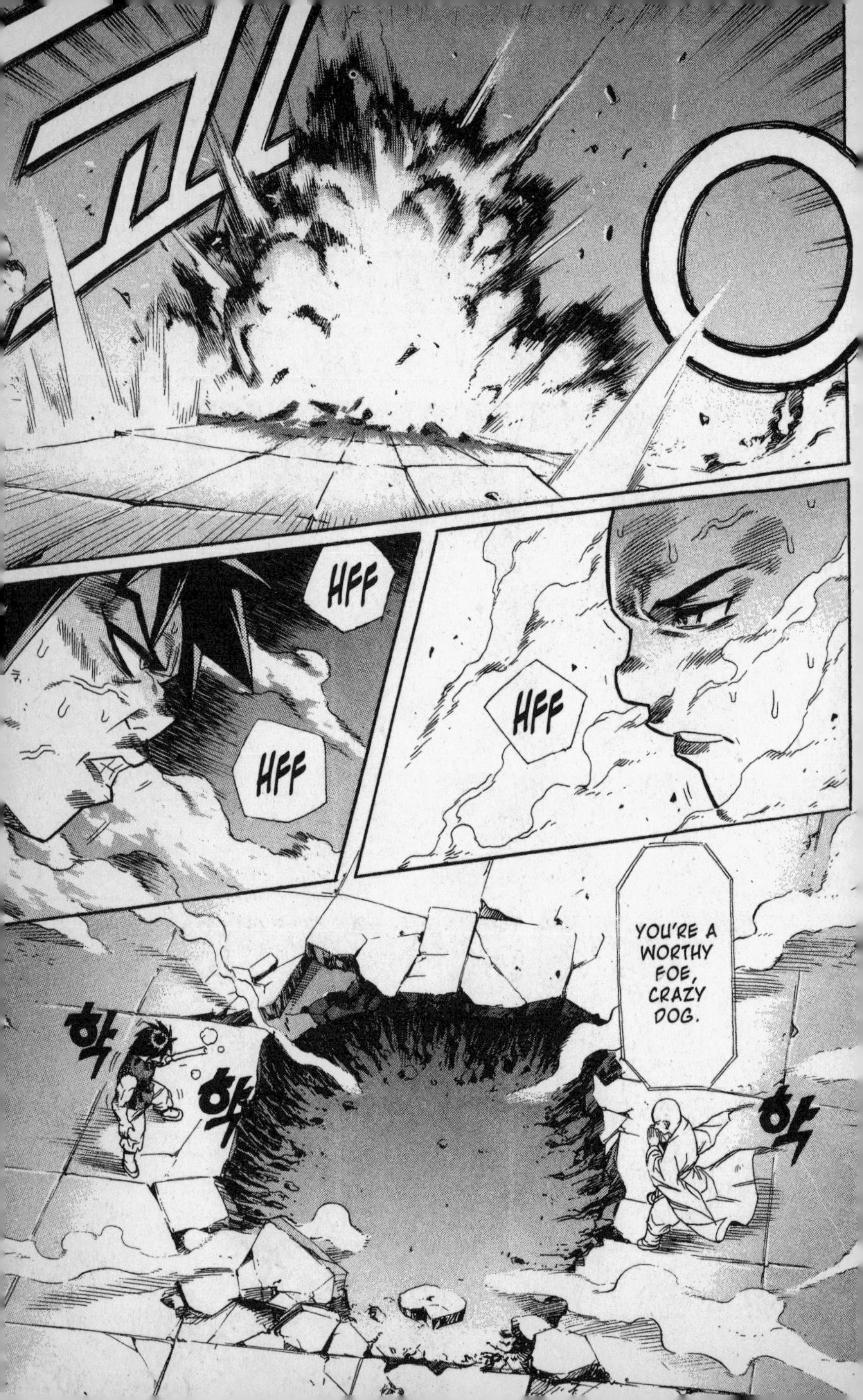
HFF
HFF
HFF
YOU'RE A WORTHY FOE, CRAZY DOG.
학
학
학

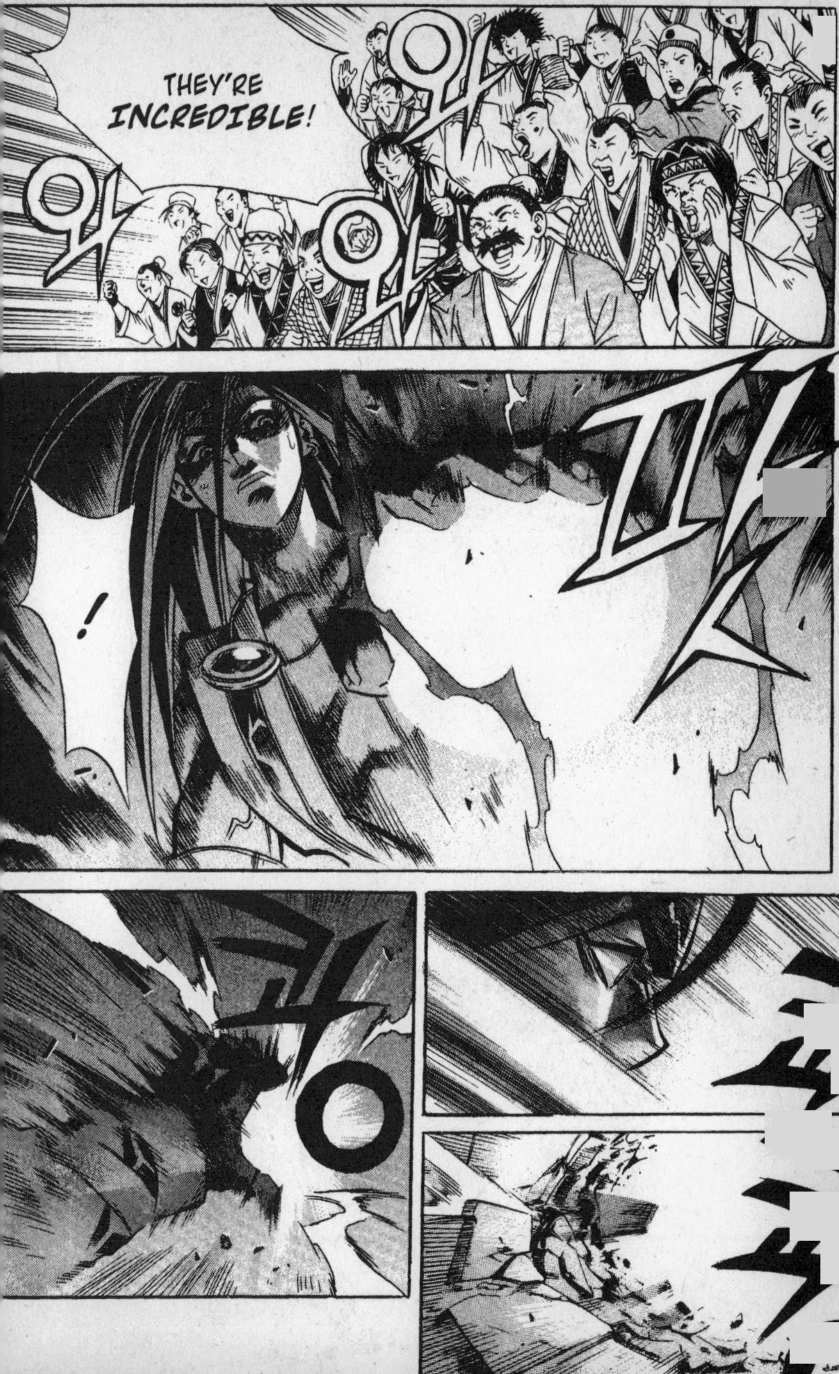
THEY'RE INCREDIBLE!
!

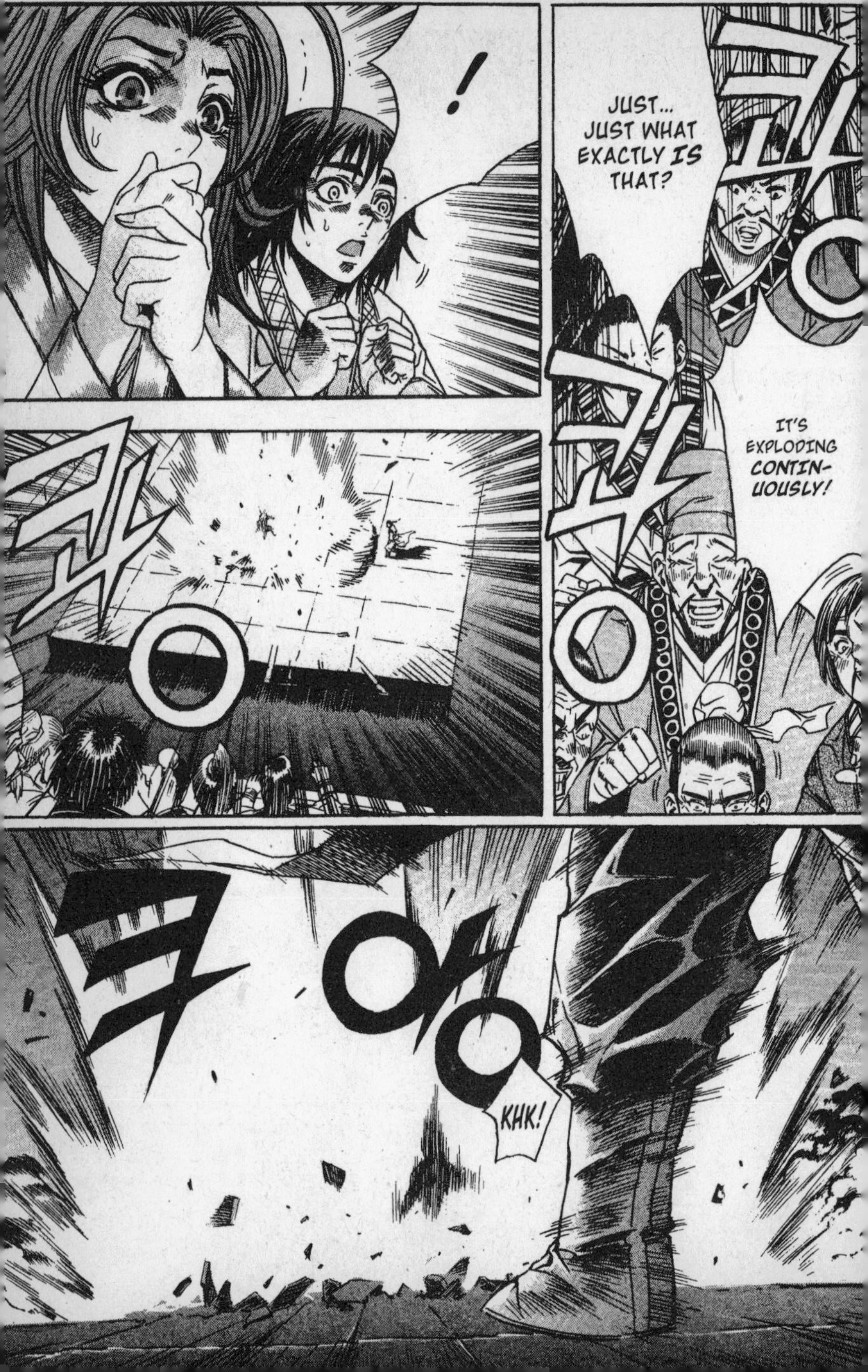
JUST... JUST WHAT EXACTLY IS THAT?
IT'S EXPLODING CONTIN-UOUSLY!
!
KHK!

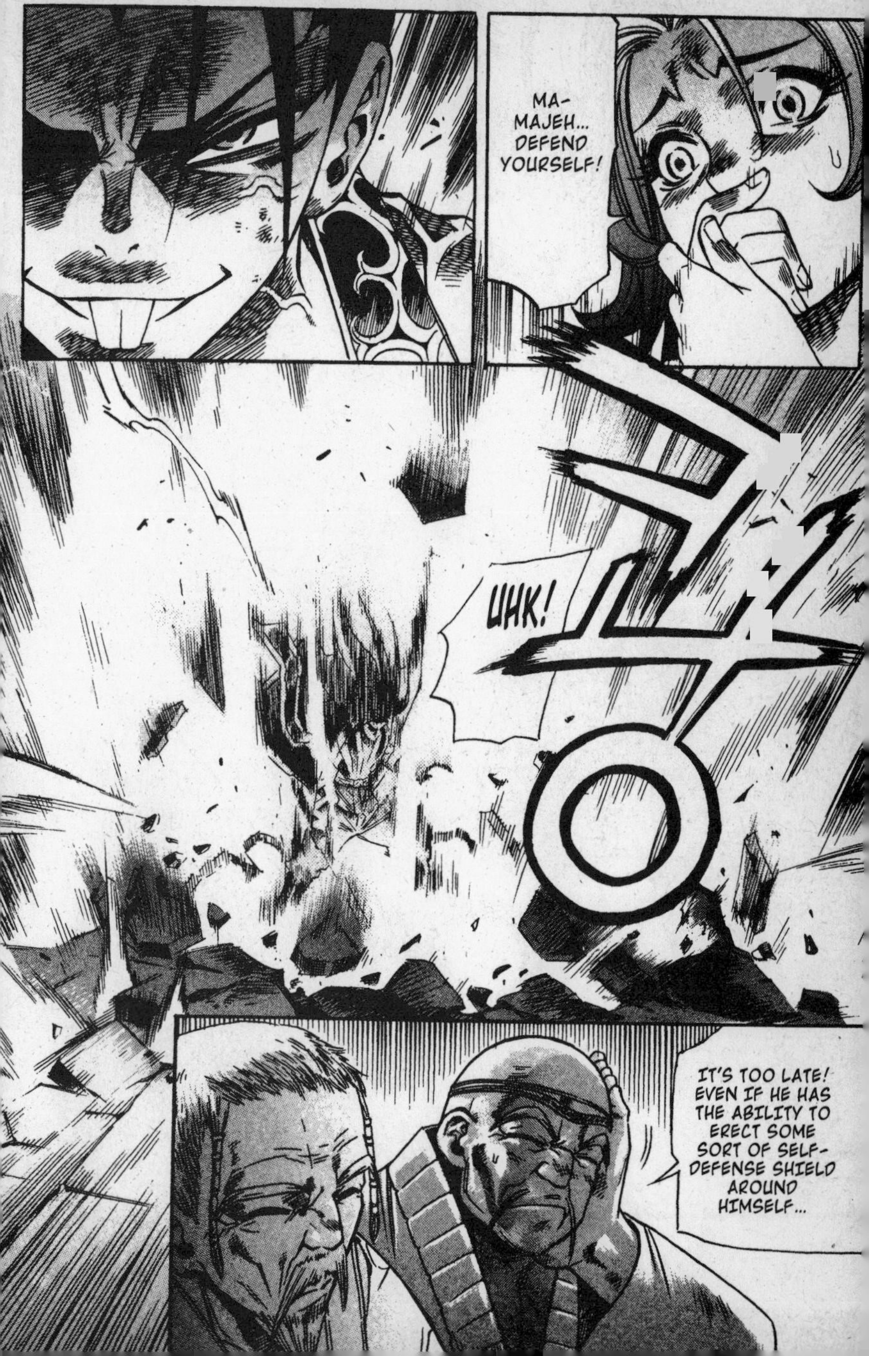
MA-MAJEH... DEFEND YOURSELF!
UHK!
IT'S TOO LATE! EVEN IF HE HAS THE ABILITY TO ERECT SOME SORT OF SELF-DEFENSE SHIELD AROUND HIMSELF...

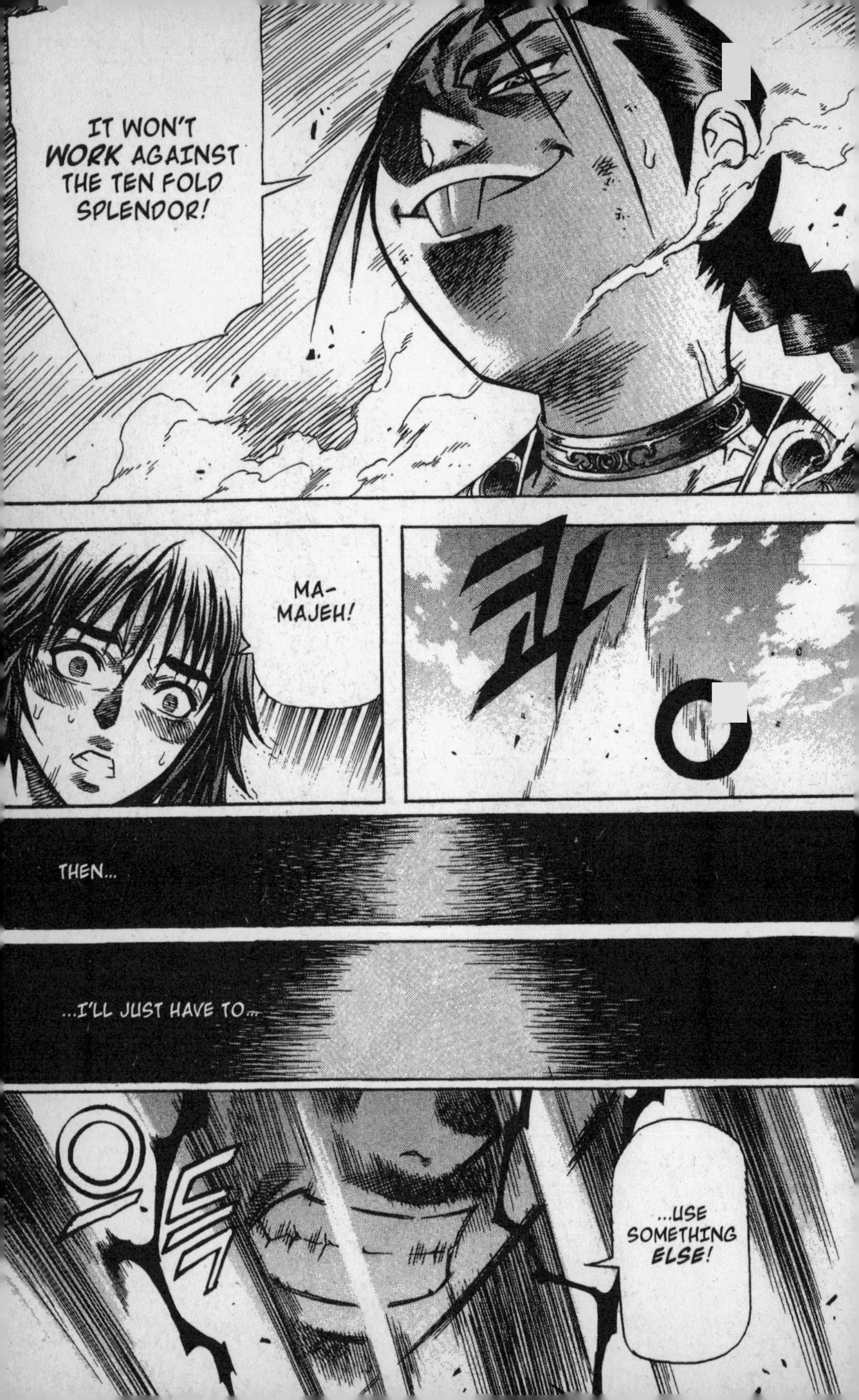
IT WON'T WORK AGAINST THE TEN FOLD SPLENDOR!
MA- MAJEH!
THEN...
...I'LL JUST HAVE TO...
...USE SOMETHING ELSE!

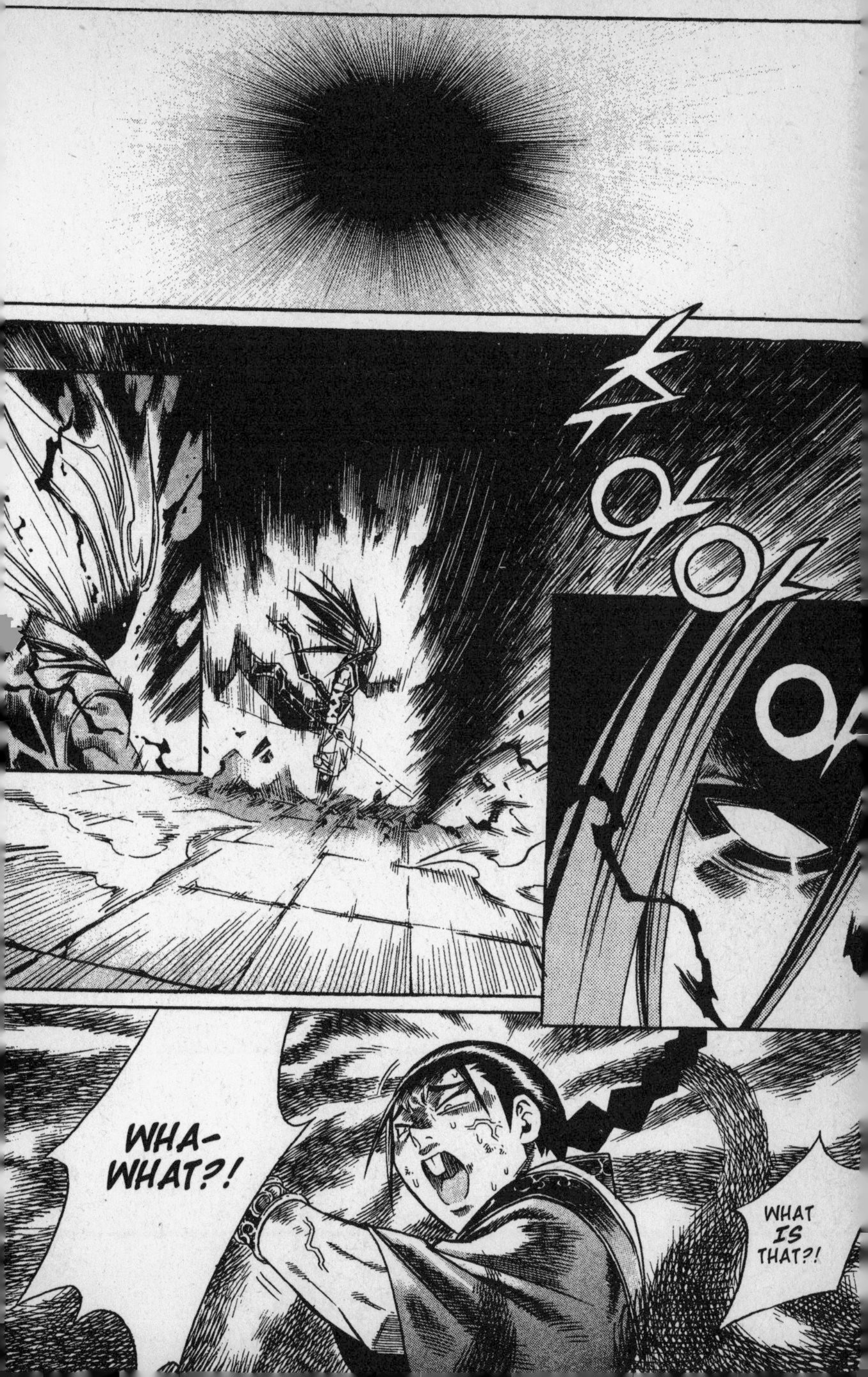
WHAT IS THAT?!
WHA- WHAT?!

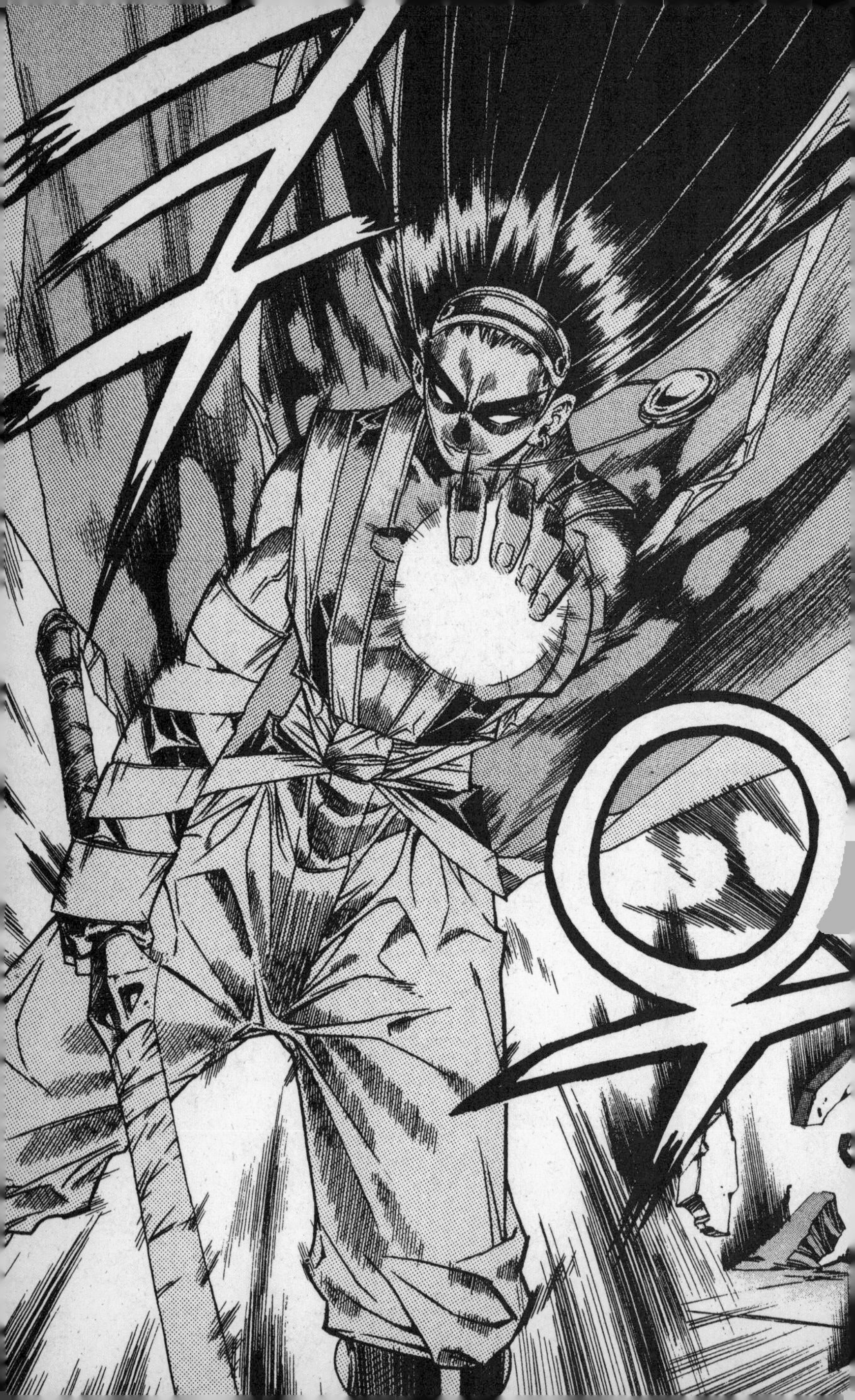

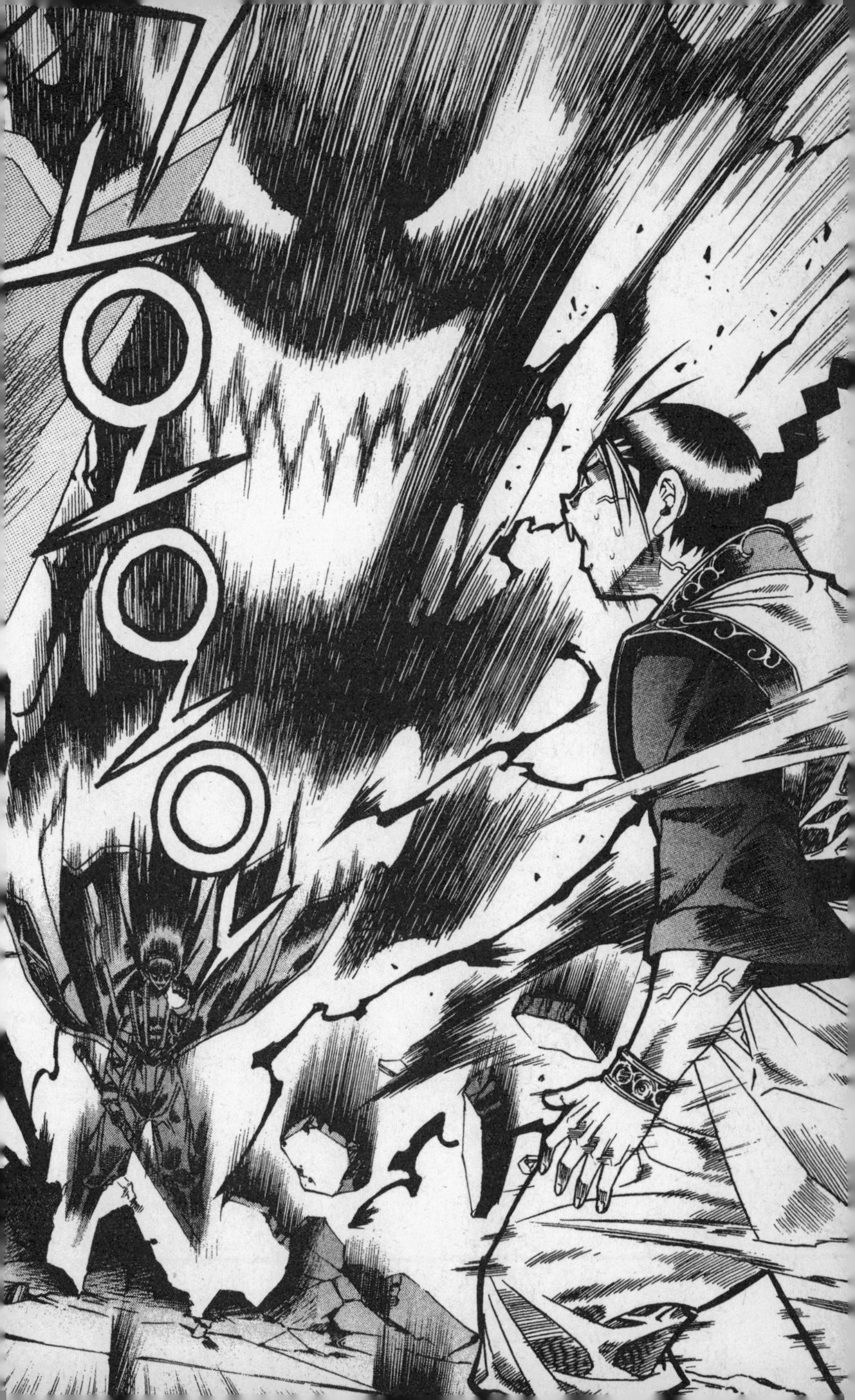

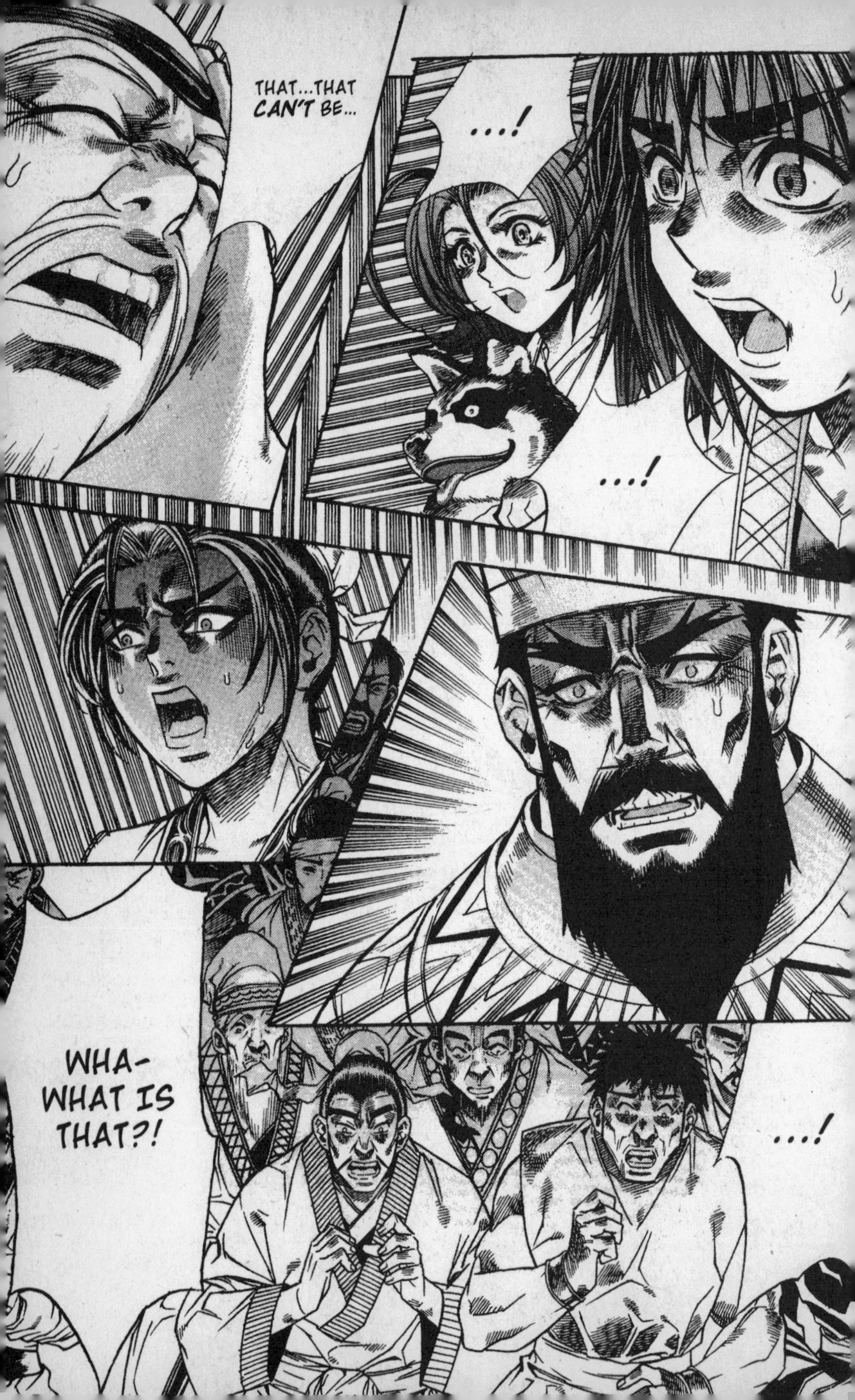
...!
...!
THAT...THAT CAN'T BE...
...!
WHA-WHAT IS THAT?!

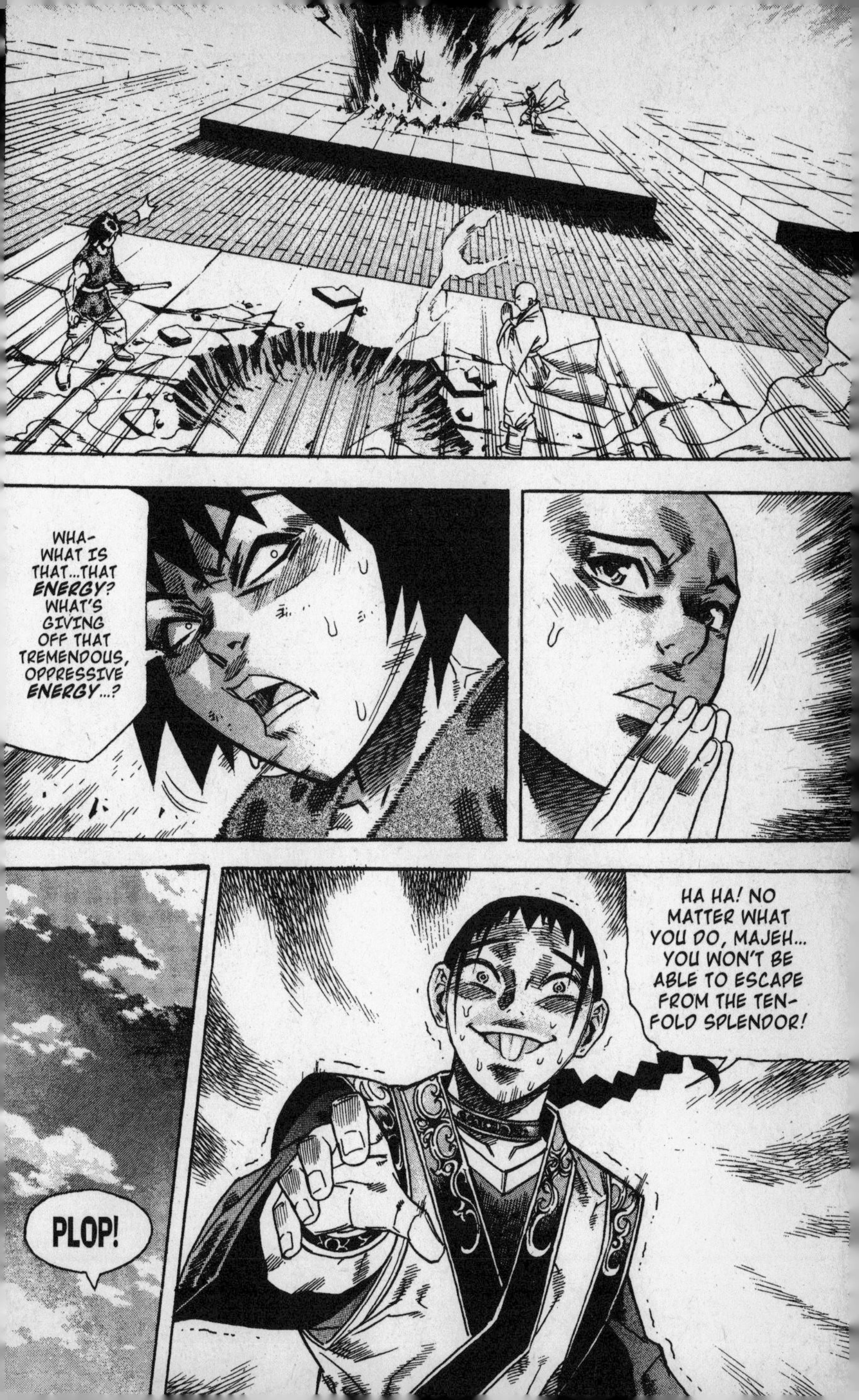
WHA- WHAT IS THAT...THAT ENERGY? WHAT'S GIVING OFF THAT TREMENDOUS, OPPRESSIVE ENERGY...?
HA HA! NO MATTER WHAT YOU DO, MAJEH... YOU WON'T BE ABLE TO ESCAPE FROM THE TEN-FOLD SPLENDOR!
PLOP!

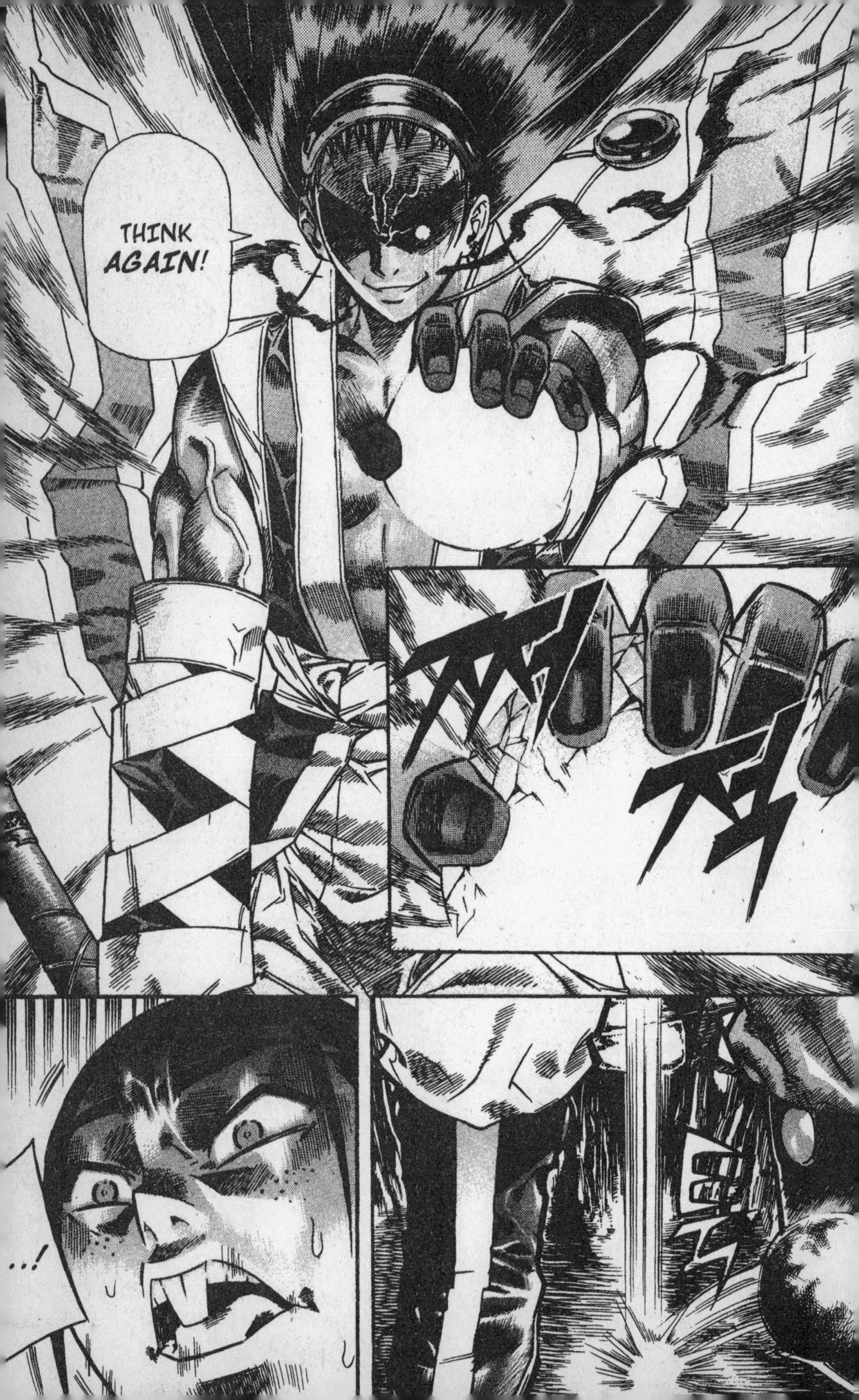
THINK AGAIN!
..!

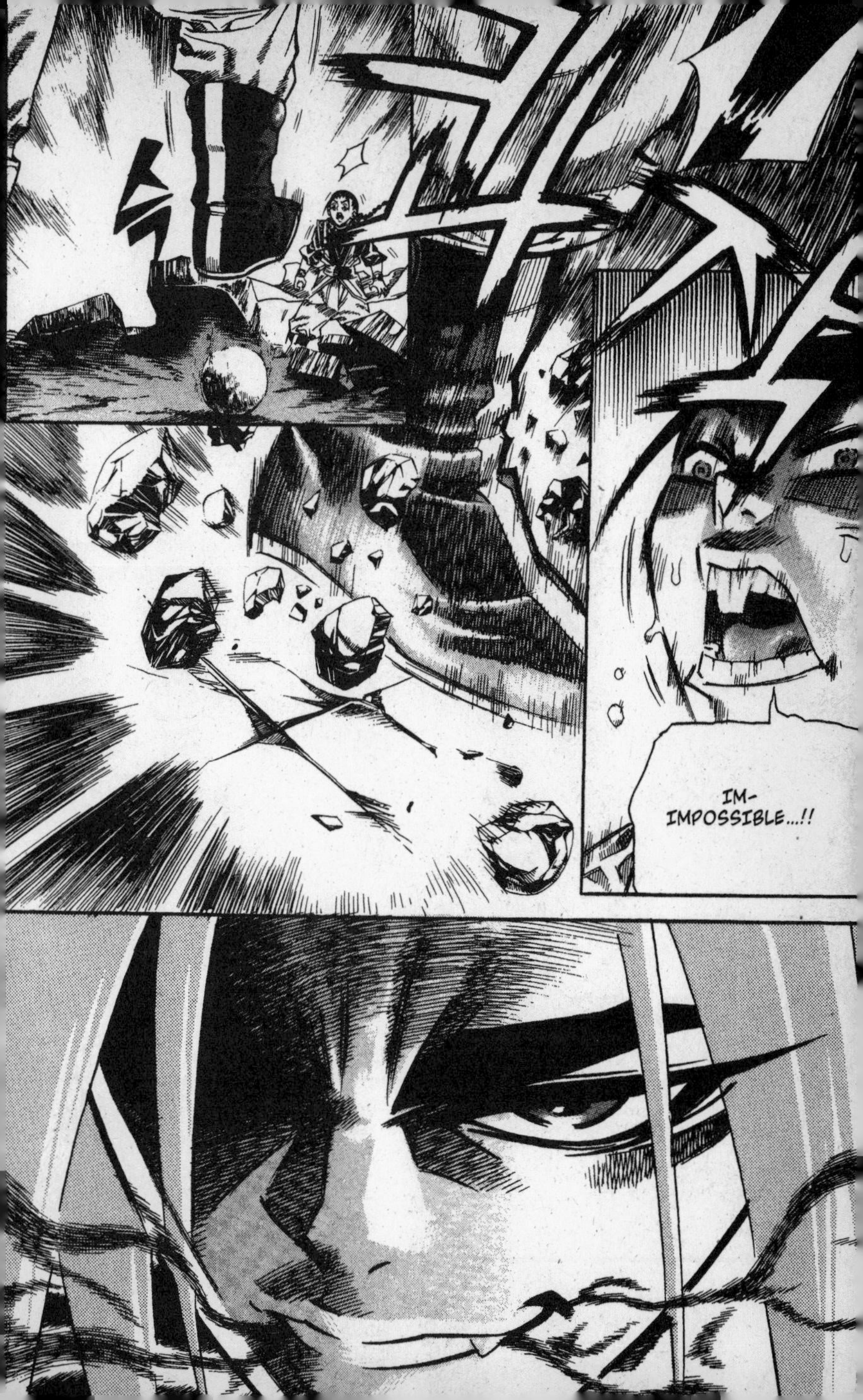
IM-
IMPOSSIBLE...!!

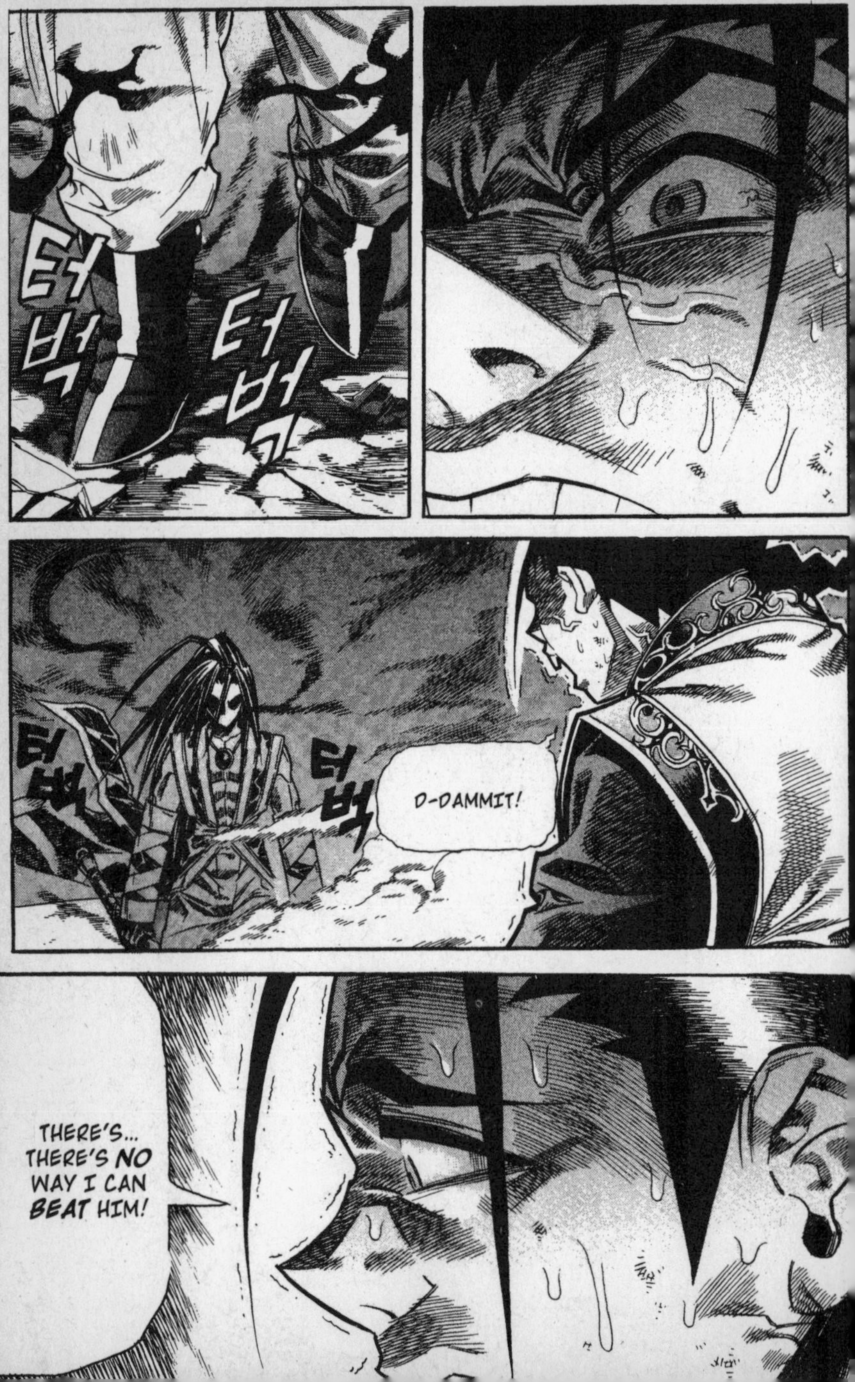
터벅
터벅
터벅
터벅
D-DAMMIT!
THERE'S...
THERE'S **NO**
WAY I CAN
BEAT HIM!

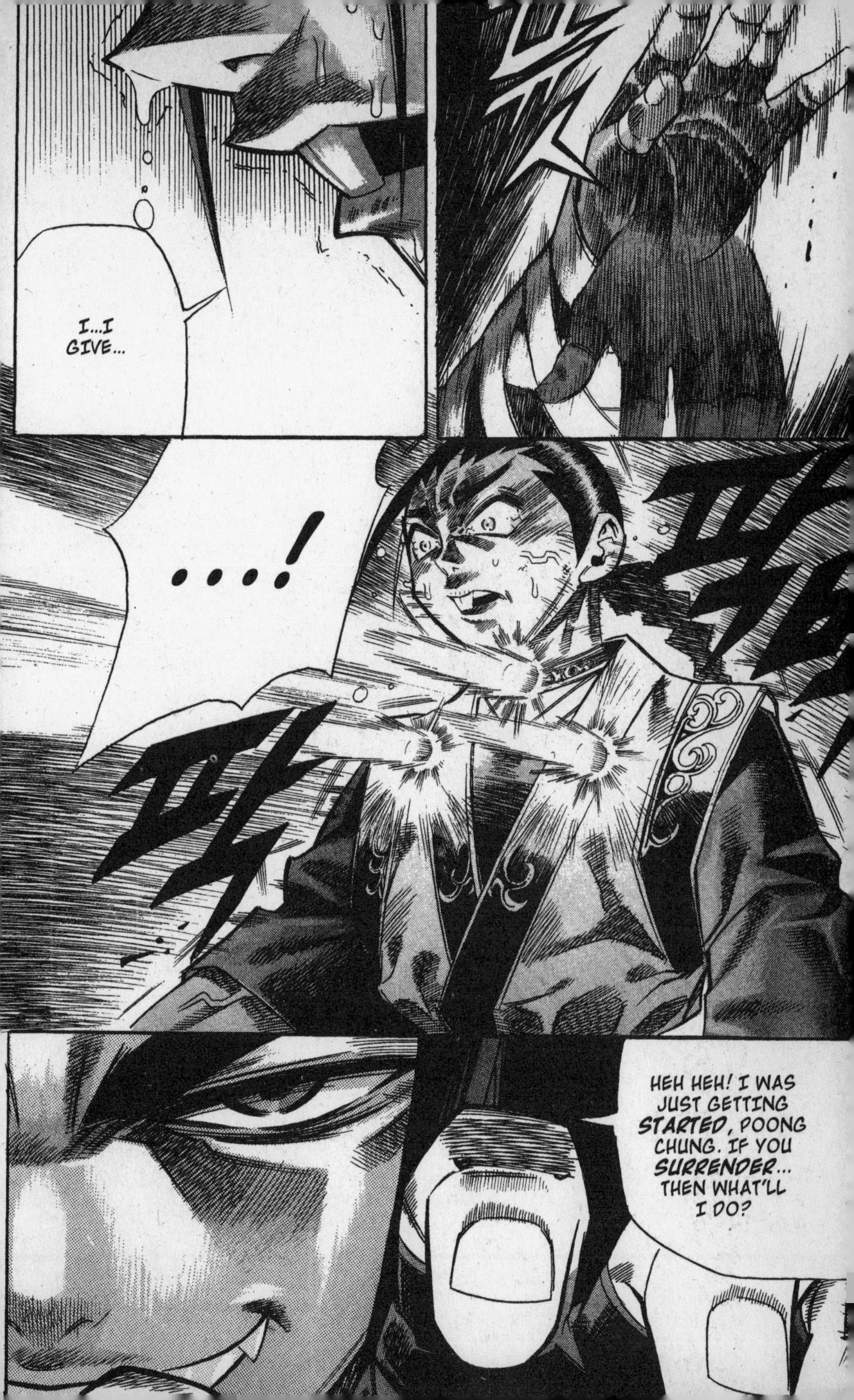
I...I GIVE...
...!
HEH HEH! I WAS JUST GETTING **STARTED**, POONG CHUNG. IF YOU **SURRENDER**... THEN WHAT'LL I DO?

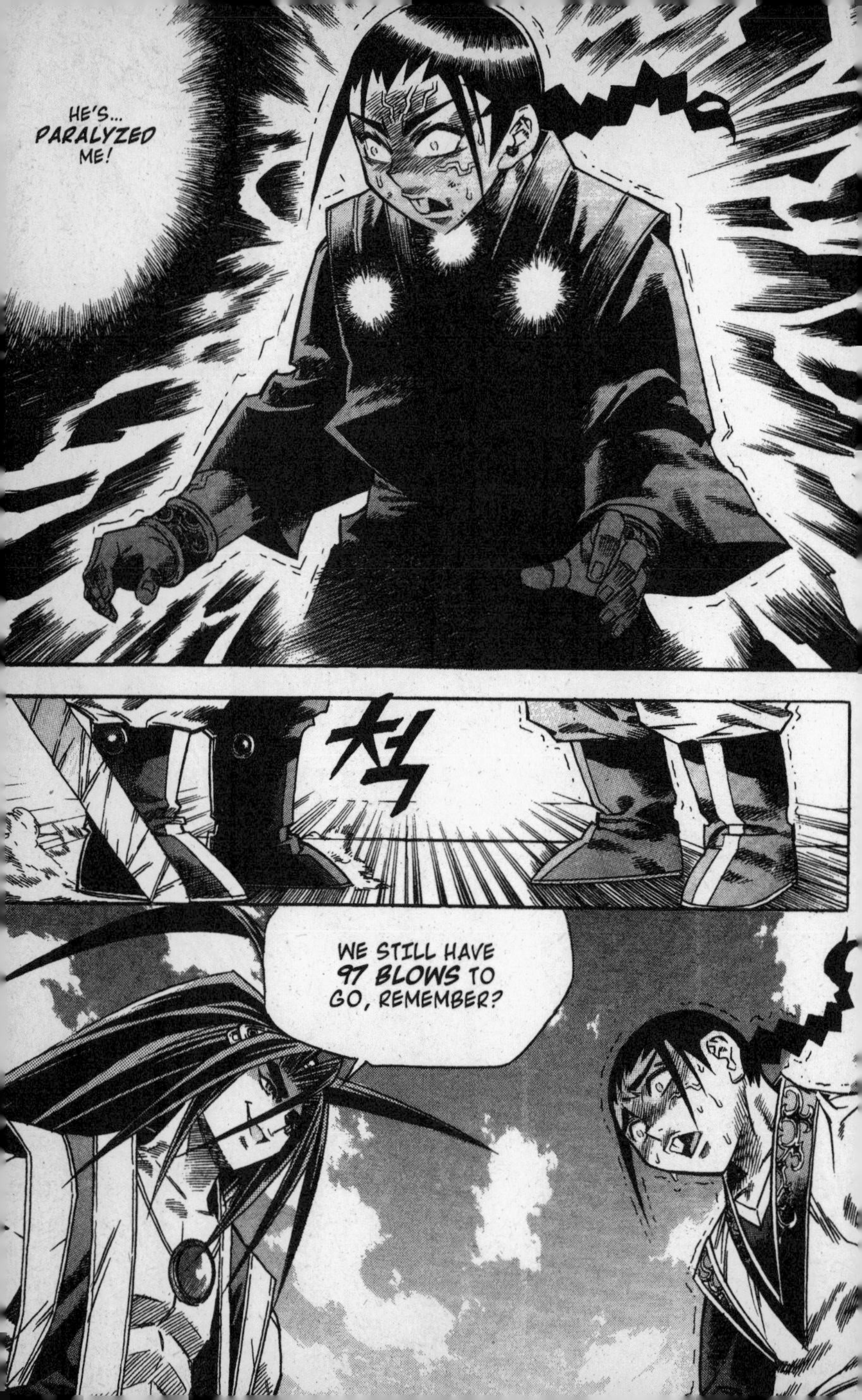
HE'S... PARALYZED ME!
척
WE STILL HAVE 97 BLOWS TO GO, REMEMBER?

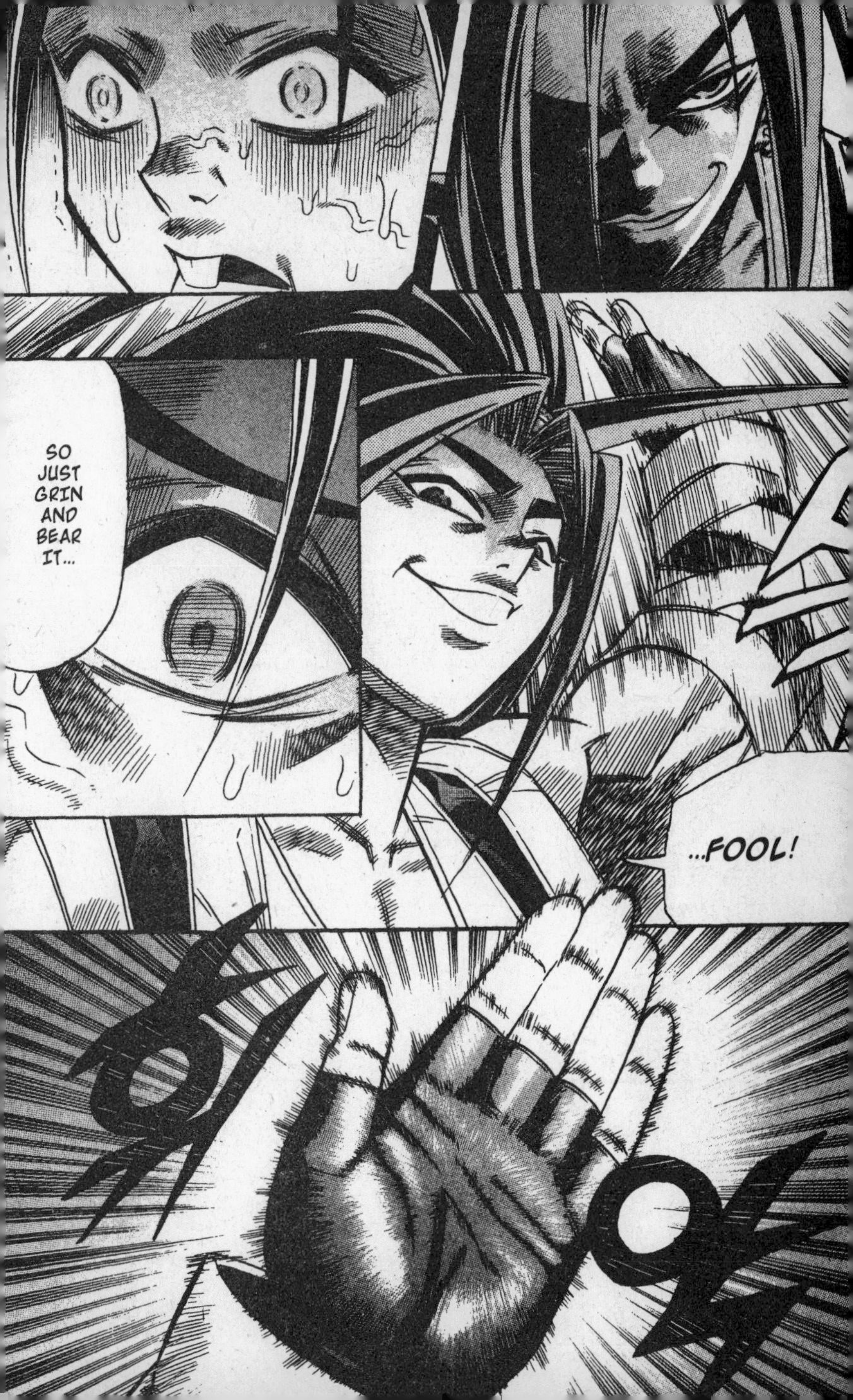
SO JUST GRIN AND BEAR IT...
...FOOL!

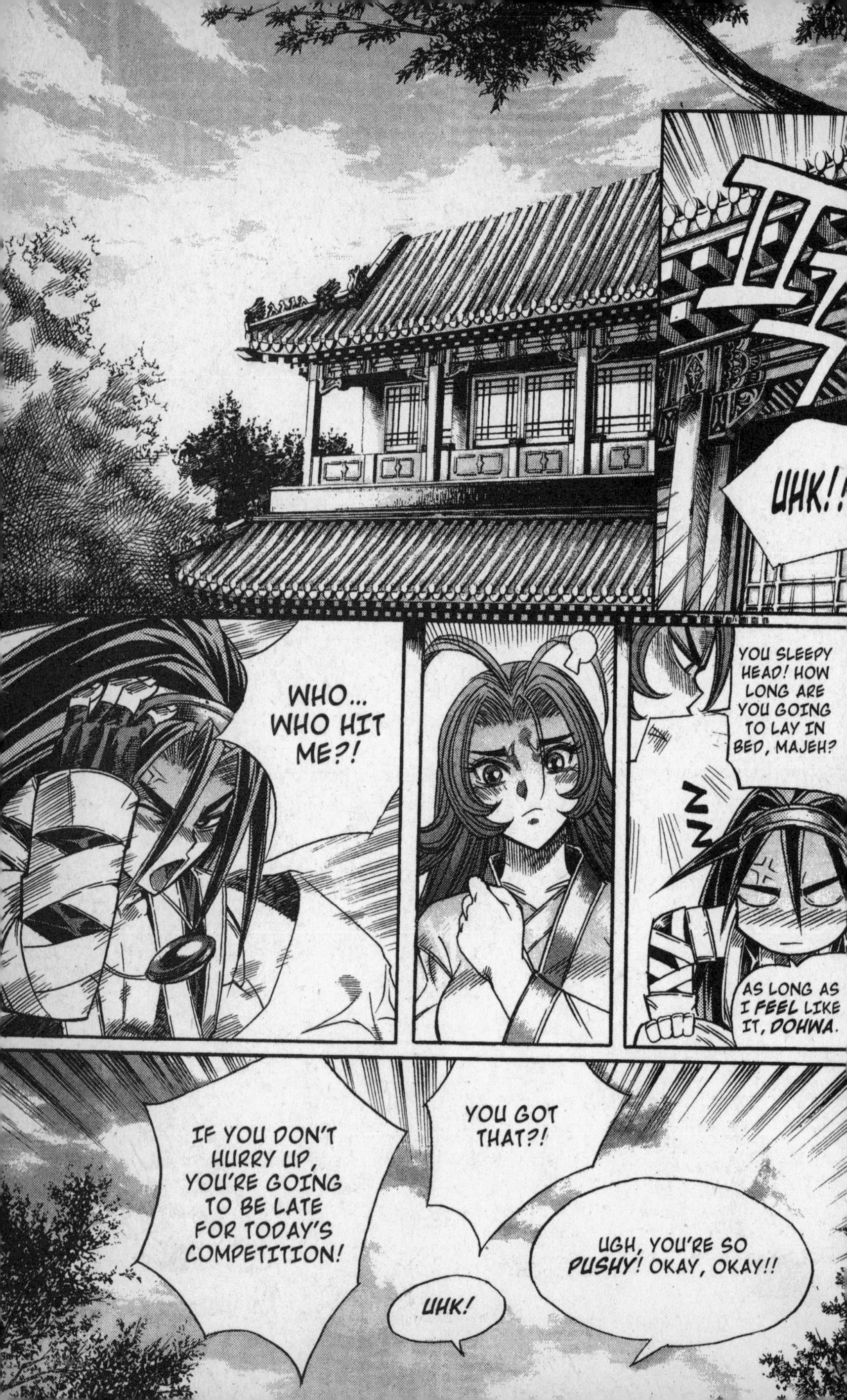
UHK!!
WHO... WHO HIT ME?!
YOU SLEEPY HEAD! HOW LONG ARE YOU GOING TO LAY IN BED, MAJEH?
AS LONG AS I *FEEL* LIKE IT, *DOHWA*.
IF YOU DON'T HURRY UP, YOU'RE GOING TO BE LATE FOR TODAY'S COMPETITION!
YOU GOT THAT?!
UHK!
UGH, YOU'RE SO *PUSHY*! OKAY, OKAY!!

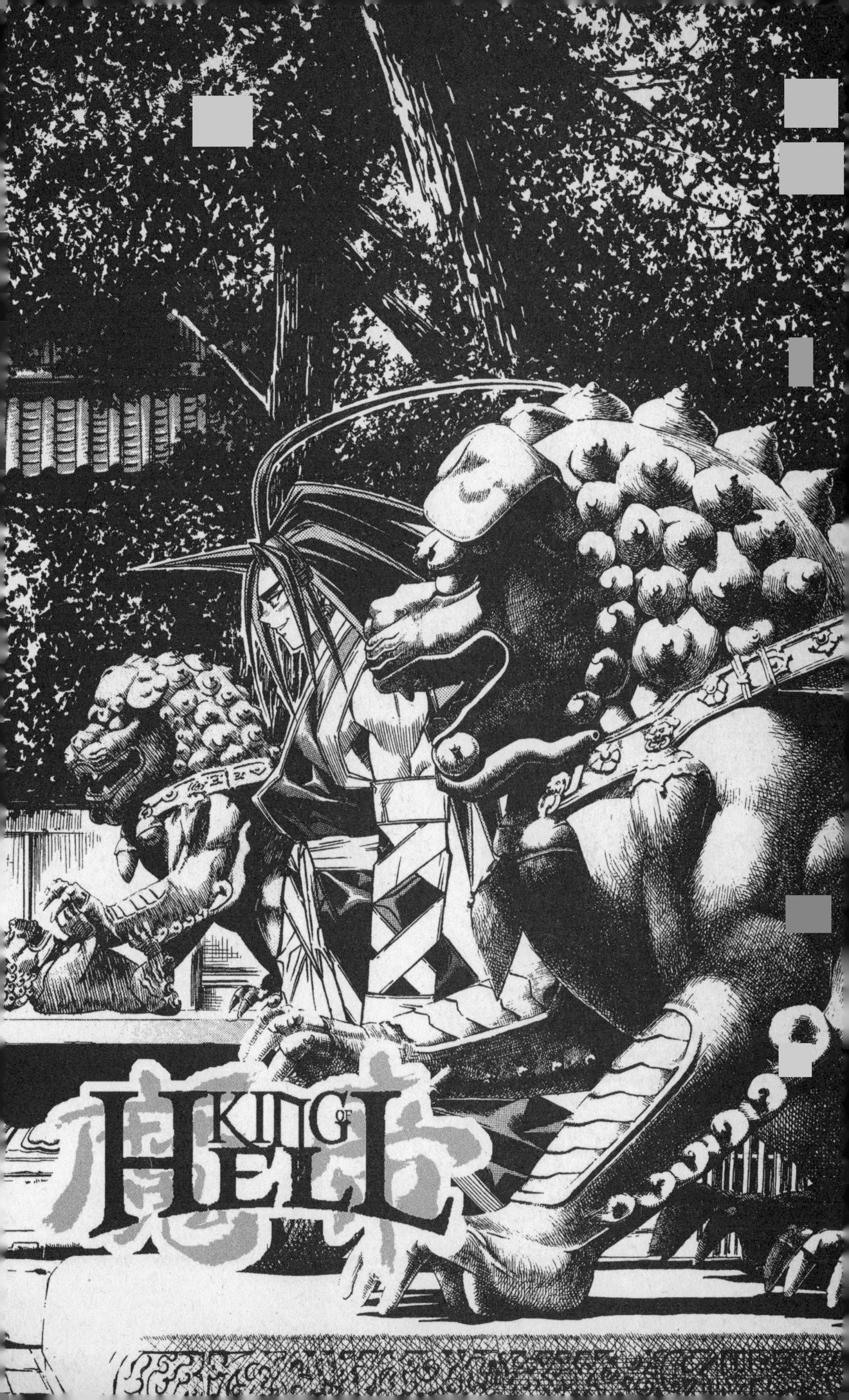
KING OF HELL

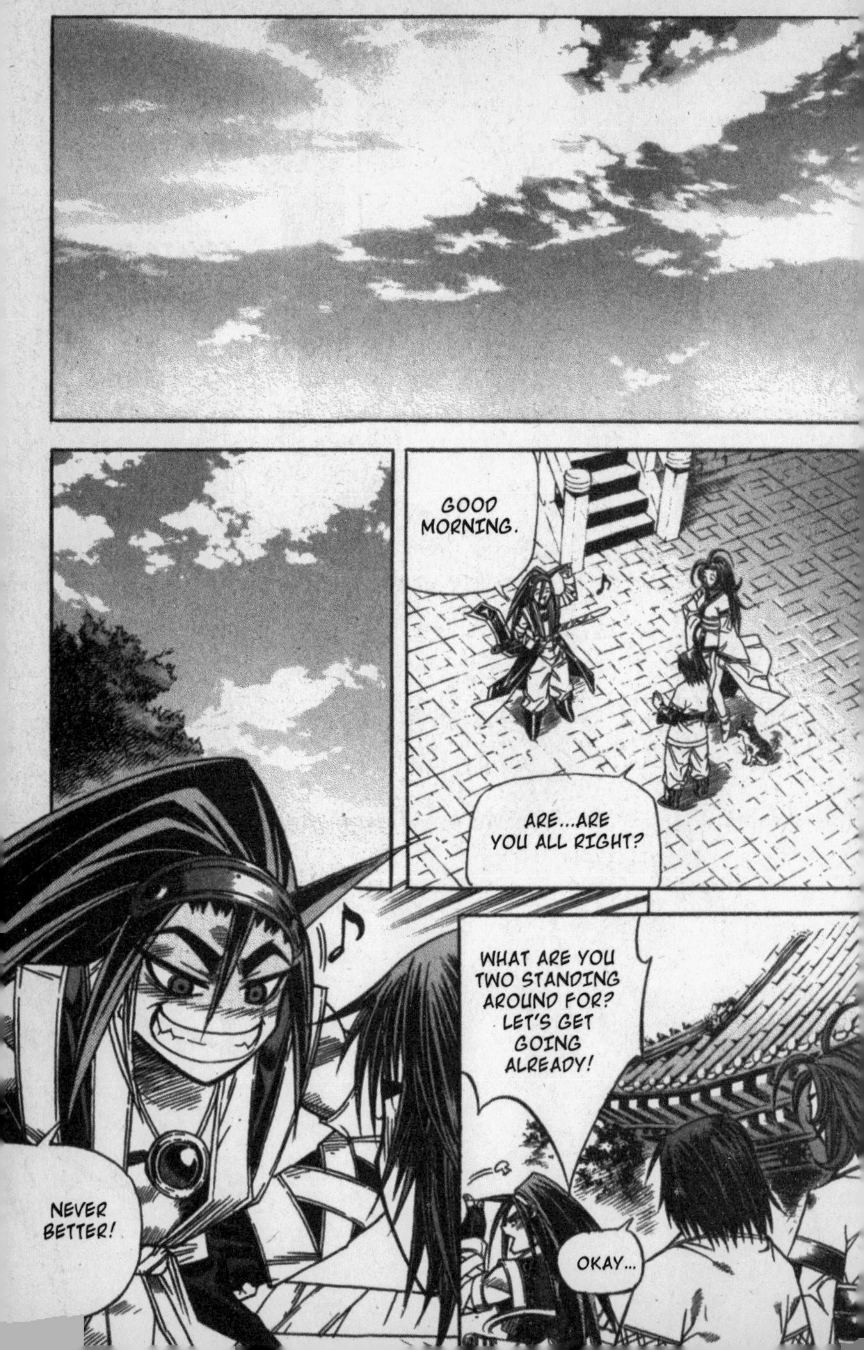
GOOD MORNING.
ARE...ARE YOU ALL RIGHT?
NEVER BETTER!
WHAT ARE YOU TWO STANDING AROUND FOR? LET'S GET GOING ALREADY!
OKAY...

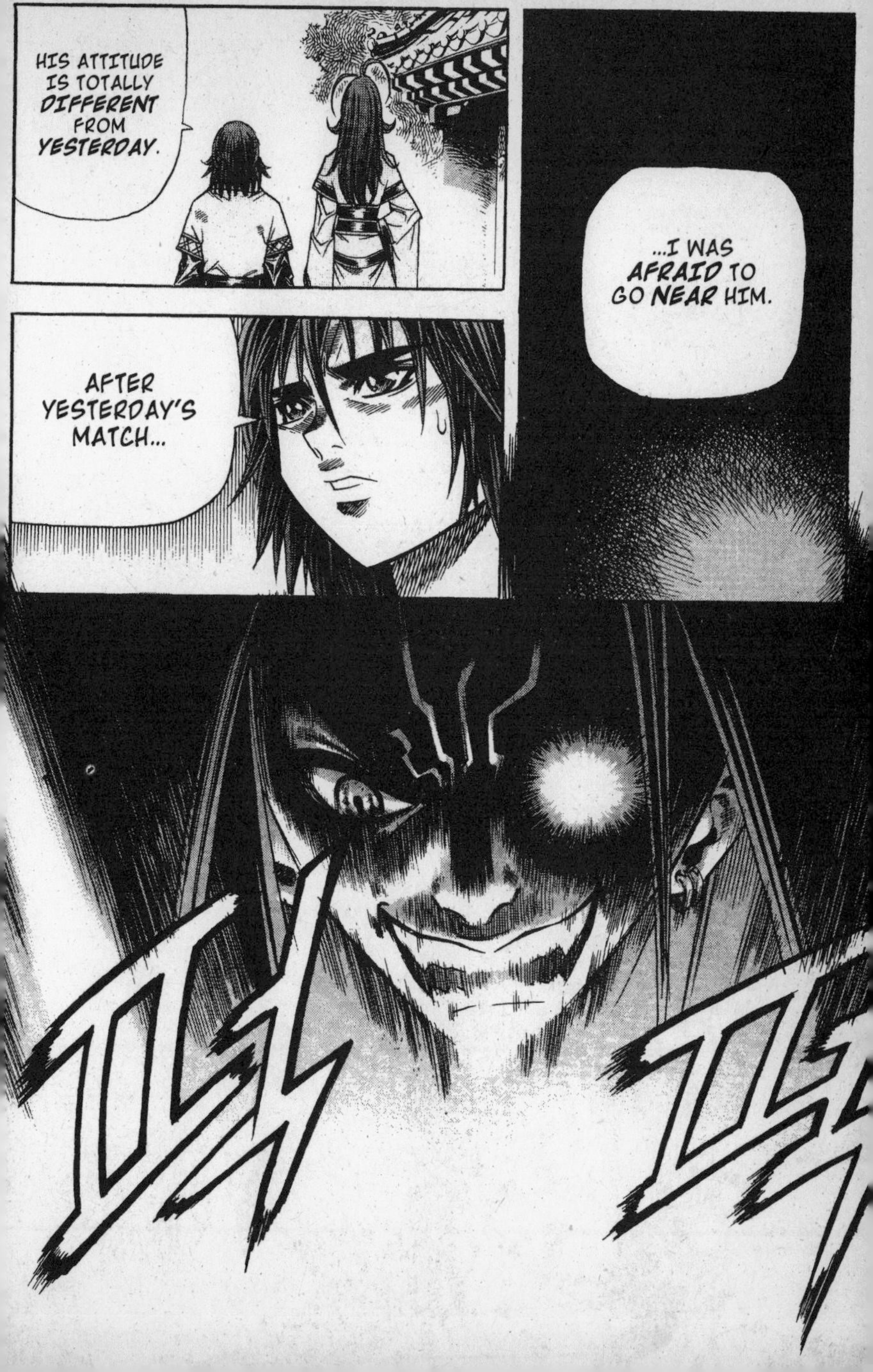
HIS ATTITUDE IS TOTALLY DIFFERENT FROM YESTERDAY.
AFTER YESTERDAY'S MATCH...
...I WAS AFRAID TO GO NEAR HIM.

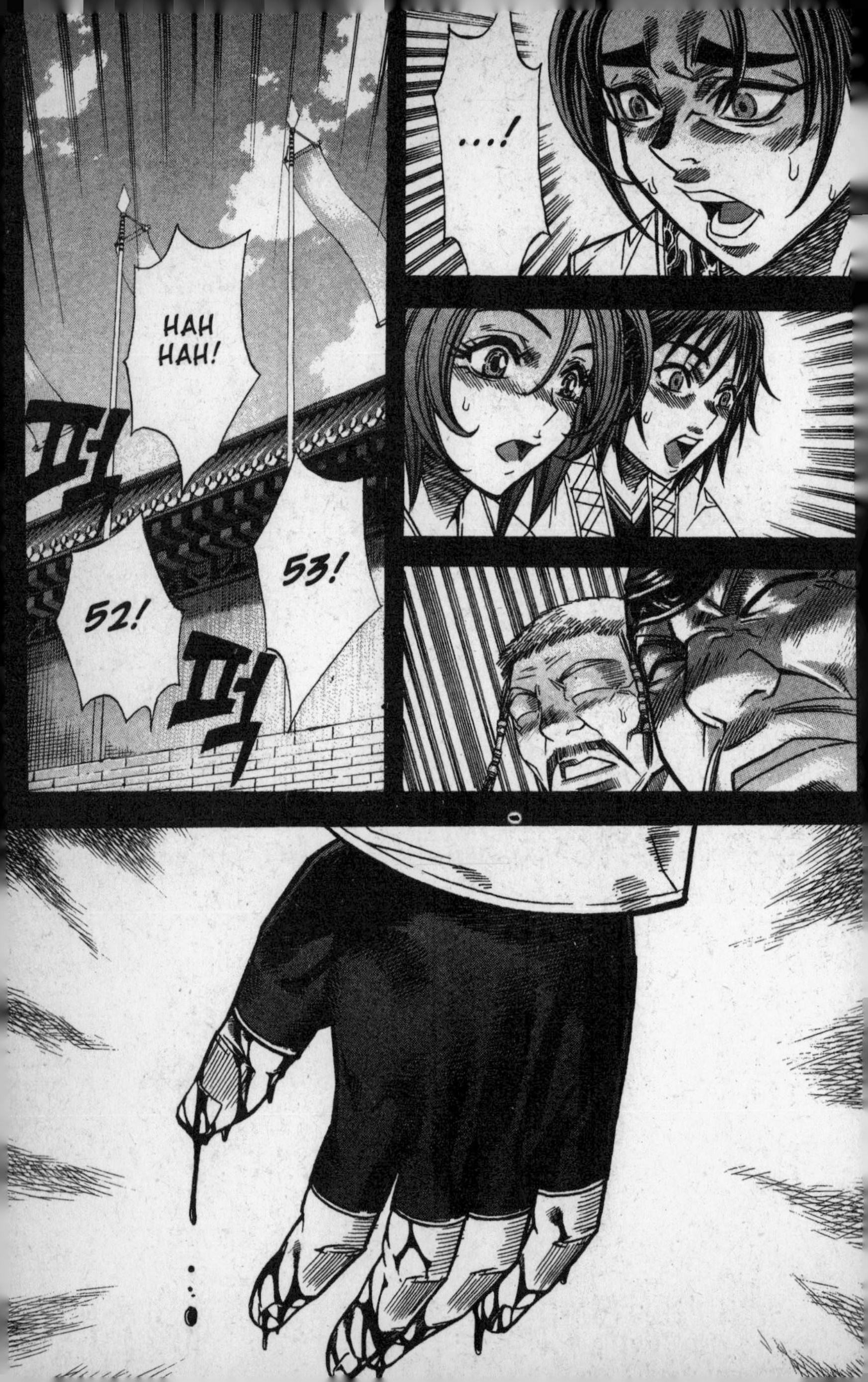
...!
HAH HAH!
53!
퍽
52!
퍽
...

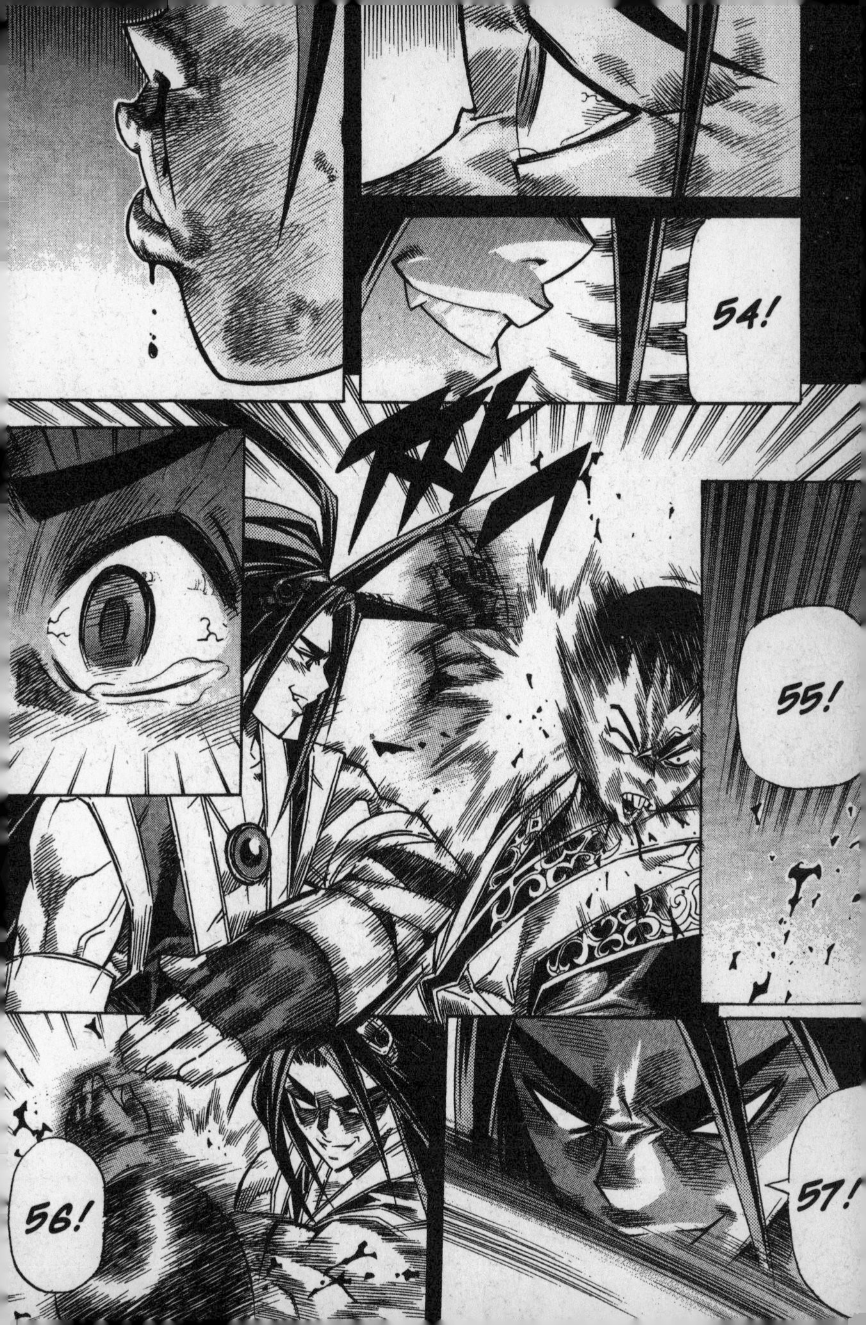
54!
55!
57!
56!

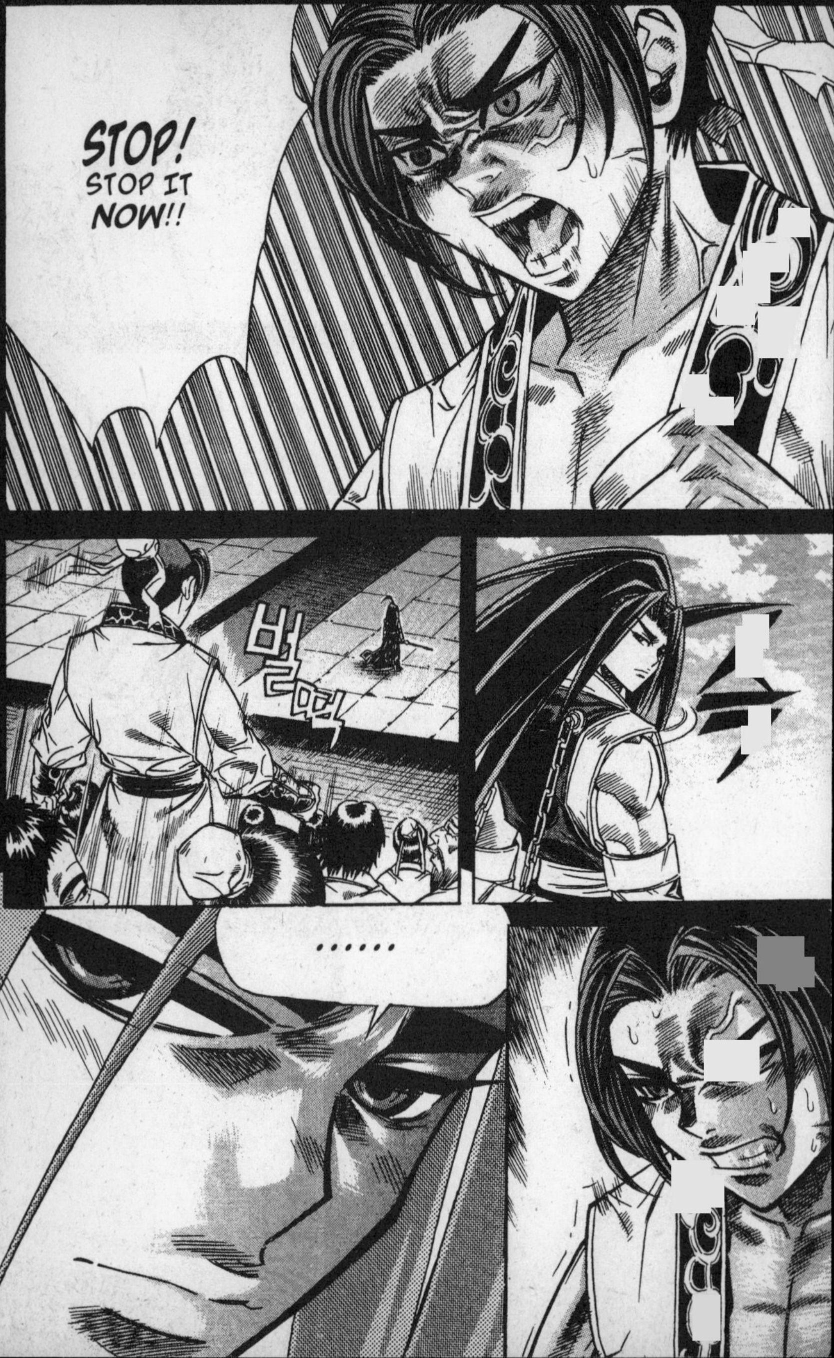
STOP! STOP IT NOW!!
벌떡
......

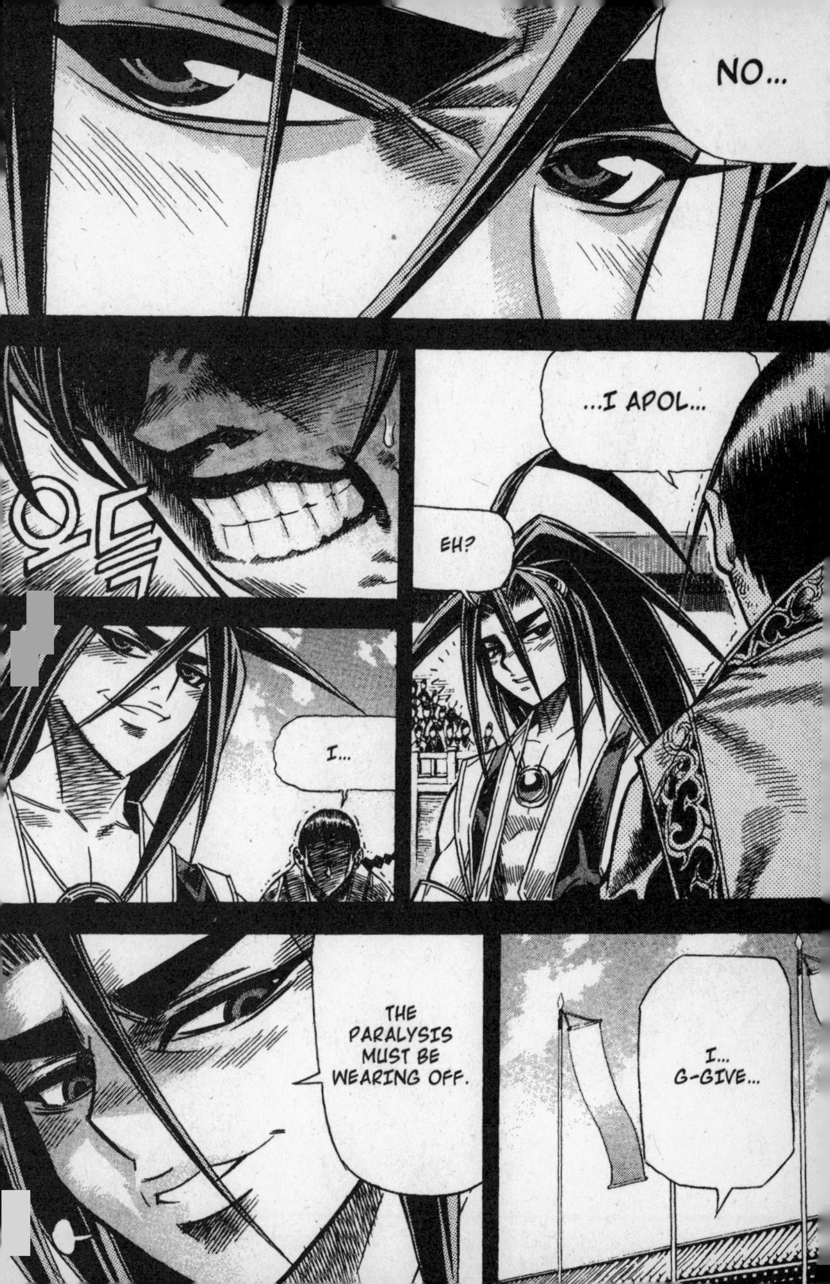
NO...
...I APOL...
EH?
I...
I...
G-GIVE...
THE PARALYSIS MUST BE WEARING OFF.

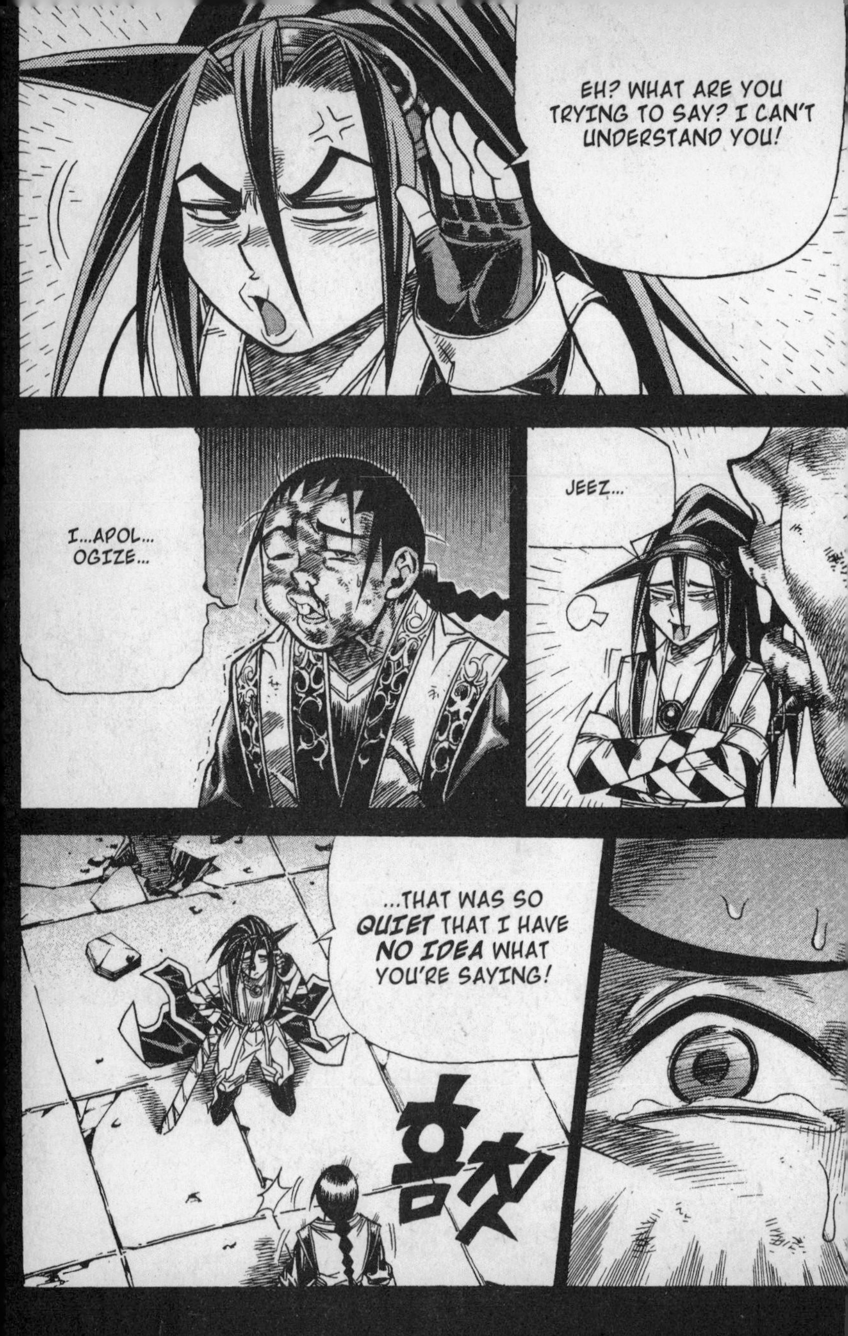
EH? WHAT ARE YOU TRYING TO SAY? I CAN'T UNDERSTAND YOU!
I...APOL... OGIZE...
JEEZ...
...THAT WAS SO *QUIET* THAT I HAVE **NO IDEA** WHAT YOU'RE SAYING!
흠칫

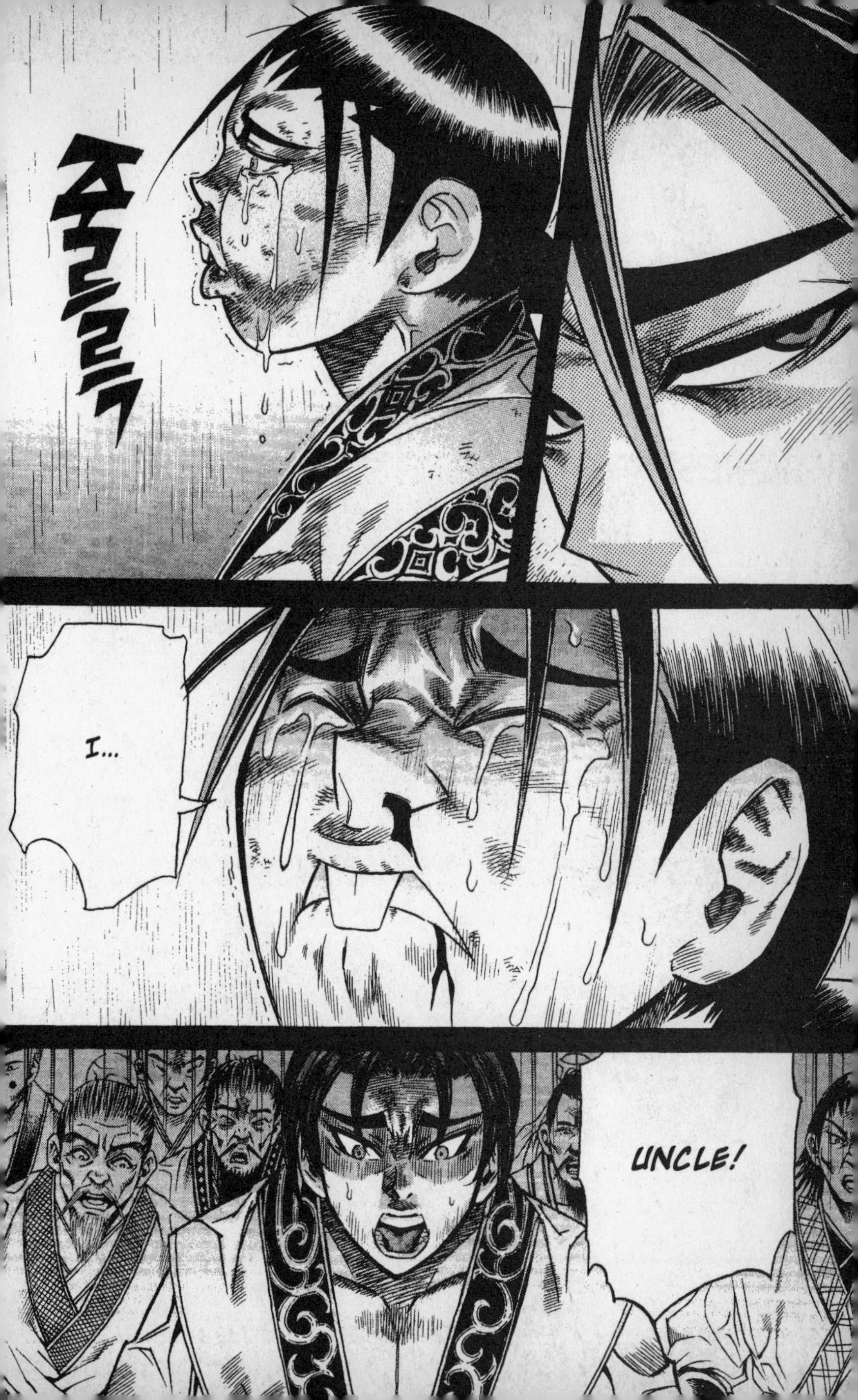
I...
UNCLE!

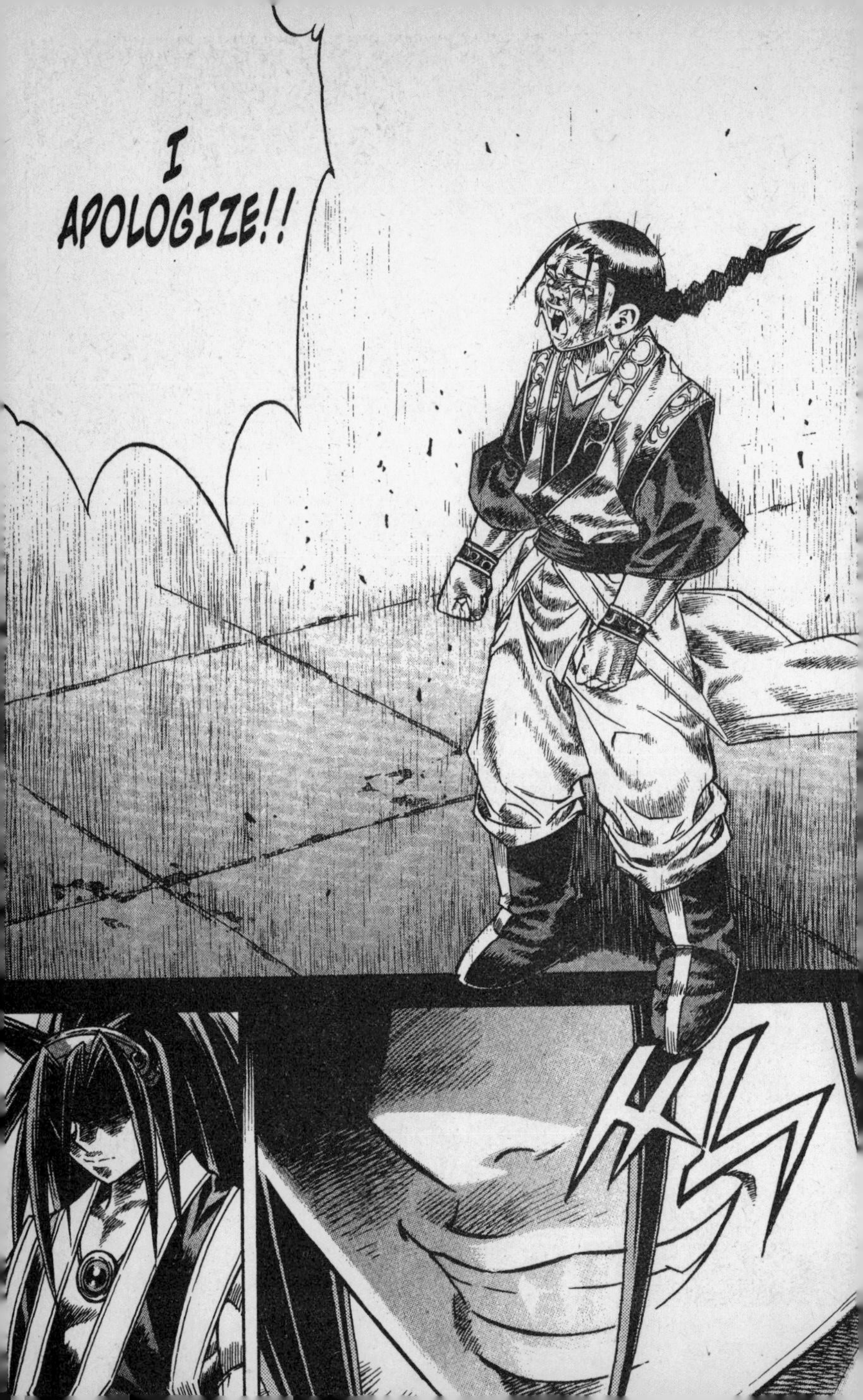
I APOLOGIZE!!

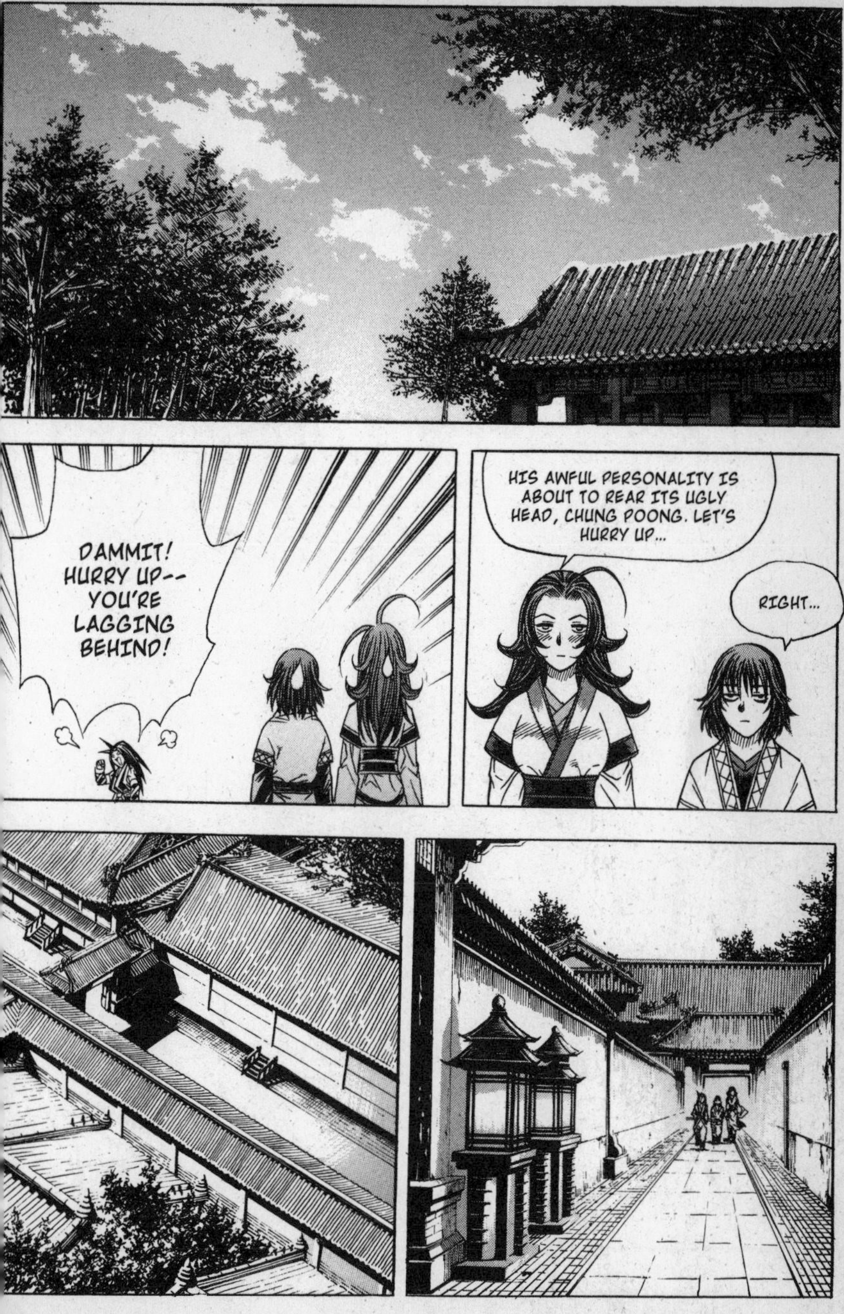
DAMMIT! HURRY UP-- YOU'RE LAGGING BEHIND!
HIS AWFUL PERSONALITY IS ABOUT TO REAR ITS UGLY HEAD, CHUNG POONG. LET'S HURRY UP...
RIGHT...

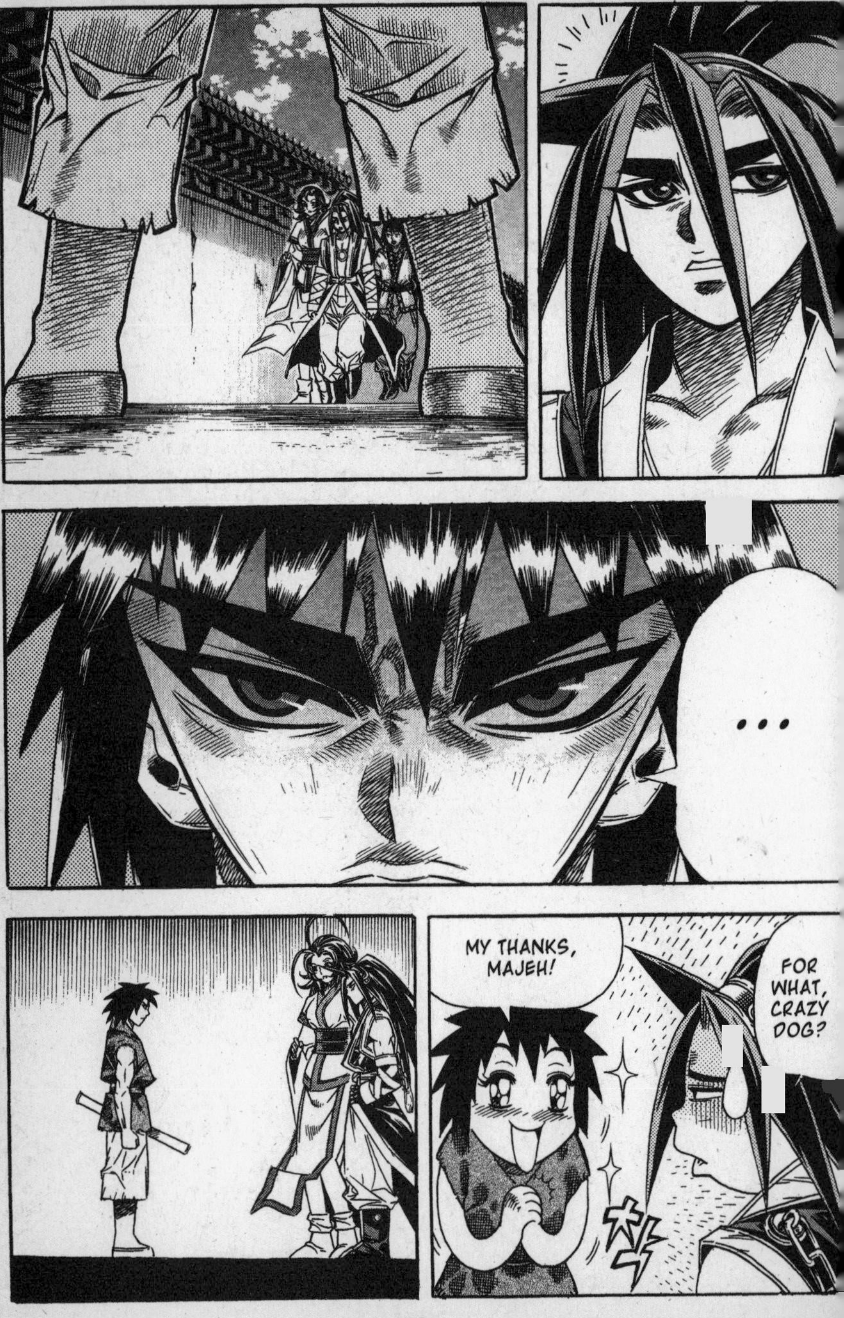
...
FOR WHAT, CRAZY DOG?
MY THANKS, MAJEH!

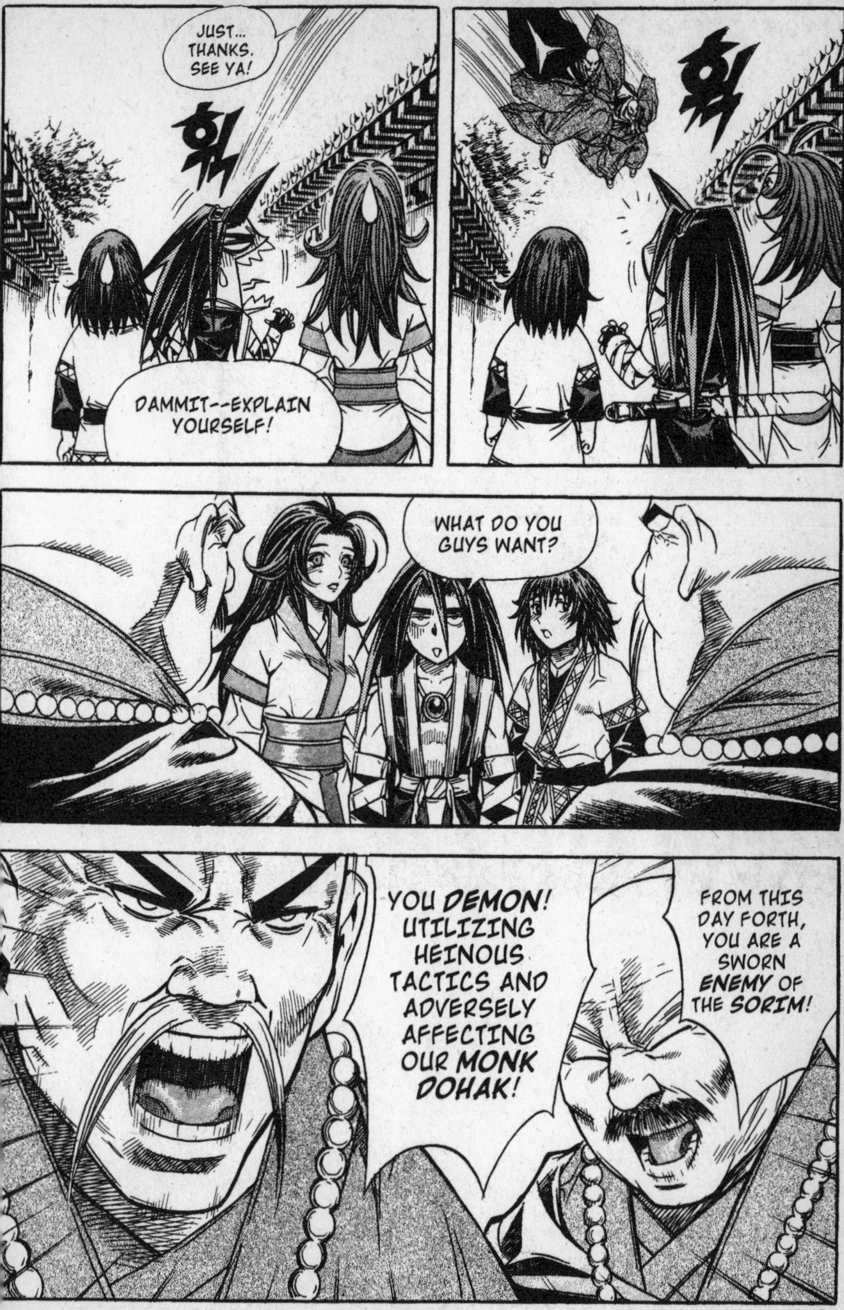
JUST... THANKS. SEE YA!
DAMMIT--EXPLAIN YOURSELF!
WHAT DO YOU GUYS WANT?
YOU DEMON! UTILIZING HEINOUS TACTICS AND ADVERSELY AFFECTING OUR MONK DOHAK!
FROM THIS DAY FORTH, YOU ARE A SWORN ENEMY OF THE SORIM!

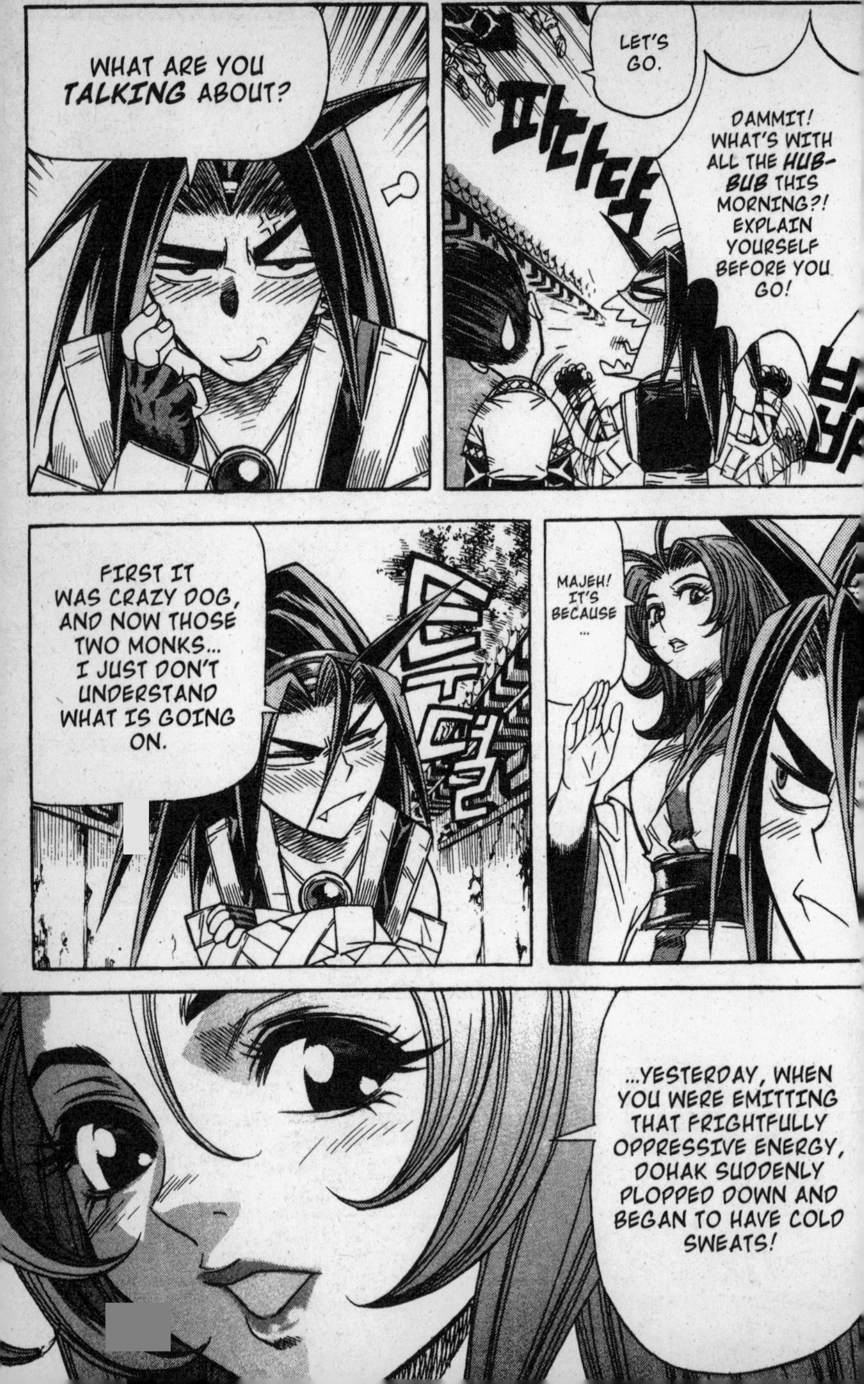
WHAT ARE YOU TALKING ABOUT?
LET'S GO.
DAMMIT! WHAT'S WITH ALL THE HUB-BUB THIS MORNING?! EXPLAIN YOURSELF BEFORE YOU GO!
FIRST IT WAS CRAZY DOG, AND NOW THOSE TWO MONKS... I JUST DON'T UNDERSTAND WHAT IS GOING ON.
MAJEH! IT'S BECAUSE ...
...YESTERDAY, WHEN YOU WERE EMITTING THAT FRIGHTFULLY OPPRESSIVE ENERGY, DOHAK SUDDENLY PLOPPED DOWN AND BEGAN TO HAVE COLD SWEATS!

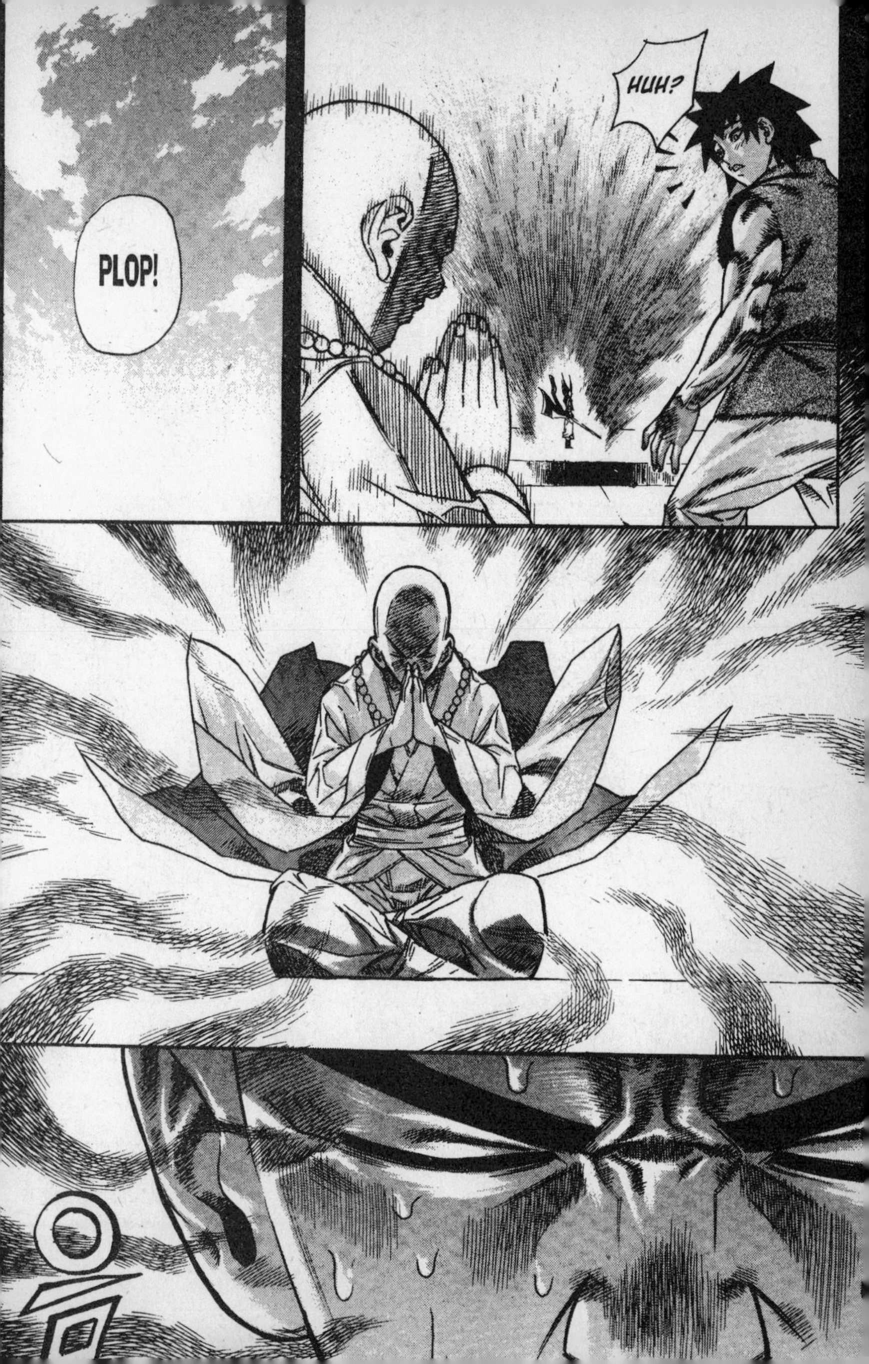
HUH?
PLOP!

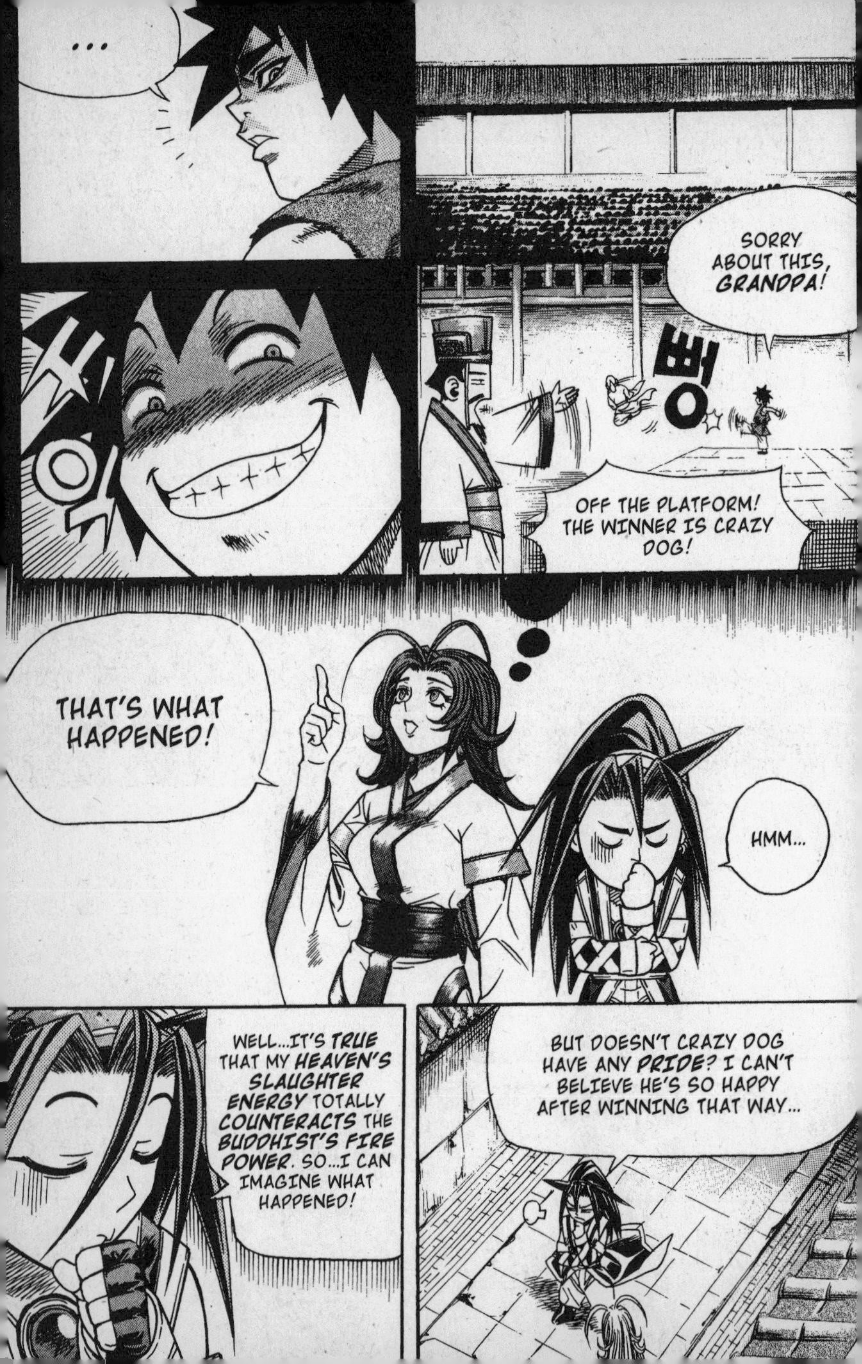
SORRY ABOUT THIS, GRANDPA!
뻥
OFF THE PLATFORM! THE WINNER IS CRAZY DOG!
...
THAT'S WHAT HAPPENED!
HMM...
BUT DOESN'T CRAZY DOG HAVE ANY PRIDE? I CAN'T BELIEVE HE'S SO HAPPY AFTER WINNING THAT WAY...
WELL...IT'S TRUE THAT MY HEAVEN'S SLAUGHTER ENERGY TOTALLY COUNTERACTS THE BUDDHIST'S FIRE POWER. SO...I CAN IMAGINE WHAT HAPPENED!

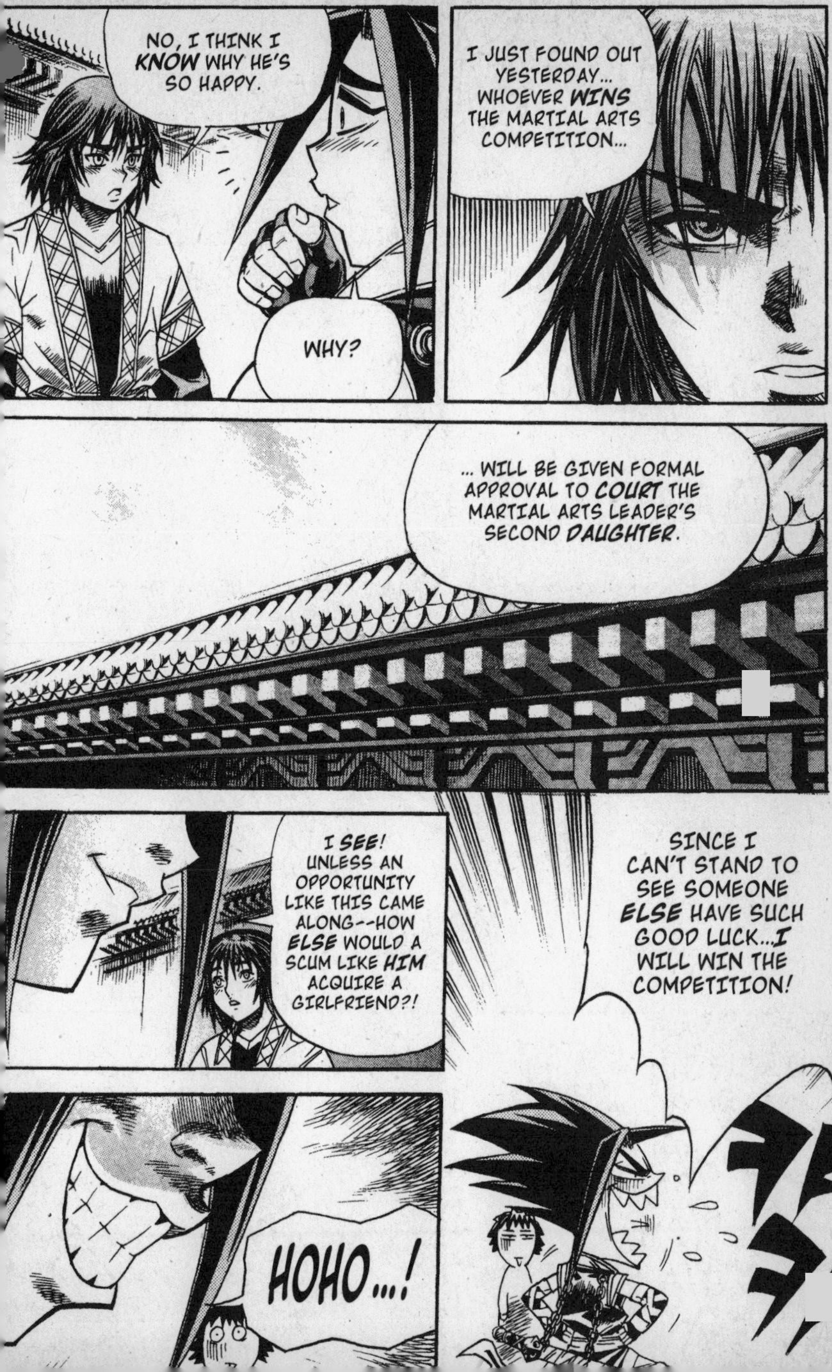
NO, I THINK I KNOW WHY HE'S SO HAPPY.
WHY?
I JUST FOUND OUT YESTERDAY... WHOEVER WINS THE MARTIAL ARTS COMPETITION...
... WILL BE GIVEN FORMAL APPROVAL TO COURT THE MARTIAL ARTS LEADER'S SECOND DAUGHTER.
I SEE! UNLESS AN OPPORTUNITY LIKE THIS CAME ALONG--HOW ELSE WOULD A SCUM LIKE HIM ACQUIRE A GIRLFRIEND?!
HOHO...!
SINCE I CAN'T STAND TO SEE SOMEONE ELSE HAVE SUCH GOOD LUCK...I WILL WIN THE COMPETITION!

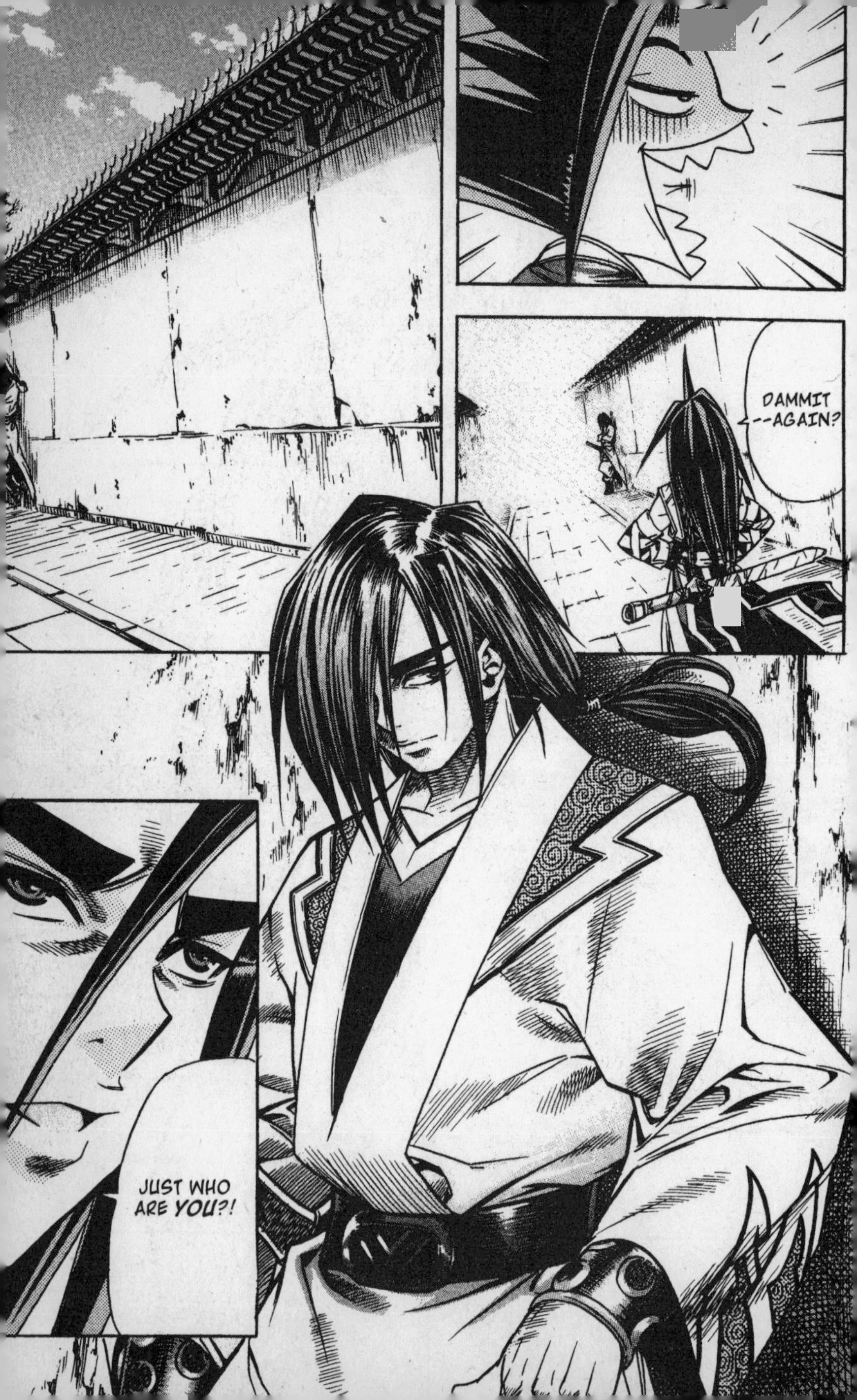
DAMMIT --AGAIN?
JUST WHO ARE YOU?!

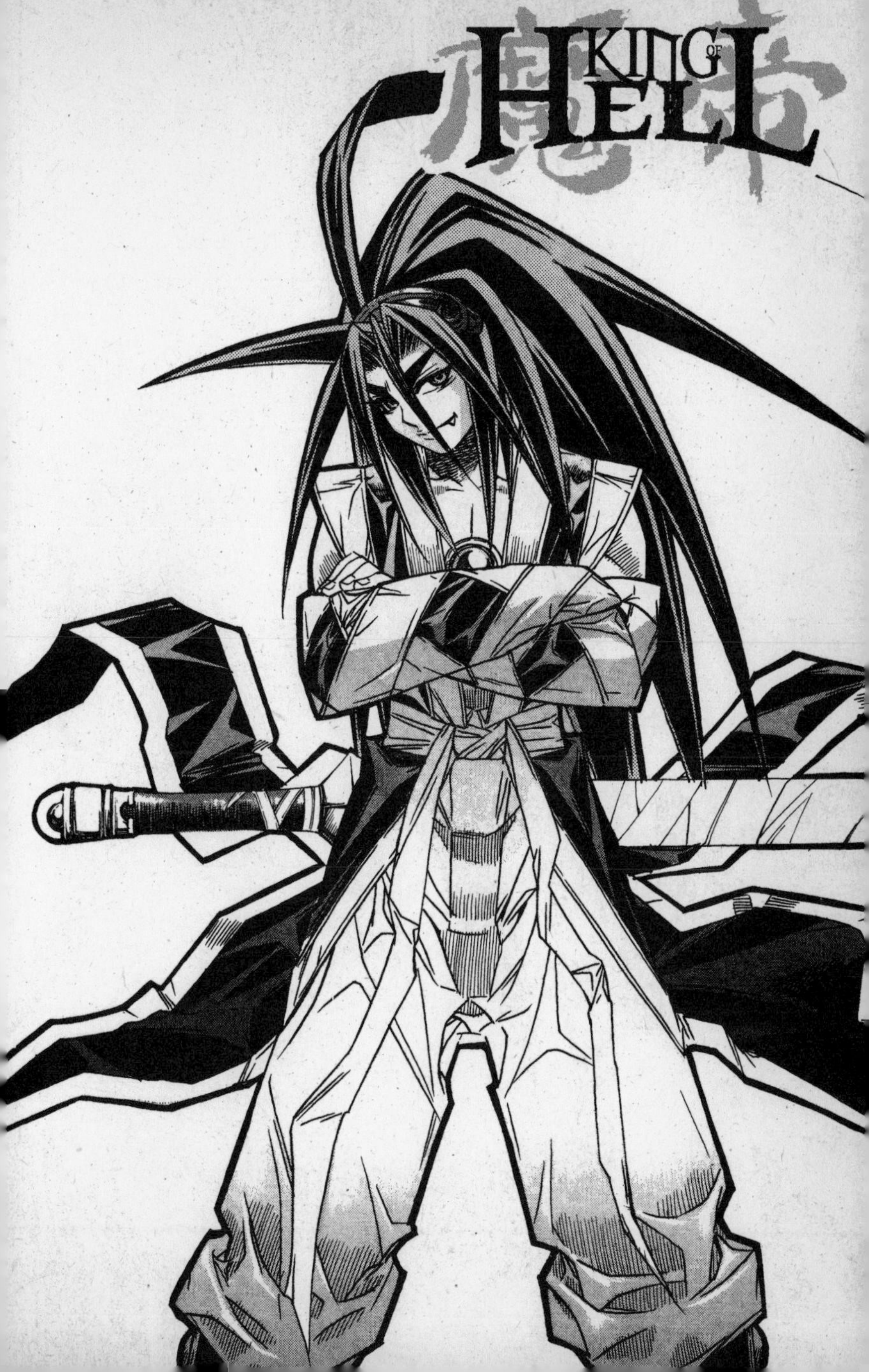
KING OF HELL

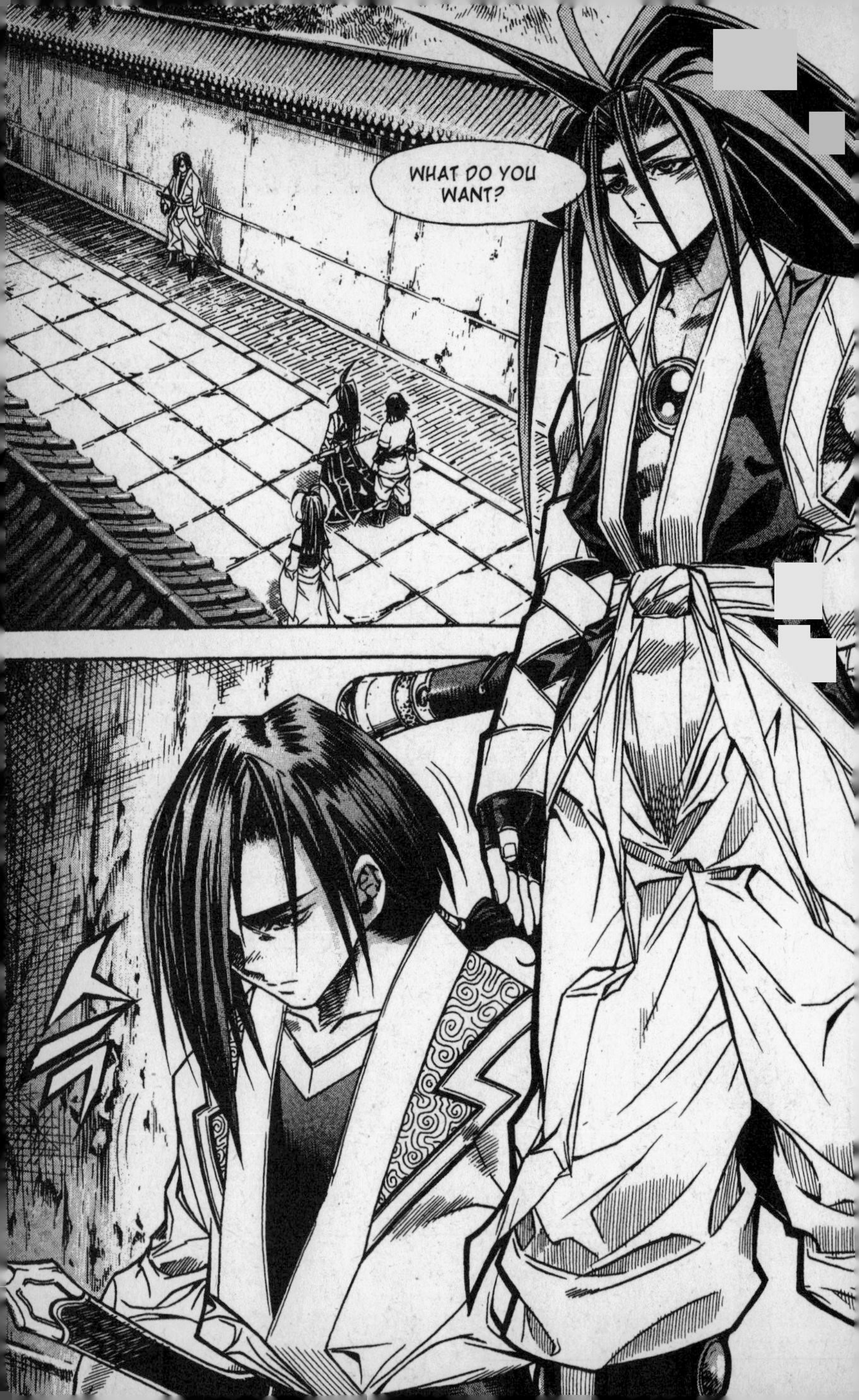
WHAT DO YOU WANT?

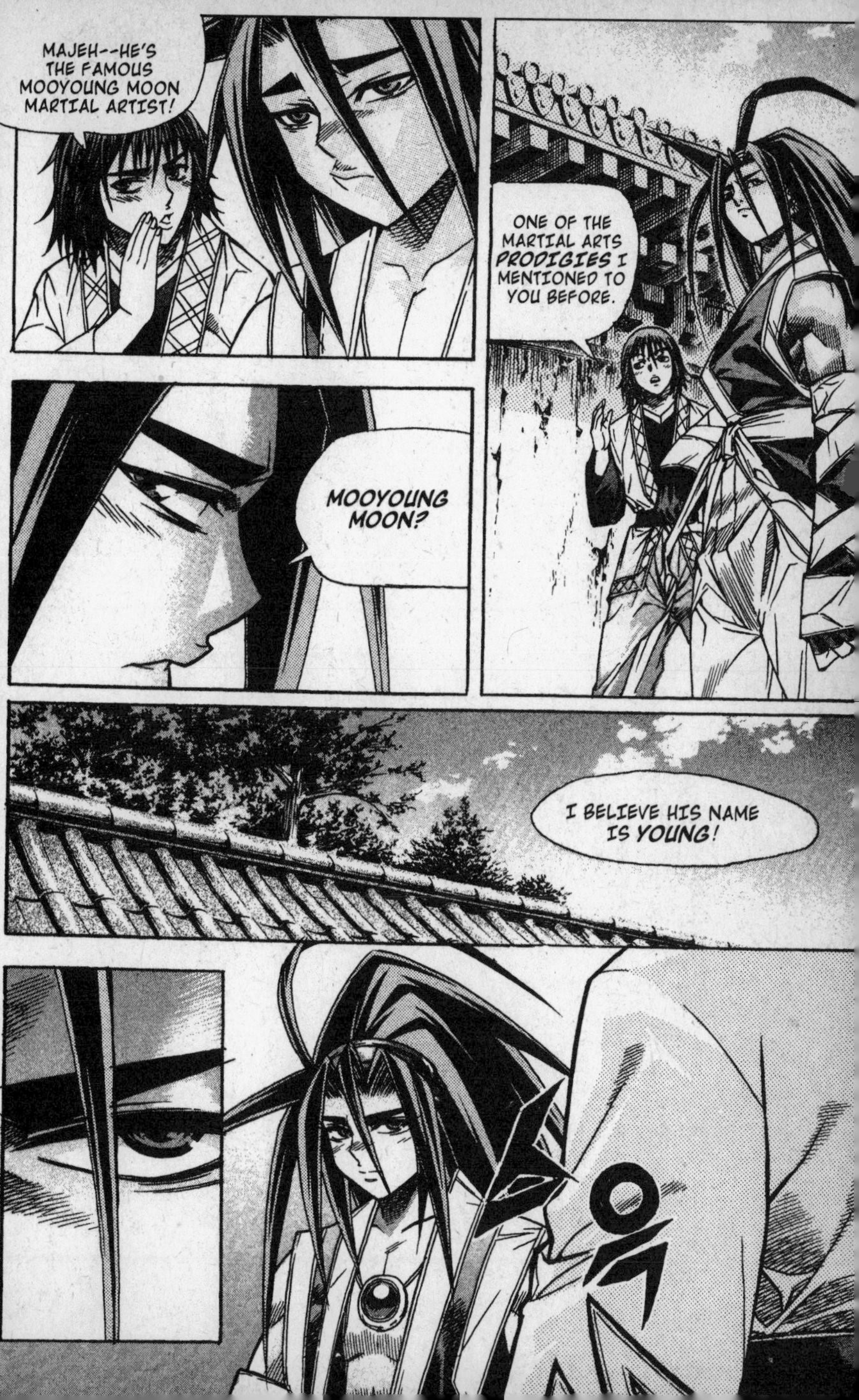
ONE OF THE MARTIAL ARTS PRODIGIES I MENTIONED TO YOU BEFORE.
MAJEH--HE'S THE FAMOUS MOOYOUNG MOON MARTIAL ARTIST!
MOOYOUNG MOON?
I BELIEVE HIS NAME IS YOUNG!

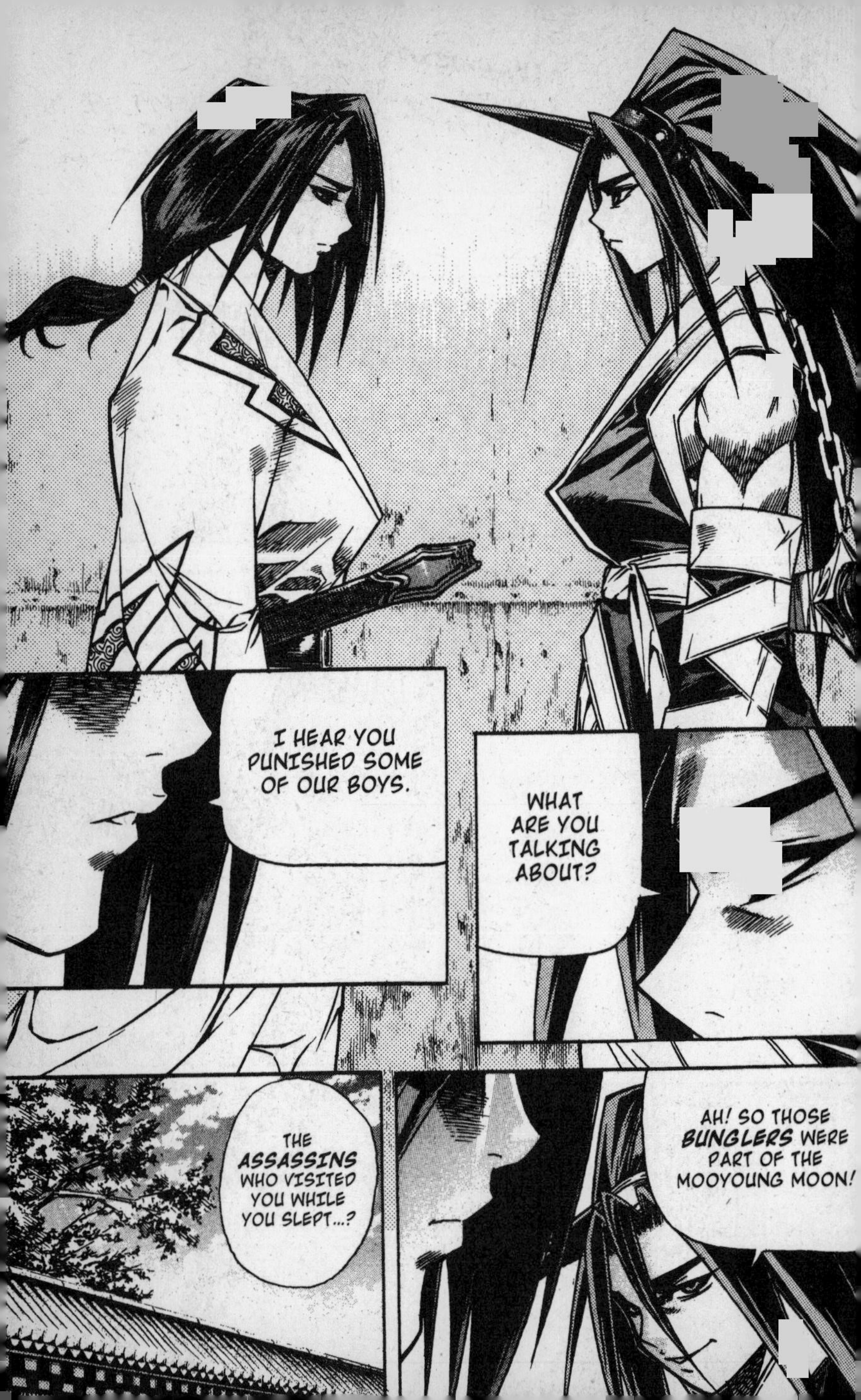
I HEAR YOU PUNISHED SOME OF OUR BOYS.
WHAT ARE YOU TALKING ABOUT?
THE ASSASSINS WHO VISITED YOU WHILE YOU SLEPT...?
AH! SO THOSE BUNGLERS WERE PART OF THE MOOYOUNG MOON!

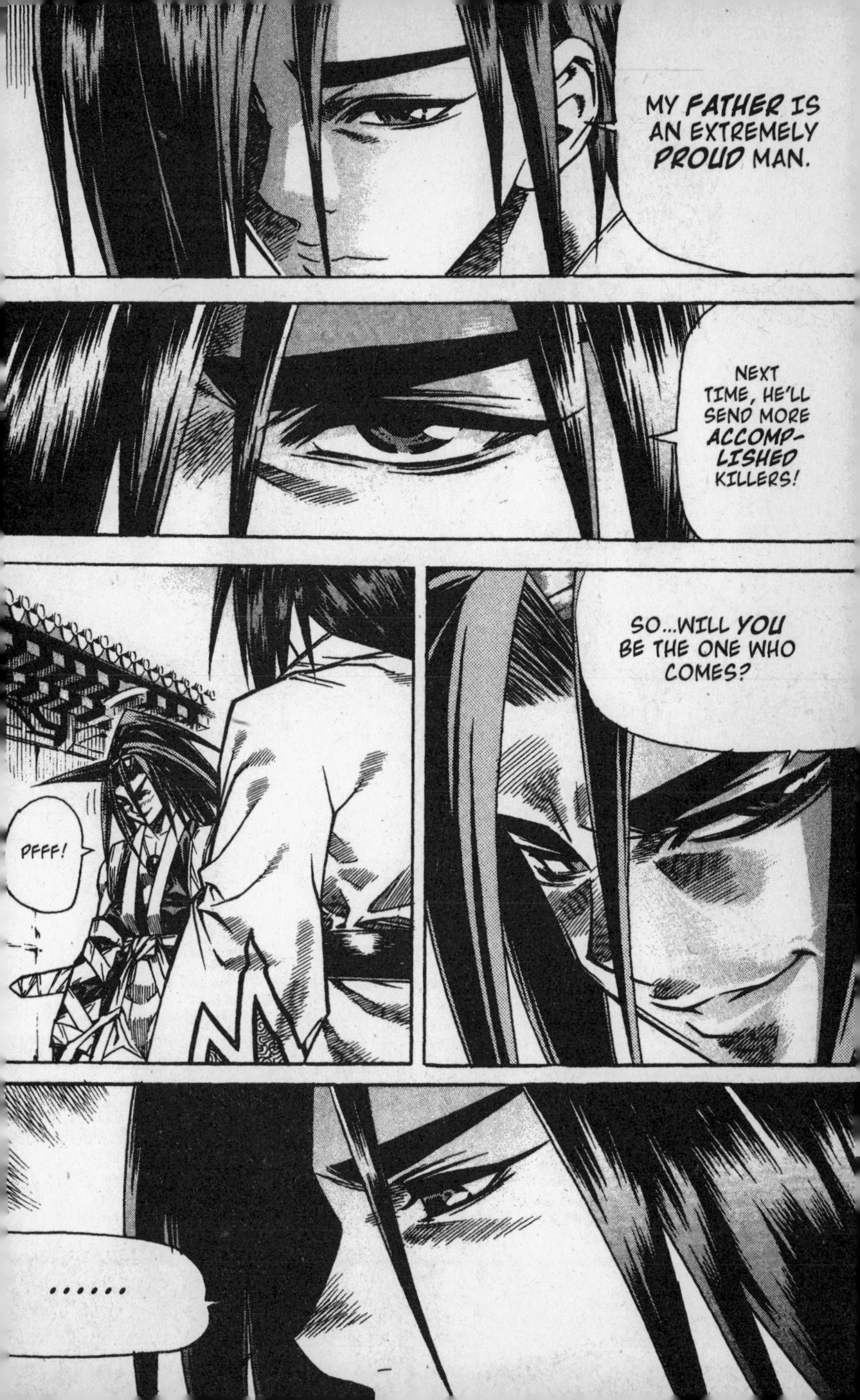
MY FATHER IS AN EXTREMELY PROUD MAN.
NEXT TIME, HE'LL SEND MORE ACCOMP-LISHED KILLERS!
SO...WILL YOU BE THE ONE WHO COMES?
PFFF!
......

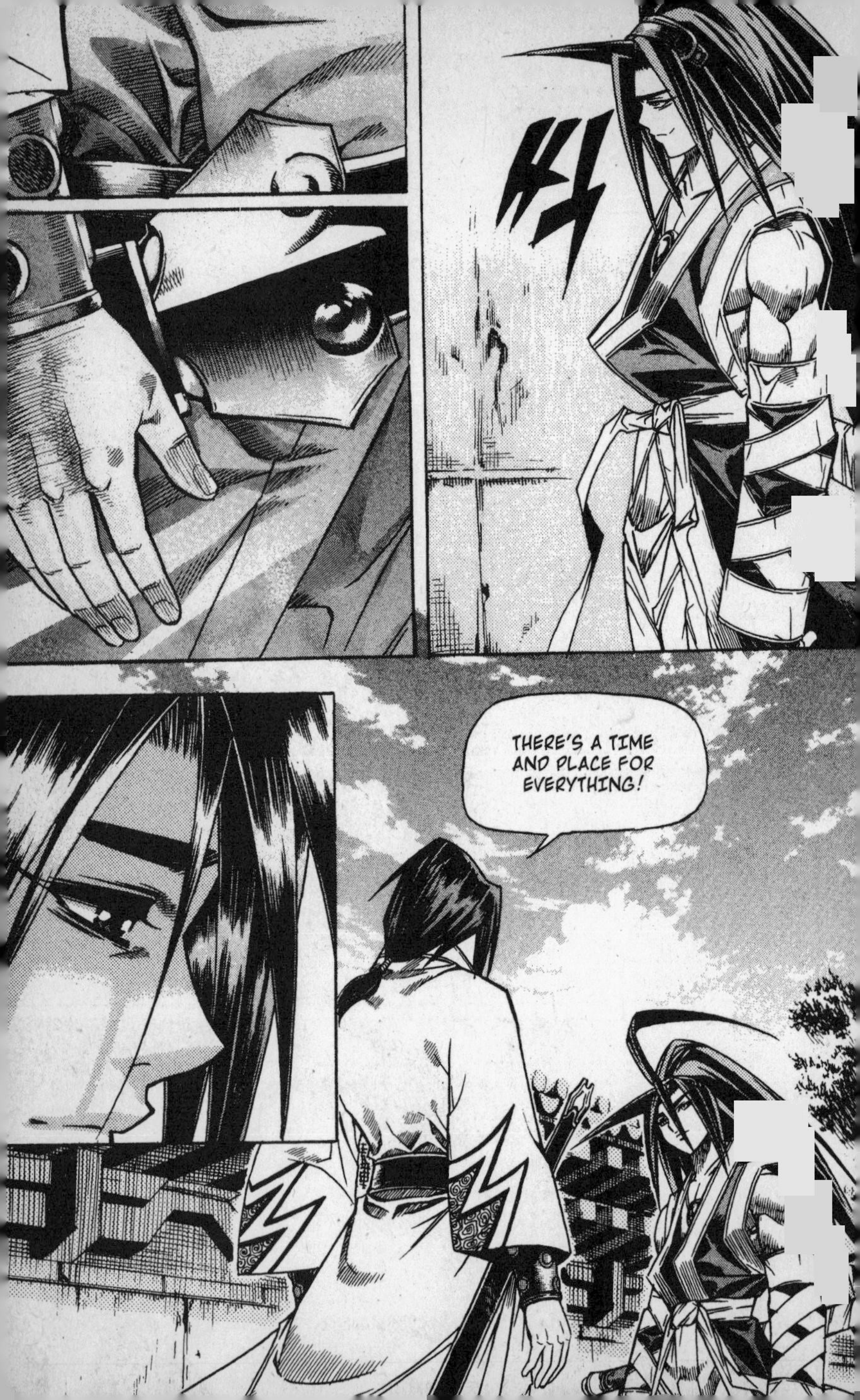
THERE'S A TIME AND PLACE FOR EVERYTHING!

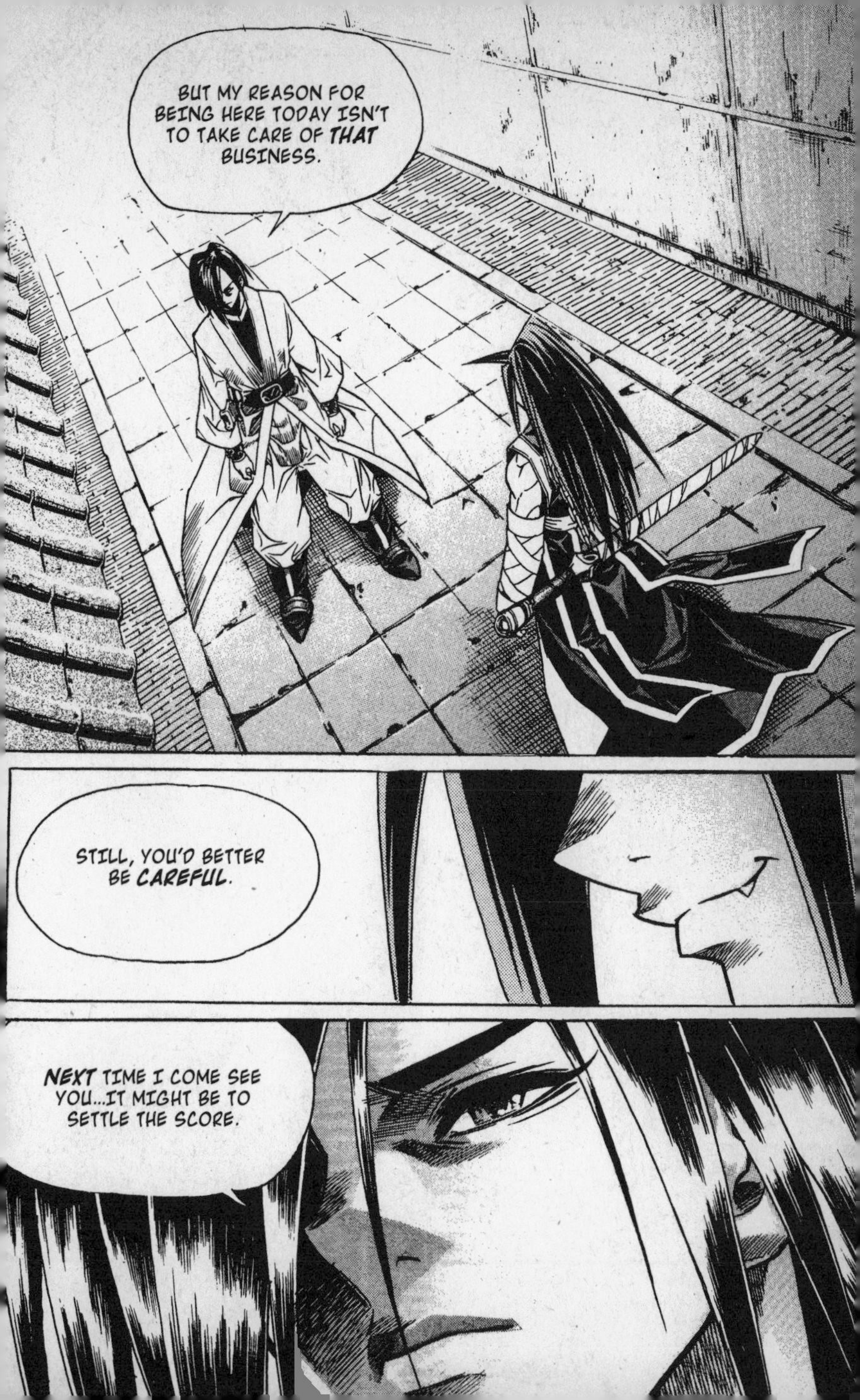
BUT MY REASON FOR BEING HERE TODAY ISN'T TO TAKE CARE OF THAT BUSINESS.
STILL, YOU'D BETTER BE CAREFUL.
NEXT TIME I COME SEE YOU...IT MIGHT BE TO SETTLE THE SCORE.

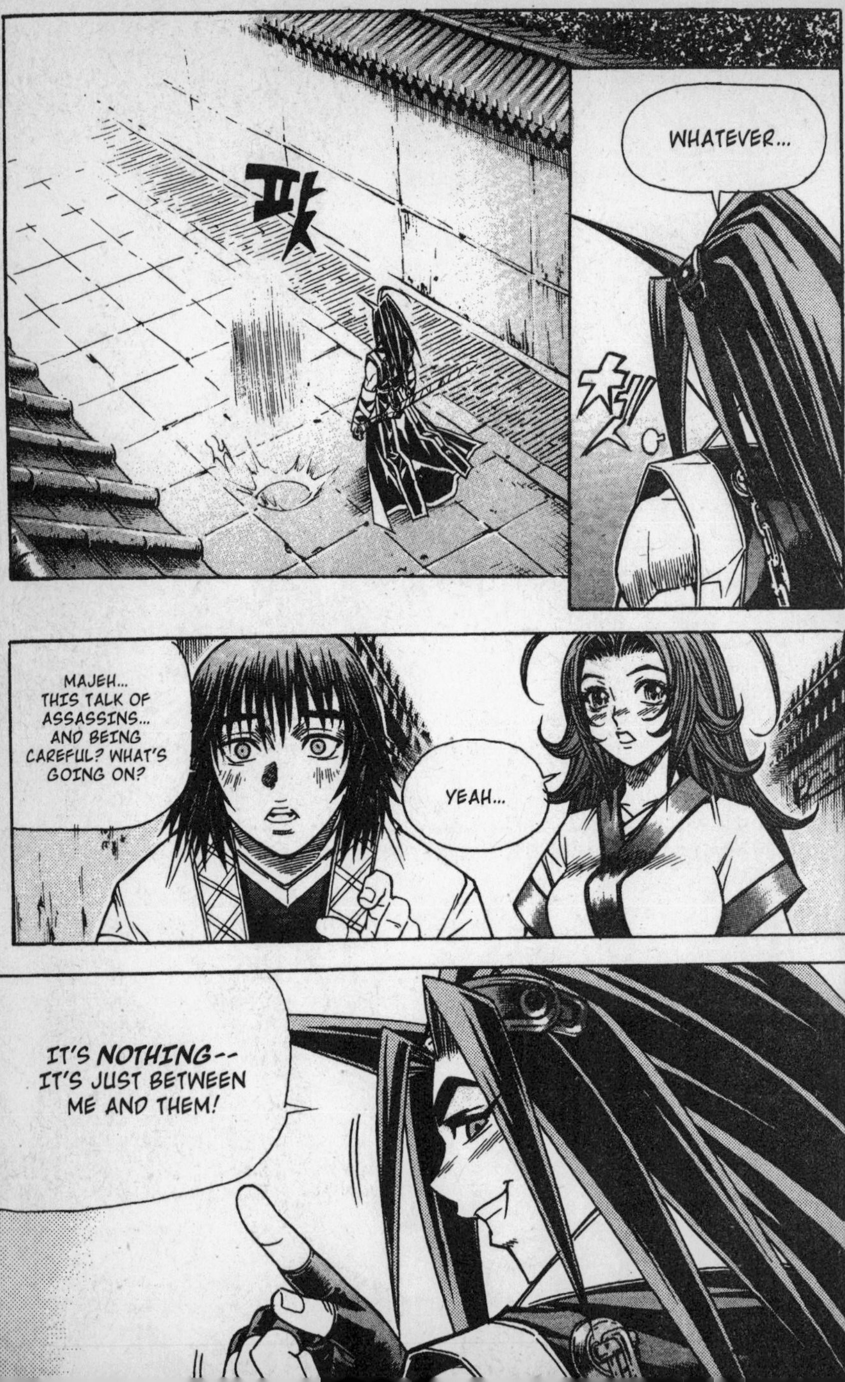

팍
WHATEVER...
MAJEH... THIS TALK OF ASSASSINS... AND BEING CAREFUL? WHAT'S GOING ON?
YEAH...
IT'S NOTHING-- IT'S JUST BETWEEN ME AND THEM!

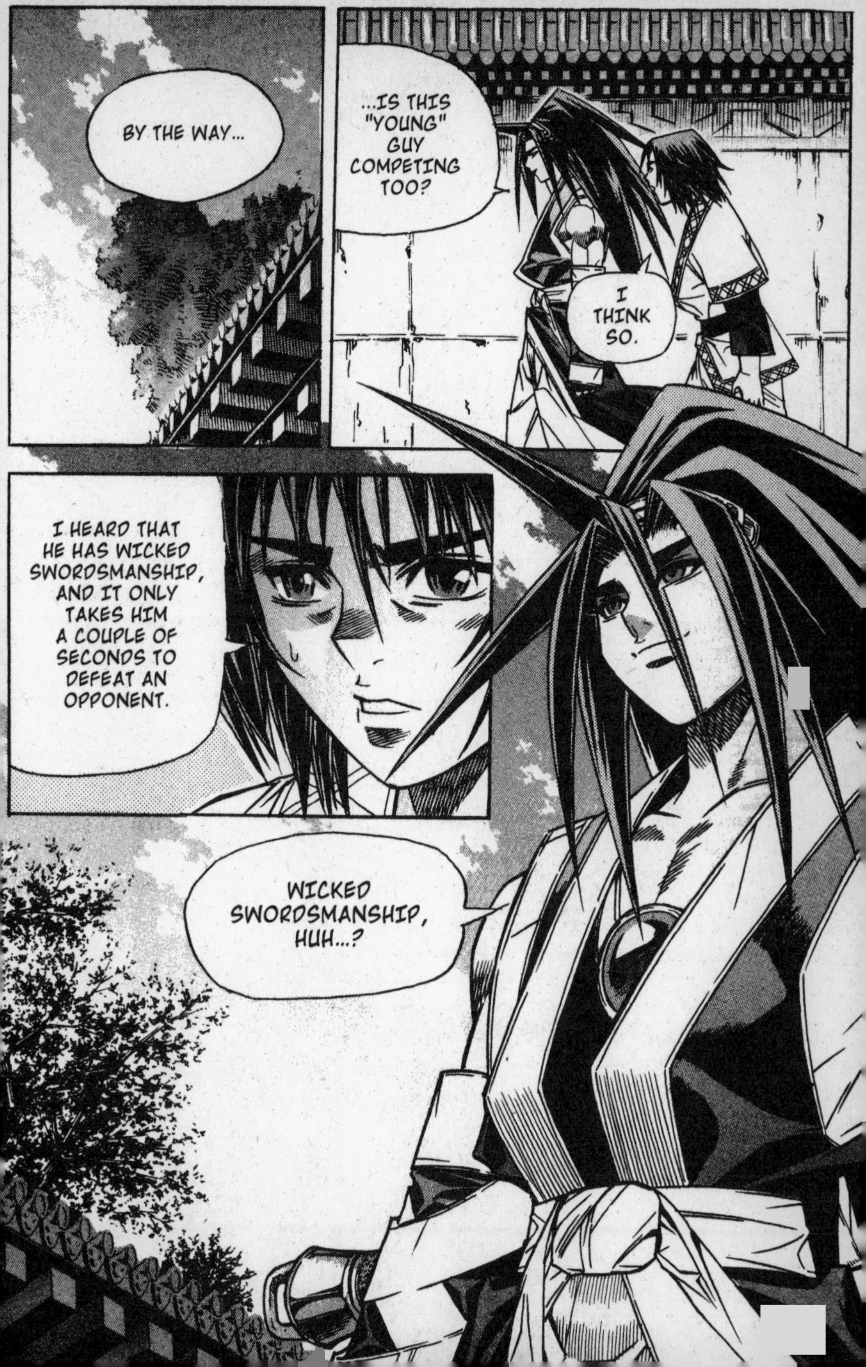
BY THE WAY...
...IS THIS "YOUNG" GUY COMPETING TOO?
I THINK SO.
I HEARD THAT HE HAS WICKED SWORDSMANSHIP, AND IT ONLY TAKES HIM A COUPLE OF SECONDS TO DEFEAT AN OPPONENT.
WICKED SWORDSMANSHIP, HUH...?

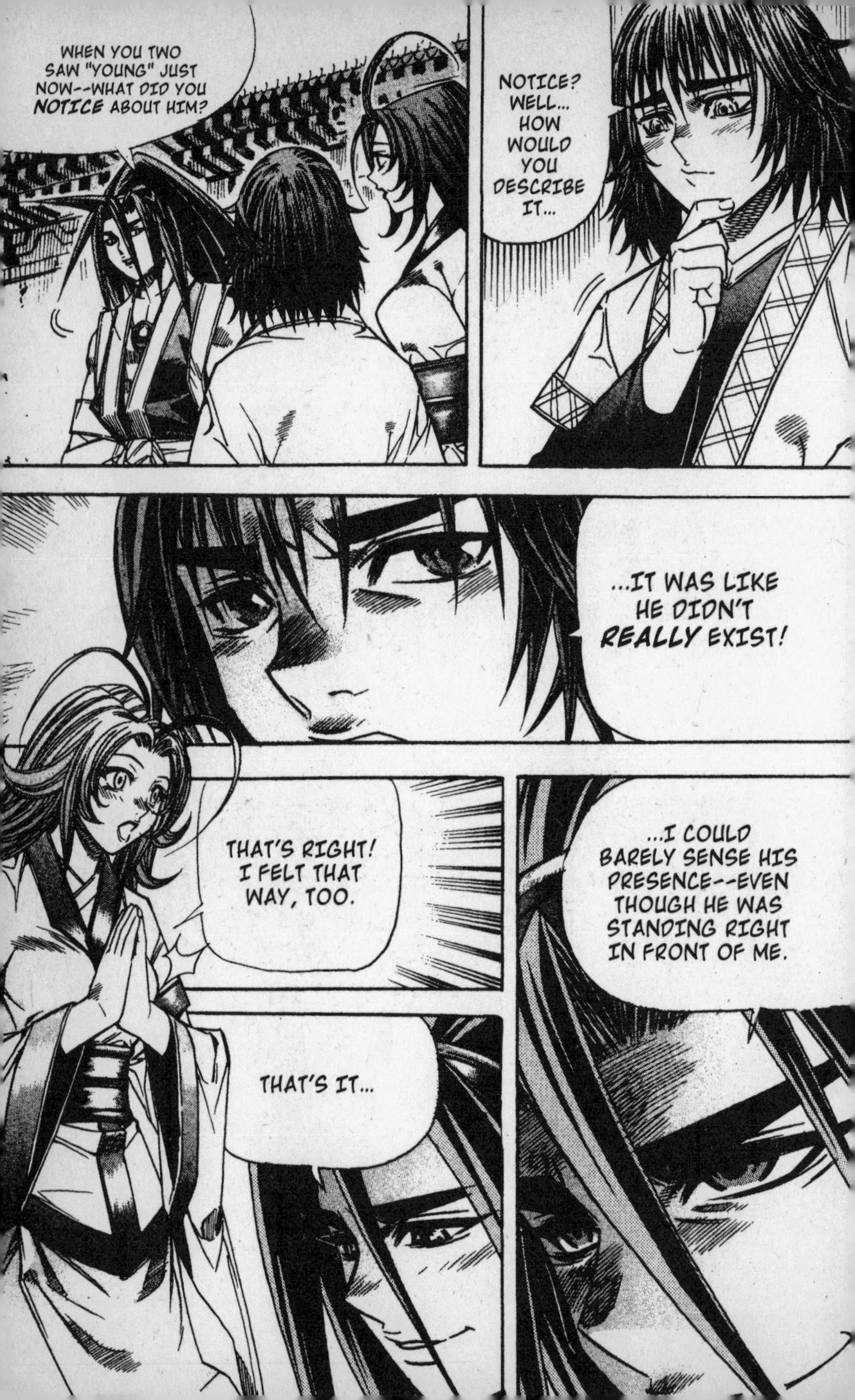
WHEN YOU TWO SAW "YOUNG" JUST NOW--WHAT DID YOU NOTICE ABOUT HIM?
NOTICE? WELL... HOW WOULD YOU DESCRIBE IT...
...IT WAS LIKE HE DIDN'T REALLY EXIST!
THAT'S RIGHT! I FELT THAT WAY, TOO.
...I COULD BARELY SENSE HIS PRESENCE--EVEN THOUGH HE WAS STANDING RIGHT IN FRONT OF ME.
THAT'S IT...

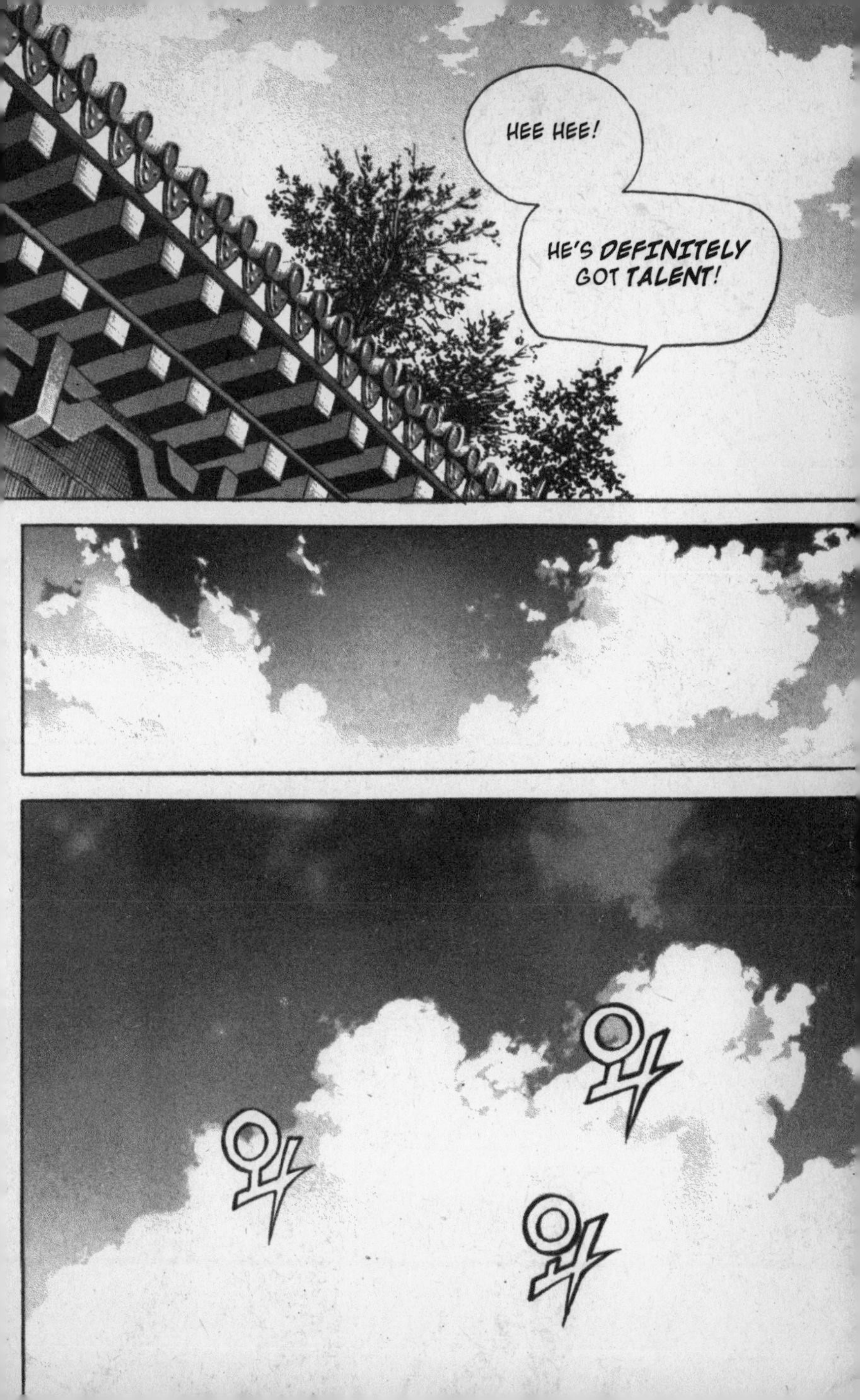
HEE HEE!
HE'S DEFINITELY GOT TALENT!
와
와
와

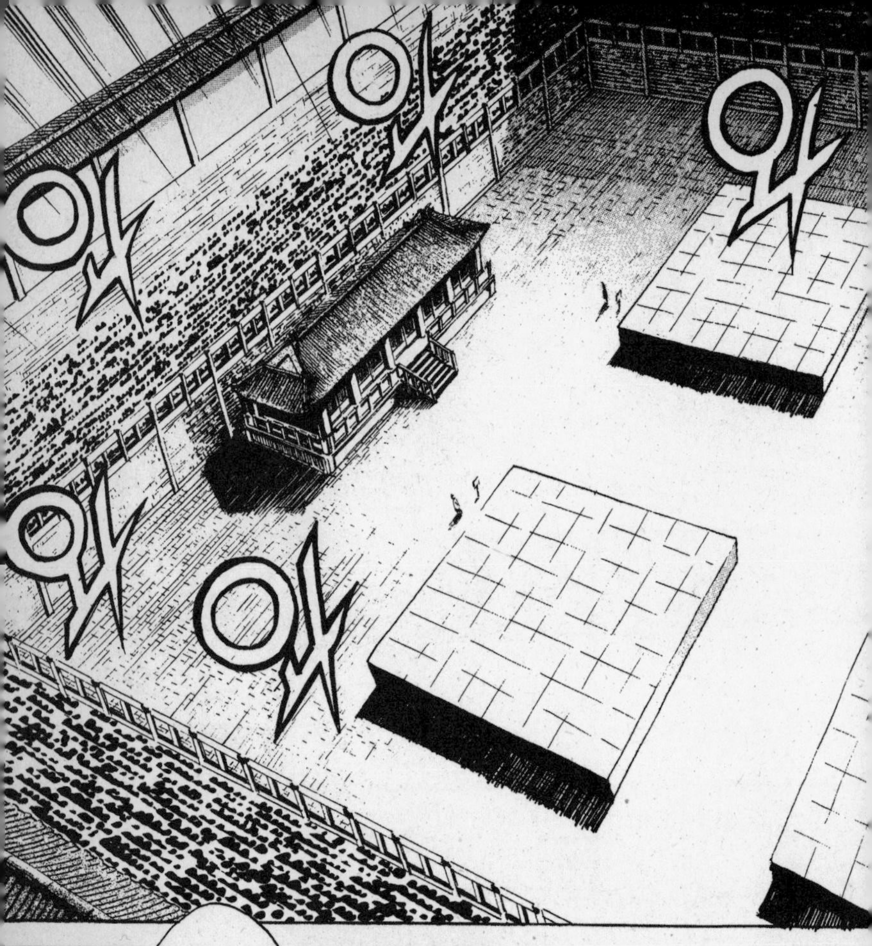

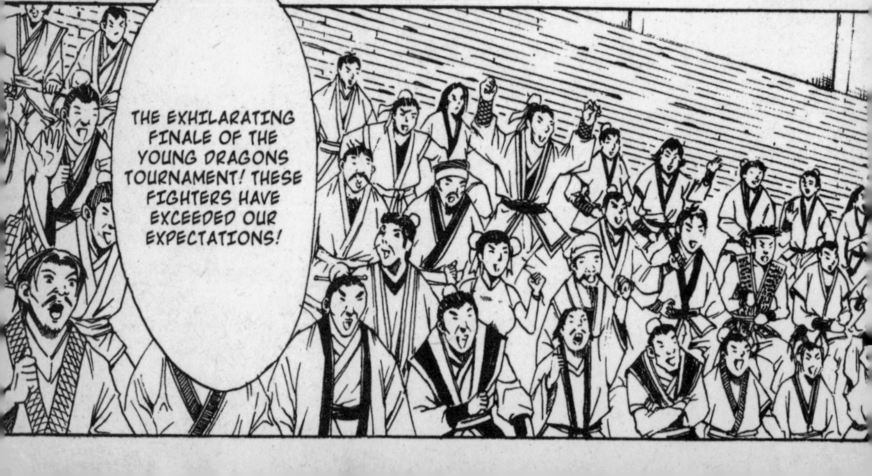
THE EXHILARATING FINALE OF THE YOUNG DRAGONS TOURNAMENT! THESE FIGHTERS HAVE EXCEEDED OUR EXPECTATIONS!

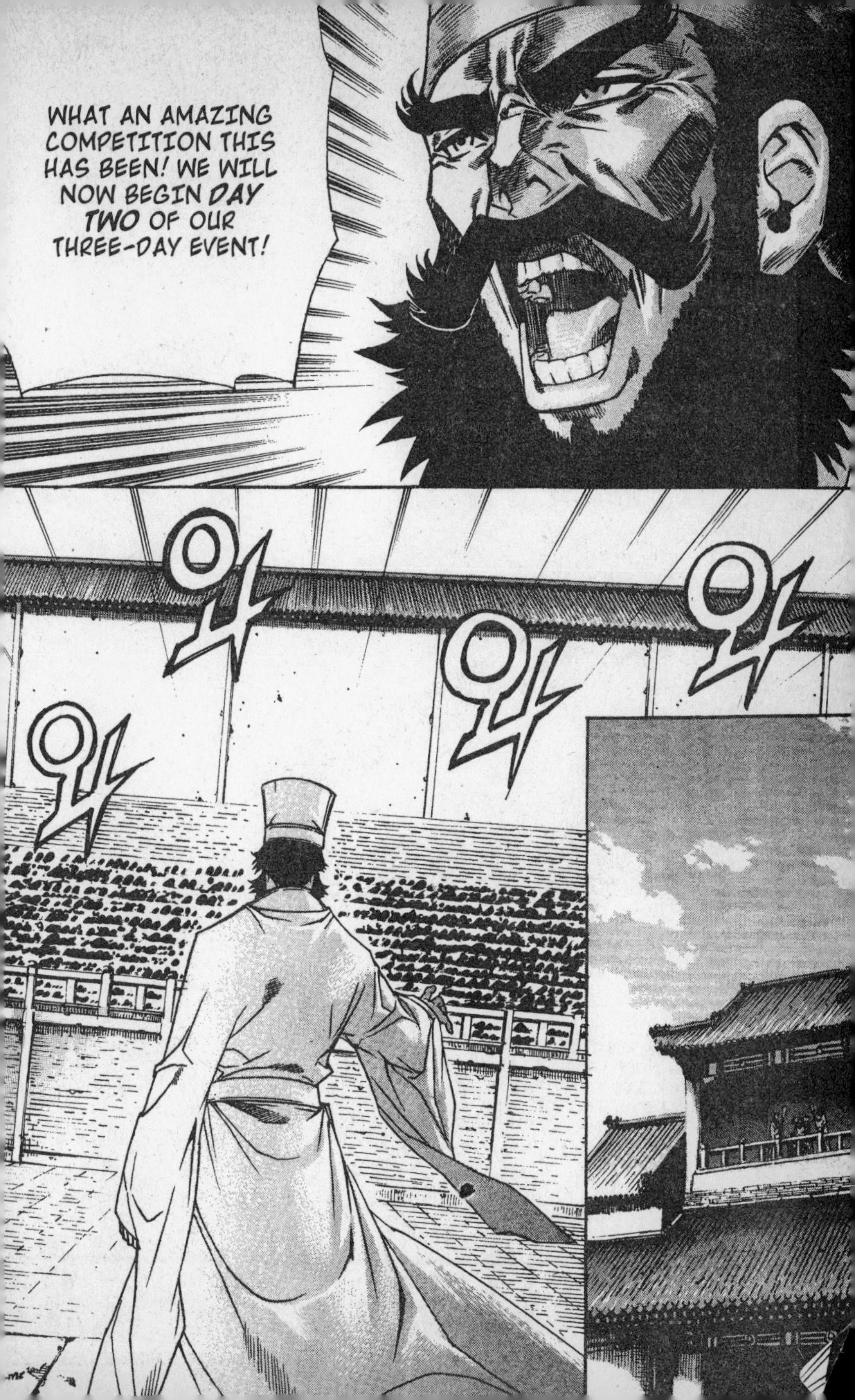
WHAT AN AMAZING COMPETITION THIS HAS BEEN! WE WILL NOW BEGIN *DAY TWO* OF OUR THREE-DAY EVENT!

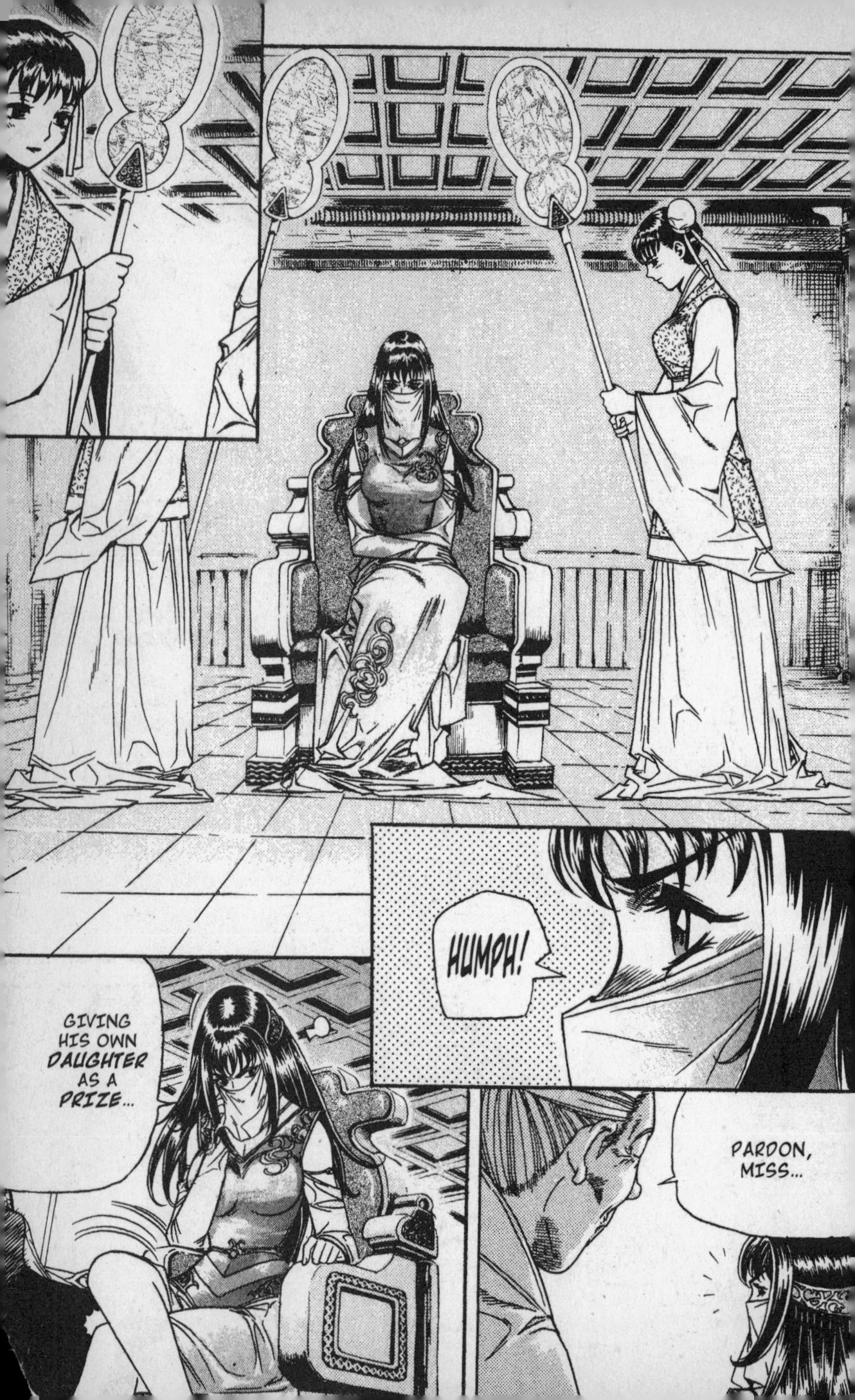
GIVING HIS OWN DAUGHTER AS A PRIZE...
HUMPH!
PARDON, MISS...

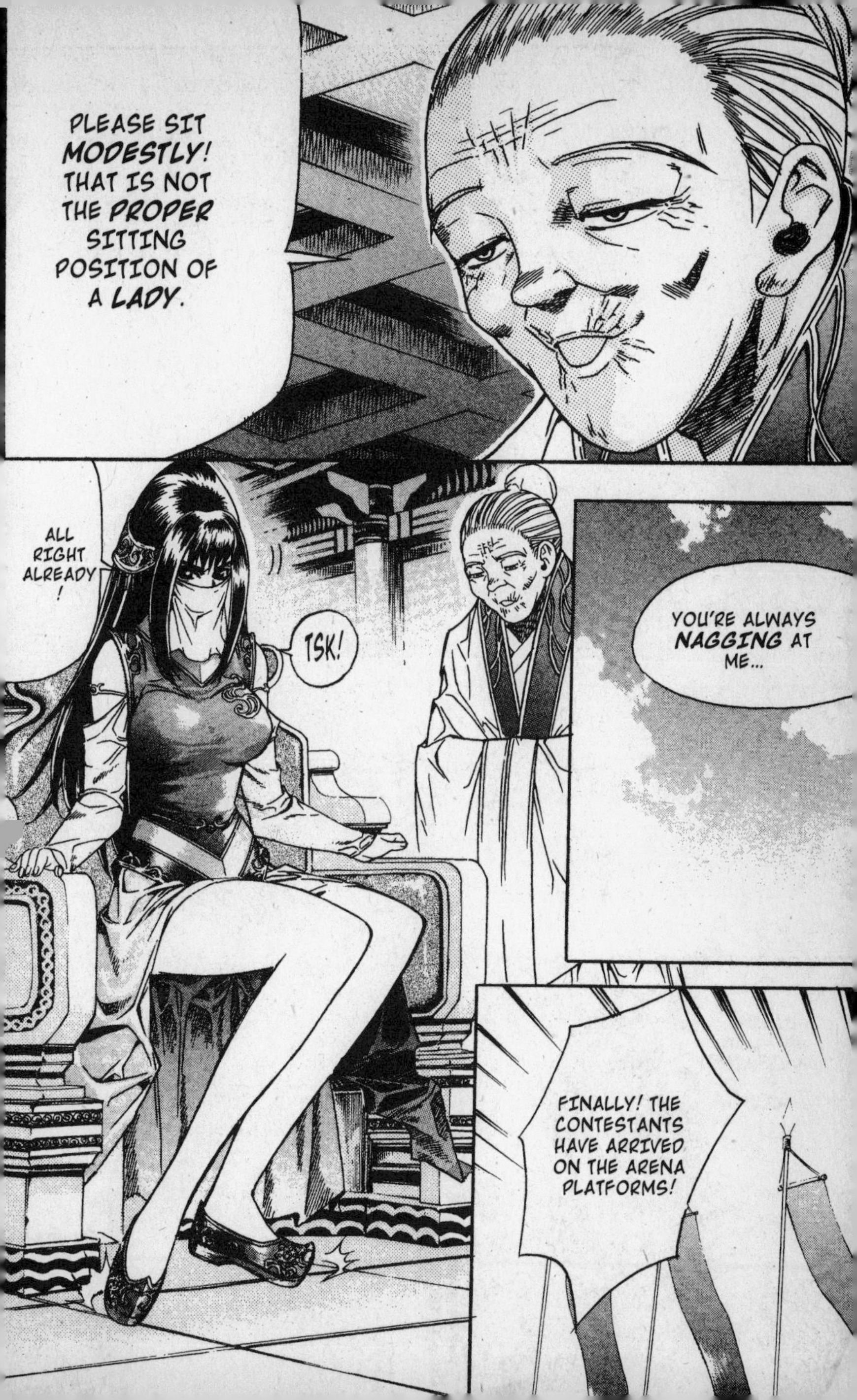

PLEASE SIT MODESTLY! THAT IS NOT THE PROPER SITTING POSITION OF A LADY.
TSK!
ALL RIGHT ALREADY!
YOU'RE ALWAYS NAGGING AT ME...
FINALLY! THE CONTESTANTS HAVE ARRIVED ON THE ARENA PLATFORMS!

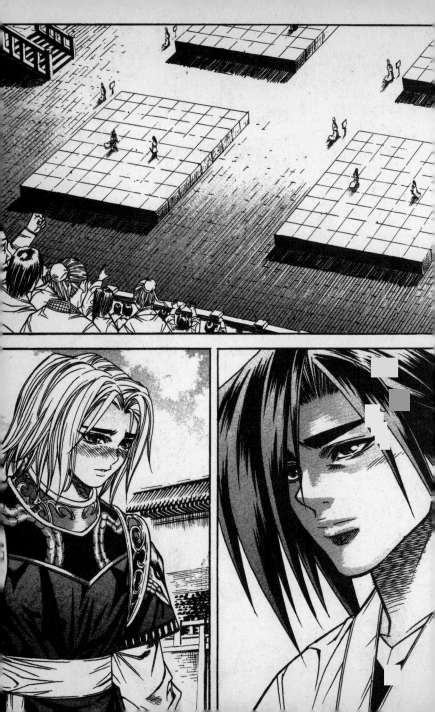

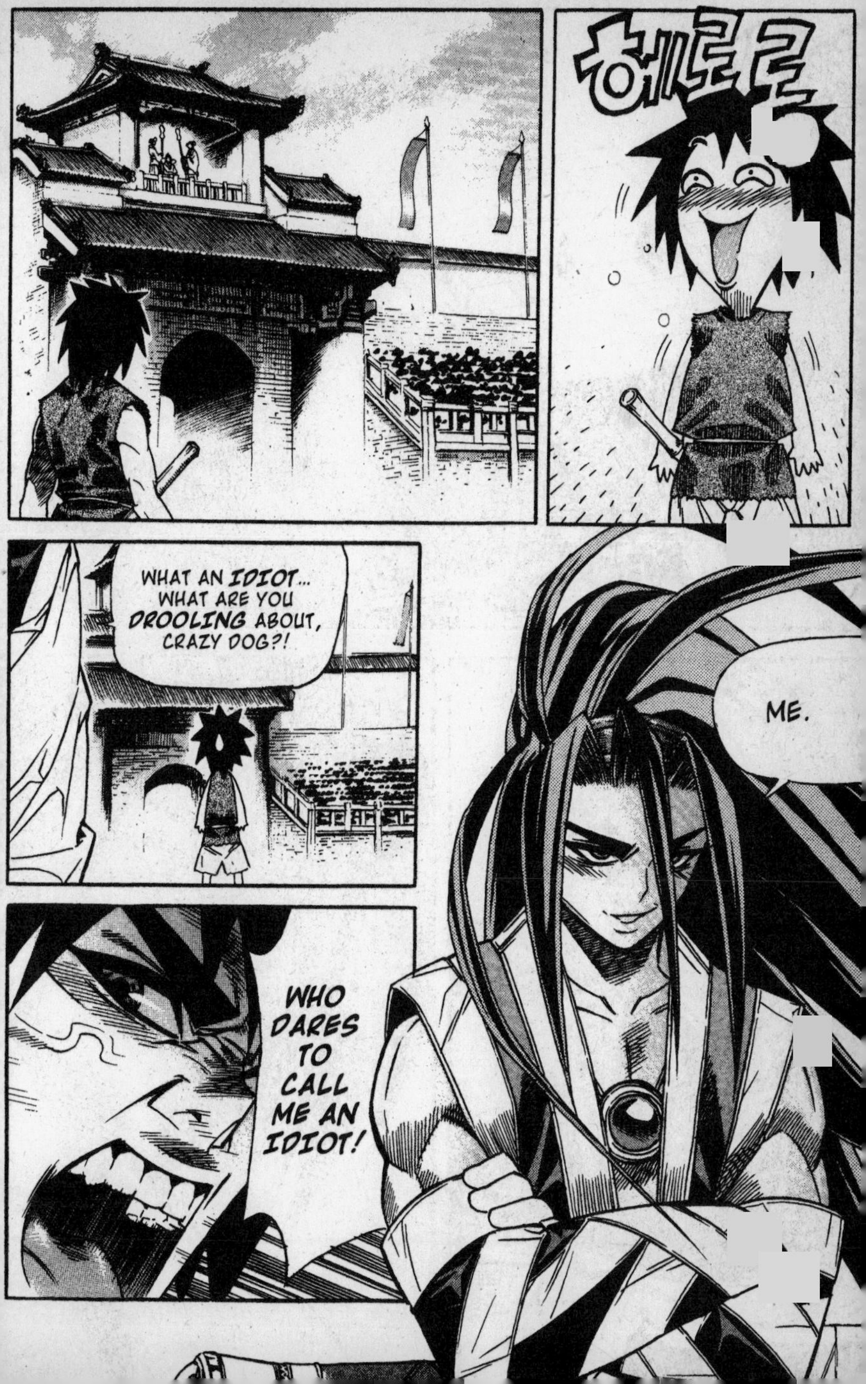
헤르르
WHAT AN IDIOT... WHAT ARE YOU DROOLING ABOUT, CRAZY DOG?!
WHO DARES TO CALL ME AN IDIOT!
ME.

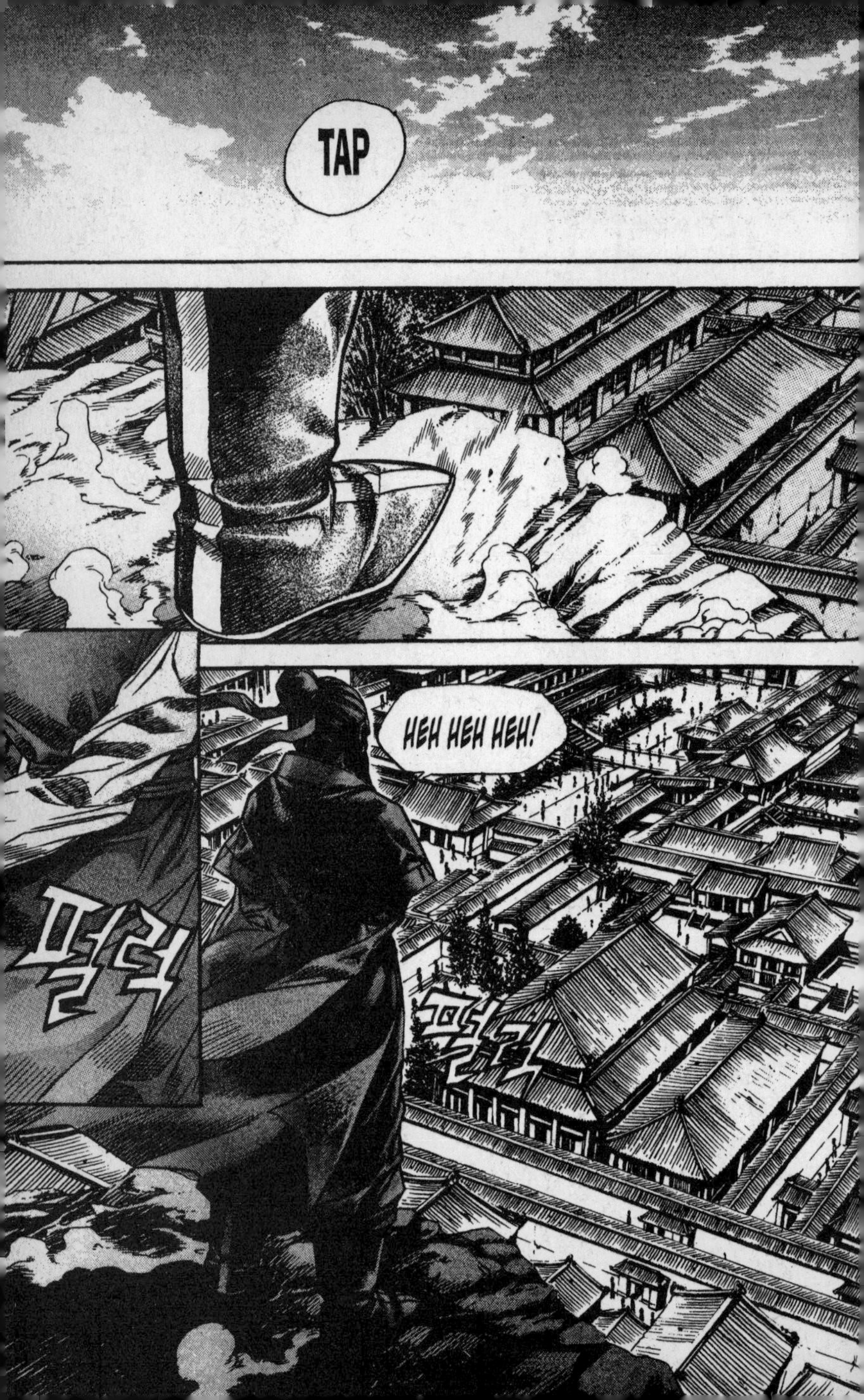
TAP
펄럭
HEH HEH HEH!
펄럭

IN THE NEXT VOLUME OF

KING OF HELL

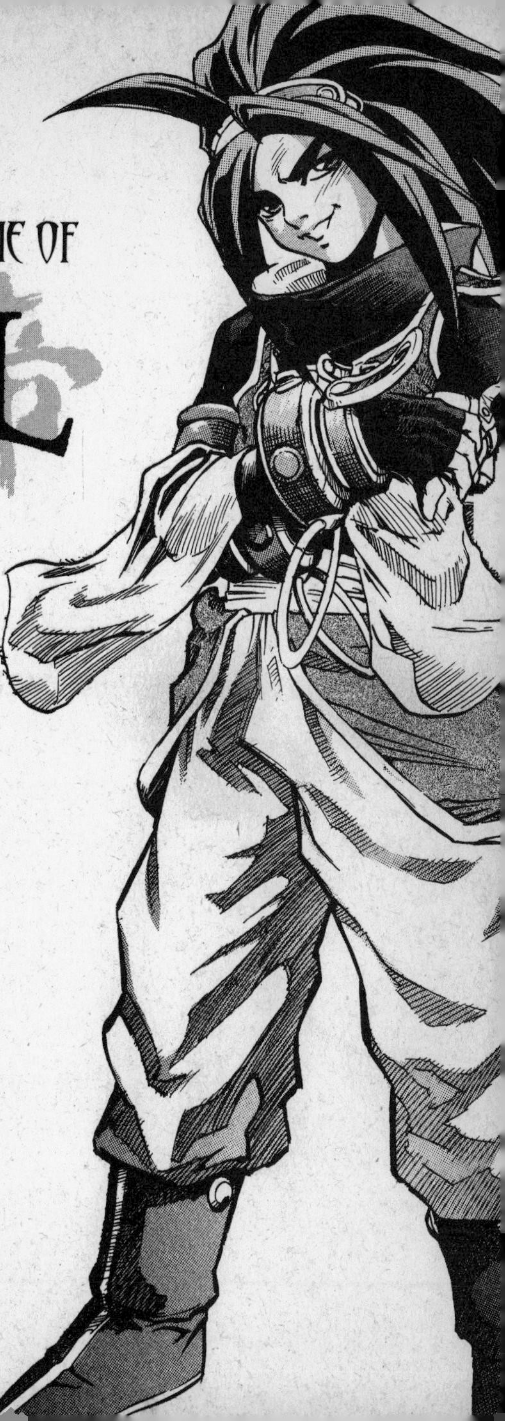

The Martial Arts Tournament continues with Young fighting Baby and Majeh vs. Crazy Dog! Though Majeh seems to have forgotten his mission to capture Hell's Most Wanted, the escaped evil souls have certainly not forgotten him!

Now that Majeh's prey is on the hunt for their hunter, does even Hell's cockiest envoy have a hope against a force of pure evil?

ALSO AVAILABLE FROM 🐾TOKYOPOP®

MANGA

.HACK//LEGEND OF THE TWILIGHT
@LARGE
ABENOBASHI: MAGICAL SHOPPING ARCADE
A.I. LOVE YOU
AI YORI AOSHI
ANGELIC LAYER
ARM OF KANNON
BABY BIRTH
BATTLE ROYALE
BATTLE VIXENS
BRAIN POWERED
BRIGADOON
B'TX
CANDIDATE FOR GODDESS, THE
CARDCAPTOR SAKURA
CARDCAPTOR SAKURA - MASTER OF THE CLOW
CHOBITS
CHRONICLES OF THE CURSED SWORD
CLAMP SCHOOL DETECTIVES
CLOVER
COMIC PARTY
CONFIDENTIAL CONFESSIONS
CORRECTOR YUI
COWBOY BEBOP
COWBOY BEBOP: SHOOTING STAR
CRAZY LOVE STORY
CRESCENT MOON
CULDCEPT
CYBORG 009
D•N•ANGEL
DEMON DIARY
DEMON ORORON, THE
DEUS VITAE
DIGIMON
DIGIMON TAMERS
DIGIMON ZERO TWO
DOLL
DRAGON HUNTER
DRAGON KNIGHTS
DRAGON VOICE
DREAM SAGA
DUKLYON: CLAMP SCHOOL DEFENDERS
EERIE QUEERIE!
ERICA SAKURAZAWA: COLLECTED WORKS
ET CETERA
ETERNITY
EVIL'S RETURN
FAERIES' LANDING
FAKE
FLCL
FORBIDDEN DANCE
FRUITS BASKET
G GUNDAM
GATEKEEPERS
GETBACKERS

GIRL GOT GAME
GRAVITATION
GTO
GUNDAM BLUE DESTINY
GUNDAM SEED ASTRAY
GUNDAM WING
GUNDAM WING: BATTLEFIELD OF PACIFISTS
GUNDAM WING: ENDLESS WALTZ
GUNDAM WING: THE LAST OUTPOST (G-UNIT)
HANDS OFF!
HAPPY MANIA
HARLEM BEAT
I.N.V.U.
IMMORTAL RAIN
INITIAL D
INSTANT TEEN: JUST ADD NUTS
ISLAND
JING: KING OF BANDITS
JING: KING OF BANDITS - TWILIGHT TALES
JULINE
KARE KANO
KILL ME, KISS ME
KINDAICHI CASE FILES, THE
KING OF HELL
KODOCHA: SANA'S STAGE
LAMENT OF THE LAMB
LEGAL DRUG
LEGEND OF CHUN HYANG, THE
LES BIJOUX
LOVE HINA
LUPIN III
LUPIN III: WORLD'S MOST WANTED
MAGIC KNIGHT RAYEARTH I
MAGIC KNIGHT RAYEARTH II
MAHOROMATIC: AUTOMATIC MAIDEN
MAN OF MANY FACES
MARMALADE BOY
MARS
MARS: HORSE WITH NO NAME
METROID
MINK
MIRACLE GIRLS
MIYUKI-CHAN IN WONDERLAND
MODEL
ONE
ONE I LOVE, THE
PARADISE KISS
PARASYTE
PASSION FRUIT
PEACH GIRL
PEACH GIRL: CHANGE OF HEART
PET SHOP OF HORRORS
PITA-TEN
PLANET LADDER
PLANETES
PRIEST

02.03.04T

ALSO AVAILABLE FROM TOKYOPOP®

PRINCESS AI
PSYCHIC ACADEMY
RAGNAROK
RAVE MASTER
REALITY CHECK
REBIRTH
REBOUND
REMOTE
RISING STARS OF MANGA
SABER MARIONETTE J
SAILOR MOON
SAINT TAIL
SAIYUKI
SAMURAI DEEPER KYO
SAMURAI GIRL REAL BOUT HIGH SCHOOL
SCRYED
SEIKAI TRILOGY, THE
SGT. FROG
SHAOLIN SISTERS
SHIRAHIME-SYO: SNOW GODDESS TALES
SHUTTERBOX
SKULL MAN, THE
SMUGGLER
SNOW DROP
SORCERER HUNTERS
STONE
SUIKODEN III
SUKI
THREADS OF TIME
TOKYO BABYLON
TOKYO MEW MEW
TRAMPS LIKE US
TREASURE CHESS
UNDER THE GLASS MOON
VAMPIRE GAME
VISION OF ESCAFLOWNE, THE
WARRIORS OF TAO
WILD ACT
WISH
WORLD OF HARTZ
X-DAY
ZODIAC P.I.

NOVELS

CLAMP SCHOOL PARANORMAL INVESTIGATORS
KARMA CLUB
SAILOR MOON
SLAYERS

ART BOOKS

ART OF CARDCAPTOR SAKURA
ART OF MAGIC KNIGHT RAYEARTH, THE
PEACH: MIWA UEDA ILLUSTRATIONS

ANIME GUIDES

COWBOY BEBOP
GUNDAM TECHNICAL MANUALS
SAILOR MOON SCOUT GUIDES

TOKYOPOP KIDS

STRAY SHEEP

CINE-MANGA™

ALADDIN
ASTRO BOY
CARDCAPTORS
CONFESSIONS OF A TEENAGE DRAMA QUEEN
DUEL MASTERS
FAIRLY ODDPARENTS, THE
FAMILY GUY
FINDING NEMO
G.I. JOE SPY TROOPS
JACKIE CHAN ADVENTURES
JIMMY NEUTRON: BOY GENIUS, THE ADVENTURES OF
KIM POSSIBLE
LILO & STITCH
LIZZIE MCGUIRE
LIZZIE MCGUIRE MOVIE, THE
MALCOLM IN THE MIDDLE
POWER RANGERS: NINJA STORM
SHREK 2
SPONGEBOB SQUAREPANTS
SPY KIDS 2
SPY KIDS 3-D: GAME OVER
TEENAGE MUTANT NINJA TURTLES
THAT'S SO RAVEN
TRANSFORMERS: ARMADA
TRANSFORMERS: ENERGON

For more information visit www.TOKYOPOP.com

02.03.04T

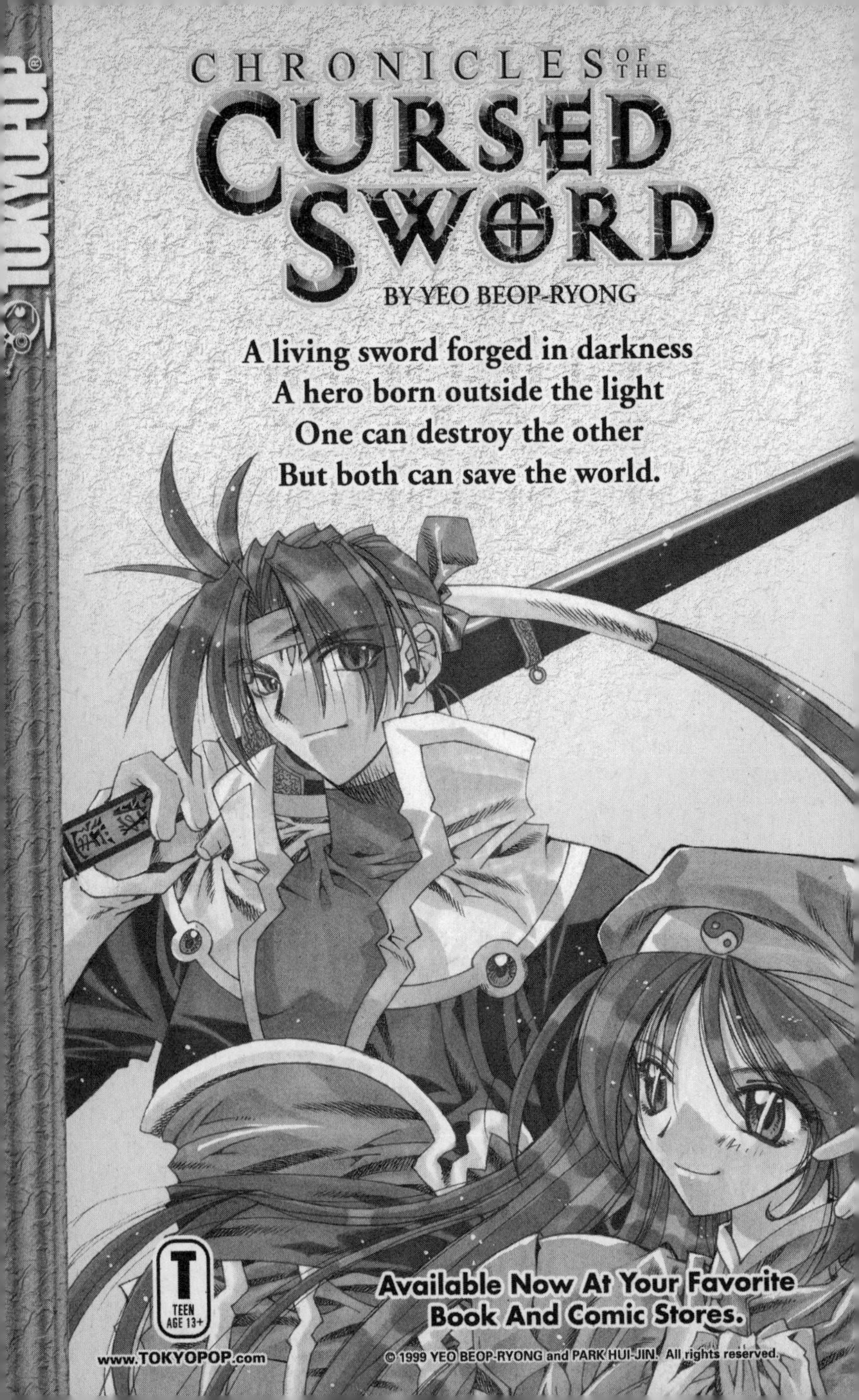
TOKYOPOP®
CHRONICLES OF THE
CURSED SWORD
BY YEO BEOP-RYONG
A living sword forged in darkness
A hero born outside the light
One can destroy the other
But both can save the world.
T
TEEN
AGE 13+
Available Now At Your Favorite
Book And Comic Stores.
www.TOKYOPOP.com
© 1999 YEO BEOP-RYONG and PARK HUI-JIN. All rights reserved.